CALIFORNIA TRAILS

D E S E R T   R E G I O N

Warning: While every effort has been made to make the 4WD trail descriptions in this book as accurate as possible, some discrepancies may exist between the text and the actual trail. Hazards may have changed since the research and publication of this edition. Adler Publishing Company, Inc., and the authors accept no responsibility for the safety of users of this guide. Individuals are liable for all costs incurred if rescue is necessary.

Printed in the United States of America

Cover photos
Clockwise from bottom left: Cerro Gordo Road, Racetrack Road, Mojave Road

Rear cover photos
From left: Racetrack Road, Ivanpah Mountains Trail

CALIFORNIA TRAILS
DESERT REGION

PETER MASSEY
JEANNE WILSON
ANGELA TITUS

ADLER
PUBLISHING

Acknowledgements

Many people and organizations have made major contributions to the research and production of this book. We owe them all special thanks for their assistance.

First, we would like to thank the following people who have played major roles in the production of this book and have been key to completing it in a timely fashion.

Cover Design Concept: **Rudy Ramos**
Editing and Proofreading: **Robin Loveman, Sallie Greenwood**
Graphic Design and Maps: **Deborah Rust**

We would also like to thank Sally Cunkelman, and the rest of the staff at the Bureau of Land Management's Barstow Field Office; staff at the California Desert Information Center in Barstow; and staff at Jawbone Station for information on the OHV area.

We are most thankful to the following organizations and people who have helped to research photographs or allowed us to publish the wonderful photographs they have taken: Lori Swingle and Coi Gehrig, Denver Public Library; Linda Fisk and Ken Hedges, San Diego Museum of Man; Dace Taube, University of Southern California; Carrie Burroughs and Karren Elsbernd, California Academy of Sciences (CalPhotos); Barbara Pitschel, Strybing Arboretum & Botanical Gardens; Tanya Hollis, Abby Bridge, and Crissa Van Vleck, California Historical Society; Professor Ron Olowin, Department of Physics and Astronomy at Saint Mary's College and curator of the Alfred Brousseau Collection.

Publishers Note: Every effort has been taken to ensure that the information in this book is accurate at press time. Please visit our website to advise us of any changes or corrections you find. We also welcome recommendations for new 4WD trails or other suggestions to improve the information in this book.

Adler Publishing Company, Inc.
1601 Pacific Coast Highway, Suite 290
Hermosa Beach, CA 90254
Phone: 800-660-5107
Fax: 310-698-0709
4WDbooks.com

ADLER
PUBLISHING

Contents

Before You Go

Why a 4WD Does It Better

The design and engineering of 4WD vehicles provide them with many advantages over normal cars when you head off the paved road:

■ improved distribution of power to all four wheels;

■ a transmission transfer case, which provides low-range gear selection for greater pulling power and for crawling over difficult terrain;

■ high ground clearance;

■ less overhang of the vehicle's body past the wheels, which provides better front- and rear-clearance when crossing gullies and ridges;

■ large-lug, wide-tread tires;

■ rugged construction (including underbody skid plates on many models).

If you plan to do off-highway touring, all of these considerations are important whether you are evaluating the capabilities of your current 4WD or are looking to buy one; each is considered in detail in this chapter.

To explore the most difficult trails described in this book, you will need a 4WD vehicle that is well rated in each of the above features. If you own a 2WD sport utility vehicle, a lighter car-type SUV, or a pickup truck, your ability to explore the more difficult trails will depend on conditions and your level of experience.

A word of caution: Whatever type of 4WD vehicle you drive, understand that it is not invincible or indestructible. Nor can it go everywhere. A 4WD has a much higher center of gravity and weighs more than a car, and so has its own consequent limitations.

Experience is the only way to learn what your vehicle can and cannot do. Therefore, if you are inexperienced, we strongly recommend that you start with trails that have lower difficulty ratings. As you develop an understanding of your vehicle and of your own taste for adventure, you can safely tackle the more challenging trails.

One way to beef up your knowledge quickly, while avoiding the costly and sometimes dangerous lessons learned from on-the-road mistakes, is to undertake a 4WD course taught by a professional. Look in the Yellow Pages for courses in your area.

Using This Book

Route Planning

The regional map on pages 24 through 27 provide a convenient overview of the trails in that portion of the state the Desert Region of California. Each 4WD trail is shown, as are major highways and towns, helping you plan various routes by connecting a series of 4WD trails and paved roads.

As you plan your overall route, you will probably want to utilize as many 4WD trails as possible. However, check the difficulty rating and time required for each trail before finalizing your plans. You don't want to be stuck 50 miles from the highway—at sunset and without camping gear, since your trip was supposed to be over hours ago—when you discover that your vehicle can't handle a certain difficult passage.

Difficulty Ratings

We utilize a point system to rate the difficulty of each trail. Any such system is subjective, and your experience of the trails will vary depending on your skill and the road conditions at the time. Indeed, any amount of rain may make the trails much more difficult, if not completely impassable.

We have rated the 4WD trails on a scale of 1 to 10—1 being passable for a normal passenger vehicle in good conditions and 10 requiring a heavily modified vehicle and an experienced driver who expects to encounter vehicle damage. Because this book is designed for owners of unmodified 4WD vehicles—who we assume do not want to damage their vehicles—most of the trails are rated 5 or lower. A few trails are included that rate as high as 7, while those rated 8 to 10 are beyond the scope of this book.

This is not to say that the moderate-rated trails are easy. We strongly recommend that inexperienced drivers not tackle trails rated at 4 or higher until they have undertaken a number of the lower-rated ones, so that they can gauge their skill level and prepare for the difficulty of the higher-rated trails.

In assessing the trails, we have always assumed good road conditions (dry road surface, good visibility, and so on). The factors influencing our ratings are as follows:

■ obstacles such as rocks, mud, ruts, sand, slickrock, and stream crossings;
■ the stability of the road surface;
■ the width of the road and the vehicle clearance between trees or rocks;
■ the steepness of the road;
■ the margin for driver error (for example, a very high, open shelf road would be rated more difficult even if it was not very steep and had a stable surface).

The following is a guide to the ratings.

Rating 1: The trail is graded dirt but suitable for a normal passenger vehicle. It usually has gentle grades, is fairly wide, and has very shallow water crossings (if any).

Rating 2: High-clearance vehicles are preferred but not necessary. These trails are dirt roads, but they may have rocks, grades, water crossings, or ruts that make clearance a concern in a normal passenger vehicle. The trails are fairly wide, making passing possible at almost any point along the trail. Mud is not a concern under normal weather conditions.

Rating 3: High-clearance 4WDs are preferred, but any high-clearance vehicle is acceptable. Expect a rough road surface; mud and sand are possible but will be easily passable. You may encounter rocks up to 6 inches in diameter, a loose road surface, and shelf roads, though these will be wide enough for passing or will have adequate pull-offs.

Rating 4: High-clearance 4WDs are recommended, though most stock SUVs are acceptable. Expect a rough road surface with rocks larger than 6 inches, but there will be a reasonable driving line available. Patches of mud are possible but can be readily negotiated; sand may be deep and require lower tire pressures. There may be stream crossings up to 12 inches deep, substantial sections of single-lane shelf road, moderate grades, and sections of moderately loose road surface.

Rating 5: High-clearance 4WDs are required. These trails have either a rough, rutted surface, rocks up to 9 inches, mud and deep sand that may be impassable for inexperienced drivers, or stream crossings up to 18 inches deep. Certain sections may be steep enough to cause traction problems, and you may encounter very narrow shelf roads with steep drop-offs and tight clearance between rocks or trees.

Rating 6: These trails are for experienced four-wheel drivers only. They are potentially dangerous, with large rocks, ruts, or terraces that may need to be negotiated. They may also have stream crossings at least 18 inches deep, involve rapid currents, unstable stream bottoms, or difficult access; steep slopes, loose surfaces, and narrow clearances; or very narrow sections of shelf road with steep drop-offs and possibly challenging road surfaces.

Rating 7: Skilled, experienced four-wheel drivers only. These trails include very challenging sections with extremely steep grades, loose surfaces, large rocks, deep ruts, and/or tight clearances. Mud or sand may necessitate winching.

Rating 8 and above: Stock vehicles are likely to be damaged and may find the trail impassable. Highly skilled, experienced four-wheel drivers only.

Scenic Ratings

If rating the degree of difficulty is subjective, rating scenic beauty is guaranteed to lead to arguments. Southern California's Desert Region contains a spectacular variety of scenery. Despite the subjectivity of attempting a comparative rating of diverse scenery, we have tried to provide a guide to the relative scenic quality of the various trails. The ratings are based on a scale of 1 to 10, with 10 being the most attractive.

Remoteness Ratings

Many trails in the Desert Region are in remote country; sometimes the trails are seldom traveled, and the likelihood is low that another vehicle will appear within a reasonable time to assist you if you get stuck or break down. We have included a ranking for remoteness of +0 through +2. Extreme summer temperatures can make a breakdown in the more remote areas a life-threatening experience. Prepare carefully before tackling the higher-rated, more remote trails (see Special Preparations for Remote Travel, page 11). For trails with a high remoteness rating, consider traveling with a second vehicle.

Estimated Driving Times

In calculating driving times, we have not allowed for stops. Your actual driving time may be considerably longer depending on the number and duration of the stops you make. Add more time if you prefer to drive more slowly than good conditions allow.

Current Road Information

All the 4WD trails described in this book may become impassable in poor weather conditions. Storms can alter roads, remove tracks, and create impassable washes. Most of the trails described, even easy 2WD trails, can quickly become impassable even to 4WD vehicles after only a small amount of rain. For each trail, we have provided a phone number for obtaining current information about conditions.

Abbreviations

The route directions for the 4WD trails use a series of abbreviations as follows:

SO	CONTINUE STRAIGHT ON
TL	TURN LEFT
TR	TURN RIGHT
BL	BEAR LEFT
BR	BEAR RIGHT
UT	U-TURN

Using Route Directions

For every trail, we describe and pinpoint (by odometer reading) nearly every significant feature along the route—such as intersections, streams, washes, gates, cattle guards, and so on—and provide directions from these landmarks. Odometer readings will vary from vehicle to vehicle, so you should allow for slight variations. Be aware that trails can quickly change in the desert. A new trail may be cut around a washout, a faint trail can be graded by the county, or a well-used trail may fall into disuse. All these factors will affect the accuracy of the given directions.

If you diverge from the route, zero your trip meter upon your return and continue along the route, making the necessary adjustment to the point-to-point odometer readings. In the directions, we regularly reset the odometer readings—at significant landmarks or popular lookouts and spur trails—so that you won't have to recalculate for too long.

Most of the trails can be started from either end, and the route directions include both directions of travel; reverse directions are printed in orange below the main directions. When traveling in reverse, read from the bottom of the table and work up.

Route directions include cross-references whenever two 4WD trails included in this book connect; these cross-references allow for an easy change of route or destination.

Each trail includes periodic latitude and longitude readings to facilitate using a global positioning system (GPS) receiver. These readings may also assist you in finding your location on the maps. The GPS coordinates are given in the format dd°mm.mm'. To save time when loading coordinates into your GPS receiver, you may wish to include only one decimal place, since in Southern California, the first decimal place equals about 165 yards and the second only about 16 yards.

Map References

We recommend that you supplement the information in this book with more-detailed maps. For each trail, we list the sheet maps and road atlases that provide the best detail for the area. Typically, the following references are given:

- Bureau of Land Management Maps
- U.S. Forest Service Maps
- *California Road & Recreation Atlas,* 2nd ed. (Medford, Oregon: Benchmark Maps, 2000)—Scale 1:300,000
- *Southern & Central California Atlas & Gazetteer,* 5th ed. (Yarmouth, Maine: DeLorme Mapping, 2000)—Scale 1:150,000
- Maptech-Terrain Navigator Topo Maps—Scale 1:100,000 and 1:24,000
- *Trails Illustrated* Topo Maps; National Geographic Maps—various scales, but all contain good detail

We recommend the *Trails Illustrated* series of maps as the best for navigating these trails. They are reliable, easy to read, and printed on nearly indestructible plastic paper. However, this series covers only a few of the 4WD trails described in this book.

The DeLorme Atlas the advantage of providing you with maps of the state at a reasonable price. Although its 4WD trail information doesn't go beyond what we provide, it is useful if you wish to explore the hundreds of side roads.

U.S. Forest Service maps lack the topographic detail of the other sheet maps and, in our experience, are occasionally out of date. They have the advantage of covering a broad area and are useful in identifying land use and travel restrictions. These maps are most useful for the longer trails.

In our opinion, the best single option by far is the Terrain Navigator series of maps published on CD-ROM by Maptech. These CD-ROMs contain an amazing level of detail because they include the entire set of 1,941 U.S. Geological Survey topographical maps of California at the 1:24,000 scale and all 71 maps at the 1:100,000 scale. These maps offer many advantages over normal maps:

- GPS coordinates for any location can be found and loaded into your GPS receiver. Conversely, if you have your GPS coordinates, your location on the map can be pinpointed instantly.
- Towns, rivers, passes, mountains, and many other sites are indexed by name so that they can be located quickly.

- 4WD trails can be marked and profiled for elevation changes and distances from point to point.
- Customized maps can be printed out.

Maptech uses 14 CD-ROMs to cover the entire state of California; they can be purchased individually or as part of a two-state package at a heavily discounted price. The CD-ROMs can be used with a laptop computer and a GPS receiver in your vehicle to monitor your location on the map and navigate directly from the display.

All these maps should be available through good map stores. The Maptech CD-ROMs are available directly from the company (800-627-7236, or on the internet at www.maptech.com).

Backcountry Driving Rules and Permits

Four-wheel driving involves special driving techniques and road rules. This section is an introduction for 4WD beginners.

4WD Road Rules

To help ensure that these trails remain open and available for all four-wheel drivers to enjoy, it is important to minimize your impact on the environment and not be a safety risk to yourself or anyone else. Remember that the 4WD clubs in California fight a constant battle with the government and various lobby groups to retain the access that currently exists.

The fundamental rule when traversing the 4WD trails described in this book is to use common sense. In addition, special road rules for 4WD trails apply:

- Vehicles traveling uphill have the right of way.
- If you are moving more slowly than the vehicle behind you, pull over to let the other vehicle by.
- Park out of the way in a safe place. Blocking a track may restrict access for emergency vehicles as well as for other recreationalists. Set the parking brake—don't rely on leaving the transmission in park. Manual transmissions should be left in the lowest gear.

Tread Lightly!

Remember the rules of the Tread Lightly! program:

■ Be informed. Obtain maps, regulations, and other information from the forest service or from other public land agencies. Learn the rules and follow them.

■ Resist the urge to pioneer a new road or trail or to cut across a switchback. Stay on constructed tracks and avoid running over young trees, shrubs, and grasses, damaging or killing them.

■ Stay off soft, wet roads and 4WD trails readily torn up by vehicles. Repairing the damage is expensive, and quite often authorities find it easier to close the road rather than repair it.

■ Travel around meadows, steep hillsides, stream banks, and lake shores that are easily scarred by churning wheels.

■ Stay away from wild animals that are rearing young or suffering from a food shortage. Do not camp close to the water sources of domestic or wild animals.

■ Obey gate closures and regulatory signs.

■ Preserve America's heritage by not disturbing old mining camps, ghost towns, or other historical features. Leave historic sites, Native American rock art, ruins, and artifacts in place and untouched.

■ Carry out all your trash, and even that of others.

■ Stay out of designated wilderness areas. They are closed to all vehicles. It is your responsibility to know where the boundaries are.

■ Get permission to cross private land. Leave livestock alone. Respect landowners' rights.

Report violations of these rules to help keep these 4WD trails open and to ensure that others will have the opportunity to visit these backcountry sites. Many groups are actively seeking to close these public lands to vehicles, thereby denying access to those who are unable, or perhaps merely unwilling, to hike long distances. This magnificent countryside is owned by, and should be available to, all Americans.

Special Preparations for Remote Travel

Due to the remoteness of some areas in California and the very high summer temperatures, you should take some special precautions to ensure that you don't end up in a life-threatening situation:

■ When planning a trip into the desert, always inform someone as to where you are going, your route, and when you expect to return. Stick to your plan.

■ Carry and drink at least one gallon of water per person per day of your trip. (Plastic gallon jugs are handy and portable.)

■ Be sure your vehicle is in good condition with a sound battery, good hoses, spare tire, spare fan belts, necessary tools, and reserve gasoline and oil. Other spare parts and extra radiator water are also valuable. If traveling in pairs, share the common spares and carry a greater variety.

■ Keep an eye on the sky. Flash floods can occur in a wash any time you see thunderheads—even when it's not raining a drop where you are.

■ If you are caught in a dust storm while driving, get off the road and turn off your lights. Turn on the emergency flashers and back into the wind to reduce windshield pitting by sand particles.

■ Test trails on foot before driving through washes and sandy areas. One minute of walking may save hours of hard work getting your vehicle unstuck.

■ If your vehicle breaks down, stay near it. Your emergency supplies are there. Your car has many other items useful in an emergency. Raise your hood and trunk lid to denote "help needed." Remember, a vehicle can be seen for miles, but a person on foot is very difficult to spot from a distance.

■ When you're not moving, use available shade or erect shade from tarps, blankets, or seat covers—anything to reduce the direct rays of the sun.

■ Do not sit or lie directly on the ground. It may be 30 degrees hotter than the air.

■ Leave a disabled vehicle only if you are positive of the route and the distance to help. Leave a note for rescuers that gives the time you left and the direction you are taking.

■ If you must walk, rest for at least 10 minutes out of each hour. If you are not normally physically active, rest up to 30 minutes out of each hour. Find shade, sit down, and prop up your feet. Adjust your shoes and socks, but do not remove your shoes—you may not be able to get them back on swollen feet.

■ If you have water, drink it. Do not ration it.

■ If water is limited, keep your mouth closed. Do not talk, eat, smoke, drink alcohol, or take salt.

■ Keep your clothing on despite the heat. It helps to keep your body temperature down and reduces your body's dehydration rate. Cover your head. If you don't have a hat, improvise a head covering.

■ If you are stalled or lost, set signal fires. Set smoky fires in the daytime and bright ones at night. Three fires in a triangle denote "help needed."

■ A roadway is a sign of civilization. If you find a road, stay on it.

■ When hiking in the desert, equip each person, especially children, with a police-type whistle. It makes a distinctive noise with little effort. Three blasts denote "help needed."

■ To avoid poisonous creatures, put your hands or feet only where your eyes can see. One insect to be aware of in Southen California is the Africanized honeybee. Though indistinguishable from its European counterpart, these bees are far more aggressive and can be a threat. They have been known to give chase of up to a mile and even wait for people who have escaped into the water to come up for air. The best thing to do if attacked is to cover your face and head with clothing and run to the nearest enclosed shelter. Keep an eye on your pet if you notice a number of bees in the area, as many have been killed by Africanized honeybees.

■ Avoid unnecessary contact with wildlife. Some mice in California carry the deadly hantavirus, a pulmonary syndrome fatal in 36 percent of human cases. Fortunately the disease is very rare—by May 2006, only 43 cases had been reported in California and 438 nationwide—but caution is still advised. Other rodents may transmit bubonic plague, the same epidemic that killed one-third of Europe's population in the 1300s. Be especially wary near sick animals and keep pets, especially cats, away from wildlife and their fleas. Another creature to watch for is the western black-legged tick, the carrier of Lyme disease. Wearing clothing that covers legs and arms, tucking pants into boots, and using insect repellent are good ways to avoid fleas and ticks.

Obtaining Permits

Backcountry permits, which usually cost a fee, are required for certain activities on public lands in California, whether the area is a national park, state park, national monument, Indian reservation, or BLM land.

Restrictions may require a permit for all overnight stays, which can include backpacking and 4WD or bicycle camping. Permits may also be required for day use by vehicles, horses, hikers, or bikes in some areas.

When possible, we include information about fees and permit requirements and where permits may be obtained, but these regulations change constantly. If in doubt, check with the most likely governing agency.

Assessing Your Vehicle's Off-Road Ability

Many issues come into play when evaluating your 4WD vehicle, although most of the 4WDs on the market are suitable for even the roughest trails described in this book. Engine power will be adequate in even the least-powerful modern vehicle. However, some vehicles are less suited to off-highway driving than others, and some of the newest, carlike sport utility vehicles simply are not designed for off-highway touring. The following information should allow you to identify the good, the bad, and the ugly.

Differing 4WD Systems

All 4WD systems have one thing in common: The engine provides power to all four wheels rather than to only two, as is typical in most standard cars. However, there are a number of differences in the way power is applied to the wheels.

The other feature that distinguishes nearly all 4WDs from normal passenger vehicles is that the gearboxes have high and low ratios that effectively double the number of gears. The high range is comparable to the range on a passenger car. The low range provides lower speed and more power, which is useful when towing heavy loads, driving up steep hills, or crawling over rocks. When driving downhill, the 4WD's low range increases engine braking.

Various makes and models of SUVs offer different drive systems, but these differences center on two issues: the way power is applied to the other wheels if one or more wheels slip, and the ability to select between 2WD and 4WD.

Normal driving requires that all four wheels be able to turn at different speeds; this allows the vehicle to turn without scrubbing its tires. In a 2WD vehicle, the front wheels (or rear wheels in a front-wheel-drive vehicle) are not powered by the engine and thus are free to turn individually at any speed. The rear wheels, powered by the engine, are only able to turn at different speeds because of the differential, which applies power to the faster-turning wheel.

This standard method of applying traction has certain weaknesses. First, when power is applied to only one set of wheels, the other set cannot help the vehicle gain traction. Second, when one powered wheel loses traction, it spins, but the other powered wheel doesn't turn. This happens because the differential applies all the engine power to the faster-turning wheel and no power to the other wheels, which still have traction. All 4WD systems are designed to overcome these two weaknesses. However,

different 4WDs address this common objective in different ways.

Full-Time 4WD. For a vehicle to remain in 4WD all the time without scrubbing the tires, all the wheels must be able to rotate at different speeds. A full-time 4WD system allows this to happen by using three differentials. One is located between the rear wheels, as in a normal passenger car, to allow the rear wheels to rotate at different speeds. The second is located between the front wheels in exactly the same way. The third differential is located between the front and rear wheels to allow different rotational speeds between the front and rear sets of wheels. In nearly all vehicles with full-time 4WD, the center differential operates only in high range. In low range, it is completely locked. This is not a disadvantage because when using low range the additional traction is normally desired and the deterioration of steering response will be less noticeable due to the vehicle traveling at a slower speed.

Part-Time 4WD. A part-time 4WD system does not have the center differential located between the front and rear wheels. Consequently, the front and rear drive shafts are both driven at the same speed and with the same power at all times when in 4WD.

This system provides improved traction because when one or both of the front or rear wheels slips, the engine continues to provide power to the other set. However, because such a system doesn't allow a difference in speed between the front and rear sets of wheels, the tires scrub when turning, placing additional strain on the whole drive system. Therefore, such a system can be used only in slippery conditions; otherwise, the ability to steer the vehicle will deteriorate and the tires will quickly wear out.

Some vehicles, such as Jeeps with Selectrac and Mitsubishi Monteros with Active Trac 4WD, offer both full-time and part-time 4WD in high range.

Manual Systems to Switch Between 2WD and 4WD. There are three manual systems for switching between 2WD and 4WD. The most basic requires stopping and getting out of the vehicle to lock the front hubs manually before selecting 4WD. The second requires you to stop, but you change to 4WD by merely throwing a lever inside the vehicle (the hubs lock automatically). The third allows shifting between 2WD and 4WD high range while the vehicle is moving. Any 4WD that does not offer the option of driving in 2WD must have a full-time 4WD system.

Automated Switching Between 2WD and 4WD. Advances in technology are leading to greater automation in the selection of two- or four-wheel drive. When operating in high range, these high-tech systems use sensors to monitor the rotation of each wheel. When any slippage is detected, the vehicle switches the proportion of power from the wheel(s) that is slipping to the wheels that retain grip. The proportion of power supplied to each wheel is therefore infinitely variable as opposed to the original systems where the vehicle was either in two-wheel drive or four-wheel drive.

In recent years, this process has been spurred on by many of the manufacturers of luxury vehicles entering the SUV market— Mercedes, BMW, Cadillac, Lincoln, and Lexus have joined Range Rover in this segment.

Manufacturers of these higher-priced vehicles have led the way in introducing sophisticated computer-controlled 4WD systems. Although each of the manufacturers has its own approach to this issue, all the systems automatically vary the allocation of power between the wheels within milliseconds of the sensors' detecting wheel slippage.

Limiting Wheel Slippage

All 4WDs employ various systems to limit wheel slippage and transfer power to the wheels that still have traction. These systems may completely lock the differentials or they may allow limited slippage before transferring power back to the wheels that retain traction.

Lockers completely eliminate the operation of one or more differentials. A locker on the center differential switches between full-time and part-time 4WD. Lockers on the front or rear differentials ensure that power remains equally applied to each set of wheels regardless of whether both have traction. Lockers may be controlled manually, by a switch or a lever in the vehicle, or they may be automatic.

The Toyota Land Cruiser offers the option of having manual lockers on all three differentials, while other brands such as the Mitsubishi Montero offer manual lockers on the center and rear differential. Manual lockers are the most controllable and effective devices for ensuring that power is provided to the wheels with traction. However, because they allow absolutely no slippage, they must be used only on slippery surfaces.

An alternative method for getting power to the wheels that have traction is to allow limited wheel slippage. Systems that work this way may be called limited-slip differentials, posi-traction systems, or in the center differential, viscous couplings. The advantage of these systems is that the limited difference they allow in rotational speed between wheels enables such systems to be used when driving on a dry surface. All full-time 4WD systems allow limited slippage in the center differential.

For off-highway use, a manually locking differential is the best of the above systems, but it is the most expensive. Limited-slip differentials are the cheapest but also the least satisfactory, as they require one wheel to be slipping at 2 to 3 mph before power is transferred to the other wheel. For the center differential, the best system combines a locking differential and, to enable full-time use, a viscous coupling.

Tires

The tires that came with your 4WD vehicle may be satisfactory, but many 4WDs are fitted with passenger-car tires. These are unlikely to be the best choice because they are less rugged and more likely to puncture on rocky trails. They are particularly prone to sidewall damage as well. Passenger vehicle tires also have a less aggressive tread pattern than specialized 4WD tires, providing less traction in mud.

For information on purchasing tires better suited to off-highway conditions, see Special 4WD Equipment, page 20.

Clearance

Road clearances vary considerably among different 4WD vehicles—from less than 7 inches to more than 10 inches. Special vehicles may have far greater clearance. For instance, the Hummer has a 16-inch ground clearance. High ground clearance is particularly advantageous on the rockier or more rutted 4WD trails in this book.

When evaluating the ground clearance of your vehicle, you need to take into account the clearance of the bodywork between the wheels on each side of the vehicle. This is particularly relevant for crawling over larger rocks. Vehicles with sidesteps have significantly lower clearance than those without.

Another factor affecting clearance is the approach and departure angles of your vehicle—that is, the maximum angle the ground can slope without the front of the vehicle hitting the ridge on approach or the rear of the vehicle hitting on departure. Mounting a winch or tow hitch to your vehicle is likely to reduce your angle of approach or departure.

If you do a lot of driving on rocky trails, you will inevitably hit the bottom of the vehicle sooner or later. When this happens, you will be far less likely to damage vulnerable areas such as the oil pan and gas tank if your vehicle is fitted with skid plates. Most manufacturers offer skid plates as an option. They are worth every penny.

Maneuverability

When you tackle tight switchbacks, you will quickly appreciate that maneuverability is an important criterion when assessing 4WD vehicles. Where a full-size vehicle may be forced to go back and forth a number of times to get around a sharp turn, a small 4WD might go straight around. This is not only easier, it's safer.

If you have a full-size vehicle, all is not lost. We have traveled many of the trails in this book in a Suburban. That is not to say that some of these trails wouldn't have been easier to negotiate in a smaller vehicle! We have noted in the route descriptions if a trail is not suitable for larger vehicles.

In Summary

Using the criteria above, you can evaluate how well your 4WD will handle off-road touring, and if you haven't yet purchased your vehicle, you can use these criteria to help select one. Choosing the best 4WD system is, at least partly, subjective. It is also a matter of your budget. However, for the type of off-highway driving covered in this book, we make the following recommendations:

■ Select a 4WD system that offers low range and, at a minimum, has some form of limited slip differential on the rear axle.

■ Use light truck, all-terrain tires as the standard tires on your vehicle. For sand and slickrock, these will be the ideal choice. If conditions are likely to be muddy, or traction will be improved by a tread pattern that will give more bite, consider an additional set of mud tires.

■ For maximum clearance, select a vehicle with 16-inch wheels or at least choose the tallest tires that your vehicle can accommodate. Note that if you install tires with a diameter greater than standard, the odometer will undercalculate the distance you have traveled. Your engine braking and gear ratios will also be affected.

■ If you are going to try the rockier 4WD trails, don't install a sidestep or low-hanging front bar. If you have the option, have underbody skid plates mounted.

■ Remember that many of the obstacles you encounter on backcountry trails are more difficult to navigate in a full-size vehicle than in a compact 4WD.

Four-Wheel Driving Techniques

Safe four-wheel driving requires that you observe certain golden rules:

- Size up the situation in advance.
- Be careful and take your time.
- Maintain smooth, steady power and momentum.
- Engage 4WD and low-range gears before you get into a tight situation.
- Steer toward high spots, trying to put the wheel over large rocks.
- Straddle ruts.
- Use gears and not just the brakes to hold the vehicle when driving downhill. On very steep slopes, chock the wheels if you park your vehicle.
- Watch for logging and mining trucks and smaller recreational vehicles, such as all-terrain vehicles (ATVs).
- Wear your seat belt and secure all luggage, especially heavy items such as tool boxes or coolers. Heavy items should be secured by ratchet tie-down straps rather than elastic-type straps, which are not strong enough to hold heavy items if the vehicle rolls.

California's 4WD trails have a number of common obstacles, and the following provides an introduction to the techniques required to surmount them.

Rocks. Tire selection is important in negotiating rocks. Select a multiple-ply, tough sidewall, light-truck tire with a large-lug tread.

As you approach a rocky stretch, get into 4WD low range to give yourself maximum slow-speed control. Speed is rarely necessary, since traction on a rocky surface is usually good. Plan ahead and select the line you wish to take. If a rock appears to be larger than the clearance of your vehicle, don't try to straddle it. Check to see that it is not higher than the frame of your vehicle once you get a wheel over it. Put a wheel up on the rock and slowly climb it, then gently drop over the other side using the brake to ensure a smooth landing. Bouncing the car over rocks increases the likelihood of damage, as the body's clearance is reduced by the suspension compressing. Running boards also significantly reduce your clearance in this respect. It is often helpful to use a "spotter" outside the vehicle to assist you with the best wheel placement.

Steep Uphill Grades. Consider walking the trail to ensure that the steep hill before you is passable, especially if it is clear that backtracking is going to be a problem.

Select 4WD low range to ensure that you have adequate power to pull up the hill. If the wheels begin to lose traction, turn the steering wheel gently from side to side to give the wheels a chance to regain traction.

If you lose momentum, but the car is not in danger of sliding, use the foot brake, switch off the ignition, leave the vehicle in gear (if manual transmission) or park (if automatic), engage the parking brake, and get out to examine the situation. See if you can remove any obstacles, and figure out the line you need to take. Reversing a couple of yards and starting again may allow you to get better traction and momentum.

If halfway up, you decide a stretch of road is impassably steep, back down the trail. Trying to turn the vehicle around on a steep hill is extremely dangerous; you will very likely cause it to roll over.

Steep Downhill Grades. Again, consider walking the trail to ensure that a steep downhill is passable, especially if it is clear that backtracking uphill is going to be a problem.

Select 4WD low range and use first gear to maximize braking assistance from the engine. If the surface is loose and you are losing traction, change up to second or third gear. Do not use the brakes if you can avoid it, but don't let the vehicle's speed get out of control. Feather (lightly pump) the brakes if you slip under braking. For vehicles fitted with ABS, apply even pressure if you start to slip; the ABS helps keep vehicles on line.

Travel very slowly over rock ledges or ruts. Attempt to tackle these diagonally, letting one wheel down at a time.

If the back of the vehicle begins to slide around, gently apply the throttle and correct the steering. If the rear of the vehicle starts to slide sideways, do not apply the brakes.

Sand. As with most off-highway situations, your tires are the key to your ability to cross sand. It is difficult to tell how well a particular tire will handle in sand just by looking at it, so be guided by the manufacturer and your dealer.

The key to driving in soft sand is floatation, which is achieved by a combination of low tire pressure and momentum. Before crossing a stretch of sand, reduce your tire pressure to between 15 and 20 pounds. If necessary, you can safely go to as low as 12 pounds. As you cross, maintain momentum so that your vehicle rides on the top of the soft sand without digging in or stalling. This may require plenty of engine power. Avoid using the brakes if possible; removing your foot from the accelerator alone is normally enough to slow or stop. Using the brakes digs the vehicle deep in the sand.

Air the tires back up as soon as you are out of the sand to avoid damage to the tires and the rims. Airing back up requires a high-quality air compressor. Even then, it is a slow process.

In the backcountry of Southern California, sandy conditions are commonplace. You will therefore find a good compressor most useful.

Slickrock. When you encounter slickrock, first assess the correct direction of the trail. It is easy to lose sight of the trail on slickrock, as there are seldom any developed edges. Often the way is marked with small cairns, which are simply rocks stacked high enough to make a landmark.

All-terrain tires with tighter tread are more suited to slickrock than the more open, luggier type tires. As with rocks, a multiple-ply sidewall is important. In dry conditions, slickrock offers pavement-type grip. In rain or snow, you will soon learn how it got its name. Even the best tires may not get an adequate grip. Walk steep sections first; if you are slipping on foot, chances are your vehicle will slip too.

Slickrock is characterized by ledges and long sections of "pavement." Follow the guidelines for travel over rocks. Refrain from speeding over flat-looking sections, as you may hit an unexpected crevice or water pocket, and vehicles bend easier than slickrock! Turns and ledges can be tight, and vehicles with smaller overhangs and better maneuver-

ability are at a distinct advantage—hence the popularity of the compacts in the slickrock mecca of Moab, Utah.

On the steepest sections, engage low range and pick a straight line up or down the slope. Do not attempt to traverse a steep slope sideways.

Mud. Muddy trails are easily damaged, so they should be avoided if possible. But if you must traverse a section of mud, your success will depend heavily on whether you have open-lugged mud tires or chains. Thick mud fills the tighter tread on normal tires, leaving the tire with no more grip than if it were bald. If the muddy stretch is only a few yards long, the momentum of your vehicle may allow you to get through regardless.

If the muddy track is very steep, uphill or downhill, or off camber, do not attempt it. Your vehicle is likely to skid in such conditions, and you may roll or slip off the edge of the road. Also, check to see that the mud has a reasonably firm base. Tackling deep mud is definitely not recommended unless you have a vehicle-mounted winch—and even then, be cautious, because the winch may not get you out. Finally, check to see that no ruts are too deep for the ground clearance of your vehicle.

When you decide you can get through and have selected the best route, use the following techniques to cross through the mud:

■ Avoid making detours off existing tracks to minimize environmental damage.

■ Select 4WD low range and a suitable gear; momentum is the key to success, so use a high enough gear to build up sufficient speed.

■ Avoid accelerating heavily, so as to minimize wheel spinning and to provide maximum traction.

■ Follow existing wheel ruts, unless they are too deep for the clearance of your vehicle.

■ To correct slides, turn the steering wheel in the direction that the rear wheels are skidding, but don't be too aggressive or you'll overcorrect and lose control again.

■ If the vehicle comes to a stop, don't continue to accelerate, as you will only spin your wheels and dig yourself into a rut. Try backing out and having another go.

■ Be prepared to turn back before reaching the point of no return.

Stream Crossings. By crossing a stream that is too deep, drivers risk far more than water flowing in and ruining the interior of their vehicles. Water sucked into the engine's air intake will seriously damage the engine. Likewise, water that seeps into the air vent on the transmission or differential will mix with the lubricant and may lead to serious problems in due course.

Even worse, if the water is deep or fast flowing, it could easily carry your vehicle downstream, endangering the lives of everyone in the vehicle.

Some 4WD manuals tell you what fording depth the vehicle can negotiate safely. If your vehicle's owner's manual does not include this information, your local dealer may be able to assist. If you don't know, then avoid crossing through water that is more than a foot or so deep.

The first rule for crossing a stream is to know what you are getting into. You need to ascertain how deep the water is, whether there are any large rocks or holes, if the bottom is solid enough to avoid bogging down the vehicle, and whether the entry and exit points are negotiable. This may take some time and involve getting wet, but you take a great risk by crossing a stream without first properly assessing the situation.

The secret to water crossings is to keep moving, but not too fast. If you go too fast, you may drown the electrics, causing the vehicle to stall midstream. In shallow water (where the surface of the water is below the bumper), your primary concern is to safely negotiate the bottom of the stream, avoiding any rock damage and maintaining momentum if there is a danger of getting stuck or of slipping on the exit.

In deeper water (between 18 and 30 inches), the objective is to create a small bow wave in front of the moving vehicle. This requires a speed that is approximately walking pace. The bow wave reduces the depth of the water around the engine compartment. If the water's surface reaches your tailpipe, select a gear that will maintain moderate engine revs to avoid water backing up into the exhaust; and do not change gears midstream.

Crossing water deeper than 25 to 30 inches requires more extensive preparation of the vehicle and should be attempted only by experienced drivers.

Snow. The trails in this book that receive heavy snowfall are closed in winter. Therefore, the snow conditions that you are most likely to encounter are an occasional snowdrift that has not yet melted or fresh snow from an unexpected storm. Getting through such conditions depends on the depth of the snow, its consistency, the stability of the underlying surface, and your vehicle.

If the snow is no deeper than about 9 inches and there is solid ground beneath it, crossing the snow should not be a problem. In deeper snow that seems solid enough to support your vehicle, be extremely cautious: If you break through a drift, you are likely to be stuck, and if conditions are bad, you may have a long wait.

The tires you use for off-highway driving, with a wide tread pattern, are probably suitable for these snow conditions. Nonetheless, it is wise to carry chains (preferably for all four wheels), and if you have a vehicle-mounted winch, even better.

Vehicle Recovery Methods

If you do enough four-wheel driving, you are sure to get stuck sooner or later. The following techniques will help you get back on the go. The most suitable method will depend on the equipment available and the situation you are in—whether you are stuck in sand, mud, or snow, or are high-centered or unable to negotiate a hill.

Towing. Use a nylon yank strap of the type discussed in the Special 4WD Equipment section below. This type of strap will stretch 15 to 25 percent, and the elasticity will assist in extracting the vehicle.

Attach the strap only to a frame-mounted tow point. Ensure that the driver of the stuck vehicle is ready, take up all but about 6 feet of slack, then move the towing vehicle away at a moderate speed (in most circumstances this means using 4WD low range in second gear) so that the elasticity of the strap is employed in the way it is meant to be. Don't take off like a bat out of hell or you risk breaking the strap or damaging a vehicle.

Never join two yank straps together with a shackle. If one strap breaks, the shackle will become a lethal missile aimed at one of the vehicles (and anyone inside). For the same reason, never attach a yank strap to the tow ball on either vehicle.

Jacking. Jacking the vehicle allows you to pack under the wheel (with rocks, dirt, or logs) or use your shovel to remove an obstacle. However, the standard vehicle jack is unlikely to be of as much assistance as a high-lift jack. We highly recommend purchasing a good high-lift jack as a basic accessory if you decide that you are going to do a lot of serious, off-highway four-wheel driving. Remember a high-lift jack is of limited use if your vehicle does not have an appropriate jacking point. Some brush bars have two built-in forward jacking points.

Tire Chains. Tire chains can be of assistance in both mud and snow. Cable-type chains provide much less grip than link-type chains. There are also dedicated mud chains with larger, heavier links than on normal snow chains. It is best to have chains fitted to all four wheels.

Once you are bogged down is not the best time to try to fit the chains; if at all possible, try to predict their need and have them on the tires before trouble arises. An easy way to affix chains is to place two small cubes of wood under the center of the stretched-out chain. When you drive your tires up on the blocks of wood, it is easier to stretch the chains over the tires because the pressure is off.

Winching. Most recreational four-wheel drivers do not have a winch. But if you get serious about four-wheel driving, this is probably the first major accessory you should consider buying.

Under normal circumstances, a winch would be warranted only for the more difficult 4WD trails in this book. Having a winch is certainly comforting when you see a difficult section of road ahead and have to decide whether to risk it or turn back. Also, major obstacles can appear when you least expect them, even on trails that are otherwise easy.

Owning a winch is not a panacea to all your recovery problems. Winching depends on the availability of a good anchor point, and electric winches may not work if they are submerged in a stream. Despite these constraints, no accessory is more useful than a high-quality, powerful winch when you get into a difficult situation.

If you acquire a winch, learn to use it properly; take the time to study your owner's manual. Incorrect operation can be extremely dangerous and may cause damage to the winch or to your anchor points, which are usually trees.

Navigation by the Global Positioning System (GPS)

Although this book is designed so that each trail can be navigated simply by following the detailed directions provided, nothing makes navigation easier than a GPS receiver.

The global positioning system (GPS) consists of a network of 24 satellites, nearly 13,000 miles in space, in six different orbital paths. The satellites are constantly moving at about 8,500 miles per hour, making two complete orbits around the earth every 24 hours.

Each satellite is constantly transmitting data, including its identification number, its operational health, and the date and time. It also transmits its location and the location of every other satellite in the network.

By comparing the time the signal was transmitted to the time it is received, a GPS receiver calculates how far away each satellite is. With a sufficient number of signals, the receiver can then triangulate its location. With three or more satellites, the receiver can determine latitude and longitude coordinates. With four or more, it can calculate altitude. By constantly making these calculations, it can determine speed and direction. To facilitate these calculations, the time data broadcast by GPS is accurate to within 40 billionths of a second.

The U.S. military uses the system to provide positions accurate to within half an inch. When the system was first established, civilian receivers were deliberately fed slightly erroneous information in order to effectively deny military applications to hostile countries or terrorists—a practice called selective availability (SA). However on May 1, 2000, in response to the growing importance of the system for civilian applications, the U.S. government stopped intentionally downgrading GPS data. The military gave its support to this change once new technology made it possible to selectively degrade the system within any defined geographical area on demand. This new feature of the system has made it safe to have higher-quality signals available for civilian use. Now, instead of the civilian-use signal having a margin of error being between 20 and 70 yards, it is only about one-tenth of that.

A GPS receiver offers the four-wheeler numerous benefits:

■ You can track to any point for which you know the longitude and latitude coordinates with no chance of heading in the wrong direction or getting lost. Most receivers provide an extremely easy-to-understand graphic display to keep you on track.

■ It works in all weather conditions.

■ It automatically records your route for easy backtracking.

■ You can record and name any location, so that you can relocate it with ease. This may include your campsite, a fishing spot, or even a silver mine you discover!

■ It displays your position, allowing you to pinpoint your location on a map.

■ By interfacing the GPS receiver directly to a portable computer, you can monitor and record your location as you travel (using the appropriate map software) or print the route you took.

However, remember that GPS units can fail, batteries can go flat, and tree cover and

tight canyons can block the signals. Never rely entirely on GPS for navigation. Always carry a compass for backup.

Special 4WD Equipment

Tires

When 4WD touring, you will likely encounter a wide variety of terrain: rocks, mud, talus, slickrock, sand, gravel, dirt, and bitumen. The immense variety of tires on the market includes many specifically targeted at one or another of these types of terrain, as well as tires designed to adequately handle a range of terrain.

Every four-wheel driver seems to have a preference when it comes to tire selection, but most people undertaking the 4WD trails in this book will need tires that can handle all of the above types of terrain adequately.

The first requirement is to select rugged, light-truck tires rather than passenger-vehicle tires. Check the size data on the sidewall: it should have "LT" rather than "P" before the number. Among light-truck tires, you must choose between tires that are designated "all-terrain" and more-aggressive, wider-tread mud tires. Either type will be adequate, especially on rocks, gravel, talus, or dirt. Although mud tires have an advantage in muddy conditions and soft snow, all-terrain tires perform better on slickrock, in sand, and particularly on ice and paved roads.

When selecting tires, remember that they affect not just traction but also cornering ability, braking distances, fuel consumption, and noise levels. It pays to get good advice before making your decision.

Global Positioning System Receivers

GPS receivers have come down in price considerably in the past few years and are rapidly becoming indispensable navigational tools. Many higher-priced cars now offer integrated GPS receivers, and within the next few years, receivers will become available on most models.

Battery-powered, hand-held units that meet the needs of off-highway driving currently range from less than $100 to a little over $300 and continue to come down in price. Some high-end units feature maps that are incorporated in the display, either from a built-in database or from interchangeable memory cards. Currently, only a few of these maps include 4WD trails.

If you are considering purchasing a GPS unit, keep the following in mind:

■ Price. The very cheapest units are likely outdated and very limited in their display features. Expect to pay from $125 to $300.

■ The display. Compare the graphic display of one unit with another. Some are much easier to decipher or offer more alternative displays.

■ The controls. GPS receivers have many functions, and they need to have good, simple controls.

■ Vehicle mounting. To be useful, the unit needs to be placed where it can be read easily by both the driver and the navigator. Check that the unit can be conveniently located in your vehicle. Different units have different shapes and different mounting systems.

■ Map data. More and more units have map data built in. Some have the ability to download maps from a computer. Such maps are normally sold on a CD-ROM. GPS units have a finite storage capacity and having the ability to download maps covering a narrower geographical region means that the amount of data relating to that specific region can be greater.

■ The number of routes and the number of sites (or "waypoints") per route that can be stored in memory. For off-highway use, it is important to be able to store plenty of waypoints so that you do not have to load coordinates into the machine as frequently. Having plenty of memory also ensures that you can automatically store your present location without fear that the memory is full.

■ Waypoint storage. The better units store up to 500 waypoints and 20 reversible routes of up to 30 waypoints each. Also consider the number of characters a GPS receiver allows you to use to name waypoints. When you try to recall a waypoint, you may have difficulty recognizing names restricted to only a few characters.

■ Automatic route storing. Most units automatically store your route as you go along and enable you to display it in reverse to make backtracking easy.

After you have selected a unit, a number of optional extras are also worth considering:

■ A cigarette lighter electrical adapter. Despite GPS units becoming more power efficient, protracted in-vehicle use still makes this accessory a necessity.

■ A vehicle-mounted antenna, which will improve reception under difficult conditions. (The GPS unit can only "see" through the windows of your vehicle; it cannot monitor satellites through a metal roof.) Having a vehicle-mounted antenna also means that you do not have to consider reception when locating the receiver in your vehicle.

■ An in-car mounting system. If you are going to do a lot of touring using the GPS, consider attaching a bracket on the dash rather than relying on a Velcro mount.

■ A computer-link cable and digital maps. Data from your GPS receiver can be downloaded to your PC; maps and waypoints can be downloaded from your PC; or if you have a laptop computer, you can monitor your route as you go along, using one of a number of inexpensive map software products on the market.

Yank Straps

Yank straps are industrial-strength versions of the flimsy tow straps carried by the local discount store. They are 20 to 30 feet long and 2 to 3 inches wide, made of heavy nylon, rated to at least 20,000 pounds, and have looped ends.

Do not use tow straps with metal hooks in the ends (the hooks can become missiles in the event the strap breaks free). Likewise, never join two yank straps together using a shackle.

CB Radios

If you are stuck, injured, or just want to know the conditions up ahead, a citizen's band (CB) radio can be invaluable. CB radios are relatively inexpensive and do not require an FCC license. Their range is limited, especially in very hilly country, as their transmission patterns basically follow lines of sight. Range can be improved using single sideband (SSB) transmission, an option on more expensive units. Range is even better on vehicle-mounted units that have been professionally fitted to ensure that the antenna and cabling are matched appropriately.

Winches

There are three main options when it comes to winches: manual winches, removable electric winches, and vehicle-mounted electric winches.

If you have a full-size 4WD vehicle—which can weigh in excess of 7,000 pounds when loaded—a manual winch is of limited use without a lot of effort and considerable time. However, a manual winch is a very handy and inexpensive accessory if you have a small 4WD. Typically, manual winches are rated to pull about 5,500 pounds.

Electric winches can be mounted to your vehicle's trailer hitch to enable them to be removed, relocated to the front of your vehicle (if you have a hitch installed), or moved to another vehicle. Although this is a very useful feature, a winch is heavy, so relocating one can be a two-person job. Consider that 5,000-pound-rated winches weigh only about 55 pounds, while 12,000-pound-rated models weigh around 140 pounds. Therefore, the larger models are best permanently front-mounted. Unfortunately, this position limits their ability to winch the vehicle backward.

When choosing among electric winches, be aware that they are rated for their maximum capacity on the first wind of the cable around the drum. As layers of cable wind onto the drum, they increase its diameter and thus decrease the maximum load the winch can handle. This decrease is significant: A winch rated to pull 8,000 pounds on a bare drum may only handle 6,500 pounds on the second layer, 5,750 pounds on the third layer, and 5,000 pounds on the fourth. Electric winches also draw a high level of current and may necessitate upgrading the battery in your 4WD or adding a second battery.

There is a wide range of mounting options—from a simple, body-mounted frame that holds the winch to heavy-duty winch bars that replace the original bumper and incorporate brush bars and mounts for auxiliary lights.

If you buy a winch, either electric or manual, you will also need quite a range of additional equipment so that you can operate it correctly:

- at least one choker chain with hooks on each end,
- winch extension straps or cables,
- shackles,
- a receiver shackle,
- a snatch block,
- a tree protector,
- gloves.

Grill/Brush Bars and Winch Bars

Brush bars protect the front of the vehicle from scratches and minor bumps; they also provide a solid mount for auxiliary lights and often high-lift jacking points. The level of protection they provide depends on how solid they are and whether they are securely mounted onto the frame of the vehicle. Lighter models attach in front of the standard bumper, but the more substantial units replace the bumper. Prices range from about $150 to $450.

Winch bars replace the bumper and usually integrate a solid brush bar with a heavy-duty winch mount. Some have the brush bar as an optional extra to the winch bar component. Manufacturers such as Warn, ARB, and TJM offer a wide range of integrated winch bars. These are significantly more expensive, starting at about $650.

Remember that installing heavy equipment on the front of the vehicle may necessitate increasing the front suspension rating to cope with the additional weight.

Portable Air Compressors

Most portable air compressors on the market are flimsy models that plug into the cigarette lighter and are sold at the local discount store. These are of very limited use for four-wheel driving. They are very slow to inflate the large tires of a 4WD vehicle; for instance, to reinflate from 15 to 35 pounds typically takes about 10 minutes for each tire. They are also unlikely to be rated for continuous use, which means that they will overheat and cut off before completing the job. If you're lucky, they will start up again when they have cooled down, but this means that you are unlikely to reinflate your tires in less than an hour.

The easiest way to identify a useful air compressor is by the price—good ones cost $200 or more. Many of the quality units feature a Thomas-brand pump and are built to last. Another good unit is sold by ARB. All these pumps draw between 15 and 20 amps and thus should not be plugged into the cigarette lighter socket but attached to the vehicle's battery with clips. The ARB unit can be permanently mounted under the hood. Quick-Air makes a range of units including a 10-amp compressor that can be plugged into the cigarette lighter socket and performs well.

Auxiliary Driving Lights

There is a vast array of auxiliary lights on the market today, and selecting the best lights for your purpose can be a confusing process.

Auxiliary lights greatly improve visibility in adverse weather conditions. Driving lights provide a strong, moderately wide beam to supplement headlamp high beams, giving improved lighting in the distance and to the sides of the main beam. Fog lamps throw a wide-dispersion, flat beam; and spots provide a high-power, narrow beam to improve lighting range directly in front of the vehicle. Rear-mounted auxiliary lights provide greatly improved visibility for backing up.

For off-highway use, you will need quality lights with strong mounting brackets. Some high-powered off-highway lights are not approved by the Department of Transportation for use on public roads.

Roof Racks

Roof racks can be excellent for storing gear, as well as providing easy access for certain weatherproof items. However, they raise the center of gravity on the vehicle, which can substantially alter the rollover angle. A roof rack is best used for lightweight objects that are well strapped down. Heavy recovery gear and other bulky items should be packed low in the vehicle's interior to lower the center of gravity and stabilize the vehicle.

A roof rack should allow for safe and secure packing of items and be sturdy enough to withstand knocks.

Packing Checklist

Before embarking on any 4WD adventure, whether a lazy Sunday drive on an easy trail or a challenging climb over rugged terrain, be prepared. The following checklist will help you gather the items you need.

Essential
- ❏ Rain gear
- ❏ Small shovel or multipurpose ax, pick, shovel, and sledgehammer
- ❏ Heavy-duty yank strap
- ❏ Spare tire that matches the other tires on the vehicle
- ❏ Working jack and base plate for soft ground
- ❏ Maps
- ❏ Emergency medical kit, including sun protection and insect repellent
- ❏ Bottled water
- ❏ Blankets or space blankets
- ❏ Parka, gloves, and boots
- ❏ Spare vehicle key
- ❏ Jumper leads
- ❏ Heavy-duty flashlight
- ❏ Multipurpose tool, such as a Leatherman
- ❏ Emergency food—high-energy bars or similar

Worth Considering
- ❏ Global Positioning System (GPS) receiver
- ❏ Cell phone
- ❏ A set of light-truck, off-highway tires and matching spare
- ❏ High-lift jack
- ❏ Additional tool kit
- ❏ CB radio
- ❏ Portable air compressor
- ❏ Tire gauge
- ❏ Tire-sealing kit
- ❏ Tire chains
- ❏ Handsaw and ax
- ❏ Binoculars
- ❏ Firearms
- ❏ Whistle
- ❏ Flares
- ❏ Vehicle fire extinguisher
- ❏ Gasoline, engine oil, and other vehicle fluids
- ❏ Portable hand winch
- ❏ Electric cooler

If Your Credit Cards Aren' t Maxed Out
- ❏ Electric, vehicle-mounted winch and associated recovery straps, shackles, and snatch blocks
- ❏ Auxiliary lights
- ❏ Locking differential(s)

Trails in the Desert Region

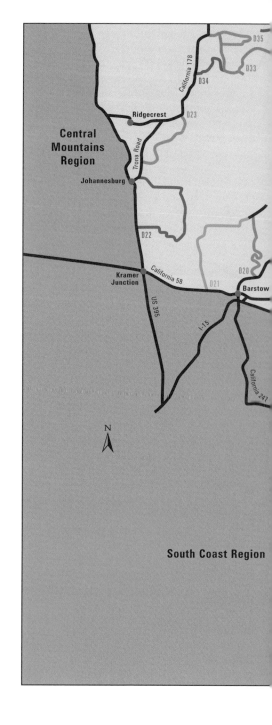

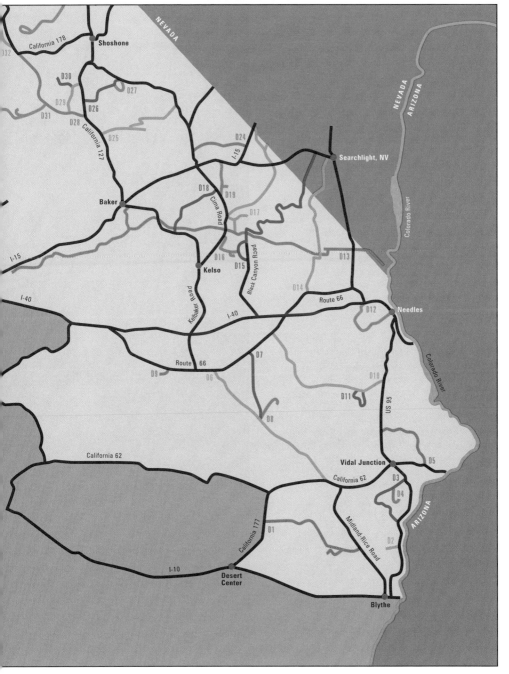

Trails in the Desert Region

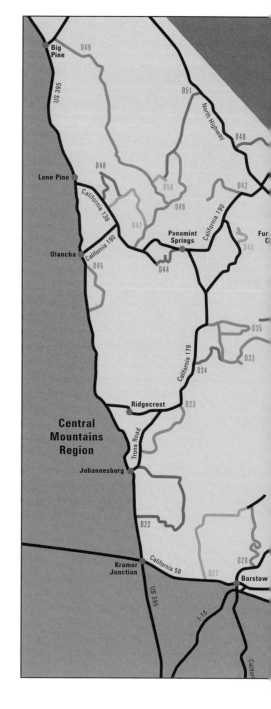

MAP CONTINUES ON PAGE 25

Palen Pass Trail

STARTING POINT: Desert Center–Rice Road (California 177), 9.7 miles south of the intersection with California 62
FINISHING POINT: Midland–Rice Road, 17.7 miles north of I-10
TOTAL MILEAGE: 33.8 miles, plus 0.9-mile spur
UNPAVED MILEAGE: 33.8 miles, plus 0.9-mile spur
DRIVING TIME: 3 hours
ELEVATION RANGE: 600–1,600 feet
USUALLY OPEN: Year-round
BEST TIME TO TRAVEL: October to June
DIFFICULTY RATING: 3
SCENIC RATING: 8
REMOTENESS RATING: +1

Special Attractions

- Trail travels a vehicle corridor through the Palen-McCoy Wilderness.
- Remains of the Arlington and Black Jack Mines.
- Midland Long-Term Visitor Area, located a short distance from the trail.

History

In the late 1800s, an Irish miner named Matthew Palen prospected the mountains of this remote desert region. His name has been attached to the wide valley at the western end of this trail as well as the pass between the Granite and Palen Mountains.

Camp Coxcomb is at the western end of Palen Pass Trail. The camp was part of General George Patton's Desert Training Center (DTC), later called the California-Arizona Maneuver Area (CAMA), established in the spring of 1942. The camp was one of 11 that spanned a combined area of nearly 18,000 square miles in California, Nevada, and Arizona. The camps, set in a harsh desert environment, were chosen to train troops for action in the same conditions they would face in North Africa during World War II.

Inca Siding

Rock enclosures on the west side of Palen Pass are left over from World War II training exercises

CAMA was declared surplus in March 1944, when the last troops were deployed and cleanup began. Hundreds of duds were located and destroyed onsite. However, because only a limited number of troops were available, an extensive search could not be undertaken. Although cleanups have occurred since then, the CAMA locations generally have surface clearance only. The public is advised not to dig below the surface and is encouraged to report finding any duds.

Palen Pass was a site used by troops from the DTC to stage practice ambushes. Divisions would carry out maneuvers against fortified positions at Palen Pass. These exercises could go on for up to four days at a time, in temperatures reaching as high as 130 degrees. They taught soldiers the importance of depending on the regiment for much needed supplies. A division could not last in such a harsh setting without water, gas, and rations. Water supplies were kept at a minimum to continually test the troops. When hiking in this region, you will likely encounter several small stone enclosures left over from these training maneuvers.

The McCoy Mountains, along the south side of this trail, were named after the operator of a local government trading post, Bill McCoy. His store was in Ehrenburg, on the Arizona side of the Colorado River. The McCoy Mountains were the site of a lost placer mine in the late 1800s. An old Papago chief, named Papuan, and his Mojave wife would always pay for goods with gold. The couple bought so much that it was estimated McCoy had acquired more than $70,000 from them. The Mojave woman had known of a gold mine in the McCoy Mountains in the 1860s, prior to meeting her husband. Together they would slip away from their camp by the Colorado River, always returning from the McCoy Mountains with gold in hand. They were known to share their treasure with other Indians, who would also shop at McCoy's trading post. Though questioned and followed by would-be claim jumpers, the chief and his wife were artists when it came to evading detection. They never revealed the location of the gold.

The Palen-McCoy Wilderness was established in 1994, encompassing 270,629 acres. Ironwood trees are predominant as you travel down the sandy wash east of Palen Pass. This forest is one of the most lush ironwood forests in California's desert. The name of the trees reflects the dense nature of the wood, which Native Americans used for tools and weapons. Seeds were part of their staple diet. Ironwoods are found in other harsh environments, such as the hot deserts of Australia; the wood is so heavy it sinks in water.

Description

Palen Pass Trail follows the marked Palen Pass Road and Arlington Mine Road. The route is marked by white posts with the road's name. Most intersections and points where there is a chance for confusion have such markers, so navigation is easy.

The trail leaves California 177 south of its intersection with California 62. It travels in a plumb line up the bajada toward the pale, jagged peaks of the mountain ranges of the Palen-McCoy Wilderness. There are many shallow wash crossings along this route; they have not been mentioned in the route directions because they are so numerous. Along the bajada, the trail traverses areas of loose, deep sand. It enters a vehicle corridor within the wilderness; vehicle travel is not permitted off the formed trail. As the trail begins the gradual ascent toward the pass, it becomes a rough formed road. The trail's difficulty rating of 3 is based upon this section on the west side of the pass. The uneven surface makes a high-clearance 4WD preferable.

Palen Pass is a gentle rise between the Granite Mountains to the north and the Palen Mountains to the south. The Granite Mountains are a popular hiking destination. The ranges are pale in color, with jagged peaks and sparse vegetation. Tailings heaps and long cuts indicate past strip-mining endeavors along the trail.

On the east side of the pass, the route joins Arlington Mine Road. This wider, once-graded road makes for easier travel. However, it can be rough in places, and gul-

Approaching Palen Pass from the west

lies and sand traps can catch the unwary. The trail descends a wide valley, with the Little Maria Mountains to the north and the McCoy Mountains to the south; both ranges rise abruptly from the broad valley floor.

East of Palen Pass, ironwoods, mesquites, and palo verdes provide habitat for coyotes, bobcats, kit foxes, gray foxes, kangaroo rats, and mountain lions.

The Arlington and Black Jack Mines are reached by a short spur. Trails within the mine areas can be confusing because they weave around many diggings, large pits, and adits over 30 feet tall. Many of these trails are unsafe or washed away. Be careful when exploring the area, whether on foot or in a vehicle.

The trail continues along the wide valley, passing the railroad siding at Inca on the Atchison, Topeka & Santa Fe Railroad, before finishing northwest of Blythe on Midland–Rice Road. A short distance south of the end of the trail is the Midland Long-Term Visitor Area, a BLM-managed area that caters to winter RV visitors. They are permitted to stop within the area between September and April with the appropriate permit. Although not as popular as Quartzsite, Arizona, the area still attracts many winter visitors.

Current Road Information
Bureau of Land Management
Palm Springs South Coast Field Office
PO Box 581260
690 West Garnet Avenue
North Palm Springs, CA 92258
(760) 251-4800

Map References
BLM   Eagle Mtns., Blythe
USGS 1:24,000   West of Palen Pass,
        Palen Pass, Arlington Mine, Little
        Maria Mtn., Inca, Big Maria Mtn. SW
        1:100,000 Eagle Mtns., Blythe
Maptech CD-ROM: San Diego/Joshua Tree
Southern & Central California Atlas & Gazetteer, pp. 110, 111
California Road & Recreation Atlas, p. 113

DESERT #1: PALEN PASS TRAIL

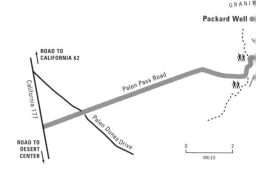

Route Directions

▼ 0.0   From Desert Center–Rice Road (California 177) at mile marker 17, 9.7 miles south of the intersection with California 62, zero trip meter and turn east on Palen Pass Road (shown on some maps as P 172). The road is marked with a BLM route marker as Palen Pass Road. There is a historical marker on the road opposite.

1.7 ▲   Trail finishes on Desert Center–Rice Road (California 177). Turn left for Desert Center; turn right for Vidal Junction.

GPS: N33°54.49′ W115°14.82′

▼ 1.0 BR Trail forks, left track can be sandier.
0.7 ▲ SO Trail rejoins.
▼ 1.2 SO Trail rejoins.
0.5 ▲ BL Trail forks, right track can be sandier.
▼ 1.7 SO Track on left and right is marked as Palen Dunes Drive by a marker post. Zero trip meter and continue into the vehicle corridor through the Palen-McCoy Wilderness.
0.0 ▲   Continue to the west.

GPS: N33°54.58′ W115°12.96′

▼ 0.0   Continue to the east.
7.9 ▲ SO Track on left and right is marked as Palen Dunes Drive by a marker post. Zero trip meter and leave vehicle corridor.

▼ 6.7 SO Trail deviates around a large washout. Follow marker posts.

1.2 ▲ SO Trail deviates around a large washout. Follow marker posts.
GPS: N33°54.19' W115°05.89'

▼ 7.1 BL Track on right gives wilderness access for foot and horse travel only.
0.8 ▲ BR Track on left gives wilderness access for foot and horse travel only.
GPS: N33°54.17' W115°05.54'

▼ 7.9 BR Track on left gives wilderness access for foot and horse travel only. Zero trip meter at sign.
0.0 ▲ Continue to the south.
GPS: N33°54.76' W115°05.21'

▼ 0.0 Continue to the east and cross through wash.
3.1 ▲ BL Cross through wash; then track on right gives wilderness access for foot and horse travel only. Zero trip meter at sign.
▼ 0.1 SO Track on left gives wilderness access for foot and horse travel only.
3.0 ▲ SO Track on right gives wilderness access for foot and horse travel only.
▼ 0.2 SO Track on right.
2.9 ▲ SO Track on left.
▼ 0.3 SO Start to cross through wide wash.
2.8 ▲ SO Exit wide wash crossing.
▼ 0.4 SO Exit wide wash crossing and wilderness corridor.
2.7 ▲ SO Enter vehicle corridor through the Palen-McCoy Wilderness and start to cross through wide wash.

▼ 0.7 SO High above the trail on the left are small rock enclosures.
2.4 ▲ SO High above the trail on the right are small rock enclosures.
GPS: N33°54.82' W115°04.61'

▼ 0.8 SO Five small stone ruins on left.
2.3 ▲ SO Five small stone ruins on right.
GPS: N33°54.86' W115°04.58'

▼ 0.9 SO Enter wash.
2.2 ▲ SO Exit wash.
▼ 1.1 SO Exit wash.
2.0 ▲ SO Enter wash.
▼ 1.4 SO Track on left; then cross through wash.
1.7 ▲ SO Cross through wash; then track on right.
▼ 1.5 SO Track on left; then track on right into mining area.
1.6 ▲ SO Track on left into mining area; then track on right.
GPS: N33°54.94' W115°03.81'

▼ 1.9 SO Cross through two washes.
1.2 ▲ SO Cross through two washes.
▼ 2.1 SO Enter wash.
1.0 ▲ SO Exit wash.
▼ 2.2 SO Exit wash.
0.9 ▲ SO Enter wash.
▼ 2.3 SO Palen Pass. Many small tracks on left and right to mines for the next 0.7 miles.
0.8 ▲ SO Palen Pass.
GPS: N33°55.23' W115°03.17'

▼ 2.4 SO Enter down wash. Track on left.
0.7 ▲ SO Track on right. Exit wash.

▼ 2.7   SO   Track on right.

0.4 ▲   SO   Track on left.

▼ 2.9   SO   Exit wash.

0.2 ▲   SO   Enter wash.

▼ 3.0   SO   Track on right; then cross through wash.

0.1 ▲   SO   Cross through wash; then track on left. Many small tracks on left and right to mines for the next 0.7 miles.

▼ 3.1   TR   Turn right onto Arlington Mine Road and zero trip meter at marker post. Wide track on left goes to Packard Well.

0.0 ▲   Continue to the southwest.
GPS: N33°55.37′ W115°02.35′

▼ 0.0   Continue to the east.

9.4 ▲   TL   Turn left onto Palen Pass Road and zero trip meter at marker post. Wide track ahead goes to Packard Well.

▼ 0.1   SO   Track on left.

9.3 ▲   SO   Track on right.

▼ 0.7   SO   Cross through wash.

8.7 ▲   SO   Cross through wash.

▼ 1.8   SO   Track on left.

7.6 ▲   SO   Track on right.
GPS: N33°54.86′ W115°00.54′

▼ 3.0   SO   Track on right.

6.4 ▲   SO   Track on left.

▼ 3.1   SO   Cross through wash.

6.3 ▲   SO   Cross through wash.
GPS: N33°54.06′ W114°59.58′

▼ 3.4   SO   Track on right.

6.0 ▲   SO   Track on left.

▼ 8.2   SO   Cross through wash.

1.2 ▲   SO   Cross through wash.
GPS: N33°50.26′ W114°57.01′

▼ 8.3   SO   Graded track on left. Continue on Arlington Mine Road.

1.1 ▲   SO   Graded track on right. Continue on Arlington Mine Road.
GPS: N33°50.23′ W114°56.92

▼ 9.1   SO   Track on left in wash. Continue on Arlington Mine Road.

0.3 ▲   SO   Track on right in wash. Continue on Arlington Mine Road.

▼ 9.4   BL   Well-used track on right. Zero trip meter at Arlington Mine Road marker.

0.0 ▲   Continue to the west.
GPS: N33°49.71′ W114°55.98′

▼ 0.0   Continue to the northeast.

1.4 ▲   BR   Well-used track on left. Zero trip meter at Arlington Mine Road marker.

▼ 0.3   SO   Track on right.

1.1 ▲   SO   Track on left.

▼ 1.0   SO   Track on left.

0.3 ▲   SO   Track on right.

▼ 1.2   SO   Track on right.

0.2 ▲   SO   Track on left.

▼ 1.4   BL   Well-used track on right is spur to Arlington and Black Jack Mines. Zero trip meter at marker post.

0.0 ▲   Continue to the northwest.
GPS: N33°49.30′ W114°54.87′

Spur to Arlington and Black Jack Mines

▼ 0.0   Proceed to the southwest.

▼ 0.1   BL   Track on right.

▼ 0.4   BR   Track on left; then track on left and track on right.
GPS: N33°49.03′ W114°55.09′

▼ 0.5   TR   Track on left. Straight ahead goes 0.1 miles to Arlington Mine pit. Turn right; then track on left goes into Arlington Mine pit.
GPS: N33°48.96′ W114°55.13′

▼ 0.8   SO   Track on left to adit.

▼ 0.9   UT   Large adit of the Black Jack Mine on left. Track on right descends to loading hopper. Road ahead is extremely rough and will stop most vehicles in a short distance. Hiking is recommended.
GPS: N33°49.00′ W114°55.46′

Continuation of Main Trail

▼ 0.0   Continue to the northeast.

3.3 ▲   BR   Well-used track on left is the spur to Arlington and Black Jack Mines. Zero trip meter at marker post.
GPS: N33°49.30′ W114°54.87′

▼ 2.1	SO	Track on left.
1.2 ▲	SO	Track on right.
▼ 2.9	SO	Wide formed road on left.
0.4 ▲	SO	Wide formed road on right.

GPS: N33°49.07' W114°51.84'

▼ 3.3	SO	Graded road on left goes to mine. Zero trip meter at route marker.
0.0 ▲		Continue to the west.

GPS: N33°48.98' W114°51.41'

▼ 0.0		Continue to the east.
7.0 ▲	BL	Graded road on right goes to mine. Zero trip meter at route marker.
▼ 0.4	SO	Track on right and track on left.
6.6 ▲	SO	Track on left and track on right.
▼ 2.5	SO	Track on left.
4.5 ▲	SO	Track on right.
▼ 3.3	SO	Track on left.
3.7 ▲	SO	Track on right.
▼ 4.2	SO	Track on right and track on left.
2.8 ▲	SO	Track on left and track on right.

GPS: N33°47.90' W114°47.10'

▼ 4.9	BL	Graded road on right. Continue on Arlington Mine Road.
2.1 ▲	SO	Graded road on left. Continue on Arlington Mine Road.
▼ 5.0	SO	Track on left.
2.0 ▲	SO	Track on right.
▼ 5.2	BL	Track on right. Bear left toward railroad crossing.
1.8 ▲	BR	Track on left. Bear right away from railroad.

GPS: N33°47.97' W114°46.03'

▼ 5.4	SO	Cross over railroad at Inca Siding.
1.6 ▲	SO	Cross over railroad at Inca Siding.

GPS: N33°48.09' W114°45.94'

▼ 7.0		Trail ends at T-intersection with paved Midland–Rice Road. Small formed road opposite. Turn left for Rice Siding and California 62; turn right for I-10 and Blythe.
0.0 ▲		Trail commences on paved Midland–Rice Road, 17.7 miles north of I-40 and the Lovekin Boulevard exit in Blythe. (Lovekin Boulevard becomes Midland–Rice Road.) Zero trip meter and turn

southwest on wide, graded dirt road, marked Arlington Mine Road by a BLM marker post. There is a notice board at the intersection and a formed road opposite.

GPS: N33°49.05' W114°44.85'

DESERT #2

Blythe Intaglios Trail

STARTING POINT: US 95, 15.3 miles north of Blythe
FINISHING POINT: Big Maria Mountains
TOTAL MILEAGE: 4.0 miles (one-way)
UNPAVED MILEAGE: 4.0 miles
DRIVING TIME: 45 minutes (one-way)
ELEVATION RANGE: 300–1,000 feet
USUALLY OPEN: Year-round
BEST TIME TO TRAVEL: October to June
DIFFICULTY RATING: 3
SCENIC RATING: 10
REMOTENESS RATING: +0

Special Attractions
- Blythe intaglios.
- Narrow ridge-top trail into the Big Maria Mountains.
- Varied vegetation and views over the Colorado River and Big Maria Mountains.

History
Paleo-Indians roamed the Colorado River region for thousands of years before the arrival of Euro-Americans. Records of these peoples' histories appear in many forms across the landscape. One of the more striking is the collection of intaglios (in-TAL-yos) situated north of Blythe. Giant human and animal figures are etched into the desert surface high above the riverbed, alongside geometrical shapes. All of the figures are bare areas on the stony hillside, with outlines made by moving patinaed stones, thereby creating the shapes.

The first report of these figures came in 1930 from George Palmer, a pilot who spotted them from the air. Upon further inspection, a

This ridge-top trail offers splendid views into the Big Maria Mountains

total of six figures in three locations were found; archaeological studies put them at approximately 1,100 years of age. The largest human figure spans about 170 feet from head to toe. Creations such as these in the United States are seldom seen and have only been found in Arizona and California. Though it is not always possible, the best way to view these intaglios is from the air.

Theories and tales about the figures' meaning or purpose have evolved throughout the years. Local Mojave and Quechan say the human figures represent Mastamho, the creator of life, and the animals represent Hatakulya, a part-lion part-person who helped at the time of creation. Religious ceremonies honoring Mastamho occurred at this location.

Pilgrimages were held along the banks of the Colorado River, with ceremonies at points such as this. The southern end of the river was referred to as the Land of the Dead. As the pilgrimage moved north, it celebrated the actions of mythic beings that were represented by intaglios along the way. When the pilgrimage reached the northern end of the great river, it was said to have entered into the Place of Creation.

Other interpretations associate the figures with astronomy, religious lore, and territorial markers. One controversial author, Erich von Daniken, put forward the theory that God was an astronaut from outer space in a number of books from the late 1960s to the present. He based his theory on the abundance of these giant figures worldwide.

Description

The Blythe intaglios are excellent examples of ancient desert art. This short trail leaves US 95 north of Blythe and passes alongside the figures. The trail is fenced on either side within the intaglio area. A couple of small parking areas mark the start of short hiking trails to the intaglios. Human figures, an animal believed to be part horse, and spiral and circular shapes can be seen.

Past the intaglio area, the trail is less used and unmarked. It follows a formed trail toward the Big Maria Mountains.

Blythe intaglio—human figure

YUMA (QUECHAN) & MOJAVE (MOHAVE)

Quechan Yellow Sky on left

The Yuma, or Quechan as they prefer to be called, trace their ancestral home to a sacred mountain near Needles, California, called Avikwamé. Sometime before Spanish explorers made contact with the tribe in 1540, they moved to the area around the confluence of the Colorado and Gila Rivers and controlled the Yuma crossing, an important passage across the Colorado River.

Conditions in the region were harsh; temperatures often exceeded 100°F. The Quechan lived along the banks of the river, moving to higher lands to avoid spring floods. Their dwellings varied from open, rectangular structures to Apache-like wickiups. They supplemented their diet of fish and wild plants by farming corn, beans, squash, and grasses in the silt left over from floods.

In the late 1700s, Spanish missionaries established two settlements near Yuma crossing. Soldiers from the missions mistreated the Indians, stealing food, supplies, and land. On July 17, 1781, Chief Palma and his brother Ygnacio Palma led their people in a revolt. Local settlements were burned to the ground and about 95 priests, settlers, and soldiers were killed. The Yuma rebellion shut down the Spanish route into Alta (Upper) California that had been created by Juan Bautista de Anza. Spanish soldiers tried to regain the lost land, but the Quechan fought them off and were never subdued.

By the 1840s, Americans began to pass through Quechan territory. At first, the Quechan were able to exploit the situation, charging travelers for passage across the Colorado River. However, non-Indian ferry companies soon challenged Quechan control of the crossing. When Indians attacked a rival ferryman, a California lawyer named John C. Morehead raised a volunteer militia and destroyed Quechan crops and boats. Skirmishes between Indians and travelers became frequent. Those who traversed the Yuma crossing did so with trepidation. Fort Yuma was built in 1850 to quell the situation, but a poor supply line and frequent attacks led to its abandonment. Not until the following year did a stronger garrison return to secure the crossing.

In 1884, the Quechan were put on a reservation along the Colorado River. Later, the Cocopah Reservation was established for them in 1917. Since then, the Quechan have had to continually battle for land. By the 1950s, the federal government had taken or sold 8,500 acres of Quechan territory. Twenty-five thousand acres of land were returned to the reservation in 1978, but the 1,000 remaining Indians still fight for water rights.

The Mojave Desert, named after this Southwestern tribe, is one of the harshest environments in the United States. Temperatures regularly exceed 100°F during the day, then drop sharply at night. The Mojave adapted to the tough conditions by settling along the banks of the lower Colorado River, an area they occupy to this day. Mojave Indians call themselves the *aha macave* (meaning "people along the water"). Near the river they were able to farm corn, pumpkins, squash, melons, and (after Spanish influence permeated the area) wheat. The runoff from melting snows in the Rocky Mountains into the Colorado River flooded their lands annually, and they adjusted their crop cycles accordingly, producing double harvests of many crops. The Mojave supplemented their diet with local game, nuts, and protein-rich fish.

Traditionally, the Mojave lived in two types of dwellings constructed from brush and earth. For the winter months they built low rectangular houses; in the summer they made open flat-roofed structures. They dressed in sandals and rabbit skin robes. Both males and females took pride in body art, adorning their bodies with tattoos and body paint. The Mojave were very interested in dreams. Interpretations of dreams exerted influence over much of their daily life.

Lithograph of three Mojave Indians in body paint

One of the Mojave's first contacts with Europeans came when Spanish explorer Juan de Oñate met with them on January 25, 1605. The Mojave Indians regaled the conquistador with strange stories, which Oñate's companion Escobar jotted down in his journal. They told about a rich island on Lake Copalla where the people wore gold bracelets, and another island whose fat, big-footed queen ruled over a tribe of bald-headed men. The stories became more and more fantastic; the most bizarre was about a tribe that purposely slept underwater. By the time Oñate left, his head was full of outlandish visions of the New World, and the Indians had eaten half of his party's horses.

However, much of the Mojave's contact with white men was less friendly. They became known as the "wild Indians" because of their frequent raids on Spanish settlers. With the Mexican Cession of 1848, and the California gold rush of the following year, more Americans were traveling through Mojave territory. When Captain Lorenzo Sitgreaves surveyed the land in 1851, the Indians attacked, killing one member of his party and wounding another. Mojave were also responsible for many ambushes and slaughters along the Beale Wagon Road. In 1858, members of the tribe massacred a group of immigrants, killing nine and wounding sixteen. In response, Fort Mohave was created and the Indian raids were steadily reduced.

A traditional Mojave boy's cardle board (left) has feathers; girl's (right) has red cloth and beads

The Mojave never signed an official treaty with the government, and they continue to live on and have rights to their homeland on the Colorado River. A congressional act in 1934 officially recognized the Fort Mojave Indian Reservation and the Colorado River Indian Reservation, though the sites were laid out as early as 1865. Today, most of the 2,900 Mojave live on the two reservations, along the California-Arizona border, or on the Fort McDowell Reservation in Maricopa County, Arizona.

At the 1.7-mile mark, the route turns down a side trail. This turn is easily missed, but if you continue straight ahead at this point, the trail continues only 0.6 miles before being blocked by the Big Maria Mountains Wilderness.

The trail crosses a wide wash, then ascends to a ridge top. It runs along the narrow spine of the ridge, overlooking a deep wash on either side. The views are dramatic. Ahead are the pale and sandy Big Maria Mountains and behind are the Colorado River and Arizona. The vegetation is varied. Ocotillos, small barrel cacti, creosote bushes, and beavertail cacti sparsely cover the slopes, but they stand out dramatically against the pale rocks.

The trail finishes at the end of the ridge, where the rugged terrain of the Big Maria Mountains will draw avid hikers farther.

Current Road Information

Bureau of Land Management
Needles Field Office
1303 South US Highway 95
Needles, CA 92363
(760) 326-7000

Map References

BLM   Blythe
USGS 1:24,000   Big Maria Mtn. SE
          1:100,000 Blythe
Maptech CD-ROM: San Diego/Joshua Tree
Southern & Central California Atlas & Gazetteer, p. 111
California Road & Recreation Atlas, p. 114

Route Directions

▼ 0.0   From US 95, 15.3 miles north of Blythe, zero trip meter and turn west

on road #52 at the BLM sign for Blythe Intaglios. The road is designated as suitable for 4WDs, ATVs, and motorbikes.
GPS: N33°48.00' W114°31.62'

▼ 0.1   SO Track on left and track on right under power lines is road #53 for 4WDs, ATVs, and motorbikes. Continue straight ahead and enter the site of the Blythe Intaglios. Please remain on the established road.

▼ 0.4   SO Parking area on right and short walk to two fenced areas containing a horse and a circular shape in one and a human figure in the other.

▼ 0.7   SO Parking area on right and short walk to fenced area containing a human figure.
GPS: N33°47.95' W114°32.29'

▼ 1.0   SO Leaving intaglio area.
GPS: N33°48.00' W114°32.61'

▼ 1.4   BR Well-used track on left.
GPS: N33°48.01' W114°33.07'

▼ 1.5   SO Cross through wash.
▼ 1.7   TR Track continues straight ahead to the edge of the Big Maria Mountains Wilderness. Turn right on unmarked track and cross through wash.
GPS: N33°48.04' W114°33.34'

▼ 3.9   SO Track on left to mine. Track on right descends to wash.
GPS: N33°48.51' W114°35.31'

▼ 4.0   Spur ends at a viewpoint of the mountains at the end of the ridge.
GPS: N33°48.52' W114°35.38'

Blythe-Vidal Old Road

STARTING POINT: US 95 at Vidal, 6.1 miles south of the intersection with California 62

FINISHING POINT: US 95, immediately south of mile marker 24.5

TOTAL MILEAGE: 22.2 miles

UNPAVED MILEAGE: 22.2 miles

DRIVING TIME: 2 hours

Elevation Range: 400–1,400 feet

USUALLY OPEN: Year-round

BEST TIME TO TRAVEL: October to June

DIFFICULTY RATING: 4

SCENIC RATING: 8

REMOTENESS RATING: +1

Special Attractions

■ Historic old road between Blythe and Vidal.
■ Road passes between two wilderness areas.

History

The old Blythe–Vidal Road reminds travelers how early routes through desert terrain developed. The old road followed the path of least resistance, traversing the gently sloping, sandy bajadas where possible and weaving a path through the more jagged interiors. No earthmoving machinery was available to remove obstacles or fill in washes. The trail skirts the high, craggy peaks of the Riverside Mountains between Blythe and Vidal, two early settlements close to the Colorado River. The original trail followed the course of Big Wash and was somewhat less circuitous than today's realigned route. Passage along the river was not always possible because floods would erode any evidence of a trail.

In 1882, Thomas Blythe took measures to curb the periodic flooding of the Colorado River, harness its waters, and avail of the exposed alluvial valley. A diversion channel was constructed and Blythe attended the ceremo-

The re-routed road now travels north up Big Wash

nious final blasting into the Colorado River in the fall of 1882. Before this, the river was up to 5 miles wide in places. The final cut was the intake point for Blythe's diversion channel. The diversion opened up land for development and settlement. Blythe appointed George Irish, a 28-year-old Englishman, to oversee his project. Blythe spent more than $80,000 to clear the land, setting up an irrigation scheme that covered an area of 40,000 acres, including a 40-acre farm actively experimenting with various crops. Blythe was enthusiastic about developing an empire on the Colorado. Fort Yuma lay just 90 miles downstream, prospectors were working the riverside mountains, settlers were coming west, and he could see the need for development.

Unfortunately, Blythe never got to see his "empire on the Colorado." He suffered a heart attack and died in San Francisco. His project fell by the wayside after his death. However, his name survives in the city that developed on the banks of the Colorado River.

The wide expanse of Rice Valley slopes to the northwest of this trail. The sandy valley and old army air base have taken their names from the Rice Siding on the floor of the valley. The siding got its name in the 1910s from Guy R. Rice, a chief engineer of the California Southern Railroad. Later, a World War II training facility was located in the heart of the valley. General George Patton conducted training maneuvers in the vicinity in 1942, choosing many such desolate locations to prepare for combat in North Africa. The only reminders of this base are shell casings, a large concrete pad, and scattered debris. A 1994 report indicates that 1,000 acres of unexploded ordnance sites were suspected on what is now designated as BLM land.

Description

The Blythe–Vidal Old Road follows a sandy path along the western and southern edge of the Riverside Mountains, starting and finishing on US 95. The trail is easy to follow. Once you find the unmarked starting point, there are adequate route markers, both BLM marker posts and older white signs, and few side trails to confuse you.

The trail's main difficulty is very loose,

very deep sand along much of its length. One particularly deep stretch is the 1.1-mile section that travels within a tributary of Big Wash. Apart from the sand, there are many steep entries to and exits from washes; good tires will help gain traction on the often scrabbly surface.

The trail leaves sleepy Vidal, and travels southwest along a loose, sandy surface, crossing Vidal Wash and traveling across Vidal Valley toward the Riverside Mountains. The difficult Desert #4: Gold Rice Mine Trail leaves this route and makes an adventurous detour for experienced drivers or mountain bikers.

The old road continues on the smaller trail, skirting the edge of the Riverside Mountains Wilderness. It travels along a tributary of Big Wash for a short distance; this section has some of the deepest sand along the entire trail. Exiting the wash, the trail follows alongside power lines through a vehicle corridor with wilderness on both sides. Sections here can be rough and uneven, and a few steeper pinches on the low-traction surface may pose a slight challenge to some. Leaving the vehicle corridor, the trail swings east along the southern side of the Riverside Mountains Wilderness toward the Colorado River. Navigation can be a challenge because the trail is often faint. Pay close attention to the route to avoid inadvertently entering the wilderness. There are more marker posts along this section to aid route finding, but it is still easy to lose your way, especially in some of the wide, tangled washes where boulders, disturbed surfaces, and vegetation conspire to hide the true route.

For the most part, though, the trail is well used and easy to follow. It ends back at US 95, opposite the Colorado River. Part of the original Blythe–Vidal Old Road is now enclosed within the wilderness. This route follows the more modern detour around these areas.

Current Road Information

Bureau of Land Management
Needles Field Office
1303 South US Highway 95
Needles, CA 92363
(760) 326-7000

Long sections of deep sand bogged down early travelers

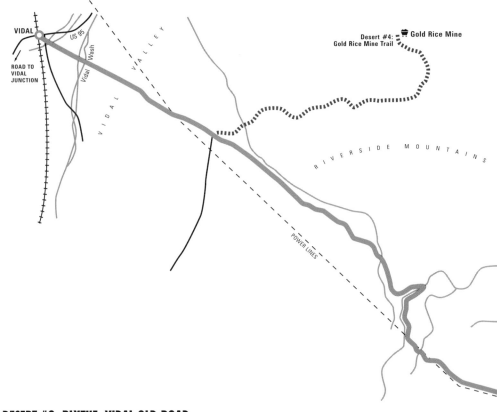

DESERT #3: BLYTHE–VIDAL OLD ROAD

Map References
BLM   Parker, Blythe
USGS 1:24,000   Vidal, Grommet, Big
      Maria Mtn. NW, Big Maria Mtn. NE,
      1:100,000 Parker, Blythe
Maptech CD-ROM: San Bernardino County/
      Mojave; San Diego/Joshua Tree
*Southern & Central California Atlas &
      Gazetteer,* pp. 101, 111
California Road & Recreation Atlas, p. 114

Route Directions

▼ 0.0   From the intersection of California 62
           and US 95 at Vidal Junction (west of
           Parker, AZ), continue southeast on US
           95 for 6 miles to Vidal. Cross over rail-
           road and proceed 0.1 miles south. Turn
           southwest onto an unmarked small,
           formed, single-track trail. The turn is
           opposite the sign for Main Street, but

it is not the wider road that runs perpendicular to US 95. It is the smaller
trail leading off at an angle to the
southwest. Zero trip meter.

3.7 ▲   Trail ends at US 95 at Vidal. Turn right
           for Blythe; turn left for Vidal Junction.
           GPS: N34°07.13′ W114°30.56′

▼ 0.2   SO Cross through wash.
3.5 ▲   SO Cross through wash.
▼ 0.3   SO Cross through wash.
3.4 ▲   SO Cross through wash.
▼ 0.4   SO Cross through wash.
3.3 ▲   SO Cross through wash.
▼ 0.6   SO Road is now marked Blythe–Vidal
           Old Road.
3.1 ▲   SO Marker post for Blythe–Vidal Old Road.
▼ 0.8   SO Start to cross through wide Vidal Wash.
2.9 ▲   SO Exit wash crossing.
▼ 1.0   SO Exit wash crossing.
2.7 ▲   SO Start to cross through wide Vidal Wash.

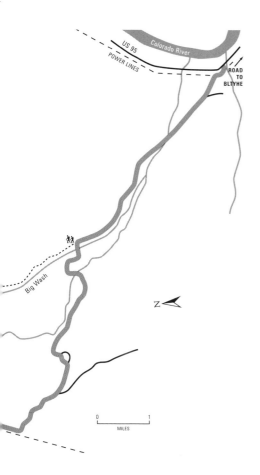

Mine Trail. Also track on left. Zero trip meter and continue straight ahead on Blythe–Vidal Road. There is a large concrete block at the intersection used as a direction marker.

▼ 3.1 SO Cross through wash.
2.1 ▲ SO Cross through wash.
▼ 3.9 SO Cross through wash.
1.3 ▲ SO Cross through wash.
GPS: N34°01.97' W114°35.73'

▼ 5.2 TR Enter a tributary of Big Wash and turn sharp right up wash, following marker for Blythe–Vidal Road. The wash forms the wilderness boundary (now on your left). Remain in wash for next 1.1 miles. Zero trip meter.
0.0 ▲ Continue to the north.
GPS: N34°01.35' W114°36.35'

▼ 0.0 Continue to the northwest up the wash.
3.9 ▲ TL Exit tributary of Big Wash, turning sharp left and climbing out of the wash, following marker for Blythe–Vidal Road. Leaving wilderness boundary. Zero trip meter.
▼ 1.1 TL Turn left out of wash alongside power lines. Trail enters a vehicle corridor through the wilderness.
2.8 ▲ TR Turn right down wash, away from power lines, following the Blythe–Vidal Road trail markers. Trail now has wilderness on the right. Remain in wash for the next 1.1 miles.
GPS: N34°01.70' W114°37.25'

▼ 1.5 SO Cross through wash.
2.4 ▲ SO Cross through wash.
▼ 2.2 SO Cross through wash.
1.7 ▲ SO Cross through wash.
▼ 2.4 SO Cross through wide wash.
1.5 ▲ SO Cross through wide wash.
▼ 3.4 SO Cross through two washes.
0.5 ▲ SO Cross through two washes.
▼ 3.7 SO Cross through wash.
0.2 ▲ SO Cross through wash.
▼ 3.8 SO Cross through wash.
0.1 ▲ SO Cross through wash.
▼ 3.9 TL Turn left onto formed trail, away from power lines, following the marker for

▼ 2.9 SO Pass under power lines, remaining on Blythe–Vidal Old Road.
0.8 ▲ SO Pass under power lines, remaining on Blythe–Vidal Old Road.
GPS: N34°05.07' W114°32.46'

▼ 3.4 BR Small track on left.
0.3 ▲ SO Small track on right.
GPS: N34°04.67' W114°32.77'

▼ 3.7 SO Track on left is Desert #4: Gold Rice Mine Trail. Also track on right. Zero trip meter and continue straight ahead on Blythe–Vidal Road. There is a large concrete block at the intersection used as a direction marker.
0.0 ▲ Continue to the northeast.
GPS: N34°04.49' W114°32.93'

▼ 0.0 Continue to the southwest.
5.2 ▲ SO Track on right is Desert #4: Gold Rice

Blythe–Vidal Road. Zero trip meter.
0.0 ▲ Continue to the north.
GPS: N33°59.79' W114°38.88'

▼ 0.0 Continue to the southeast.
4.8 ▲ TR Turn right onto formed trail under power lines, following the marker for Blythe–Vidal Road. Zero trip meter. The wilderness boundary is on the right.
▼ 0.1 SO Cross through two washes.
4.7 ▲ SO Cross through two washes.
▼ 0.4 BL Track on right. Follow route marker and cross through wash.
4.4 ▲ BR Cross through wash; then track on left. Follow route marker.
▼ 1.2 BL Track on right.
3.6 ▲ SO Track on left.
GPS: N33°59.09' W114°38.24'

▼ 1.8 BL Track on right. Follow marker for Blythe–Vidal Old Road.
3.0 ▲ SO Track on left. Follow marker for Blythe–Vidal Old Road.
▼ 2.0 TL Drop down and turn left up wash.
2.8 ▲ TR Turn right and exit wash at route marker.
GPS: N34°58.98' W114°37.50'

▼ 2.1 BR Bear right, exiting wash at route marker. Track on left also leaves wash.
2.7 ▲ TL Enter wash and turn left down wash. Track ahead exits wash.
▼ 3.1 BR Bear right, following route marker. This intersection is faint and easily missed. Trail now heads across a wide area of desert pavement and is indistinct. Watch for route markers.
1.7 ▲ SO Continue straight ahead at trail marker.
GPS: N33°58.65' W114°36.59'

▼ 3.7 SO Cross through wash.
1.1 ▲ SO Cross through wash.
▼ 3.8 SO Cross through two washes.
1.0 ▲ SO Cross through two washes. Trail now heads across a wide area of desert pavement and is indistinct. Watch for route markers.
GPS: N33°58.49' W114°36.02'

▼ 3.9 SO Start to cross through wide wash.
0.9 ▲ SO Exit wide wash.

▼ 4.0 BR Exit wash and bear right to cross through another wash.
0.8 ▲ BL Cross through wash; then bear left and start to cross through wide wash. Wilderness boundary is on right. Be sure you don't inadvertently enter the wilderness area.
GPS: N33°58.62' W114°35.94'

▼ 4.1 SO Cross through two washes.
0.7 ▲ SO Cross through two washes.
▼ 4.2 SO Cross through wash.
0.6 ▲ SO Cross through wash.
▼ 4.3 SO Track on left.
0.5 ▲ SO Track on right.
▼ 4.8 BR Bear right, remaining on Blythe–Vidal Road. Track on left is for foot and horse travel only and enters the wilderness. Zero trip meter at wilderness access sign.
0.0 ▲ Continue to the west.
GPS: N33°58.48' W114°35.38'

▼ 0.0 Continue to the southeast.
4.6 ▲ BL Bear left, remaining on Blythe–Vidal Road. Track on right is for foot and horse travel only and enters the wilderness. Zero trip meter at wilderness access sign. Trail now follows along wilderness boundary on the right.
▼ 1.5 SO Cross through wash.
3.1 ▲ SO Cross through wash.
▼ 2.1 SO Cross through Big Wash.
2.5 ▲ SO Cross through Big Wash.
GPS: N33°57.20' W114°33.94'

▼ 2.2 SO Trail moves away from wilderness boundary on left; then cross through wash. Track on right and track on left up and down wash.
2.4 ▲ SO Cross through wash. Track on right and track on left up and down wash. Riverside Mountains Wilderness boundary is now on right of trail.
GPS: N33°57.09' W114°33.85'

▼ 2.9 SO Cross through wash. Track on left and track on right up and down wash.
1.7 ▲ SO Cross through wash. Track on left and track on right up and down wash.

▼ 3.1	BR	Track on left; then cross through wash.
1.5 ▲	SO	Cross through wash; then track on right. Continue on Blythe-Vidal Road.
▼ 3.3	SO	Track on left.
1.3 ▲	SO	Track on right.
▼ 3.7	SO	Track on left.
0.9 ▲	SO	Track on right.
▼ 3.8	BL	Well-used track on right. Bear left toward Colorado River.
0.8 ▲	BR	Well-used track on left. Follow marker for Blythe–Vidal Road.

GPS: N33°56.06′ W114°32.96′

▼ 4.0	BR	Track on left.
0.6 ▲	SO	Track on right.
▼ 4.1	BR	Track on left.
0.5 ▲	SO	Track on right.
▼ 4.3	TR	T-intersection along power lines.
0.3 ▲	TL	Turn left away from power lines at marker for Blythe–Vidal Road.

GPS: N33°55.78′ W114°32.49′

▼ 4.4	BL	Descend steeply into large sandy wash.
0.2 ▲	SO	End of climb out of wash. Continue alongside power lines.
▼ 4.5	TL	Turn left down wash toward Colorado River.
0.1 ▲	TR	Turn right and climb high embankment out of wash alongside power lines.
▼ 4.6		Trail ends at US 95. Turn left for California 62 and Parker, AZ; turn right for Blythe.
0.0 ▲		Trail commences on US 95, 9 miles south of Wilson Road and immediately south of mile marker 24.5. Zero trip meter and turn southwest up wide sandy wash. Track is unmarked.

GPS: N33°55.63′ W114°32.36′

DESERT #4

Gold Rice Mine Trail

STARTING POINT: Desert #3: Blythe–Vidal Old Road, 3.7 miles south of US 95

FINISHING POINT: Gold Rice Mine

TOTAL MILEAGE: 6.2 miles (one-way)

UNPAVED MILEAGE: 6.2 miles

DRIVING TIME: 1.5 hours (one-way)

ELEVATION RANGE: 900–1,200 feet

USUALLY OPEN: Year-round

BEST TIME TO TRAVEL: October to June

DIFFICULTY RATING: 6

SCENIC RATING: 8

REMOTENESS RATING: +1

Special Attractions

■ Remains of the Gold Rice and Jean Mines.

■ Trail travels a vehicle corridor within the Riverside Mountains Wilderness.

■ Remote and challenging trail for stock vehicles and mountain bikes.

History

The famous lawman Wyatt Earp frequented the nearby settlements of Vidal, on the Atchison, Topeka & Santa Fe Railroad, and Earp, on the Colorado River. Earp was born in Illinois in 1848 and gradually moved west as opportunities arose in the 1870s. He developed a reputation as a fearless frontier lawman in places such as Prescott, Arizona, and Wichita and Dodge City, Kansas. He may also be remembered as a survivor of the gunfight at the O.K. Corral in Tombstone, Arizona. His addiction for mining and a spot of gambling took him and his wife, Josie, to many gold mining camps throughout the Southwest.

Between 1897 and 1902, the couple operated a saloon in Alaska at the peak of the Klondike gold rush. Even though it was a very profitable period for them, they decided to return to the Southwest to mining boom towns. Wyatt prospected heavily at the base of the mountains around Vidal, establishing a home in the town. He discovered gold and copper veins on many claims, although his investments from earlier ventures proved sufficient for both him and his wife. They spent the hot summers in the Hollywood area, befriending many movie stars. They would return to work their claims in the cooler winter months. Wyatt Earp passed away in Los Angeles in 1929 at the age of 80. Josie survived him by 15 years.

The mines in this region are important roosting sites for bats. Field studies of bats in California and Arizona go back to the

Broken chisel heads testify to the hardness of the rock at Jean Mine

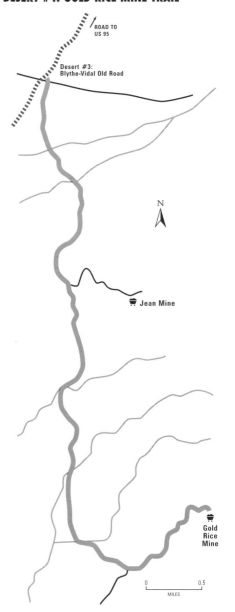

1860s. Studies in the 1950s and 1960s showed that banded bats, found in mines close to this trail, were from as far away as eastern Arizona. Bats usually roost in small crevices, such as small drill holes found in mining tunnels. As more bats join in, they tend to cluster around the location of the first group in the drill holes, even though they are less protected and sheltered on the walls of the mine.

Description

Gold Rice Mine Trail travels along a roughly formed trail through a vehicle corridor in the Riverside Mountains Wilderness. The first couple of miles are easygoing, but the farther along the trail, the tougher it becomes. Much of the trail travels along a very narrow shelf road that is barely wide enough for a full size vehicle to venture through. The roughness of the trail surface further compounds the problem. The surface offers little in the way of traction at times, and approaches and departures from some of the wash crossings are very steep. This trail has no alternate exit, so be confident in your vehicle's and your ability to retrace your steps before committing yourself. The trail sees little traffic, so help could be a long time coming.

A side trail leads 1 mile to the Jean Mine. Little remains here except for three shafts and some tailings.

The main trail continues into the Riverside Mountains before curling northeast to finish at the Gold Rice Mine. The final mile of the trail is the most difficult. This is where the trail earns its 6 rating. Rock crawling along the narrow shelf road, off-camber side slopes, and steep climbs make up the final section. An amazing amount of work must have been put in to construct such a sturdy and stable shelf road. Along its length you can see evidence of the dry

The rugged Riverside Mountains challenged early road builders

stone embankment supporting it as it contours its way above the wash.

The Gold Rice Mine has three shafts, an adit, and tailings. Concrete foundations are probably the remains of a mill. Hiking around this region is rough but very rewarding.

Current Road Information
Bureau of Land Management
Needles Field Office
1303 South US Highway 95
Needles, CA 92363
(760) 326-7000

Map References
BLM   Parker
USGS 1:24,000 Vidal
        1:100,000 Parker
Maptech CD-ROM: San Bernardino
        County/Mojave
Southern & Central California Atlas &
        Gazetteer, p. 101
California Road & Recreation Atlas, p. 114

Route Directions

▼ 0.0   From Desert #3: Blythe–Vidal Old Road, 3.7 miles from the northern end at Vidal, zero trip meter at the large concrete block marker and proceed east on well-used, unmarked trail. Riverside Mountains Wilderness starts on the right at the intersection.
GPS: N34°04.49′ W114°32.93′

▼ 0.1   TR Turn right on sandy trail and pass "Riverside Mountains Wilderness Area Ahead" sign.

▼ 0.6   SO Cross through wide wash.

▼ 1.0   SO Cross through wide wash.

▼ 2.1   SO Unmarked track on left goes 1 mile to the Jean Mine. Zero trip meter. This short track is rated 6 for difficulty because of steep entrances and exits at gullies and off-camber sections.
GPS: N34°02.93′ W114°32.69′

▼ 0.0   Continue to the southeast on main trail.

▼ 1.1	SO	Cross through wash.
▼ 1.7	SO	Cross through two washes.
▼ 1.8	SO	Cross through wash.
▼ 2.2	SO	Start to cross through wide wash.
▼ 2.3	SO	Exit wash crossing.
▼ 2.5	BL	Drop down to enter wash and bear left up wash.
		GPS: N34°00.97′ W114°32.61′

▼ 2.6	BR	Exit wash to the right.
▼ 2.8	SO	Cross through wash.
▼ 3.0	TL	T-intersection. Zero trip meter and turn left, heading uphill.
		GPS: N34°00.77′ W114°32.16′

▼ 0.0		Continue to the northeast.
▼ 0.9	SO	Cross over wash on rocky waterfall.
▼ 1.1		Trail ends at the Gold Rice Mine.
		GPS: N34°01.19′ W114°31.39′

DESERT #5

Whipple Mountains Trail

STARTING POINT: US 95, 15.9 miles south of Havasu Lake Road
FINISHING POINT: California 62, 7 miles west of Earp
TOTAL MILEAGE: 23.4 miles
UNPAVED MILEAGE: 23.4 miles
DRIVING TIME: 3.5 hours
ELEVATION RANGE: 800–2,000
USUALLY OPEN: Year-round
BEST TIME TO TRAVEL: October to June
DIFFICULTY RATING: 3
SCENIC RATING: 8
REMOTENESS RATING: +1

Special Attractions

- Remains of many old mining camps.
- Rockhounding for chalcedony.
- Remote, easy-to-follow desert trail, popular with ATVs and 4WDs.

History

As a lieutenant in the Corps of U.S. Topographical Engineers, Amiel W. Whipple assisted in the early exploration of California.

In 1853, Whipple's expedition left Fort Smith, Arkansas, with a party of about 70 men. Whipple's group was one of several survey parties sent out to find a route for a transcontinental railroad. The epic journey, which ran close to the thirty-fifth parallel, ultimately took the survey party to Los Angeles. The journey was difficult, and it tested all the men involved. By the time the explorers reached the Colorado River, most of their wagons had been abandoned.

The Mojave guided the expedition through the Colorado River region. The group might not have made it across the river without this assistance. After crossing the river, the expedition suffered its only casualty; Paiute Indians killed one of the herders who had fallen behind with the stock.

Although a more northerly route was chosen for the first transcontinental railroad, the expedition successfully mapped a lot of previously unknown territory. In 1856, federal funding was used to improve the Whipple Trail. The Atchison, Topeka & Santa Fe Railroad would eventually follow much of Whipple's route from Albuquerque, New Mexico, to California.

The rugged Whipple Mountains were the scene of gold mining during the Southwest's early prospecting days. The remoteness of the mountains that bear the lieutenant's name, combined with the harsh weather of this locale, kept many from entering the region. Although several mines can be seen along this trail, the mountains have remained relatively undisturbed by people. The American Eagle Mine, also known as the New American Mine, was discovered in 1875 and produced copper and gold. The Whipple Mining District was further developed in the 1930s and early 1940s. Native gold was found in several mines along with oxidized copper and iron minerals. The gold was found in narrow quartz veins that ran through gneiss and metamorphic rocks of the Precambrian era.

Description

The trail through the Whipple Mountains runs between US 95 and the Colorado River.

Headframe at the American Eagle Mine

Approaches to washes can change frequently after storms

It passes through some remote desert areas that are more reminiscent of Arizona than California.

The trail leaves US 95 along a well-used, but unmarked, trail. There is a marker post for the Heritage Trail 1 mile to the north of the trail's beginning. The Heritage Trail joins the route described below, but it is seldom used and overgrown in places. Most vehicles seem to follow the route described here.

The route travels over desert pavement toward the prominent Pyramid Butte. It then wraps around the butte to the east. Many small trails leave from the main route in this region. Some of them access popular rockhounding areas to the north, where it is possible to find chalcedony. The pale-colored rock is easy to see against the darker desert pavement. It will take a bit of hunting, though, to find the more prized chalcedony roses.

As you get farther along the trail, there are fewer side trails and the major intersections are well marked. Spur trails lead off a short distance to the Gold Hill Mine and the Gold

Standard Mine. Little remains of these mines except some collapsed timber structures, adits, shafts, and tailings.

The trail joins Needles–Parker Road, which runs down a loose, gravelly wash for much of the way. A short loop off this section takes you past the American Eagle Mine, where there are a couple of headframes and other structures, before rejoining Needles–Parker Road back in the wash.

For the most part, the formed trail is well within the capabilities of any high-clearance stock SUV, but after heavy rains, conditions can change quickly. There are some remote, but exposed, backcountry campsites along the trail, although campers will find the surfaces uneven.

The final part of the trail remains on Needles–Parker Road as it exits the wash, crossing the sloping bajada toward US 95. Teddy bear chollas, brittlebush, creosote, and occasional ocotillos dot the stony alluvial fan.

The trail crosses an underground section of the Colorado River Aqueduct and finishes on US 95 between Vidal Junction and Earp.

Blue copper rock at the Gold Standard Mine

DESERT #5: WHIPPLE MOUNTAINS TRAIL

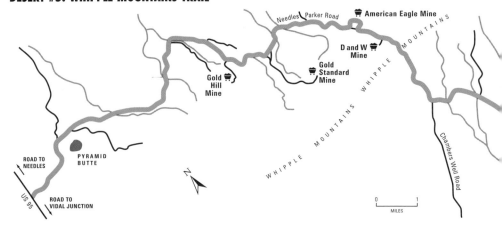

Current Road Information
Bureau of Land Management
Needles Field Office
1303 South US Highway 95
Needles, CA 92363
(760) 326-7000

Map References
BLM   Parker
USGS 1:24,000   Savahia Peak SW,
        Savahia Peak, Whipple Mtn. SW,
        Parker NW
        1:100,000 Parker
Maptech CD-ROM: San Bernardino
        County/Mojave
*Southern & Central California Atlas &
    Gazetteer,* p. 101
California Road & Recreation Atlas, p. 115

Route Directions

▼ 0.0   From US 95, 15.9 miles south of
              Havasu Lake Road, 0.1 miles south of
              mile marker 2, zero trip meter and turn
              east on unmarked formed trail that
              leaves across a stretch of desert
              pavement.

8.0 ▲   Trail ends at T-intersection with paved
              US 95. Turn right for Needles; turn left
              for Vidal Junction.
              GPS: N34°19.21′ W114°39.11′

▼ 1.3   SO   Pyramid Butte is the taller of the two
                 hills on the right.

6.7 ▲   SO   Pyramid Butte is the taller of the two
                 hills on the left.

▼ 1.7   BR   Faint track straight ahead and to the
                 left. Bear right and proceed along the
                 north face of Pyramid Butte.

6.3 ▲   BL   Faint track straight ahead and to the
                 right. Bear left and proceed around the
                 west side of Pyramid Butte.
                 GPS: N34°19.91′ W114°37.81′

▼ 2.0   BL   Track on right. Follow Heritage Trail
                 mile marker 587.2. Pyramid Butte is
                 immediately south of the trail.

6.0 ▲   SO   Track on left. Pyramid Butte is immedi-
                 ately south of the trail.
                 GPS: N34°19.95′ W114°37.45′

▼ 2.2   BR   Small track on left. There is a rock-
                 hounding area for chalcedony to the
                 north along this trail.

5.8 ▲   SO   Small track on right. There is a rock-
                 hounding area for chalcedony to the
                 north along this trail.

▼ 2.3   SO   Small track on right.

5.7 ▲   SO   Small track on left.

▼ 2.4   SO   Cross through wash.

5.6 ▲   SO   Cross through wash.

▼ 2.8   SO   Small track on left.

5.2 ▲   SO   Small track on right.

▼ 3.1   SO   Well-used track on right.

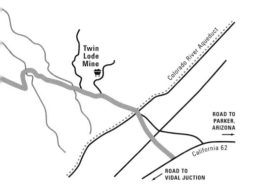

4.9 ▲   BR   Well-used track on left.
         GPS: N34°19.71′ W114°36.40′

▼ 3.4   SO   Cross through wash. Many wash
             crossings for the next 2.9 miles.
4.6 ▲   SO   Cross through wash.
▼ 6.3   SO   Cross through wash.
1.7 ▲   SO   Cross through wash. Many wash
             crossings for the next 2.9 miles.
         GPS: N34°20.29′ W114°33.92′

▼ 7.2   SO   Well-used track on left.
0.8 ▲   SO   Well-used track on right.
         GPS: N34°19.86′ W114°33.16′

▼ 8.0   TL   T-intersection. Track on left is Heritage
             Trail, suitable for 4WDs, ATVs, and
             motorbikes. Track on right, which goes
             0.2 miles to the Gold Hill Mine, is suit-
             able for 4WDs, ATVs, and motorbikes.
             Zero trip meter and turn left, following
             marker for the Heritage Trail.
0.0 ▲   Continue to the northwest.
         GPS: N34°19.22′ W114°32.89′

▼ 0.0   Continue to the northeast.
1.2 ▲   TR   Track ahead, which goes 0.2 miles
             to the Gold Hill Mine, is suitable for
             4WDs, ATVs, and motorbikes. Zero trip
             meter and turn right onto unmarked,
             well-used trail.
▼ 0.2   SO   Cross through wash.

1.0 ▲   SO   Cross through wash.
▼ 0.3   SO   Diggings on left.
0.9 ▲   SO   Diggings on right.
         GPS: N34°19.03′ W114°32.70′

▼ 0.5   SO   Cross through wash.
0.7 ▲   SO   Cross through wash.
▼ 0.6   SO   Enter wash.
0.6 ▲   SO   Exit wash.
▼ 0.7   BR   Small track on left out of wash.
             Exit wash.
0.5 ▲   BL   Small track on right out of wash.
             Enter wash.
         GPS: N34°19.11′ W114°32.46′

▼ 1.0   SO   Cross through wash.
0.2 ▲   SO   Cross through wash.
▼ 1.2   BL   Track straight ahead, which goes 1.6
             miles to the Gold Standard Mine, is
             suitable for 4WDs, ATVs, and motor-
             bikes. Zero trip meter and bear left.
             Remain on the marked Heritage Trail.
0.0 ▲   Continue to the west.
         GPS: N34°18.87′ W114°32.05′

▼ 0.0   Continue to the northeast.
1.7 ▲   BR   Track on left, which goes 1.6 miles to
             the Gold Standard Mine, is suitable for
             4WDs, ATVs, and motorbikes. Zero trip
             meter and bear right on well-used,
             unmarked trail.
▼ 0.1   SO   Start to cross through wide wash.
1.6 ▲   SO   Exit wide wash.
▼ 0.3   SO   Exit wash crossing. Track on right joins
             trail to the Gold Standard Mine; then
             cross through wash.
1.4 ▲   BR   Cross through wash; then track on left
             joins the trail to the Gold Standard Mine.
             Start to cross through wide wash.
         GPS: N34°18.96′ W114°31.81′

▼ 0.8   SO   Cross through wash.
0.9 ▲   SO   Cross through wash.
▼ 1.0   SO   Cross through wash.
0.7 ▲   SO   Cross through wash.
▼ 1.2   SO   Cross through wash.
0.5 ▲   SO   Cross through wash.
▼ 1.7   TR   T-intersection with trail in the wash. It
             is marked as Needles Parker Road to
             the right and left, suitable for 4WDs,

ATVs, and motorbikes. It is also marked as the Heritage Trail to the left. Small trail straight ahead, exiting wash. Zero trip meter and turn right onto Needles–Parker Road, traveling up the wash.

0.0 ▲ Continue to the west.
GPS: N34°18.93' W114°30.58'

▼ 0.0 Continue to the southeast.
1.2 ▲ TL Needles–Parker Road continues ahead in the wash at the marker. It is also now signed for the Heritage Trail, suitable for 4WDs, ATVs, and motorbikes. Small track on right out of wash and well-used formed trail on left out of wash. Zero trip enter and turn left onto unmarked, well-used, formed trail exiting the wash.

▼ 1.1 SO Exit wash.
0.1 ▲ SO Enter down wash.
▼ 1.2 TL Needles–Parker Road continues ahead in wash. Turn left away from wash, following marker for the American Eagle Mine. Trail is suitable for 4WDs, ATVs, and motorbikes. Zero trip meter.

0.0 ▲ Continue to the northwest.
GPS: N34°18.32' W114°29.75'

▼ 0.0 Continue to the northeast.
3.5 ▲ TR T-intersection with Needles–Parker Road, running in the wash. Turn right to rejoin this road and zero trip meter.
▼ 0.2 SO Track on right.
3.3 ▲ SO Track on left.
▼ 0.3 SO American Eagle Mine on left. Headframe and concrete foundations remain.
3.2 ▲ SO American Eagle Mine on right. Headframe and concrete foundations remain.
GPS: N34°18.35' W114°29.59'

▼ 0.4 TR Track ahead goes to white wooden headframe and shed. Turn right down wash.
3.1 ▲ TL Track on right goes to white wooden headframe and shed. Turn left out of wash.
▼ 0.7 TL T-intersection with–Needles Parker Road. Turn left down wash, rejoining this road.

2.8 ▲ TR Turn right up unmarked trail in side wash to loop past the American Eagle Mine. Needles–Parker Road continues ahead.
GPS: N34°18.20' W114°29.70'

▼ 1.3 SO Track on left.
2.2 ▲ SO Track on right.
▼ 1.4 SO Track on right is D and W Mine Track, suitable for 4WDs, ATVs, and motorbikes.
2.1 ▲ SO Track on left is D and W Mine Track, suitable for 4WDs, ATVs, and motorbikes.
GPS: N34°17.72' W114°29.25'

▼ 3.4 SO Exit wash to the left.
0.1 ▲ SO Enter up wash.
▼ 3.5 BL Track on right is Chambers Well Road, suitable for 4WDs, ATVs, and motorbikes. Zero trip meter and remain on marked Needles–Parker Road.
0.0 ▲ Continue to the north.
GPS: N34°16.08' W114°29.07'

▼ 0.0 Continue to the southeast.
5.5 ▲ SO Track on left is Chambers Well Road, suitable for 4WDs, ATVs, and motorbikes. Zero trip meter and remain on marked Needles–Parker Road.
▼ 0.3 SO Cross through wash.
5.2 ▲ SO Cross through wash.
▼ 0.4 SO Cross through wash.
5.1 ▲ SO Cross through wash.
▼ 1.3 SO Cross through wash; then track on left.
4.2 ▲ SO Track on right; then cross through wash.
▼ 1.4 SO Cross through wash.
4.1 ▲ SO Cross through wash.
▼ 3.0 SO Cross through wash.
2.5 ▲ SO Cross through wash.
GPS: N34°14.15' W114°27.15'

▼ 3.5 SO Cross through wash.
2.0 ▲ SO Cross through wash.
▼ 3.8 SO Enter wash.
1.7 ▲ SO Exit wash.
▼ 3.9 SO Exit wash.
1.6 ▲ SO Enter wash.
▼ 4.1 SO Cross through wash. Many wash crossings for the next 1.4 miles.
1.4 ▲ SO Cross through wash.
▼ 4.8 SO Leaving Whipple Mountains Wilderness boundary on left.

0.7 ▲	SO	Whipple Mountains Wilderness boundary now on right.
▼ 5.0	SO	Small track on left.
0.5 ▲	SO	Small track on right.

GPS: N34°13.46′ W114°25.98′

▼ 5.2	SO	Track on left.
0.3 ▲	SO	Track on right.
▼ 5.3	SO	Cross through wide wash.
0.2 ▲	SO	Cross through wide wash.
▼ 5.5	SO	Unmarked, well-used track on left goes 0.8 miles to Twin Lode Mine and wilderness boundary. Zero trip meter.
0.0 ▲		Continue to the northwest. Many wash crossings for the next 1.4 miles.

GPS: N34°13.09′ W114°25.59′

▼ 0.0		Continue to the southeast.
2.3 ▲	BL	Unmarked, well-used track on right goes 0.8 miles to Twin Lode Mine and wilderness boundary. Bear left on unmarked trail and zero trip meter.
▼ 0.7	BL	Track on right.
1.6 ▲	SO	Track on left.
▼ 0.9	SO	Cross over graded water pipeline road, remaining on small formed trail; then track on left.
1.4 ▲	SO	Track on right; then cross over graded water pipeline road, remaining on small formed trail.

GPS: N34°12.41′ W114°25.05′

▼ 1.0	SO	Small track on left.
1.3 ▲	BR	Small track on right.
▼ 1.6	SO	Track on left and track on right is pipeline road.
0.7 ▲	SO	Track on left and track on right is pipeline road.
▼ 2.3		Trail ends at intersection with California 62. Turn right for Vidal Junction; turn left for Parker, AZ.
0.0 ▲		Trail commences on California 62, 7 miles west of Earp, which is immediately on the California side of the Colorado River. Trail is 0.1 miles west of mile marker 135. Zero trip meter and turn north on well-used, unmarked formed trail.

GPS: N34°11.12′ W114°24.95′

Cadiz Road

STARTING POINT: California 62 at the Freda Railroad Siding, 23 miles west of Vidal Junction

FINISHING POINT: National Trails Highway (Route 66) at Chambless

TOTAL MILEAGE: 47.1 miles

UNPAVED MILEAGE: 42.8 miles

DRIVING TIME: 2 hours

ELEVATION RANGE: 600–1,400 feet

USUALLY OPEN: Year-round

BEST TIME TO TRAVEL: September to June

DIFFICULTY RATING: 1

SCENIC RATING: 8

REMOTENESS RATING: +1

Special Attractions

- Cadiz Dunes Wilderness sand dunes.
- Marble Mountain Fossil Beds Area of Critical Environmental Concern (ACEA).
- Broad, sweeping views of the Ward and Cadiz Valleys and the old salt works.

History

The Atlantic & Pacific Railroad constructed the line through Cadiz at the northern end of this trail in 1883. The company also named the location. The names of the railroad sidings across this section of the Mojave Desert run alphabetically from the east—Amboy, Bristol, (Saltus Siding came later), Cadiz, Danby, Essex, Fenner, Goffs, and Homer. The line eventually became part of the Atchison, Topeka & Santa Fe Railroad.

Just northwest of Cadiz Siding is an old marble quarry noted for its unusual fossils. The quarry site now known as Marble Mountain Fossil Beds has a fossil of one of the earliest known animals, called trilobites, to have a skeleton and eyes. When the dry Bristol Lake was part of an ancient Cambrian sea, it was habitat for a number of creatures, including trilobites. These animals were small marine crustaceans somewhat like today's horseshoe crabs. The fragile na-

Sodium and calcium chloride processing works at the dry Danby Lake

ture of the fossils makes the discovery and observation of a complete trilobite quite difficult. Some may be fortunate enough to see tiny specks that are thought to be trilobite eggs.

The Calevanto marble mine at the fossil beds was worked from 1937 to 1939. Marble from the quarry was used in the San Francisco Customs House and the Oxnard and Gardena post offices.

Bristol and Cadiz Lakes (west of this trail) are dried-out basins, remains of a wet period some time in the past. Weathering of the surrounding mountains lined the lakebeds with salts, mainly calcium chloride and sodium. The evaporation of the waters over time has encrusted the lakebeds with concentrated salts. These salts have been collected in both lakes at different times. Bristol has produced so much that a railroad siding was named Saltus in 1915.

The dry lake area is noted for chloride mining operations, which have been ongoing since the early part of the twentieth century. Trenches are dug on the lakebed, filled with a brine solution pumped from wells, then allowed to concentrate by evaporation. Calcium chloride is shipped as a liquid concentrate for the agricultural industry. The other product, sodium chloride, is used for table salt and is an essential chemical in many industrial processes.

Midway along the trail, at Chubbuck, are the remains of several large limestone mines and quarries that operated in the 1920s. The equipment used in these mines was freighted in by the Sugar Lime Rock Company, which ran the Baxter and Ballardi claim north of Baxter. When the Baxter mines closed down, the equipment was moved to Chubbuck.

Bristol Lake has fooled many a lost traveler or wishful prospector in the summer (or even winter) heat. The enormous dry lake develops spectacular mirages. Visions of water seem to shimmer at the base of the rugged Bullion Mountains.

Description

Cadiz Road is a wide, graded road that links California 62 with the National Trails Highway (Route 66). The road is sandy and loose along its length, and suitable for a carefully driven passenger vehicle in dry weather. Patches of loose sand, gullies, and occasional washouts may make some drivers wish for a high-clearance vehicle. The road may be impassable when wet, even to a 4WD vehicle, because the deep sand traps turn to greasy mud. The road is often washboardy from low maintenance.

The trail follows alongside the Atchison, Topeka & Santa Fe Railroad for most of its length. There are many small railroad maintenance tracks leading off from the main trail; these are not mentioned in the route directions unless there is a chance for confusion with the main trail.

To the west, the trail offers views of Danby Lake in the wide Ward Valley. The Iron Mountains are farther west, and the Old Woman Mountains are to the north. The salt works can be seen at various points along the way.

The Cadiz Dunes can be reached by a 5-mile spur trail. Hikers can continue to explore farther into the wilderness area.

Current Road Information

Bureau of Land Management
Needles Field Office
1303 South US Highway 95
Needles, CA 92363
(760) 326-7000

Map References

BLM Amboy, Sheep Hole Mtns., Parker
USGS 1:24,000 Arica Mtn., Sablon,
        Danby Lake, East of Milligan,
        Milligan, Chubbuck, Cadiz Lake
        NE, Cadiz Lake NW, Cadiz
        Summit, Cadiz
        1:100,000 Amboy, Sheep Hole
        Mtns., Parker
Maptech CD-ROM: San Bernardino
        County/Mojave
Southern & Central California Atlas &
        Gazetteer, pp. 100, 99, 85
California Road & Recreation Atlas,
        pp. 107, 113

DESERT #6: CADIZ ROAD

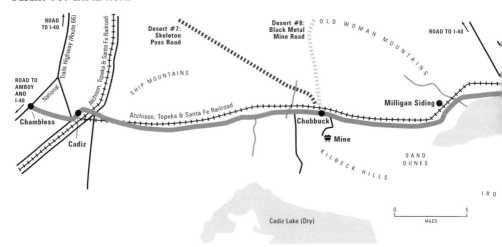

Route Directions

▼ 0.0　From California 62 at the Freda Railroad Siding, 23 miles west of Vidal Junction and 0.7 miles west of mile marker 103, zero trip meter and turn north on graded dirt road. The road is unsigned, but has a yellow "Not maintained by San Bernardino County" sign at the start. If approaching from the east, the sign is immediately before a left-hand bend.

13.8 ▲　Trail ends on California 62 at Freda Railroad Siding. Turn left for Vidal Junction and Parker, AZ; turn right for Twentynine Palms.
GPS: N34°06.42′ W114°55.90′

▼ 0.6　SO Cross through wash. Atchison, Topeka & Santa Fe Railroad joins on the right.

13.2 ▲　SO Railroad tracks leave on the left.

▼ 1.4　SO Cross through wash.

12.4 ▲　SO Cross through wash.

▼ 2.6　SO Cross through wash.

11.2 ▲　SO Cross through wash.
GPS: N34°08.24′ W114°57.47

▼ 3.5　SO Cross through wash.

10.3 ▲　SO Cross through wash.

▼ 4.2　SO Cross through wash.

9.6 ▲　SO Cross through wash.
GPS: N34°09.37′ W114°58.57′

▼ 5.1　SO Cross through wash.

8.7 ▲　SO Cross through wash.

▼ 6.1　SO Cross through wash.

7.7 ▲　SO Cross through wash.

▼ 6.7　SO Cross through wash.

7.1 ▲　SO Cross through wash.

▼ 7.6　SO Cross through wash.

6.2 ▲　SO Cross through wash.

▼ 9.4　SO Track on right.

4.4 ▲　SO Track on left.
GPS: N34°12.74′ W115°02.49′

▼ 10.5　SO Track on right.

3.3 ▲　SO Track on left.

▼ 11.2　SO Cross through wash.

2.6 ▲　SO Cross through wash.

▼ 11.6　SO Cross through wash.

2.2 ▲　SO Cross through wash.

▼ 12.6　SO Graded road on left and graded road on right along pipeline.

1.2 ▲　SO Graded road on left and graded road on right along pipeline.
GPS: N34°14.40′ W115°05.14′

▼ 13.8　SO Graded road on left and graded road on right under power lines. Left goes 8 miles to California 62; right goes 50 miles to I-40. Zero trip meter.

0.0 ▲　Continue to the southeast.
GPS: N34°15.06′ W115°06.19′

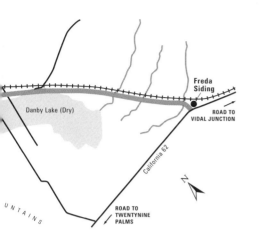

▼ 0.0   Continue to the northwest and cross through wash. Road is now marked as Cadiz Road

4.2 ▲   SO   Cross through wash; then graded road on left and graded road on right under power lines. Right goes 8 miles to California 62; left goes 50 miles to I-40. Zero trip meter.

▼ 2.9   SO   Graded road on left under power lines and graded road on right; then entrance into dry lake mining operations on right.

1.3 ▲   SO   Entrance into dry lake mining operations on left; then road on left. Road on right under power lines.

GPS: N34°16.56′ W115°08.73′

Explosives bunker at the Chubbuck Mines

▼ 3.0   SO   Track on left.
1.2 ▲   SO   Track on right.
▼ 3.4   SO   Cross through wash.
0.8 ▲   SO   Cross through wash.
▼ 3.9   SO   Track on left.
0.3 ▲   SO   Track on right.
▼ 4.1   SO   Milligan Siding on right at small sign.
0.1 ▲   SO   Milligan Siding on left at small sign.

GPS: N34°16.59' W115°10.08'

▼ 4.2   SO   Wide graded road on left. Road on right crosses railroad. Zero trip meter.
0.0 ▲   Continue to the east.

GPS: N34°16.60' W115°10.20'

▼ 0.0   Continue to the west.
9.1 ▲   SO   Wide graded road on right. Road on left crosses railroad. Zero trip meter.
▼ 0.2   SO   Cross through wash; then track on right along railroad.
8.9 ▲   SO   Track on left along railroad; then cross through wash.
▼ 1.4   SO   Graded road on left.
7.7 ▲   SO   Graded road on right.

GPS: N34°16.71' W115°11.60'

▼ 3.3   SO   Cross through wash.
5.8 ▲   SO   Cross through wash.
▼ 4.2   SO   Cross through wash.
4.9 ▲   SO   Cross through wash.
▼ 6.3   SO   Cross through wash.
2.8 ▲   SO   Cross through wash.
▼ 7.2   SO   Cross through wash.
1.9 ▲   SO   Cross through wash.
▼ 7.7   SO   Cross through wash.
1.4 ▲   SO   Cross through wash.
▼ 8.3   SO   Graded road on left goes 1 mile to mine and workings.
0.8 ▲   SO   Graded road on right goes 1 mile to mine and workings.

GPS: N34°21.26' W115°16.68'

▼ 9.1   SO   Track on left; then cross through wash; then track on right is Desert #7: Skeleton Pass Road, which leaves at an angle and crosses the railroad. Marker for the trail is set back from Cadiz Road. Zero trip meter.
0.0 ▲   Continue to the southeast and cross through wash; then track on right.

GPS: N34°21.84' W115°17.14'

▼ 0.0   Continue to the northwest.
7.3 ▲   SO   Track on left is Desert #7: Skeleton Pass Road, which leaves at an acute angle and crosses the railroad. Marker for the trail is set back from Cadiz Road. Zero trip meter.
▼ 0.5   SO   Cross through wash.
6.8 ▲   SO   Cross through wash.
▼ 0.8   SO   Track on right follows alongside rail line.
6.5 ▲   SO   Track on left follows alongside rail line.
▼ 1.4   SO   Track on right follows alongside rail line.
5.9 ▲   SO   Track on left follows alongside rail line.
▼ 1.6   SO   Cross through wash.
5.7 ▲   SO   Cross through wash.
▼ 1.7   SO   Track on left leads toward Cadiz Lake along edge of the Cadiz Dunes Wilderness.
5.6 ▲   SO   Track on right leads toward Cadiz Lake along edge of the Cadiz Dunes Wilderness.

GPS: N34°22.92' W115°18.42'

▼ 2.0   SO   Cross through wash.
5.3 ▲   SO   Cross through wash.
▼ 2.9   SO   Track on right.
4.4 ▲   SO   Track on left.
▼ 4.1   SO   Track on right.
3.2 ▲   SO   Track on left.
▼ 4.3   SO   Cross through wash.
3.0 ▲   SO   Cross through wash.
▼ 5.7   SO   Track on right.
1.6 ▲   SO   Track on left.
▼ 6.0   SO   Track on right.
1.3 ▲   SO   Track on left.
▼ 6.7   SO   Cross through wash.
0.6 ▲   SO   Cross through wash.

GPS: N34°25.40' W115°23.12'

▼ 7.3   SO   Well-used track on left is CZ 332, which leads to the edge of the Cadiz Dunes and is suitable for 4WDs, ATVs, and motorbikes. Zero trip meter.
0.0 ▲   Continue to the southeast.

GPS: N34°25.61' W115°23.53'

▼ 0.0   Continue to the northwest.
6.4 ▲   SO   Well-used track on right is CZ 332, which leads to the edge of the Cadiz

Dunes and is suitable for 4WDs, ATVs, and motorbikes. Zero trip meter.

▼ 0.4 SO Cross through wash.
6.0 ▲ SO Cross through wash.
▼ 1.0 SO Track on right.
5.4 ▲ SO Track on left.
▼ 1.3 SO Cross through wash.
5.1 ▲ SO Cross through wash.
▼ 1.9 SO Track on right.
4.5 ▲ SO Track on left.
▼ 2.1 SO Cross through wash.
4.3 ▲ SO Cross through wash.
▼ 2.7 SO Cross through wash.
3.7 ▲ SO Cross through wash.
▼ 2.9 SO Cross through wash.
3.5 ▲ SO Cross through wash.
▼ 3.5 SO Cross through wash.
2.9 ▲ SO Cross through wash.
▼ 4.7 SO Cross through wash.
1.7 ▲ SO Cross through wash.
GPS: N34°28.41' W115°27.43'

▼ 5.3 SO Cross through wash.
1.1 ▲ SO Cross through wash.
▼ 6.0 SO Track on left to pipeline works and track on right; then cross through wash.
0.4 ▲ SO Cross through wash; then track on right to pipeline works and track on left.
▼ 6.2 SO Cadiz Pump Station on left.
0.2 ▲ SO Cadiz Pump Station on right.
GPS: N34°29.32' W115°28.45'

▼ 6.4 BR Graded road on left; then track on right and track on left along rail line. Cross over rail line and zero trip meter.
0.0 ▲ Continue to the south. Track on left and track on right along rail line; then bear left past graded road on right.
GPS: N34°29.50' W115°28.58'

▼ 0.0 Continue to the north. Track on left and track on right along rail line.
6.3 ▲ BL Track on right and track on left along rail line. Cross over rail line and zero trip meter.
▼ 0.1 SO Track on right.
6.2 ▲ SO Track on left.
▼ 1.5 SO Track on left.
4.8 ▲ SO Track on right.

▼ 2.0 SO Cadiz. Graded road on left. Graded road on right goes along rail line to Danby. Cross over railroad. Two tracks on left and two tracks on right. Road is now paved. Remain on paved road, ignoring tracks on right and left.
4.3 ▲ SO Cadiz. Road turns to graded dirt. Two tracks on left and two tracks on right. Cross over the Atchison, Topeka & Santa Fe Railroad. Graded road on left goes along rail line to Danby. Graded road on right.
GPS: N34°31.10' W115°29.59'

▼ 2.3 SO Track on right goes to Marble Mountain Fossil Beds ACEC.
4.0 ▲ SO Track on left goes to Marble Mountain Fossil Beds ACEC.
GPS: N34°31.29' W115°29.73'

▼ 3.2 TR Road on left goes to Cadiz Siding.
3.1 ▲ TL Road straight ahead goes to Cadiz Siding.
▼ 6.3 Trail ends on National Trails Highway (Route 66) at Chambless. Turn right for I-40; turn left for Amboy.
0.0 ▲ Trail commences on National Trails Highway (Route 66) at Chambless, 11.2 miles west of Amboy. Zero trip meter and turn southeast on paved Cadiz Road at sign.
GPS: N34°33.71' W115°32.59'

DESERT #7

Skeleton Pass Road

STARTING POINT: National Trails Highway (Route 66), 23.5 miles east of Amboy
FINISHING POINT: Desert #6: Cadiz Road, 20 miles south of Chambless
TOTAL MILEAGE: 20.3 miles
UNPAVED MILEAGE: 20.3 miles
DRIVING TIME: 1.5 hours
ELEVATION RANGE: 1,100–1,600 feet
USUALLY OPEN: Year-round
BEST TIME TO TRAVEL: September to June
DIFFICULTY RATING: 2
SCENIC RATING: 8
REMOTENESS RATING: +1

Special Attractions

- Rockhounding for opalite in the Ship Mountains.
- Views of the rugged Old Woman Mountains and Cadiz Valley.

History

The ruins at the Danby intersection on Route 66 are all that remains of the old Justice Court building, gas station, and garage from the 1930s. The famous Route 66 was a long strip of tarmac that stretched a total 2,278 miles from Chicago to Santa Monica. Migrants from the Dust Bowl packed up their jalopies and headed west in search of opportunity. Some fell by the wayside, because conditions were harsh for automobiles of the day. Small business enterprises along Route 66 offered support to those who failed. For some migrants who were down to their last resources, this meant selling their automobiles to buy food. Weather conditions and elevation changes made progress along this route almost impossible for the ill-prepared.

In 1926, the nation adopted a numbered route system, thus bringing Route 66 to life. By 1936, Route 66 was completely paved. The road was decommissioned 49 years later when major sections of the route were replaced, relocated, renamed, and updated.

The Vulcan Mine, just over a mile west of Skeleton Pass in the Ship Mountains, was a gold and copper mine established in 1898. Close by are the remains of the Ship Mountain Mine, an old iron mine.

Description

Skeleton Pass Road is a roughly graded dirt road that travels from National Trails Highway (Route 66) to join the wider, graded dirt road in Cadiz Valley. Along the way, it travels down the wide, sloping bajada between the jagged peaks of the Old Woman Mountains and the Ship Mountains, passing through a varied landscape vegetated with creosote bush and cactus.

Rockhounding areas in the Ship Mountains containing the multicolored opalite can be reached from this trail. The trail borders the Old Woman Mountains Wilderness on its

DESERT #7: SKELETON PASS ROAD

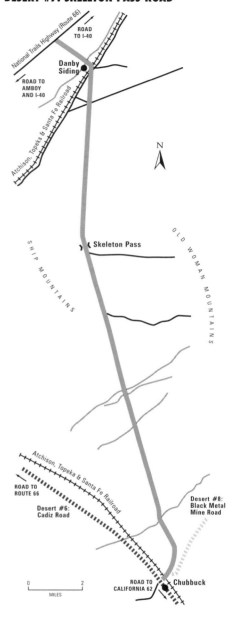

western edge. It is easygoing in dry weather and suitable for high-clearance 2WD vehicles.

Current Road Information

Bureau of Land Management
Needles Field Office
1303 South US Highway 95
Needles, CA 92363
(760) 326-7000

Trains still pass by Danby Siding but do not stop anymore

Map References

BLM   Amboy, Sheep Hole Mtns.
USGS 1:24,000   Danby, Skeleton Pass,
        Cadiz Lake NE, Chubbuck
        1:100,000 Amboy, Sheep Hole Mts.
Maptech CD-ROM: San Bernardino
        County/Mojave
*Southern & Central California Atlas &
        Gazetteer,* pp. 85, 99
California Road & Recreation Atlas, p. 107

Route Directions

▼ 0.0   From National Trails Highway (Route
            66), 23.5 miles east of Amboy, zero
            trip meter and turn southeast on grad-
            ed dirt Danby Road at sign.
1.6 ▲   Trail ends at Danby on paved National
            Trails Highway (Route 66). Turn right
            for I-40; turn left for Amboy.
            GPS: N34°38.92′ W115°22.19′

▼ 1.4   SO Cross through wash.
0.2 ▲   SO Cross through wash.
▼ 1.6   TR Track on right and track on left along
            rail line; then cross over rail line at
            Danby Siding; then 4-way intersection.
            Zero trip meter at intersection and turn
            right onto Skeleton Pass Road, which
            is marked by a BLM marker
            and is suitable for 4WDs, ATVs, and
            motorbikes.
0.0 ▲   Continue to the northwest. Track on
            left and track on right along rail line.
            GPS: N34°38.11′ W115°20.65′

▼ 0.0   Continue to the south. Track on right
            follows rail line.
5.1 ▲   TL Track on left follows rail line; then 4-
            way intersection. This is Danby Siding.
            Zero trip meter. Turn left and cross
            over rail line.
▼ 1.3   SO Two tracks on right and two tracks on
            left along pipeline.

ROUTE 66

If you ever plan to motor west
Travel my way, take the highway that's the best,
Get your kicks on Route 66!

It winds from Chicago to L. A.
More than two thousand miles all the way.
Get your kicks on Route 66!

—"Route 66" by Bobby Troup, 1946

 Route 66 was the idea of Tulsa, Oklahoma, highway commissioner Cyrus Stevens Avery, who wanted a road that would link his state to the metropolises of Chicago and Los Angeles. Avery was asked by the U.S. Bureau of Public Works to develop a system of interstate highways. On November 11, 1926, Route 66 was created, weaving together hundreds of existing roads. Improvements to the route, touted as "The Mother Road" and the "Main Street of America," began immediately. By 1936 the entire route from Chicago to Santa Monica was paved. Its completed length was 2,278 miles, 320 of which wound through California.

Beginning on the shore of Lake Michigan and stretching across eight states before concluding on the shore of the Pacific Ocean, Route 66 helped link California to the rest of the nation. Towns along the route prospered, providing gasoline, lodging, and cheap food to weary long-distance travelers. The very first McDonald's restaurant was opened on Route 66 in San Bernardino in 1940.

John Steinbeck made the fabled road a backdrop for his Pulitzer Prize-winning novel, *The Grapes of Wrath* (1939), chronicling the journeys of a family moving to California from Dust Bowl-era Oklahoma. Thousands of "Okies" used the route to escape the devastating drought that hit the Great Plains during the 1930s. From 1960 to 1964, Route 66 was the setting for a popular television series of the same name. Route 66, starring Martin Milner and George Maharis, followed two companions as they traveled through America's heartland in their red Corvette. Bobby Troup's song "Route 66" was recorded by several musical acts, including the Rolling Stones.

Gradually, Route 66 was superseded by new interstate highways, most notably Interstate 40. Towns began to dwindle as stores lost business. In 1984, Route 66 was officially decommissioned. Today the route, known as National Trails Highway, is seeing a resurgence of use as tourists, many of them Europeans or RV drivers who are retired, cruise its remains seeking a lost America. Ghost towns and glimpses of kitsch Americana make a trip along the remaining stretches of the road an interesting experience. The California Historic Route 66 Association was formed to protect and provide information in the Golden State. Several of the trails in this book begin on Route 66.

3.8 ▲ SO Two tracks on right and two tracks on left along pipeline.

▼ 5.1 SO Pipeline works on left. Track on left and track on right along pipeline. Zero trip meter and continue straight ahead, following sign to Skeleton Pass. Route is now a small, formed trail. The Old Woman Mountains Wilderness is now on the left of the trail.

0.0 ▲ Continue to the north. The Old Woman Mountains Wilderness is no longer on the right.

GPS: N34°33.48' W115°20.93'

▼ 0.0 Continue to the south and cross through wash.

1.5 ▲ SO Cross through wash; then pipeline works on right. Track on right and track on left along pipeline. Zero trip meter and continue straight ahead, following sign to Danby. Road is now wide and graded.

▼ 1.2 SO Pass through the gap of Skeleton Pass. Ship Mountains are to the right (west).

0.3 ▲ SO Pass through the gap of Skeleton Pass. Ship Mountains are to the left (west).

▼ 1.5 SO Track on left travels along a vehicle corridor up Carbonate Gulch into the Old Woman Mountains Wilderness. Zero trip meter.

0.0 ▲ Continue to the north.

GPS: N34°32.17' W115°20.67'

▼ 0.0 Continue to the south.

2.2 ▲ SO Track on right travels along a vehicle corridor up Carbonate Gulch into the Old Woman Mountains Wilderness. Zero trip meter.

▼ 2.2 SO Track on left travels a vehicle corridor into the Old Woman Mountains Wilderness to private property. Zero trip meter.

0.0 ▲ Continue to the north.

GPS: N34°30.24' W115°19.94'

▼ 0.0 Continue to the south.

9.9 ▲ SO Track on right travels a vehicle corridor into the Old Woman Mountains Wilderness to private property. Zero trip meter.

▼ 1.2 SO Cross through wash.

8.7 ▲ SO Cross through wash.

▼ 2.6 SO Start to cross through two washes.

7.3 ▲ SO Exit washes.

GPS: N34°27.95' W115°19.11'

▼ 2.7 SO Exit washes.

7.2 ▲ SO Start to cross through two washes.

▼ 4.0 SO Cross through wash.

5.9 ▲ SO Cross through wash.

▼ 4.1 SO Cross through wash.

5.8 ▲ SO Cross through wash.

▼ 7.5 SO Cross through wash.

2.4 ▲ SO Cross through wash.

GPS: N34°23.73' W115°17.50'

▼ 9.8 SO Track on left is Desert #8: Black Metal Mine Road, suitable for 4WDs, ATVs, and motorbikes.

0.1 ▲ BL Track on right is Desert #8: Black Metal Mine Road, suitable for 4WDs, ATVs, and motorbikes.

GPS: N34°21.93' W115°17.13'

▼ 9.9 Cross over railroad; then track on right. Trail finishes on graded dirt Desert #6: Cadiz Road. Track straight ahead.

0.0 ▲ Trail commences on graded dirt Desert #6: Cadiz Road, 20 miles south of Chambless. Zero trip meter and turn north on well-used formed trail, marked with a brown post as Skeleton Pass Road, suitable for 4WDs, ATVs, and motorbikes. The marker is set back from Cadiz Road. Immediately track on left; then cross over railroad.

GPS: N34°21.84' W115°17.15'

DESERT #8

Black Metal Mine Road

STARTING POINT: Desert #7: Skeleton Pass Road at Chubbuck, 0.1 miles from southern end at Desert #6: Cadiz Road

FINISHING POINT: Black Metal Mine

TOTAL MILEAGE: 7.1 miles

UNPAVED MILEAGE: 7.1 miles

DRIVING TIME: 30 minutes
ELEVATION RANGE: 1,100–2,700 feet
USUALLY OPEN: Year-round
BEST TIME TO TRAVEL: September to May
DIFFICULTY RATING: 3
SCENIC RATING: 8
REMOTENESS RATING: +1

Special Attractions

- Remains of the Black Metal Mine.
- Route travels a vehicle corridor into the Old Woman Mountains Wilderness.
- General location where the Old Woman Meteorite was found in 1975.

History

The Black Metal Mine lies at the southern end of the Old Woman Mountains, a little-traveled part of the Mojave Desert. In 1975, three prospectors roaming the surrounding mountains made an unusual find. They noticed a boulder that did not match any of the surrounding rocks on the mountainside and were instantly drawn to it. Further investigation suggested the boulder might in fact be a valuable meteorite. So the prospectors filed a mining claim on the site, which was within BLM jurisdiction. Unfortunately for the prospectors, meteorites are not locatable minerals under the definition of mining laws. In fact, any meteorite that lands on federal property is considered an item of national scientific interest. The Smithsonian Institution in Washington, D.C., became the official organization concerned with this rare find. The rock was dubbed the Old Woman Meteorite after the location in which it was found.

Remains of the Black Metal Mine

Caution! The timber-lined shaft of Black Metal Mine is deep

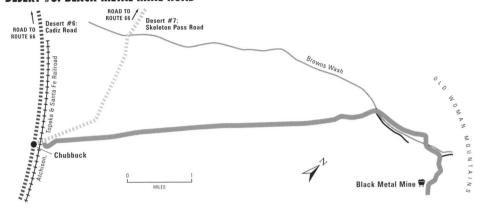

A meteoroid is a mass of rock or metal traveling in space. When one enters the earth's atmosphere, it is referred to as a meteor. The earth's gravity forces it to travel at high speeds, causing friction with the atmosphere, and resulting in extremely high temperatures. Most meteors burn up on entry and may be seen at night as a streak in the sky. Those that survive entry to land on the earth's surface are referred to as meteorites; most end up as tiny particles the size of a grain of sand. More than 90 percent of meteorites are made up of stone that blends well among other rocks. A few (as low as 6 percent) meteorites are made up of iron and nickel. These are easily spotted because they stand out from surrounding rocks.

The Old Woman Meteorite definitely stood out among the surrounding rocks, and a site inspection of the boulder by Dr. Roy Clarke of the Smithsonian Institution confirmed that it was an iron meteorite. The task of removing it from this remote desert mountain range was beyond the capabilities of any earthmoving machinery. So the U.S. Marine Corps was brought in to assess the possibility of moving it. Special equipment was lowered by helicopter, and an experienced rigging team managed to place an extra heavy-duty webbed netting around the three-ton meteorite. A Marine Heavy Helicopter Squadron helicopter then airlifted the meteorite to a truck for transport to Barstow.

The Old Woman Meteorite was taken to the Smithsonian for further research and display. It was determined the meteorite consisted of two previously known metals that had never been seen together before, thereby making this a rare find indeed.

Two copies of the Old Woman Meteorite have been made. One moves around the nation for public display; the other can usually be seen at the Barstow BLM office. The original is on permanent display at the California Desert Information Center in Barstow, where children love to test the meteorite's strong magnetism with demonstrational magnets. The Old Woman Meteorite is the second largest meteorite ever found in the United States.

Description

The Black Metal Mine is reached via a vehicle corridor through the Old Woman Mountains Wilderness. The trail is fairly short, and its only difficulty comes from the deep, loose sand in Browns Wash. The trail is a spur that begins near the intersection of Desert #6: Cadiz Road and Desert #7: Skeleton Pass Road. It crosses a sandy bajada, climbing gradually toward the mountains before entering Browns Wash. The trail travels through a wider valley before leaving the wash to finish at the Black Metal Mine. The remains of an old cabin, a deep timber-lined shaft, and a wooden loading hopper can be seen at the mine site.

The mountains are home to bighorn sheep and desert tortoises, and the area is an important habitat for many species of raptors.

Current Road Information
Bureau of Land Management
Needles Field Office
1303 South US Highway 95
Needles, CA 92363
(760) 326-7000

Map References
BLM   Sheep Hole Mts.
USGS 1:24,000 Chubbuck, Cadiz Lake
        NE, Sheep Camp Spring
        1:100,000 Sheep Hole Mtns.
Maptech CD-ROM: San Bernardino
        County/Mojave
*Southern & Central California Atlas &
        Gazetteer,* pp. 99, 100
California Road & Recreation Atlas, p. 107

Route Directions

▼ 0.0   From Desert #7: Skeleton Pass Road
         at Chubbuck, 0.1 miles north of the
         intersection with Desert #6: Cadiz
         Road, zero trip meter and turn north-
         east on formed dirt trail marked with a
         brown route marker as Black Metal
         Mine Road. Trail is suitable for 4WDs,
         ATVs, and motorbikes.
         GPS: N34°21.93' W115°14.13'

▼ 5.0   SO Enter line of Browns Wash. Track on
         right up wash.
         GPS: N34°25.66' W115°14.06'

▼ 5.3   SO Track forks and immediately rejoins.
▼ 6.3   BR Bear right across main wash. Track on
         left continues up wash.
         GPS: N34°25.99' W115°12.84'

▼ 6.5   BR Track on right; then track on left; then
         bear right in front of old wooden post
         and exit wash.
         GPS: N34°25.86' W115°12.65'

▼ 6.6   SO Track on right.
▼ 6.9   BL Trail passes through remains of the
         Black Metal Mine—old cabin on right
         and various wooden structures.
         GPS: N34°25.61' W115°12.61'

▼ 7.1   Trail ends at a saddle that overlooks
         the next valley in the Old Woman
         Mountains.
         GPS: N34°25.48' W115°12.46'

DESERT #9

Amboy Crater Road

STARTING POINT: National Trails Highway
(Route 66), 1.7 miles west of Amboy,
1.1 miles west of intersection with
Amboy Road
FINISHING POINT: Amboy Crater
TOTAL MILEAGE: 1.7 miles (one-way)
UNPAVED MILEAGE: 1.7 miles
DRIVING TIME: 30 minutes
ELEVATION RANGE: 700 feet
USUALLY OPEN: Year-round
BEST TIME TO TRAVEL: September to June
DIFFICULTY RATING: 4
SCENIC RATING: 9
REMOTENESS RATING: +0

Special Attractions
■ The volcanic Amboy Crater.
■ Spectacular hiking trail to the crater rim.

History
Amboy Crater, one of the younger cinder
cones in the region, measures 250 feet high
and approximately 1,500 feet in diameter.
Cinder cones are formed by explosive volcanic eruptions that can last from a few short
weeks to years. The volcanos produce lava
that can burst through the side or base of a
cone because the cone's walls are too fragile to
contain the pooling lava. Amboy Crater
shows signs of lava having escaped from the
base. The western side of the cone seems to
have floated away with the lava.
    Basalt lava flows around Amboy Crater
have a mixture of forms, some are aa surfaces and others are smoother sections called
pahoehoe. Both terms are Hawaiian, where
people are well and truly versed in volcanic
eruptions. The temperature of a lava flow
determines whether it will have a rough or

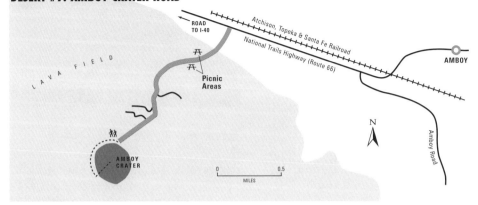

smooth finish. More steam within a flow will yield a smoother pahoehoe surface.

Radiocarbon dating has not been carried out at this cone. Carbon dating is usually performed on wood that has been caught in an eruption; with no wood to examine, no answer can be given. Recent observations and estimates by geologists suggest that the volcano is anywhere from 500 to 6,000 years old. Earlier estimates dated the age between 50,000 to 100,000 years old.

Medicine wheels, such as the one on the facing page, were made by Indians to mark sacred spaces. Ceremonies were held in and around them because they were thought to hold great power.

Amboy Siding is located at the northern end of the salt-encrusted Bristol Lake. The settlement was established with the construction of the Atlantic & Pacific Railroad in 1883. Though little happened in this remote location, it was strategically placed on what was to become the famous Route 66. In the 1930s, Buster Burris and his partner Roy opened a service station at this railroad siding and old road junction. The town flourished to support a school, café, motel, and major repair shop. These services catered to the increasing traffic of the 1940s. Amboy's population neared 100 at its peak in the late 1940s.

The town's days were numbered with the construction of Interstate 40. The new and faster highway took passing motor trade to the north, leaving Amboy a quiet, forgotten little town. Amboy faded; property was hard to sell, and some people ended up walking away from their properties. Burris stuck with the vanishing railroad settlement, whether or not by choice is hard to say. He ended up owning most of the nearly abandoned settlement.

A reawakening of interest in classic travel routes across the nation, in particular old Route 66 (also referred to as National Trails Highway), has brought attention to many small abandoned towns along quiet stretches of the route. In the late 1990s, Burris finally sold out to a duo from the East Coast. White and his partner Wilson are slowly returning a 1940s atmosphere to this once important desert crossroads. Many people are starting to appreciate the remote feeling of this gas station and motel in the depths of the sweltering Mojave Desert.

Description

This very short trail travels to the base of the towering, black cinder cone of Amboy Crater. The first 0.7 miles of the trail can be tackled by a carefully driven passenger vehicle, but it is rough and slow going with embedded black lava rock.

Past a small parking area, the trail is marked for 4WD vehicles only; passenger vehicles should stop here. The trail continues to twist and snake its way to the base of the cone. The embedded lava rock makes for a rough ride and is very hard on tires. However the trail is not technically difficult. It is

Medicine wheel in the lava flow en route to Amboy Crater

marked sporadically with brown route markers, which are useful because the trail is often indistinct and a couple of incorrect trails can confuse the navigator.

The trail wraps around the cone for a short distance before finishing at the start of a hiking trail that climbs to the crater, passing through a wide opening in the wall to climb an additional 144 feet to the narrow rim. The hike is not recommended on windy days because the path at the top is extremely narrow. This loose climb offers the reward of panoramic views over the Cadiz Valley and Bristol Mountains. Allow one to two hours for the round-trip hike if you park your vehicle at the start of the 4WD section. Note that the trail going straight up the north rim of the crater is being reclaimed; it should not be attempted.

Current Road Information

Bureau of Land Management
Needles Field Office
1303 South US Highway 95
Needles, CA 92363
(760) 326-7000

Map References

BLM   Amboy
USGS   1:24,000   Amboy Crater
        1:100,000 Amboy
Maptech CD-ROM: San Bernardino
        County/Mojave
Southern & Central California Atlas &
        Gazetteer, p. 84
California Road & Recreation Atlas, p. 106

Route Directions

▼ 0.0   Trail commences on National Trails Highway (Route 66) 1.7 miles west of Amboy, 1.1 miles west of the intersection with Amboy Road. Zero trip meter and turn south on formed trail at BLM sign for Amboy Crater National Natural Landmark.
        GPS: N34°33.61′ W115°46.43′

▼ 0.3   SO   Picnic table on right.
▼ 0.5   SO   Picnic table and information board on left.
        GPS: N34°33.40′ W115°46.76′

Amboy Crater rises abruptly above the surrounding lava flow

The walls of Amboy Crater stand high above the Mojave Desert floor

▼ 0.7 BL Bear left, following sign for crater. Trail is marked 4x4 only past this point for 4WDs, ATVs, and motorbikes.
GPS: N34°33.39' W115°46.91'

▼ 1.0 SO Track on left.
GPS: N34°33.19' W115°47.03'

▼ 1.2 BL Track on right.
▼ 1.3 SO Trail crosses flat desert pavement. In reverse this point is marked with a brown exit marker.
GPS: N34°33.02' W115°47.03'

▼ 1.4 TL Track on right.
GPS: N34°32.99' W115°47.11'

▼ 1.6 BR Trail forks and immediately rejoins.
▼ 1.7 Trail ends at the base of Amboy Crater. Return the way you came. A hiking trail begins here and wraps around the base before climbing to the crater.
GPS: N34°32.86' W115°47.33'

Sunflower Spring Road

STARTING POINT: National Trails Highway (Route 66) at Essex, 6 miles south of I-40
FINISHING POINT: US 95, 23 miles south of Needles
TOTAL MILEAGE: 45 miles, plus 1.7-mile spur to Golden Fleece Mine
UNPAVED MILEAGE: 45 miles, plus 1.7-mile spur
DRIVING TIME: 6 hours
ELEVATION RANGE: 1,400–3,400 feet
USUALLY OPEN: Year-round
BEST TIME TO TRAVEL: October to June
DIFFICULTY RATING: 4
SCENIC RATING: 10
REMOTENESS RATING: +2

Special Attractions

■ Long, exceedingly remote trail passing the boundaries of four wilderness areas.
■ Trail follows a section of the East Mojave Heritage Trail.

- Chalcedony roses and agate on either side of Turtle Mountain Road.
- Old Woman Statue.

History

Camp Essex was located just north of Essex, between the Clipper and the Piute Mountains, at the northern end of this trail. The camp spanned both sides of Essex Road and covered an area of more than 31,000 acres. Interstate 40 runs through the northern section of the old camp. The rest area on Interstate 40 occupies the old garrison area.

Camp Essex was acquired as a Desert Training Center in 1943. The camp included the area previously occupied by Camp Clipper, which had been established in 1942. Clipper was occupied by the 33rd Infantry Division from March 28 to July 17, 1943. Camp Clipper, located in the western section of the newer camp, was abandoned when Camp Essex was completed. The new camp was active from November 1943 to January 1944. It was declared surplus in March 1944. A 500,000-gallon water tank was the only permanent structure. An airstrip occupying 85 acres was also constructed. It was used by spotter planes and routine flights. All other structures were temporary.

In May 1944, more than 300 Italian prisoners of war were given the task of removing artillery duds from the ranges. However, a clean bill of health in regards to unexploded rounds may never occur. Time has eroded most traces of the camp's layout and most of the leftovers seem to be bullets rather than bombs. Surface activity is all that is allowed in the area nowadays.

The trail leaves Essex and heads south into the Old Woman Mountains. These rugged mountains got their name from a rock formation close to Sunflower Spring. When viewed side-on, the formation somewhat resembles an old woman bent over a wash tub. Several mines are visible in the Old Woman Mountains. The Blue Bugle Mine consisted of eight claims, including the Florence claim, and was on the north side of the mountain range in the Danby Mining District. Three quartz veins were worked to

depths of 160 feet. Ore was processed north of Lancaster at Rosamond that assayed at $50 per ton. The Florence claim reportedly returned up to $200 per ton in gold.

Description

Sunflower Spring Road is a long, very remote trail with sweeping desert vistas, hiking access into four wilderness areas, and the solitude of the east Mojave Desert. The trail borders the Piute Mountains Wilderness, Old Woman Mountains Wilderness, Turtle Mountains Wilderness, and Stepladder Mountains Wilderness, making it an excellent trail for hikers who wish to explore these remote areas on foot.

The trail leaves the small settlement of Essex a few miles south of I-40 on Route 66. Gas is available at the freeway exit at Fenner. For the first few miles, the wide, though unmaintained, road is used to service a pipeline's workings. It travels in a broad, flat valley with the Old Woman Mountains to the south, the Little Piute Mountains to the southeast, and the Piute Mountains to the east.

Once past the pipeline workings, the trail follows a small, sandy formed road that skirts the eastern boundary of the Old Woman Mountains Wilderness. A short spur travels 1.7 miles in a vehicle corridor into the wilderness, passing the workings of the Golden Fleece Mine to finish at a spot with views down Willow Springs Canyon.

The trail continues south, joining the East Mojave Heritage Trail. It descends gradually, twisting its way along the eastern bajada of the Old Woman Mountains and crossing many deep and sandy washes. The approaches to some of these washes can be steep and eroded. Some will test a vehicle's wheel articulation and traction. This spectacular area of desert vegetation is one of the most scenic sections along the trail.

Near Sunflower Wash, the distinctive, conically shaped Pilot Peak can be seen to the east. Beyond it are distant views to the Stepladder Mountains. Old Woman Statue can be seen to the west. The rock shape resembles a cloaked and stooping old woman.

The trail now gradually descends a long and gently sloping, sandy bajada down to

Shaft of the Golden Fleece Mine

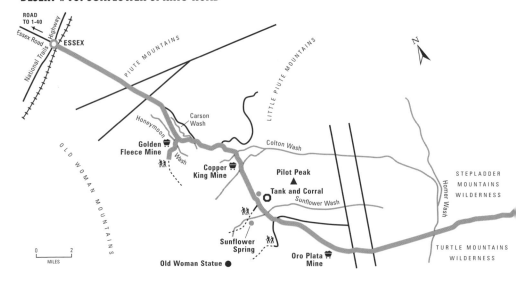

the broad Ward Valley. This section has some of the loosest and deepest sand on the trail. In the forward direction, it is not too bad, but heading uphill in the reverse direction, the sand can quickly bog a vehicle down. The yuccas along the edge of the Old Woman Mountains disappear and the valley floor becomes covered with creosote bush and little else. The eastern side of the valley, as you ascend into the Turtle Mountains, has a firmer surface.

The trail enters a vehicle corridor between the Stepladder Mountains Wilderness on the left and the Turtle Mountains Wilderness on the right. The jagged peaks of the Turtle Mountains rise up to the south, and as you crest a slight rise, the Chemehuevi Mountains and Whipple Mountains are visible to the east. Looking back to the west you can see over Ward Valley to the Old Woman Mountains.

The trail continues as a rough, well-used formed trail as it passes both ends of Desert #11: Lost Arch Inn Trail, which loops farther into the Turtle Mountains. Staghorn chollas and ocotillos can now be seen among the creosote bush. They give a brilliant display in the spring.

The final 10 miles of the route follow the wider, formed Turtle Mountain Road. This is often washboardy and has loose sand, particularly where it crosses the wide Chemehuevi Wash, a short distance before it ends at US 95. Rock hounds may like to hunt for agate and chalcedony roses in the washes and along Turtle Mountain Road.

Campers will find plenty of sites along this trail. A nice spot near the end of the trail is situated in the trees at Chemehuevi Wash. The best and most scenic spots are in the Turtle Mountains and at the southern end of Sunflower Spring Road. Campers will notice that all the spots tend to be rocky.

Current Road Information

Bureau of Land Management
Needles Field Office
1303 South US Highway 95
Needles, CA 92363
(760) 326-7000

Map References

BLM   Amboy, Sheep Hole Mtns., Parker, Needles
USGS 1:24,000   Essex, Old Woman Statue, Painted Rock Wash, Wilhelm Spring, West of Mohawk Spring, Mohawk Spring, Savahia Peak NW, Snaggletooth

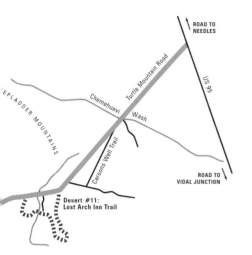

ROAD TO
NEEDLES

US 95

Turtle Mountain Road

Chemehuevi

Wash

EPLADDER MOUNTAINS

Carsons Well Trail

ROAD TO
VIDAL JUNCTION

Desert #11:
Lost Arch Inn Trail

1:100,000 Amboy, Sheep Hole
Mtns., Parker, Needles
Maptech CD-ROM: San Bernardino
County/Mojave
*Southern & Central California Atlas &
Gazetteer*, pp. 86, 100, 101, 87
California Road & Recreation Atlas,
pp. 107, 115

Route Directions

▼ 0.0   At Essex, 6 miles south of the Fenner exit on I-40, zero trip meter at the intersection of Essex Road and National Trails Highway (Route 66). Turn southeast on graded dirt road, alongside the Essex Post Office.

4.6 ▲   Trail ends on National Trails Highway (Route 66) at Essex. Continue straight ahead for I-40; turn right for Fenner.

     GPS: N34°44.10′ W115°14.69′

▼ 0.1   SO   Cross over rail line.
4.5 ▲   SO   Cross over rail line.
▼ 0.2   SO   Track on left and right; then cattle guard.
4.4 ▲   SO   Cattle guard; then track on left and right.
▼ 4.6   SO   Track on left and track on right is gas pipeline road. Zero trip meter.
0.0 ▲   Continue to the northwest.

     GPS: N34°40.87′ W115°11.50′

▼ 0.0   Continue to the southeast.
3.9 ▲   SO   Track on left and track on right is gas pipeline road. Zero trip meter.
▼ 1.0   SO   Track on left and track on right is gas pipeline road. Pipeline valves at intersection.
2.9 ▲   SO   Track on left and track on right is gas pipeline road. Pipeline valves at intersection.

     GPS: N34°40.16′ W115°10.78′

▼ 1.5   SO   Track on left and track on right is gas pipeline road. Trail ahead is now marked with a brown route marker as Sunflower Spring Road, suitable for 4WDs, ATVs, and motorbikes.
2.4 ▲   SO   Track on left and track on right is gas pipeline road.

     GPS: N34°39.83′ W115°10.44′

▼ 2.2   BR   Well-used track on left.
1.7 ▲   SO   Well-used track on right.

     GPS: N34°39.31′ W115°10.02′

▼ 2.5   SO   Cross through the three channels of Carson Wash.
1.4 ▲   SO   Cross through the three channels of Carson Wash.
▼ 3.7   SO   Track on left.
0.2 ▲   SO   Track on right.

     GPS: N34°37.99′ W115°09.94′

▼ 3.9   SO   Well-used track on right is spur to Golden Fleece Mine. Intersection is unmarked. Zero trip meter.
0.0 ▲   Continue to the northwest.

     GPS: N34°37.75′ W115°09.86′

Spur to Golden Fleece Mine

▼ 0.0   Proceed to the southwest.
▼ 0.1   SO   Track on left rejoins main trail.
▼ 0.3   SO   Cross through Honeymoon Wash.

     GPS: N34°37.62′ W115°10.06′

▼ 0.6   SO   Diggings of the Golden Fleece Mine on right and left; then cross through wash.

     GPS: N34°37.48′ W115°10.28′

▼ 1.4　BR　Bear right onto smaller trail. Track on left goes to gate—foot and horse travel only past the gate into the Old Woman Mountains Wilderness.
　　　　GPS: N34°36.98′ W115°10.85′

▼ 1.7　UT　Spur ends at a tight turnaround below the hill. Views into Willow Springs Canyon.
　　　　GPS: N34°37.03′ W115°11.05′

Continuation of Main Trail

▼ 0.0　　　Continue to the southeast.
2.6 ▲　SO　Well-used track on left is spur to Golden Fleece Mine. Intersection is unmarked. Zero trip meter.
　　　　GPS: N34°37.75′ W115°09.86′

▼ 0.1　BL　Small track on right joins spur trail. Track straight ahead goes to well.
2.5 ▲　SO　Track on sharp left goes to well. Small track on left joins spur trail.

▼ 0.2　SO　Track on right to well.
2.4 ▲　SO　Track on left to well.
▼ 0.3　SO　Cross through wash.
2.3 ▲　SO　Cross through wash.
▼ 0.4　BL　Track on right to well.
2.2 ▲　BR　Track on left to well.
　　　　GPS: N34°37.49′ W115°09.56′

▼ 0.5　SO　Cross through wash.
2.1 ▲　SO　Cross through wash.
▼ 0.6　SO　Cross through wash.
2.0 ▲　SO　Cross through wash.
▼ 1.0　SO　Cross through Carson Wash; then well-used track on left.
1.6 ▲　BL　Well-used track on right; then cross through Carson Wash.
　　　　GPS: N34°37.33′ W115°09.06′

▼ 1.2　SO　Enter wash.
1.4 ▲　SO　Exit wash.
▼ 1.3　SO　Exit wash.
1.3 ▲　SO　Enter wash.
▼ 1.4　SO　Cross through wash.
1.2 ▲　SO　Cross through wash.

Granite outcroppings near Painted Rock Wash

▼ 1.5   SO   Trail forks and immediately rejoins.

1.1 ▲   SO   Trail forks and immediately rejoins.

▼ 2.6   BR   Track on left and ahead is marked with a brown route marker as East Mojave Heritage Trail, suitable for 4WDs, ATVs, and motorbikes. Sunflower Spring Road is ahead. Zero trip meter.

0.0 ▲   Continue to the west.

GPS: N34º36.66' W115º07.77'

▼ 0.0   Continue to the east.

4.2 ▲   SO   Track on right is marked with a brown route marker as East Mojave Heritage Trail, suitable for 4WDs, ATVs, and motorbikes. Sunflower Spring Road is straight ahead. Zero trip meter.

▼ 0.1   SO   Cross through wash.

4.1 ▲   SO   Cross through wash.

▼ 0.6   SO   Small track on left.

3.6 ▲   SO   Small track on right.

▼ 0.9   SO   Cross through wash.

3.3 ▲   SO   Cross through wash.

▼ 1.0   SO   Cross through wash.

3.2 ▲   SO   Cross through wash.

GPS: N34º36.05' W115º07.04'

▼ 1.1   SO   Track on left.

3.1 ▲   SO   Track on right.

▼ 1.2   SO   Old vehicle trail on right enters wilderness and goes 0.1 miles to the Copper King Mine—foot and horse travel only. Track on left.

3.0 ▲   SO   Old vehicle trail on left enters wilderness and goes 0.1 miles to the Copper King Mine—foot and horse travel only. Track on right.

GPS: N34º35.89' W115º07.06'

▼ 1.4   SO   Cross through wash.

2.8 ▲   SO   Cross through wash.

▼ 1.6   BR   Track on left.

2.6 ▲   SO   Track on right.

▼ 1.7   SO   Track on left.

2.5 ▲   SO   Track on right.

▼ 1.8   SO   Cross through deep Colton Wash.

2.4 ▲   SO   Cross through deep Colton Wash.

GPS: N34º35.46' W115º07.05'

▼ 3.8   SO   Cross through wash.

0.4 ▲   SO   Cross through wash.

▼ 3.9   SO   Well and corral on left.

0.3 ▲   SO   Well and corral on right.

GPS: N34º33.57' W115º06.92'

▼ 4.1   SO   Cross through wash.

0.1 ▲   SO   Cross through wash.

▼ 4.2   SO   Track on left. Track on right goes 0.5 miles to a slightly closer view of Old Woman Statue. Hikers and horses can continue past this point on the old vehicle trail. Zero trip meter.

0.0 ▲   Continue to the north.

GPS: N34º33.30' W115º06.89'

▼ 0.0   Continue to the south.

1.1 ▲   SO   Track on right. Track on left goes 0.5 miles to a slightly closer view of Old Woman Statue. Hikers and horses can continue past this point on the old vehicle trail. Zero trip meter.

▼ 0.5   SO   Campsite on right; then start to cross through wide Sunflower Wash.

0.6 ▲   SO   Exit wide wash crossing; then campsite on left.

▼ 0.6   SO   Exit wide wash crossing.

0.5 ▲   SO   Start to cross through wide Sunflower Wash.

GPS: N34º32.83' W115º06.76'

▼ 1.0   BR   Track on left.

0.1 ▲   SO   Track on right.

▼ 1.1   BL   Closure gate on right; then track on right travels 3 miles to the start of a hiking trail toward Old Woman Statue and good bouldering opportunities in a natural rock amphitheater. Zero trip meter.

0.0 ▲   Continue to the northwest past closure gate on left.

GPS: N34º32.48' W115º06.51'

▼ 0.0   Continue to the southeast.

4.8 ▲   BR   Track on left travels 3 miles to the start of a hiking trail toward Old Woman Statue and good bouldering opportunities in a natural rock amphitheater. Zero trip meter.

▼ 0.2   BR   Track on sharp left is East Mojave Heritage Trail; then second track on left.

4.6 ▲   BL   Track on right; then second track on

Loose, deep sand in Ward Valley

right is East Mojave Heritage Trail.
GPS: N34°32.40' W115°06.29'

▼ 3.3 SO Cross through wash.
1.5 ▲ SO Cross through wash.
▼ 3.4 SO Cross through wash. Track on left
        down wash.
1.4 ▲ SO Cross through wash. Track on right
        down wash.
▼ 3.8 SO Oro Plata Mine workings on right.
1.0 ▲ SO Oro Plata Mine workings on left.
        GPS: N34°30.10' W115°03.71'

▼ 4.0 SO Cross through wash.
0.8 ▲ SO Cross through wash.
▼ 4.7 SO Track on right.
0.1 ▲ SO Track on left.
▼ 4.8 TL T-intersection with graded road under
        power lines. Zero trip meter and follow
        along power lines.
0.0 ▲   Continue to the southwest away from
        power lines.
        GPS: N34°29.75' W115°02.79'

▼ 0.0   Continue to the north.
11.6 ▲ TR Turn right onto smaller, formed trail
        marked East Mojave Heritage Trail and
        zero trip meter.
▼ 0.1 TR Small track on left. Turn right onto
        smaller, formed trail marked East
        Mojave Heritage Trail and leave power
        lines.
11.5 ▲ TL Small track ahead. Turn left onto grad-
        ed road under power lines.
        GPS: N34°29.81' W115°02.76'

▼ 1.2 SO Cross through wash; then track on left
        and track on right. Start of Turtle
        Mountains Wilderness on right.
10.4 ▲ SO Track on right and track on left; then
        cross through wash. End of Turtle
        Mountains Wilderness on left.
        GPS: N34°29.30' W115°01.71'

▼ 4.6 SO Cross through Homer Wash.
7.0 ▲ SO Cross through Homer Wash.
        GPS: N34°28.96' W114°58.05'

▼ 5.8   SO   Start of the Stepladder Mountains Wilderness on left. Trail now enters a vehicle corridor between the two wilderness areas.

5.8 ▲   SO   Exit vehicle corridor between the wilderness areas. Turtle Mountains Wilderness is on the left.

GPS: N34°28.92′ W114°56.79′

▼ 6.0   SO   Cross through wash.
5.6 ▲   SO   Cross through wash.
▼ 6.5   SO   Cross through wash.
5.1 ▲   SO   Cross through wash.
▼ 7.3   SO   Cross through wash.
4.3 ▲   SO   Cross through wash.
▼ 7.7   SO   Cross through wash.
3.9 ▲   SO   Cross through wash.
▼ 8.3   SO   Cross through wash.
3.3 ▲   SO   Cross through wash.
▼ 9.9   SO   Cross through wash.
1.7 ▲   SO   Cross through wash.
▼ 10.4 SO   Saddle. Ruins of a stone chimney on left. Views ahead over the Chemehuevi Valley and the Whipple Mountains.

1.2 ▲   SO   Saddle. Ruins of a stone chimney on right. Views ahead over Ward Valley and the Old Woman Mountains.

GPS: N34°28.69′ W114°52.11′

▼ 11.6 SO   Track on right is western end of Desert #11: Lost Arch Inn Trail. There is a mailbox on a post at the intersection, but it is otherwise unmarked. Zero trip meter.

0.0 ▲   Continue to the west.

GPS: N34°28.52′ W114°50.83′

▼ 0.0   Continue to the east.

2.0 ▲   BR   Track on left is western end of Desert #11: Lost Arch Inn Trail. There is a mailbox on a post at the intersection, but it is otherwise unmarked. Zero trip meter.

▼ 0.6   SO   Cross through wash.
1.4 ▲   SO   Cross through wash.
▼ 0.9   SO   Track on right.
1.1 ▲   SO   Track on left.
▼ 2.0   TL   Cross through wash; then T-intersection. To the right is marked Lost Arch Inn, suitable for 4WDs, ATVs, and

motorbikes. This is the eastern end of Desert #11: Lost Arch Inn Trail. To the left is the continuation of the East Mojave Heritage Trail. Zero trip meter and remain on the East Mojave Heritage Trail.

0.0 ▲   Continue to the northwest.

GPS: N34°28.12′ W114°48.79′

▼ 0.0   Continue to the northeast.

10.2 ▲ TR   Turn right onto formed trail and cross through wash, remaining on the marked East Mojave Heritage Trail. Ahead is marked Lost Arch Inn, suitable for 4WDs, ATVs, and motorbikes. This is the eastern end of Desert #11: Lost Arch Inn Trail. Zero trip meter.

▼ 0.5   SO   Track on right.
9.7 ▲   SO   Track on left.
▼ 4.3   SO   Track on right is Carsons Well Trail, suitable for 4WDs, ATVs, and motorbikes.

5.9 ▲   SO   Track on left is Carsons Well Trail, suitable for 4WDs, ATVs, and motorbikes.

GPS: N34°29.77′ W114°44.57′

▼ 5.0   SO   Track on right; then cross through wide, sandy Chemehuevi Wash.

5.2 ▲   SO   Cross through wide, sandy Chemehuevi Wash; then track on left.

GPS: N34°30.05′ W114°43.85′

▼ 5.2   SO   Cross through wash.
5.0 ▲   SO   Cross through wash.
▼ 10.2   Trail ends at T-intersection with US 95. Turn left for Needles; turn right for Vidal Junction.

0.0 ▲   Trail commences on US 95, 1.6 miles south of the intersection with Havasu Lake Road, 23 miles south of Needles, and 0.4 miles south of mile marker 36. Zero trip meter and turn southwest on wide dirt road, marked with a white post as Turtle Mountain Road. Road is also marked with a brown BLM route marker as East Mojave Heritage Trail, suitable for 4WDs, ATVs, and motorbikes.

GPS: N34°32.01′ W114°38.82′

Lost Arch Inn Trail

STARTING POINT: Desert #10: Sunflower
Spring Road, 10.2 miles west of US 95
FINISHING POINT: Desert #10: Sunflower
Spring Road, 12.2 miles west of US 95
TOTAL MILEAGE: 7.7 miles
UNPAVED MILEAGE: 7.7 miles
DRIVING TIME: 1 hour
ELEVATION RANGE: 1,600–2,000 feet
USUALLY OPEN: Year-round
BEST TIME TO TRAVEL: October to May
DIFFICULTY RATING: 3
SCENIC RATING: 8
REMOTENESS RATING: +0

Special Attractions
- Rockhounding for opalite, chalcedony roses, agate, and jasper.
- Lost Arch Inn cabins.
- Hiking trail to Mohawk Spring petroglyph.
- Can be combined with Desert #10: Sunflower Spring Road.

History
Mohawk Spring, located about half a mile east of this trail, was a known water source to the Indians who roamed the region. Though the spring is hardly a trickle these days, it was once an important camp in the dry, rugged Turtle Mountains. The meaning behind the unusual abstract petroglyph near the spring is unclear. Prospectors sought out the spring because it was a valuable water source when traversing this difficult region of volcanic spires.

Mopah Spring, south of the Lost Arch Inn near the Mopah Peaks, has California fan palms that were planted in 1924. This spring was also a camp for the Palco-Indians who left petroglyphs in the region. Some depict human figures possibly embracing one another. Others are abstract arrangements. Some of the concentric circles may have been added by soldiers or ranch hands at the turn of the twentieth century, though they do resemble Chumash sun motifs. The clear depiction of

hands may indicate the site was of ceremonial importance or supernatural significance. The entire ancient Mopah Range and the Cheme-huevi people who passed through are the subjects of ongoing historical and archaeological studies.

Dating the petroglyphs, like all others, is difficult. Experts studying the evolving stages of the patina on such rocks date the art somewhere between the 1500s and early 1800s. The Chemehuevi were forced into reservations in the 1880s. Their population may have rarely exceeded 1,000 because the harsh environment could not support great numbers. A census taken in 1902 of the people on the Chemehuevi Reservation counted just 32.

By the late 1800s, ranchers were adding their own creations to the rocky region. Then came the prospectors' additions in the early 1900s. World War II brought General George Patton and his troops to the region, and an airstrip was constructed. Bullets can still be found on the mountainside.

The name of the inn comes from its association with the Lost Arch Mine, which produced lode gold. The cabins at Lost Arch Inn were the home of Charley Brown and his mining partner, Jesse Craik. The two men prospected for gold and silver in the northern section of the Turtle Mountains for many years. These cabins were their home from 1922 to 1948. Although they are referred to as an inn, these cabins are barely standing.

Description
This trail describes a loop, starting and finishing near the eastern end of Desert #10: Sunflower Spring Road. The start of the trail is marked with a brown route marker. The trail follows a well-used, formed trail as far as the two old cabins known as the Lost Arch Inn. The cabins are in fair condition; one is timber, the other corrugated iron, and they stand side by side on a slight rise in the desert.

Access as far as the cabins is easy. They can normally be reached in a high-clearance 2WD vehicle. There is one wash crossing that may need some care depending on how eroded it is after recent rains. Past the cabin, the trail is smaller and a high-clearance 4WD is

An old mailbox marks the west end of Lost Arch Inn Trail

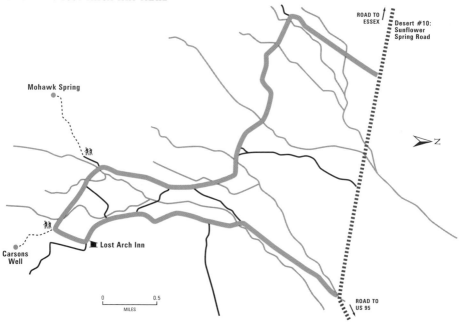

recommended. One wash crossing in particular is eroded and lumpy; it requires good clearance and wheel articulation.

The trail sees much less use past the cabins as it follows along the edge of the wilderness boundary. The hiking trails to Carsons Well and Mohawk Spring are just off the vehicle route.

The vehicle route is very quiet, and the traveler is rewarded with good views of the Turtle Mountains. The trail passes through a popular rockhounding area, where opalite, chalcedony roses, agate, and jasper can be found. These rocks are most common in the washes below Mohawk Spring.

Navigation can be a little confusing along this part of the trail. The signs stop just after the cabins and there are many small unmarked trails to choose from. Many of the side trails rejoin after a short distance. A GPS unit is very helpful along this section.

Campers will find some good remote sites, although those using tents will find it very rocky.

The trail ends back on Desert #10: Sunflower Spring Road at an old mailbox that now serves as a drop off point for travelers'

messages. How the mailbox got there is a mystery; maybe it served as a drop off point for miners' mail or maybe it was just placed there for messages.

Current Road Information

Bureau of Land Management
Needles Field Office
1303 South US Highway 95
Needles, CA 92363
(760) 326-7000

Map References

BLM   Parker
USGS 1:24,000 Mohawk Spring
        1:100,000 Parker
Maptech CD-ROM: San Bernardino
        County/Mojave
Southern & Central California Atlas & Gazetteer, p. 100
California Road & Recreation Atlas, p. 107

Route Directions

▼ 0.0   From Desert #10: Sunflower Spring Road, 10.2 miles from the easterly end at US 95, zero trip meter and turn southwest on formed trail marked Lost Arch Inn, suitable for 4WDs, ATVs, and motorbikes. Sunflower Spring Road bears northwest at this point.

2.6 ▲   Trail ends at intersection with Desert #10: Sunflower Spring Road. Turn left to continue along this trail to Essex; continue straight ahead to exit 10.2 miles to US 95.

GPS: N34°28.12' W114°48.79'

▼ 1.0   SO Cross through wash.

1.5 ▲   SO Cross through wash.

▼ 1.1   BL Well-used track on right. Remain on Lost Arch Inn Trail and cross through wash.

1.5 ▲   SO Cross through wash; then well-used track on left.

GPS: N34°27.37' W114°49.52'

▼ 1.4   SO Track on left.

1.2 ▲   SO Track on right.

▼ 1.9   SO Track on left.

0.7 ▲   SO Track on right.

Rugged and unusual rock formations form a dramatic backdrop for buckhorn chollas along the trail

▼ 2.0 SO Track on left.
0.6 ▲ SO Track on right.
▼ 2.1 SO Track on right; then cross through wash.
0.5 ▲ BR Cross through wash; then trail forks.
　　　　 Track on left.
　　　　 GPS: N34°26.52′ W114°49.66′

▼ 2.3 SO Track on left; then cross through wash; then track on right.
0.3 ▲ BR Track on left; then cross through wash; then track on right.
▼ 2.5 SO Track on left to concrete foundations.
0.1 ▲ SO Track on right to concrete foundations.
▼ 2.6 TR Two cabins on left—one timber and one corrugated iron—are Lost Arch Inn. Small track straight ahead goes a short distance to the wilderness boundary. Zero trip meter and turn right, following the trail marker for Carsons Well.
0.0 ▲ Continue to the west.
　　　　 GPS: N34°26.14′ W114°49.41′

▼ 0.0 Continue to the south.
5.1 ▲ TL Two cabins ahead—one timber and one corrugated iron—are Lost Arch Inn. Small track on right goes a short distance to the wilderness boundary. Zero trip meter and turn left onto well-used, unmarked trail.
▼ 0.3 TR Well-used track on left goes 0.1 miles to Carsons Well Trail for hikers and horses only.
4.8 ▲ TL Well-used track straight ahead goes 0.1 miles to Carsons Well Trail for hikers and horses only.
　　　　 GPS: N34°25.86′ W114°49.54′

▼ 0.4 SO Enter down line of wash. Trail continues to the northwest and looks somewhat less used.
4.7 ▲ SO Exit line of wash.
▼ 0.8 SO Well-used track on right.
4.3 ▲ SO Well-used track on left.
　　　　 GPS: N34°26.13′ W114°49.94′

▼ 0.9 SO Drop down and cross through deep wash; then track on left goes a short distance to diggings that are popular with rock hounds. Follow the small

wash on foot southwest from the diggings for other good rockhounding areas.
4.2 ▲ SO Track on right is second entrance to diggings. Trail then drops down and crosses through deep wash.
　　　　 GPS: N34°26.17′ W114°50.00′

▼ 1.0 SO Track on left is second entrance to diggings.
4.1 ▲ SO Track on right goes a short distance to diggings that are popular with rock hounds. Follow the small wash southwest from the diggings for other good rockhounding areas.
▼ 1.1 BR Track on left into mine workings.
4.0 ▲ BL Track on right into mine workings.
　　　　 GPS: N34°26.28′ W114°50.10′
▼ 1.7 SO Track on right.
3.4 ▲ BR Track on left.
　　　　 GPS: N34°26.83′ W114°49.87′

▼ 1.9 SO Unmarked 5-way intersection. Continue straight ahead to the northwest. The remains of a timber and corrugated iron cabin are at the intersection.
3.2 ▲ SO Unmarked 5-way intersection. Continue straight ahead to the southeast. The remains of a timber and corrugated iron cabin are at the intersection.
　　　　 GPS: N34°26.96′ W114°49.89′

▼ 2.1 BL Track on right.
3.0 ▲ SO Track on left.
▼ 2.2 SO Cross through wash.
2.9 ▲ SO Cross through wash.
▼ 2.4 SO Cross through wash.
2.7 ▲ SO Cross through wash.
▼ 2.6 SO Well-used track on right; then second track on right.
2.5 ▲ SO Track on left; then second well-used track on left.
　　　　 GPS: N34°27.37′ W114°50.17′

▼ 2.7 SO Cross through wash.
2.4 ▲ SO Cross through wash.
▼ 3.1 SO Cross through wash.
2.0 ▲ SO Cross through wash.
▼ 3.2 SO Track on right.
1.9 ▲ BR Track on left.

▼ 3.3　SO　Cross through wash.

1.8 ▲　SO　Cross through wash.

▼ 4.0　SO　Cross through wide wash.

1.1 ▲　SO　Cross through wide wash.

▼ 4.1　TR　Climb short wash embankment and turn right. To the left and straight ahead is the Turtle Mountains Wilderness boundary.

1.0 ▲　TL　To the right and straight ahead is the Turtle Mountains Wilderness boundary. Turn left at small stone cairn in open area of desert pavement and descend to a wash. Intersection is easily missed in this direction.
　　　　GPS: N34°27.84′ W114°51.45′

▼ 4.7　SO　Cross through wash.

0.4 ▲　SO　Cross through wash.

▼ 5.1　　　Trail ends at T-intersection with Desert #10: Sunflower Spring Road at the mailbox. Trail is unmarked. Turn left to continue along Sunflower Spring Road to Essex; turn right to exit northeast to US 95.

0.0 ▲　　　Trail commences near the eastern end of Desert #10: Sunflower Spring Road, 12.1 miles from US 95 and 1.9 miles west of the eastern end of the Lost Arch Inn Trail. Zero trip meter and turn south on formed trail. There is an old mailbox on a post at the intersection. Otherwise the trail is unmarked.
　　　　GPS: N34°28.52′ W114°50.83′

DESERT #12

Eagle Pass Trail

STARTING POINT: Broadway, in the center of Needles

FINISHING POINT: Intersection of US 95 and I-40

TOTAL MILEAGE: 23.4 miles

UNPAVED MILEAGE: 22.9 miles

DRIVING TIME: 2.5 hours

ELEVATION RANGE: 500–2,200 feet

USUALLY OPEN: Year-round

BEST TIME TO TRAVEL: September to May

DIFFICULTY RATING: 3

SCENIC RATING: 8

REMOTENESS RATING: +1

Special Attractions

- Rockhounding for jasper.
- Trail is part of the East Mojave Heritage Trail.
- Remote trail traveling along desert washes.

History

Needles was established in 1869 as a port on the Colorado River. Native Americans, Spanish explorers, and the arrival of the railroad were influences that led to the town's development.

　　The Mojave have lived in the valley by the Colorado River for generations. Their trails, petroglyphs, pictographs, and mortise-working areas are evidence of their long residence in this area. Spanish padre Francisco Garcés passed through the site of Needles guided by the Mojave in 1776. Their trail followed alongside the river at this point. Fur trapper Jedediah Smith also used this trail in 1826. He was the first American to make a crossing of the Colorado River at what was later to be named Needles.

　　In the mid to late 1800s, steamboats plied the river, carrying passengers and freight. Needles developed as a supply center for mining prospectors and settlers in the region. By 1883, the Atlantic & Pacific Railroad had established a station on the Arizona side of the river. Later that year, they transferred operations to the California side, stating that it better suited their needs as a future division depot. The railroad soon replaced the steamboats.

　　The name Needles was derived from peaks near the town. Early railroad survey crews mentioned these prominent features, to the east and south of the locality, as a reference point. The name seemed appropriate when the post office was established in 1869.

　　Needles flourished as the railroad depot grew in importance. Soon highways brought automobiles and, like many desert locations, spawned a multitude of motels and restaurants. The ornate two-story Garces Building by the railroad resembles a Southern mansion, inviting all who passed by. Today, the mansion awaits restoration. It was part of a series of Harvey Houses that were built along the Santa Fe Railroad system from Chicago to Los Angeles. These welcoming houses provided meals to rail passengers and crews along their long journey to the West Coast.

Early bridges were quite often washed away in floods. Dams and dredging on the Colorado River in the 1950s allowed more control of the river. This encouraged agriculture and further development of the town. Less flooding meant a more stable embankment and vegetation. It also made the river water clearer, which attracted recreationists. The river has since become one of the city's biggest attractions.

Description

Eagle Pass is an easy loop trail from Needles that can be done in half a day. The loop follows part of the long East Mojave Heritage Trail, the full length of which is no longer open to vehicle travel.

The trail leaves from the center of Needles and almost immediately travels along a loose, gravelly trail toward the Sacramento Mountains. It enters a canyon that climbs gently toward Eagle Pass. The towering bulk of Eagle Peak is immediately to the north. The vegetation is a mixture of sage, smoke trees, Mojave yuccas, chollas, and barrel cacti.

From Eagle Pass, the trail enters Crestview Wash and travels mainly in the line of the wash. One short stretch swings onto the ridge to cross a section of desert pavement that is studded with teddy bear chollas. The route can be hard to see along this section, but small cairns mark the way.

The trail's difficulty rating comes from the loose, soft wash beds that can make travel slow. In addition, there is one rocky descent over a shallow waterfall that requires careful wheel placement to ensure that your vehicle's underbody is not scraped on unforgiving rock. However, this section is extremely short.

The trail continues along Crestview Wash to join a pipeline road that runs alongside I-

40. It finishes a short distance later at the intersection of US 95 and I-40.

Current Road Information

Bureau of Land Management
Needles Field Office
1303 South US Highway 95
Needles, CA 92363
(760) 326-7000

Map References

BLM   Needles
USGS 1:24,000   Needles, Needles SW,
      Flattop Mtn., Bannock
      1:100,000 Needles
Maptech CD-ROM: San Bernardino
      County/Mojave
Southern & Central California Atlas & Gazetteer, pp. 87, 86
California Road & Recreation Atlas, p. 115

Route Directions

▼ 0.0   From the main street, Broadway, in
             Needles, zero trip meter and turn
             southwest on L Street. Pass under the
             freeway (I-40) and immediately turn
             right onto paved Eagle Pass Road.
6.7 ▲   Turn left onto L Street and pass under
             freeway (I-40). Trail ends at the inter-
             section with Broadway in the center
             of Needles.
             GPS: N34°50.52′ W114°36.68′

▼ 0.5   SO   Road turns to roughly graded dirt.
             Cross over embankment.
6.2 ▲   SO   Cross over embankment. Road is
             now paved.
▼ 0.6   BL   Cross through wash; then bear left
             (west) up main trail. Small track on
             right.
6.1 ▲   SO   Small track on left. Cross through wash;
             then head east toward embankment.
             GPS: N34°50.67′ W114°37.16′

▼ 0.7   SO   Two tracks on right. Remain on
             main trail.
6.0 ▲   SO   Two tracks on left. Remain on main trail.
▼ 1.2   SO   Track on left and track on right.
5.5 ▲   SO   Track on left and track on right.

GPS: N34°50.43' W114°37.69'

▼ 1.9   SO   Cross through wash. Track on left
             in wash.
4.8 ▲   SO   Cross through wash. Track on right
             in wash.
▼ 2.3   SO   Track on left.
4.4 ▲   SO   Track on right.
▼ 3.4   SO   Track on right.
3.3 ▲   SO   Track on left.
             GPS: N34°48.90' W114°39.25

▼ 6.6   SO   Track on left.
0.1 ▲   SO   Track on right.
▼ 6.7   SO   Track on left on top of embankment.
             Zero trip meter.
0.0 ▲   Continue to the east.
             GPS: N34°47.08' W114°41.93'

▼ 0.0   Continue to the west.
3.6 ▲   SO   Track on right on top of embankment.
             Zero trip meter.
▼ 0.1   SO   Track on left.
3.5 ▲   SO   Track on right.
▼ 0.2   SO   Cross over embankment. Track on left
             on top of embankment. Enter line of
             wash up canyon.
3.4 ▲   SO   Exit line of wash and canyon. Cross
             over embankment. Track on right on
             top of embankment.
▼ 1.4   SO   Track on right; then second track on
             right into mine diggings.
2.2 ▲   SO   Track on left into mine diggings; then
             second track on left.
             GPS: N34°46.92' W114°43.35'

▼ 2.3   SO   Track on left.
1.3 ▲   SO   Track on right.

Eagle Peak sits on the northwest side of Eagle Pass

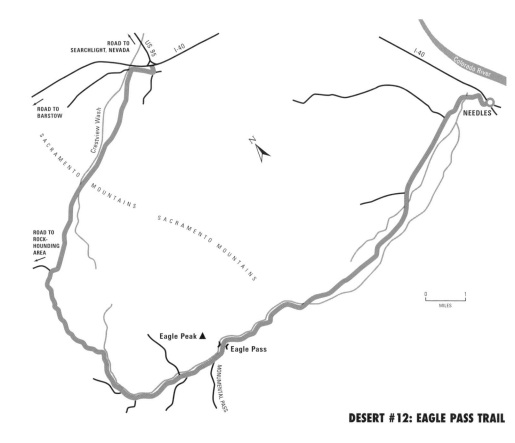

DESERT #12: EAGLE PASS TRAIL

▼ 2.6   SO   Track on right.
1.0 ▲   SO   Track on left.

▼ 3.3   SO   Eagle Pass. The pass is not at the top, but in a narrow section of the canyon. Exit canyon.
0.3 ▲   SO   Eagle Pass. The pass is not at the top, but in a narrow section of the canyon. Enter canyon.
        GPS: N34°46.31′ W114°44.90′

▼ 3.6   BR   Well-used track on left is Monumental Pass, suitable for 4WDs, ATVs, and motorbikes. Zero trip meter and continue onto Crestview Wash, marked as suitable for 4WDs, ATVs, and motorbikes.
0.0 ▲   Continue to the north.
        GPS: N34°46.19′ W114°45.14′

▼ 0.0   Continue to the southwest.
6.8 ▲   SO   Well-used track on right is Monumental Pass, suitable for 4WDs, ATVs, and motorbikes. Zero trip meter and continue straight ahead toward Eagle Pass.

▼ 0.3   BR   Track on left.
6.5 ▲   SO   Track on right.

▼ 0.8   SO   Track on left out of wash.
6.0 ▲   SO   Track on right out of wash.
        GPS: N34°45.95′ W114°45.94′

▼ 0.9   BL   Track on right up wash.
5.9 ▲   SO   Second entrance to track on left up wash.
        GPS: N34°45.97′ W114°46.03′

▼ 1.0   SO   Second entrance to track on right.
5.8 ▲   BR   Track on left.

▼ 2.2   BR   Track on left up wash. Follow sign for Crestview Wash.
4.6 ▲   BL   Bear left down main wash. Track on right up wash.
        GPS: N34°45.68′ W114°47.31′

▼ 2.6   SO   Well-used track on left up side wash. Continue in main wash.

Canyon walls close in as you approach Eagle Pass

Atlantic & Pacific Railroad

Although it began slowly, the Atlantic & Pacific Railroad would eventually make significant contributions for trade and the settling of California. The company eventually completed the third transcontinental railroad, laying tracks as far as the Southern Pacific line in Mojave. The company was organized in 1866 to build a railroad from Springfield, Missouri, to Albuquerque, New Mexico, and then to the Pacific by way of the thirty-fifth parallel route first surveyed by Amiel W. Whipple in 1854. By 1873, after only 327 miles of track had been laid in Missouri and eastern Oklahoma, financial difficulties forced the railroad into bankruptcy.

Early in 1880, the Atchison, Topeka & Santa Fe Railroad Company was laying tracks toward Albuquerque on its way to connecting with the Southern Pacific Railroad at Deming, New Mexico. However, it was keen to establish a more direct route to California. In January 1880, the Atchison, Topeka & Santa Fe joined with the St. Louis and San Francisco Railway Company to rescue the Atlantic & Pacific by financing the stalled expansion of its tracks westward from Albuquerque. The small town of Gallup, New Mexico (which was settled in 1880 as a Westward Overland Stagecoach stop), became the construction headquarters of the railway. In fact, the town was named after David L. Gallup, the railroad paymaster.

Laying tracks through desert is not an easy feat, and it certainly wasn't for the Atlantic & Pacific. Water sources were needed, so storage reservoirs had to be constructed along the route. The line did have one thing going for it—an abundance of trees that could be used for railroad ties. Although construction was arduous, the surveys proved to be so good that today the track continues along most of the original route's 575 miles. (Recently there was only a slight change in course to allow for double-tracking.)

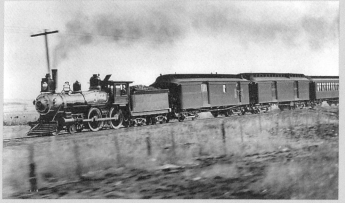

An Atchison, Topeka & Santa Fe steam engine

While the Atlantic & Pacific was hard at work, the Southern Pacific Railroad beat it to the quick by completing its own line to Needles (named after a group of needlelike peaks in nearby Arizona). Although the Southern Pacific had built its line over the proposed route of the Atlantic & Pacific, begrudgingly, a compromise between the two was reached. The Atlantic & Pacific could lease that portion of the Southern Pacific line in order to enter California. Thus, the thirty-fifth parallel transcontinental line was completed in August 1883, and yet the Southern Pacific was able to retain its monopoly over railroad access into California.

In June 1897, after having been forced into bankruptcy for a second time, the Atlantic & Pacific was sold at foreclosure to the recently reorganized Atchison, Topeka & Santa Fe Railway Company.

4.2 ▲ SO Well-used track on right up side wash.
Continue in main wash.
GPS: N34°45.90′ W114°47.66′

▼ 2.9 BL Trail skirts the rise of a shallow water-fall in the wash; then track on right.
Remain in wash.

3.9 ▲ SO Track on left; then trail skirts the rise of a shallow waterfall in the wash.
Remain in wash.

▼ 3.7 BL Bear left steeply out of wash.

3.1 ▲ BR Drop down and bear right in wash.
GPS: N34°46.66′ W114°47.96′

▼ 4.3 SO Enter down line of Crestview Wash.

2.5 ▲ SO Exit line of wash.
GPS: N34°47.00′ W114°48.40′

▼ 6.8 TR Small track on left; then track on left up side wash goes approximately 3 miles to a rockhounding area. Turn right, continuing down main wash, and zero trip meter.

0.0 ▲ Continue to the southwest, small track on right.
GPS: N34°48.79′ W114°48.93′

▼ 0.0 Continue to the east.

6.3 ▲ TL Track on right up side wash goes approximately 3 miles to a rockhound-ing area. Turn left, continuing up main wash, and zero trip meter.

▼ 0.4 BR Bear right out of wash, following trail marker.

5.9 ▲ BL Bear left up wash.
GPS: N34°48.97′ W114°48.64′

▼ 0.5 SO Enter down wash.

5.8 ▲ BR Bear right out of wash.

▼ 0.6 BR Rocky descent; then bear right down main wash.

5.7 ▲ BL Bear left out of wash up rocky ascent, following trail marker.
GPS: N34°49.07′ W114°48.54′

▼ 3.4 BL Track on right.

2.9 ▲ SO Track on left.
GPS: N34°51.12′ W114°47.04′

▼ 5.5 TR T-intersection with the pipeline road.

Turn right alongside freeway; then track on left passes under freeway.
Leave wash.

0.8 ▲ TL Track on right passes under freeway; then turn left onto formed trail up wash, marked Crestview Wash, suit-able for 4WDs, ATVs, and motorbikes.
GPS: N34°52.69′ W114°45.89′

▼ 6.2 TL 4-way intersection. Track straight ahead and to the right.

0.1 ▲ TR Turn sharp right at 4-way intersection.
Track on left and graded road straight ahead.
GPS: N34°52.54′ W114°45.25′

▼ 6.3 Trail ends at US 95 exit on the south side of I-40. Searchlight and Las Vegas are straight ahead on US 95. Take I-40 eastbound for Needles, westbound for Barstow.

0.0 ▲ Trail commences at the intersection of US 95 and I-40 at the freeway exit, 9 miles west of Needles. Proceed to the south side of the freeway, zero trip meter, and head south on graded dirt road.
GPS: N34°52.64′ W114°45.26′

<hr>

DESERT #13

Mojave Road

STARTING POINT: Needles Highway, NV, 0.7 miles north of California-Nevada state line
FINISHING POINT: I-15, at the Harvard Road exit, 24 miles east of Barstow
TOTAL MILEAGE: 128.6 miles
UNPAVED MILEAGE: 123.5 miles
DRIVING TIME: 2 days minimum, 3 or more preferably
ELEVATION RANGE: 900–5,200 feet
USUALLY OPEN: Year-round
BEST TIME TO TRAVEL: October to May
DIFFICULTY RATING: 4 (the majority is rated 2 or 3)
SCENIC RATING: 10
REMOTENESS RATING: +1

Special Attractions

- Historic Mojave Road route, including the sites of Fort Piute, The Caves, Rock Spring, Triangle Intaglios, and more.
- Unparalleled variety of Mojave Desert scenery and natural attractions, including Soda Lake and Afton Canyon.

History

The Mojave Trail was once a trade route used by various Indian cultures between the Colorado River and the Pacific Ocean. Rock Spring was a crucial link in a chain of desert springs that allowed early inhabitants to cross the Mojave Desert.

In 1854, Army Engineer Lieutenant Amiel W. Whipple led an exploration party along the Mojave Trail, seeking a transcontinental train route along the thirty-fifth parallel. He named Rock Spring and other features along the way for navigating purposes. Whipple saw an old Chemehuevi crop of corn and melons at what was later to become Fort Piute (also known as Fort Pah-Ute).

In 1857, the U.S. War Department hired explorer Edward Fitzgerald Beale and his camels to survey and establish a wagon road from New Mexico to the banks of the Colorado River. Although not required by his contract, Beale pushed farther west along the Mojave Trail and established a route through this part of California.

During the 1860s, five army posts were established approximately a day's ride apart, spanning the Mojave Desert from Camp Cady near Barstow to Fort Mohave on the Colorado River. Never officially established as a fort, Pah-Ute Creek, as it was commonly called, did house a small number of troops from November 17, 1867 to May 3, 1868. As many as 18 enlisted men from Company D, Ninth U.S. Infantry served at the remote hot spot. The small fort still stands on a low rise above Piute Spring wash, its thick stone walls having stood the test of time. A rock corral of a later date is also at the site.

Camp Rock Spring was established on December 20, 1866. It provided mail carriers and travelers safe escort across the desert, a dangerous and difficult task for all concerned

in this remote area. Harsh conditions meant that Camp Rock Spring had one of the highest desertion rates of any army post. Its remote location made it very difficult to get adequate food, supplies, water, and medical attention. Rationing was strict. Lack of fresh foods led to outbreaks of scurvy. Morale was low and there was little to do at times. When the mail route was moved, the army post was no longer needed and its soldiers were moved to other duties. The camp was closed on January 2, 1868.

Farther east, Marl Spring was originally called Pozos de San Juan de Dios (Spanish for "Wells of St. John of God"). On March 8, 1776, Fray Francisco Garcés rested there and named the wells while on his journey from Mission San Xavier del Bac in Tucson, Arizona, to Mission San Gabriel, in present-day Los Angeles. Garcés passed by the spring on his return journey, resting there again on May 22 of the same year.

Mojave Road was an important route for the people of Los Angeles because it linked the town with Prescott, Arizona, a prominent settlement at that time. However, by 1883 the road became obsolete because of the completion of the Southern Pacific Railroad from Needles, on the Colorado River, to Mojave. The railroad intersected with the old Mojave Trail at Barstow.

In 1894, the Rock Spring Land and Cattle Company, later known as Ox Ranch, controlled most of the area's water. Battles erupted between homesteaders and ranchers over water rights. The last gunfight over water rights occurred at Government Holes in 1925. A hired hand named Bill Robertson, who was good with his gun, was positioned at the holes to protect the ranchers' water. An ex-hired hand named Matt Burts, also good with a gun, was passing by when his car radiator needed a top-up. According to witnesses in the car, conversation between the two men seemed pleasant. However, the end result was a shootout at a cabin near the holes. Both men died.

From the 1910s to 1940, many families were attracted to the Lanfair area by land available under homestead laws and a wetter

Large Joshua trees in the Lanfair Valley

than average weather period. Farming seemed feasible to the newcomers, and many acres were cleared for agricultural purposes. However, the difficulties of farming in this extreme environment drove many away with little return for their years of hard labor improving the lands and building cabins. Many moved out without fulfilling the homestead requirements that would allow them to patent the land. If they were lucky, they would sell their improvements to the next hopeful homesteader. Many such cleared areas are passed along Mojave Road with little regeneration occurring in places.

Though snow is not always associated with the eastern Mojave region, the winter of 1937 was certainly a reminder of how isolated this region is when extreme weather strikes. Ed Clark and his daughter Clara were homesteaders near the Grotto Hills, just north of Mojave Road in Lanfair Valley. Snow began piling up around their home forcing the Clarks to sit out the bad weather with only a little food. Their Model-T truck could not cope with the depth of snow, and they were unable to get to Needles to purchase their monthly supplies. The Clarks battled to survive freezing temperatures in their small cabin. They ate chicken feed when their food ran out. Fortunately for them, Al Mosher and Alan Cane arrived from the Providence Ranch in Round Valley. They had battled the deep snow for hours, digging and ramming the deep wall of snow with their 1928 Chevy truck to rescue the Clarks. Ranchers lost many head of cattle in the snowstorm. In one instance, some 50 head were trapped in a box canyon where they all perished.

Only 12 years later an even worse snowstorm stranded homesteaders in drifts that were 5 to 12 feet deep in places. Winds reportedly reached 40 miles an hour, driving the powder-dry snow up and over ranchers' homes. Air Force flights over the region reported seeing few buildings, just white drifting snow. Some folks communicated with air rescue by writing OK in the snow. Plowing attempts were futile with snowdrifts repacking roads within a half hour of clearing them.

Black Canyon Road disappeared as blowing snow filled the canyon to the top, leaving it impassable for six weeks.

Borax mining in Death Valley required a better transportation system than the famed 20-mule teams that hauled borax to market in the late 1800s. This resulted in the construction of the Tonopah & Tidewater Railroad from Ludlow to Sperry, and later on to Beatty, Nevada. The railroad was constructed across the wide flats of Soda Lake and Silver Lake in 1906. The line was laid directly on the floor of the dry lakebeds. In 1922, Silver Lake filled to a depth of nearly 3 feet. The railroad, which had already been raised in 1915 because of rising waters, was abandoned and rerouted for 5 miles along the eastern shore. Sailboats completed the picture on Silver Lake that year.

Mojave Indians lived at Soda Springs on the western shore of Soda Lake for at least 7,000 years. At the end of World War II, Zzyzx Mineral Springs was developed as a resort. The 200-mile trip from Los Angeles to the popular resort was quite a distance in the days of gasoline rationing. Doc Springer established his reputation by providing good food and many activities, such as swimming, hiking, horseback riding, shuffle board, and hunting for Indian artifacts (in the days before this was illegal). Electricity for the resort was supplied by World War II surplus diesel generators. Most of the food was grown on site and rabbits were raised for their meat. In the 1960s, Doc Springer's health products came under scrutiny, and he was accused of misleading the public about the quality of his health foods.

Afton Canyon, also known as Cave Canyon for a time, offered early travelers refuge in its caves. The canyon is the result of massive erosion combined with possible faulting. Prehistoric Lake Manix covered an immense area of more than 200 square miles, mainly along the course of the Mojave River, and connected the Cronese Lakes with Soda Lake and Silver Lake. The drainage of the prehistoric lake seems to have been the force behind the deep, rapid erosion of Afton Canyon. It may have been triggered by an

Little Cowhole Mountain rises above the aptly named Soda Lake

earthquake, which would account for the off-set layers in the canyon.

Afton Caves were an important way station on the old government road between Soda Springs and Fort Cady, where travelers could get supplies and protection from Indians. The Caves, a series of deep rock shelters, were used by Indians before the arrival of Euro-Americans. At least one of the caves is large enough to shelter wagons.

The Arbuckle Mine, later known as the Cliffside Mine, found high on the south side of Afton Canyon, mined magnesite for use in steel mills and smelters during World War I.

Description

Mojave Road is a long, extremely remote trail for 4WD vehicles that generally follows the historic route of the Mojave Trail. The trail can be traveled in two long days, though it is best to allow three days so you have time to explore the many points of interest along the way. It is best suited for people intending to camp. Although accommodations are available at Laughlin, NV, Baker, and Barstow, they require long detours from the trail.

Camping is allowed almost anywhere. There are developed campgrounds a short distance from the trail at Hole-in-the-Wall and

Mid Hills within the Mojave National Preserve. In addition, primitive camping is allowed anywhere that has been previously used as a campsite.

The beginning of Mojave Road is on the banks of the Colorado River in the Fort Mohave Indian Reservation opposite the site of Fort Mohave, Arizona. However, the road is partially blocked by agriculture on the Indian reservation. For ease of access, the route described here starts 3 miles from the river on Needles Highway.

The trail is marked along its length by cairns that were placed by the Friends of the Mojave Road. The forward (westbound) route directions describe the cairns as on the right; in the reverse (eastbound) direction, they are on the left. The cairns are placed at every intersection, but some are hard to spot and they should not be relied upon. In the Rasor OHV Area, they are absent from many intersections. In addition, some sections are marked by BLM trail markers.

The overall difficulty rating for the trail is a 4. However the majority of the trail is easier, only rating a 2 or a 3 for difficulty. Even these easier sections require 4WD to negotiate the loose, deep sand.

The trail leaves Needles Highway and travels up a wash toward the Dead Mountains. The trail surface for this section is generally loose sand interspersed with rocky sections. The trail crosses through the Dead Mountains, descending into the shallow Piute Valley on the western side. After crossing US 95, the trail gradually ascends toward the Piute Range. The original route past Fort Piute is blocked to vehicle travel by a wilderness area. A short, rough spur leads 1.9 miles to the old fort. Stone walls remain and there are some good, primitive campsites scattered around the fort. Piute Spring is a short distance upstream, accessible by the Fort Piute/Piute Spring Loop Hiking Corridor.

Half a mile before you reach the fort, the remains of a stone cabin and corral are alongside the wash below the trail. Hike down to view the cabin and take particular note of the corner stones; they have small rock art designs etched into them.

The main trail crests the Piute Range before descending into the Lanfair Valley. Mojave Road is not the commonly traveled route in this area; graded roads parallel much of the rougher, eroded trail. Longer vehicles will need to take extra care along this section. Deep gullies and moguls make it easy to catch a rear overhang or lift a wheel. Parts of this section reach a 4 rating for difficulty.

The Lanfair Valley has abundant and beautiful Mojave Desert vegetation. Joshua trees, the signature plant of the Mojave Desert, mingle with Mojave yuccas, chollas, greasewoods, and prickly pears.

The historic military site of Rock Spring is close to the deep, sandy Watson Wash, one of the many sections of loose, deep sand along the trail. A few stone walls remain at Camp Rock Spring. The spring is a short distance farther up the canyon. It is surrounded by numerous petroglyphs, many of which are faint.

Another important historic site is Government Holes. Today, there is a well and a corral at the site; a tank still bears the markings of the Ox Cattle Company. A short distance west of Government Holes, the trail rejoins Cedar Canyon Road and follows it to the intersection with paved Kelso–Cima Road.

West of Kelso–Cima Road, the trail skirts the edge of the Marl Mountains, passing close to Marl Spring. This section of trail resembles a roller coaster as it undulates over moguls to cross Aikens Mine Road, part of Desert #18: Cima Dome Trail.

West of Cima Dome Trail, the route follows along Willow Wash. The sand here can be deep, and you may need to lower tire pressures. The trail rounds Seventeen Mile Point and travels in a plumb line down to the dry Soda Lake, which can be seen almost shimmering in the desert heat, far below in the valley at the foot of the Soda Mountains.

In wet weather, or immediately after rain, the trail across Soda Lake can be impassable. The thick, gooey mud quickly clogs tire treads and bogs down vehicles. On the flat lakebed, there is nothing to winch off, and it can be hard to get out of trouble. Exercise caution and be prepared to turn back and take the alternate route via Baker to the north. After crossing the fence line through Volunteer Gate, there is a short section of deep, rutty sand traps. This can be difficult both in very dry and very wet weather. The track leading north from Volunteer Gate is the alternate way around Soda Lake. It travels to Baker, avoiding the soft surface of the lakebed. From Baker you can take I-15 westbound for 11 miles and then travel south on Rasor Road for 5.1 miles to rejoin Mojave Road.

The trail across Soda Lake is marked by green stakes as well as occasional cairns. There are several deep channels that cut across the otherwise flat surface, so resist the temptation to speed. Remain close to the green posts to minimize tire tracks across this fragile area. Some sections of the lakebed can be muddy at any time of year. Midway across the lake is the Travelers or Government Cairn. Over the years, many travelers have added to this large cairn.

The far side of the lake is marked by The Granites, large granite boulders near the old Tonopah & Tidewater Railroad grade that make a pleasant place to camp. The site of Zzyzx (pronounced ZIE-zix) can be seen to the north, marked by palm trees and other splashes of green. The site, which has had an interesting history over the years, is now a desert center. Note that there is no through road from Mojave Road through Zzyzx to I-15.

The mud of Soda Lake is very caustic to vehicles. It is a good idea to wash your

Stone cabin alongside the trail is on private property

vehicle thoroughly as soon as possible after completing this trail. Don't forget about the underbody.

Mojave Road passes through the Rasor OHV Area. There are many small tracks to the right and left through the open area. This is one of the hardest sections to navigate. After the shallow, rocky Shaw Pass, the road drops into the sand dunes area of the Mojave River floodplain. Some of the deepest sand along the trail is encountered here; vehicles will need to lower tire pressures. From Shaw Pass to Basin Road, the trail is rated a 4 for difficulty. The road is poorly marked, and the large number of ever-shifting trails means it is impossible to give precise directions. The major trail intersections are noted. There are a few cairns along this section as well. Try to remain on the main trail, heading generally west-southwest in the forward direction. It is helpful to set the GPS GoTo feature to the coordinates on graded dirt Basin Road. If traveling the road in reverse it is even more difficult. There are several well-used trails that fork away from the correct one at a shallow angle. The coordinates for Shaw Pass are helpful to use as the GoTo point.

You will inevitably cross Basin Road at some point if you head generally west. If you do not see the well-used trail leading off from the west side, which is marked with a cairn, it is simple enough to scout up and down the road for a short distance until you find it.

West of Basin Road is one of the most dramatic sections of the trail. It descends through the narrow Afton Canyon. The Mojave River is crossed several times here. For most of the year there is a few inches of water in the channel, but there are two crossings near the lower end that usually have depths of a couple feet.

The road shares the canyon with a railroad, at times running right alongside the tracks. The canyon walls are narrow and brightly colored. The BLM has designated the route an Open Route, and it is marked with marker posts.

The Caves, an important stopping point along Mojave Road, are no longer accessible by vehicle. It is a short hike through the tamarisk to the caves. The river crossing at this point is one of two that can be deeper than normal. If in doubt, check the depth before proceeding.

The Afton Canyon BLM Campground is a popular overnight stop. Rock hounds are particularly fond of this spot because it is a good place to look for agate, calcite, chalcedony, and jasper in the nearby washes. Pyramid Canyon is a good spot, and so is under the railroad trestle opposite the campground. The campground has picnic tables and fire rings; there are shade ramadas over the picnic tables. A fee is charged for overnight camping, but day use is free.

Past the campground, the trail enters the Mojave River channel. The sand here is also deep and loose. A worthwhile detour is to take the side trail and short hike that leads on top of a mesa alongside the wash. The short scramble to the top of the mesa is rewarded by approximately 20 triangular shaped intaglios—etchings made into the desert pavement. Do not walk on the intaglios, as this will damage them.

The Mojave Road continues in the wash before turning up Manix Canyon to exit to the graded road at Manix, and then on to the intersection with I-15.

Current Road Information
National Park Service
Mojave National Preserve
2701 Barstow Road
Barstow, CA 92311
(760) 252-6100

Bureau of Land Management
Needles Field Office
1303 South US Highway 95
Needles, CA 92363
(760) 326-7000

Map References
BLM   Davis Dam, Ivanpah, Soda Mtns., Newberry Springs
USGS   1:24,000   Mt. Manchester, East of Homer Mtn., Homer Mtn., Signal Hill, Hackberry Mt., Grotto Hills, Pinto Valley, Mid Hills, Cima,

Marl Mtn., Indian Spring, Seventeenmile Point, Soda Lake North, Soda Lake South, Crucero Hill, Cave Mtn., Dunn, Hidden Valley West, Manix, Harvard Hill 1:100,000 Davis Dam, Ivanpah, Soda Mtns., Newberry Springs
Maptech CD-ROM: San Bernardino County/Mojave
Southern & Central California Atlas & Gazetteer, pp. 73, 72, 71, 70, 69, 82
Nevada Atlas & Gazetteer, p. 72
California Road & Recreation Atlas, pp. 99, 98, 97, 96, 105
Trails Illustrated, Mojave National Preserve (256)

Route Directions

▼ 0.0   From Needles Highway in Nevada, 0.7 miles north of the California state line, zero trip meter and turn southwest on formed sandy trail leading up a wide wash. A short distance off the highway is a Mojave Road trail marker, designating the trail suitable for 4WDs, ATVs, and motorbikes.

5.4 ▲   Trail ends on Needles Highway. Turn right for Needles; turn left for Laughlin, NV.
       GPS: N35°03.08' W114°40.57'

▼ 0.4   SO   Pass under power lines; track on right and left.
5.0 ▲   SO   Pass under power lines; track on right and left.
▼ 0.5   SO   Track on left.
4.9 ▲   SO   Track on right.
▼ 0.8   BL   Track on left; then enter main line of wash. Two tracks on right down wash.
4.6 ▲   BR   Exit main line of wash. Two tracks on left down wash. Track on right.
       GPS: N35°03.33' W114°41.31'

▼ 1.3   SO   Track on left.
4.1 ▲   SO   Track on right.
▼ 1.6   BR   Well-used track on left. Bear right under power lines.
3.8 ▲   SO   Track on right. Leave power lines.
       GPS: N35°03.58' W114°42.10'

▼ 1.7   SO   Track on right.
3.7 ▲   SO   Track on left.
▼ 1.8   BR   Track on right; then bear right past track on left and track straight ahead.
3.6 ▲   SO   Two tracks on right; then track on left.
       GPS: N35°03.79' W114°42.23'

▼ 2.0   SO   Track on left.
3.4 ▲   SO   Track on right.
▼ 2.1   BR   Track on left continues up wash. Follow Mojave Road trail marker; then track on left.
3.3 ▲   SO   Track on right; then second track on right up wash. There is a Mojave Road trail marker at this intersection.
       GPS: N35°03.95' W114°42.32'

▼ 2.6   SO   Track on left.
2.8 ▲   SO   Track on right.
▼ 2.7   SO   Track on left.
2.7 ▲   SO   Track on right.
▼ 2.9   BL   Track on right. Follow Mojave Road trail marker away from power lines.
2.5 ▲   SO   Track on left. Continue alongside power lines.
       GPS: N35°04.61' W114°42.84'

▼ 3.2   SO   Small track on left.
2.2 ▲   SO   Small track on right.
▼ 3.3   TR   Track on left. Turn right, remaining on main trail up wash.
2.1 ▲   TL   Track straight ahead. Turn left, remaining on main trail away from wash.
       GPS: N35°04.37' W114°43.07'

▼ 5.1   BR   Track on left.
0.3 ▲   SO   Track on right.
       GPS: N35°05.55' W114°44.22'

▼ 5.4   SO   Staggered intersection under power lines. Follow Mojave Road marker. Well-used track on left and right. Zero trip meter.
0.0 ▲   Continue to the east.
       GPS: N35°05.81' W114°44.45'

▼ 0.0   Continue to the west.
5.3 ▲   SO   Staggered intersection under power lines. There is a Mojave Road marker

at the intersection. Well-used track on left and right. Zero trip meter.

▼ 0.9 BR Well-used track on right; then immediately bear right, following Mojave Road marker. Well-used track on left.

4.4 ▲ BR Well-used track on right; then immediately bear right past well-used track on left.

GPS: N35°06.23' W114°45.29'

▼ 2.1 SO Enter San Bernardino County, CA. State line is unmarked.

3.2 ▲ SO Enter Clark County, NV. State line is unmarked.

▼ 2.2 BL Well-used track on right. Exit line of wash.

3.1 ▲ BR Well-used track on left. Enter line of wash.

GPS: N35°06.90' W114°46.40'

▼ 2.4 SO Track on right.

2.9 ▲ SO Track on left.

▼ 2.8 SO Track on right and track on left; then cross through wash.

2.5 ▲ SO Cross through wash; then track on left and track on right.

▼ 2.9 SO Cross Von Schmidt Boundary of 1873.

2.4 ▲ SO Cross Von Schmidt Boundary of 1873.

▼ 4.7 SO Road on right into private property; then track on left.

0.6 ▲ SO Track on right; then road on left into private property.

GPS: N35°06.76' W114°49.03'

▼ 4.8 SO Track on right.

0.5 ▲ SO Track on left.

▼ 5.3 SO Track on right; then intersection with US 95. Zero trip meter and cross paved highway onto formed trail on the west side. If anyone wants to join the trail at this point, this intersection is 0.1 miles south of mile marker 76 and 4.4 miles south of California-Nevada state line.

0.0 ▲ Continue to the east. Immediately track on left.

GPS: N35°06.77' W114°49.70'

▼ 0.0 Continue to the west.

6.9 ▲ SO Intersection with US 95. Zero trip meter and cross paved highway onto graded road on east side. If anyone

wants to join the trail at this point, this intersection is 0.1 miles south of mile marker 76 and 4.4 miles south of California-Nevada state line.

▼ 0.8 SO Track on right; then cattle guard.

6.1 ▲ SO Cattle guard; then track on left.

GPS: N35°06.78' W114°50.62'

▼ 1.6 SO Small track on left.

5.3 ▲ SO Small track on right.

▼ 2.1 SO Start to cross through wide wash.

4.8 ▲ SO Exit wash crossing.

GPS: N35°06.77' W114°52.05'

▼ 2.2 SO Exit wash crossing.

4.7 ▲ SO Start to cross through wide wash.

▼ 2.3 SO Cross through Piute Wash.

4.6 ▲ SO Cross through Piute Wash.

▼ 2.5 SO Track on left and track on right.

4.4 ▲ SO Track on left and track on right.

GPS: N35°06.77' W114°52.47'

▼ 4.0 SO Small track on right and benchmark on left.

2.9 ▲ SO Small track on left and benchmark on right.

GPS: N35°06.82' W114°54.14'

▼ 4.6 SO Cross through wash.

2.3 ▲ SO Cross through wash.

▼ 4.8 SO Cross through wash.

2.1 ▲ SO Cross through wash.

▼ 5.8 SO Track on left and track on right.

1.1 ▲ SO Track on left and track on right.

GPS: N35°06.74' W114°56.12'

▼ 6.9 TL Turn left onto graded road alongside power lines. Track ahead is spur to Fort Piute. Zero trip meter.

0.0 ▲ Continue to the northeast on formed trail.

GPS: N35°06.73' W114°57.20'

Spur to Fort Piute

▼ 0.0 Continue to the southwest.

▼ 1.1 SO Campsite on left and track on right.

GPS: N35°06.83' W114°58.23'

▼ 1.4 SO Old corral on left and old stone house.

GPS: N35°06.84' W114°58.55'

▼ 1.8   SO   Campsite on left; then site of Fort Piute on right. A plaque marks the site.
GPS: N35°06.87' W114°59.05'

▼ 1.9   UT   Spur ends just downstream from the spring. Hiking trail continues past this point.
GPS: N35°06.86' W114°59.10'

Continuation of Main Trail

▼ 0.0   Continue to the south on graded road.

1.4 ▲   TR   Turn right onto formed trail, leaving power lines behind. Track on left is spur to Fort Piute. Zero trip meter.
GPS: N35°06.73' W114°57.20'

▼ 0.5   SO   Cross through wash.
0.9 ▲   SO   Cross through wash.
▼ 0.9   SO   Track on left and track on right to tank.
0.5 ▲   SO   Track on right and track on left to tank.
▼ 1.1   SO   Cross through wash.
0.3 ▲   SO   Cross through wash.
▼ 1.4   TR   4-way intersection. Turn right, leaving power lines. Zero trip meter.
0.0 ▲   Continue to the north alongside power lines.
GPS: N35°05.47' W114°57.26'

▼ 0.0   Continue to the west, away from power lines.
3.8 ▲   TL   4-way intersection. Turn left and follow alongside power lines. Zero trip meter.
▼ 2.3   SO   Cross through wash.
1.5 ▲   SO   Cross through wash.
▼ 3.7   SO   Cresting ridge of the Piute Range.
0.1 ▲   SO   Cresting ridge of the Piute Range.
▼ 3.8   TR   Cattle guard; then turn right onto graded road. Track straight ahead is Desert #14: East Lanfair Valley Trail, which joins Mojave Road at this point. Zero trip meter.
0.0 ▲   Continue to the east.
GPS: N35°05.68' W115°01.11'

▼ 0.0   Continue to the northeast.
0.5 ▲   TL   T-intersection. Turn left over cattle guard. Zero trip meter. Track on right is Desert #14: East Lanfair Valley Trail,

which leaves Mojave Road at this point.

▼ 0.5   TL   4-way intersection. Track on right joins Fort Piute/Piute Spring Loop Hiking Corridor. Ahead is Desert #14: East Lanfair Valley Trail, which leaves Mojave Road at this point. Zero trip meter.
0.0 ▲   Continue to the south.
GPS: N35°05.98' W115°00.78'

▼ 0.0   Continue to the west.
6.8 ▲   TR   4-way intersection. Track ahead joins Fort Piute/Piute Spring Loop Hiking Corridor. Track on left is Desert #14: East Lanfair Valley Trail, which joins Mojave Road at this point. Zero trip meter.
▼ 0.8   SO   Cross through wash.
6.0 ▲   SO   Cross through wash.
▼ 1.9   SO   Faint track on right.
4.9 ▲   SO   Faint track on left.
▼ 2.0   SO   Cross through Sacramento Wash.
4.8 ▲   SO   Cross through Sacramento Wash.
GPS: N35°06.35' W115°02.88'

▼ 2.2   BL   Well-used graded track on left; then tank on right. Immediately bear left past track on right.
4.6 ▲   BL   Track on left; then tank on left. Bear left, leaving well-used graded track on right.
GPS: N35°06.43' W115°03°11'

▼ 3.1   SO   Track on right and track on left.
3.7 ▲   SO   Track on left and track on right.
GPS: N35°06.64' W115°04.08'

▼ 4.0   SO   Cross through wash.
2.8 ▲   SO   Cross through wash.
▼ 4.1   SO   Track on left and track on right.
2.7 ▲   SO   Track on left and track on right.
▼ 4.5   SO   4-way intersection with graded road. Remain on formed trail.
2.3 ▲   SO   4-way intersection with graded road. Remain on formed trail.
GPS: N35°06.88' W115°05.59'

▼ 4.9   SO   Cross through wash.
1.9 ▲   SO   Cross through wash.

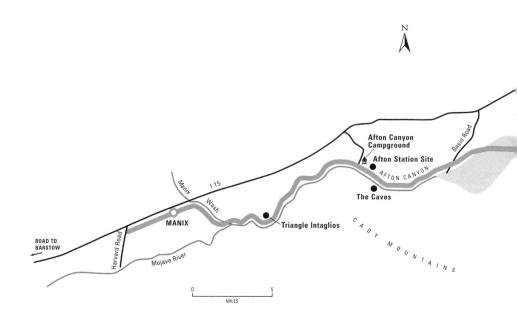

▼ 5.3 SO Dip; then cross through wash.
1.5 ▲ SO Cross through wash; then dip.
▼ 5.8 SO Track on right to old bus and shelter.
1.0 ▲ SO Track on left to old bus and shelter.
         GPS: N35°07.13′ W115°06.88′

▼ 6.0 SO Track on right and track on left.
0.8 ▲ SO Track on right and track on left.
▼ 6.6 TR T-intersection at fence line.
0.2 ▲ TL Leave fence. Track continues straight ahead.
         GPS: N35°07.34′ W115°07.72′

▼ 6.8 TL T-intersection at corner of fence. Track on right. Zero trip meter.
0.0 ▲ Continue to the south.
         GPS: N35°07.58′ W115°07.71′

▼ 0.0 Continue to the west.
3.3 ▲ TR Turn right at corner of fence, remaining alongside fence line. Track continues

ahead. Zero trip meter.
▼ 0.6 SO Cross through wash.
2.7 ▲ SO Cross through wash.
▼ 0.9 BR Bear right at cairns onto well-used, but eroded trail. Track continues along fence line.
2.4 ▲ SO Track on right at cairns. Continue alongside fence line.
         GPS: N35°07.60′ W115°08.72′

▼ 1.6 BR Track on right; then immediately bear right at cairn past track on left.
1.7 ▲ BR Track on right; then immediately bear right at cairn past track on left.
         GPS: N35°07.78′ W115°09.39′

▼ 2.0 SO Track on left and track on right.
1.3 ▲ SO Track on left and track on right.
         GPS: N35°07.89′ W115°09.86′

▼ 3.3 SO Cross over wide, graded Lanfair Road.

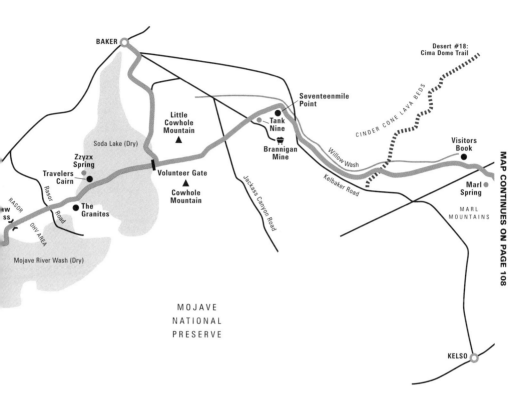

Zero trip meter and continue on small formed trail.

0.0 ▲ Continue to the east.

GPS: N35°08.32' W115°11.16'

▼ 0.0 Continue to the west.

6.7 ▲ SO Cross over wide, graded Lanfair Road. Zero trip meter and continue on small formed trail.

▼ 1.3 SO Cross through wash. Grotto Hills are on the right.

5.4 ▲ SO Cross through wash. Grotto Hills are on the left.

▼ 1.7 SO Track on right.

5.0 ▲ SO Track on left.

▼ 1.9 SO Graded road on right and left.

4.8 ▲ SO Graded road on right and left.

GPS: N35°08.37' W115°13.19'

▼ 2.0 SO Cross through wash.

4.7 ▲ SO Cross through wash.

▼ 3.8 SO Well-used track on right and left.

2.9 ▲ SO Well-used track on right and left.

GPS: N35°08.40' W115°15.30'

▼ 3.9 SO Track on right to stone cabin on private property.

2.8 ▲ SO Track on left to stone cabin on private property.

GPS: N35°08.41' W115°15.40'

▼ 5.9 SO Dam on left.

0.8 ▲ SO Dam on right.

▼ 6.3 SO Cross through wash. Track on right and track on left up and down wash.

0.4 ▲ SO Cross through wash. Track on left and track on right up and down wash.

▼ 6.7 BR Bear right onto wide, graded Cedar Canyon Road. Zero trip meter.

0.0 ▲ Continue to the northeast.

GPS: N35°08.74' W115°18.47'

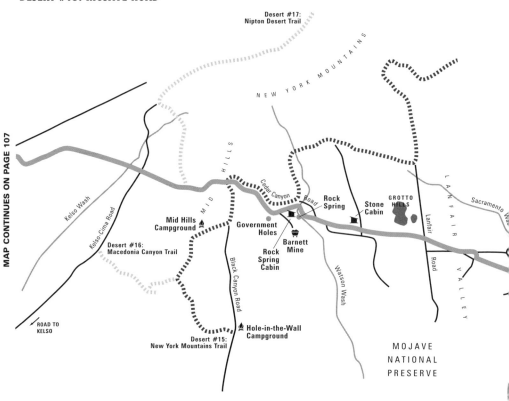

MAP CONTINUES ON PAGE 107

▼ 0.0   Continue to the west on graded road. Immediately track on right.

1.6 ▲   BL   Track on left; then bear left onto well-used, formed trail and zero trip meter.

▼ 0.4   BL   Bear left onto small, formed trail marked by a cairn.

1.2 ▲   BR   Bear right onto wide, graded Cedar Canyon Road.
         GPS: N35°08.85′ W115°18.84′

▼ 0.5   SO   Start to descend to Watson Wash.

1.1 ▲   SO   Climb out of Watson Wash.

▼ 0.8   BR   Bear right up Watson Wash.

0.8 ▲   BL   Bear left out of wash and climb toward Cedar Canyon Road.

▼ 1.3   BR   Bear right out of main wash. Looking to the left at this point you can see Rock Spring Cabin on top of the ridge above the wash. Immediately turn left. A BLM information board can be seen on the left.

0.3 ▲   BL   Turn right at T-intersection; then immediately bear left down main Watson Wash.
         GPS: N35°09.18′ W115°19.60′

▼ 1.4   SO   Parking area and information board on left for Camp Rock Spring; then track on right.

0.2 ▲   BR   Track on left; then parking area and information board on right for Camp Rock Spring.
         GPS: N35°09.20′ W115°19.63′

▼ 1.5   TL   Join graded Cedar Canyon Road and turn left.

0.1 ▲   TR   Turn right onto small formed trail down Watson Wash.
         GPS: N35°09.37′ W115°19.74′

▼ 1.6   SO   Track on right is Desert #15: New York Mountains Trail. The two trails

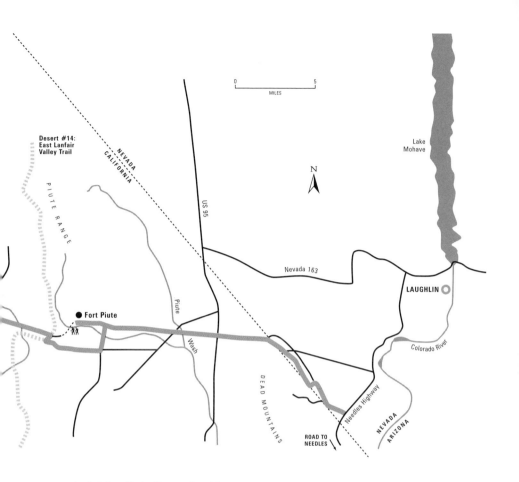

both follow Cedar Canyon Road for a short distance. Zero trip meter.

0.0 ▲ Continue to the east.

GPS: N35°09.43' W115°19.90'

▼ 0.0 Continue to the west.

2.2 ▲ SO Track on left is Desert #15: New York Mountains Trail, which leaves to the north at this point. Zero trip meter.

▼ 0.1 BL Bear left onto smaller graded road. The intersection is unmarked.

2.1 ▲ SO Join wide, graded Cedar Canyon Road.

GPS: N35°09.39' W115°20.08'

▼ 0.3 SO 4-way intersection. Track on left goes to old stone cabin above Rock Spring; then second track on left.

1.8 ▲ SO Track on right; then 4-way intersection. Track on right goes to old stone cabin above Rock Spring.

GPS: N35°09.33' W115°20.15'

▼ 0.7 SO Cross through wash.

1.5 ▲ SO Cross through wash.

GPS: N35°09.23' W115°20.57'

▼ 1.1 SO Track on left.

1.1 ▲ SO Track on right.

▼ 1.4 BL Track on right. Track on left goes to the Barnett Mine; then second track on right.

0.8 ▲ SO Track on left. Track on right goes to the Barnett Mine; then second track on left.

▼ 1.6 SO Track on left.

0.6 ▲ SO Track on right.

▼ 1.7 TR Track on left is private road. Well, tank, and corral at Government Holes.

0.5 ▲ TL Track on right is private road. Well, tank, and corral at Government Holes.

GPS: N35°08.84' W115°21.50'

▼ 1.8   BL   Pass through two wire gates; then bear left past small track on right.

0.4 ▲   BR   Small track on left; then bear right and pass through two wire gates.

▼ 1.9   BL   Track on right.

0.3 ▲   BR   Track on left.

▼ 2.1   SO   Cross through wash.

0.1 ▲   SO   Cross through wash.

▼ 2.2   TL   T-intersection with wide graded Cedar Canyon Road. Zero trip meter.

0.0 ▲   Continue to the southeast.

       GPS: N35°09.18′ W115°21.68′

▼ 0.0   Continue to the west.

3.3 ▲   TR   Turn right onto small formed trail, leaving Cedar Canyon Road. Intersection is unmarked. Zero trip meter.

▼ 0.1   SO   Track on right.

3.2 ▲   SO   Track on left.

▼ 0.3   SO   Track on right; then cattle guard.

3.0 ▲   SO   Cattle guard; then track on left.

▼ 0.7   SO   Track on right.

2.6 ▲   SO   Track on left.

▼ 1.7   SO   Track on right; then cattle guard; then second track on right.

1.6 ▲   SO   Track on left; then cattle guard; then second track on left.

▼ 2.4   SO   Track on right.

0.9 ▲   SO   Track on left.

▼ 3.3   SO   Graded road on left is continuation of Desert #15: New York Mountains Trail, which diverges from Mojave Road and follows Black Canyon Road. Zero trip meter.

0.0 ▲   Continue to the northeast.

       GPS: N35°10.45′ W115°24.65′

▼ 0.0   Continue to the southwest.

2.8 ▲   SO   Graded road on right is Desert #15: New York Mountains Trail, which joins Mojave Road at this point. Road on right is marked Black Canyon Road. Zero trip meter. Desert #15: New York Mountains Trail now follows Mojave Road for a short distance.

▼ 0.3   SO   Cross through wash.

2.5 ▲   SO   Cross through wash.

▼ 1.3   SO   Pipeline track on left and right.

1.5 ▲   SO   Pipeline track on left and right.

▼ 2.0   SO   Cross through wash.

0.8 ▲   SO   Cross through wash.

▼ 2.2   SO   Track on right joins pipeline road.

0.6 ▲   SO   Track on left joins pipeline road.

▼ 2.7   SO   Track on right.

0.1 ▲   SO   Track on left.

▼ 2.8   SO   Track on right is Desert #17: Nipton Desert Road. Zero trip meter.

0.0 ▲   Continue to the east.

       GPS: N35°09.83′ W115°27.41′

▼ 0.0   Continue to the west.

2.9 ▲   SO   Track on left is Desert #17: Nipton Desert Road. Zero trip meter.

▼ 0.3   SO   Track on left.

2.6 ▲   SO   Track on right.

▼ 0.9   SO   Road is paved.

2.0 ▲   SO   Road turns to graded dirt.

▼ 2.2   SO   Track on left.

0.7 ▲   SO   Track on right.

▼ 2.9   SO   Cattle guard; then cross over railroad tracks. Then cross over paved Kelso–Cima Road. There is a historical marker at the intersection. Zero trip meter.

0.0 ▲   Continue to the east on paved road, following sign to Providence Mountain State Recreation Area. Cross over railroad tracks; then cattle guard.

       GPS: N35°10.57′ W115°30.48′

▼ 0.0   Continue to the west on formed trail and cross cattle guard.

7.9 ▲   SO   Cattle guard; then cross over paved Kelso–Cima Road. There is a historical marker at the intersection. Zero trip meter.

▼ 0.1   SO   Cattle guard.

7.8 ▲   SO   Cattle guard.

▼ 0.4   SO   Start to cross through the many-channeled Kelso Wash.

7.5 ▲   SO   End of wash crossings.

▼ 0.8   SO   End of wash crossings.

7.1 ▲   SO   Start to cross through the many-channeled Kelso Wash.

▼ 2.2   SO   Cross through wash.

5.7 ▲   SO   Cross through wash.

       GPS: N35°10.71′ W115°31.28′

▼ 4.5   SO   Track on left.

3.4 ▲   SO   Track on right.

▼ 5.1   BL   Track on right.

2.8 ▲   BR   Track on left.

▼ 5.9 SO Track on left.
2.0 ▲ SO Track on right.
▼ 7.1 SO Track on left and track on right along power line.
0.8 ▲ SO Track on left and track on right along power line.
GPS: N35°10.51' W115°37.99'

▼ 7.9 TR Track on left goes 0.1 miles to Marl Spring. Zero trip meter.
0.0 ▲ Continue to the northeast.
GPS: N35°10.20' W115°38.77'

▼ 0.0 Continue to the north.
3.2 ▲ TL T-intersection. Track on right goes 0.1 miles to Marl Spring. Zero trip meter.
▼ 0.1 SO Stone foundations on left.
3.1 ▲ SO Stone foundations on right.
GPS: N35°10.24' W115°38.77'

▼ 1.5 SO Track on left and track on right under power lines.
1.7 ▲ SO Track on left and track on right under power lines.
GPS: N35°11.00' W115°39.79'

▼ 3.2 SO Mojave Road visitors book on right on a metal post. Zero trip meter.
0.0 ▲ Continue to the northeast.
GPS: N35°11.12' W115°41.52'

▼ 0.0 Continue to the southwest.
4.8 ▲ SO Mojave Road visitors book on left on a metal post. Zero trip meter.
▼ 0.2 SO Cattle guard.
4.6 ▲ SO Cattle guard.
▼ 0.5 SO Cattle guard.
4.3 ▲ SO Cattle guard.
GPS: N35°11.01' W115°42.06'

▼ 4.8 SO Trail crosses graded dirt Aikens Mine Road, part of Desert #18: Cima Dome Trail. Zero trip meter.
0.0 ▲ Continue to the east.
GPS: N35°10.38' W115°46.61'

▼ 0.0 Continue to the west.
6.2 ▲ SO Trail crosses graded dirt Aikens Mine Road, part of Desert #18: Cima Dome Trail. Zero trip meter.

▼ 0.3 SO Enter line of Willow Wash.
5.9 ▲ SO Exit line of Willow Wash.
▼ 1.2 BL Trail forks, but rejoins in a short distance.
5.0 ▲ BR Trail forks, but rejoins in a short distance.
GPS: N35°09.84' W115°47.73'

▼ 2.7 SO Track on left and track on right.
3.5 ▲ SO Track on left and track on right.
GPS: N35°10.13' W115°49.24'

▼ 4.7 SO Track on right and track on left.
1.5 ▲ SO Track on left and track on right.
GPS: N35°11.07' W115°51.04'

▼ 6.2 SO Cross over paved Kelbaker Road and zero trip meter. Intersection has small cairns marking it. Baker, which has fuel, food, and accommodations, is approximately 14 miles to the right.
0.0 ▲ Continue to the southeast.
GPS: N35°11.94' W115°52.29'

▼ 0.0 Continue to the northwest.
6.0 ▲ SO Cross over paved Kelbaker Road and zero trip meter. Intersection has small cairns marking it. Baker, which has fuel, food, and accommodations, is approximately 14 miles to the left.
▼ 1.2 SO Track on left.
4.8 ▲ SO Track on right.
▼ 2.0 SO Track on right.
4.0 ▲ BR Track on left.
▼ 2.4 SO Exit line of wash.
3.6 ▲ SO Enter line of wash.
▼ 3.7 SO Tank Nine—few scattered remains.
2.3 ▲ SO Tank Nine—few scattered remains.
GPS: N35°12.50' W115°55.12'

▼ 3.8 SO Track on left to Brannigan Mine and track on right.
2.2 ▲ SO Track on right to Brannigan Mine and track on left.
▼ 6.0 SO Track on left and track on right at old tank is Jackass Canyon Road (also referred to as Kelso Road on some maps). Zero trip meter.
0.0 ▲ Continue to the northeast.
GPS: N35°11.21' W115°57.18'

▼ 0.0   Continue to the southwest.
4.6 ▲   SO Track on left and track on right at old tank is Jackass Canyon Road (also referred to as Kelso Road on some maps). Zero trip meter.
▼ 2.0   SO Well-used track on right.
2.6 ▲   BR Well-used track on left.
         GPS: N35°10.15′ W115°58.94′

▼ 2.6   SO Track on left and track on right.
2.0 ▲   SO Track on left and track on right.
▼ 2.7   SO Track on right.
1.9 ▲   SO Track on left.
▼ 3.0   SO Well-used track on left. Cowhole Mountain on left and Little Cowhole Mountain on right.
1.6 ▲   SO Well-used track on right. Cowhole Mountain on right and Little Cowhole Mountain on left.
         GPS: N35°09.83′ W115°59.92′

▼ 3.6   SO Two tracks on right.
1.0 ▲   BR Two tracks on left.
         GPS: N35°09.71′ W116°00.58′

▼ 3.7   SO Well-used road on left.
0.9 ▲   BL Well-used road on right.
         GPS: N35°09.69′ W115°00.67′

▼ 3.8   BL Well-used road on right.
0.8 ▲   SO Well-used road on left.
▼ 4.0   BL Track on right.
0.6 ▲   SO Track on left.
▼ 4.3   SO Track on right.
0.3 ▲   SO Track on left.
▼ 4.6   SO Well-used track on right is alternate exit to Baker, should Soda Lake be impassable. Zero trip meter. Cross cattle guard and pass through Volunteer Gate.
0.0 ▲   Continue to the northeast.
         GPS: N35°09.48′ W116°01.65′

Alternate Exit via Baker (Avoids Soda Lake)

▼ 0.0   From the east side of Volunteer Gate, on the eastern edge of Soda Lake, zero trip meter and proceed northeast on well-used track.

7.6 ▲   Trail joins Mojave Road. Turn right to cross Soda Lake; turn left for Kelbaker Road.
▼ 0.4   BL Bear left after corral. Track on right and mine on right.
7.2 ▲   BR Bear right at corral. Track on left and mine on left.
         GPS: N35°09.76′ W116°01.79′

▼ 0.6   SO Start to cross dry bed of Soda Lake. This trail stays close to the edge.
7.0 ▲   SO Exit lakebed.
▼ 1.3   SO Exit lakebed. Fence line is now on left.
6.3 ▲   SO Start to cross dry bed of Soda Lake. This trail stays close to the edge.
         GPS: N35°10.48′ W116°02.29′

▼ 2.8   SO Well-used track on left and track on right.
4.8 ▲   SO Well-used track on right and track on left.
         GPS: N35°11.81′ W116°02.30′

▼ 3.4   SO Cross through wash.
4.2 ▲   SO Cross through wash.
▼ 3.9   SO 4-way intersection with graded road.
3.7 ▲   SO 4-way intersection with graded road.
         GPS: N35°12.85′ W116°02.29′

▼ 4.1   SO Cross through wash.
3.5 ▲   SO Cross through wash.
▼ 4.5   SO Cross through wash.
3.1 ▲   SO Cross through wash.
▼ 4.6   BL Track on right.
3.0 ▲   SO Track on left.
         GPS: N35°13.45′ W116°02.34′

▼ 4.7   SO Track on right; then wire gate.
2.9 ▲   SO Wire gate; then track on left.
▼ 5.5   SO Cross through wash.
2.1 ▲   SO Cross through wash.
▼ 5.7   SO Track on right along fence line. Continue straight ahead with fence on right.
1.9 ▲   SO Track on left along fence line. Leave fence line.
▼ 6.0   SO Track on left.
1.6 ▲   SO Track on right.
▼ 6.2   SO Graded road on right into works area. Join graded road heading toward Baker.

1.4 ▲   BR   Bear right onto smaller graded road.
Road on left goes into works area.
GPS: N35°14.14′ W116°03.73′

▼ 6.4   SO   Track on left.
1.2 ▲   SO   Track on right.
▼ 6.8   SO   Track on left and track on right along pipeline.
0.8 ▲   SO   Track on left and track on right along pipeline.
▼ 7.6   TL   Turn left onto paved Kelbaker Road. Zero trip meter.
0.0 ▲   Continue to the south.
GPS: N35°15.40′ W116°03.42′

▼ 0.0   Continue to the west.
0.8 ▲   TR   Turn right onto wide graded road. Zero trip meter.
▼ 0.8   Exit route finishes at east side of I-15 on the edge of Baker. Proceed 11 miles west on I-15 to Rasor Road exit. Continue south on Rasor Road for 5.1 miles to rejoin Mojave Road west of Soda Lake. Mojave Road cannot be accessed via Zzyzx Spring (also called Soda Spring).
0.0 ▲   Alternate route around Soda Lake starts in Baker at the east side of I-15 at the Kelbaker Road exit. Zero trip meter and proceed east on paved Kelbaker Road.
GPS: N35°15.74′ W116°04.28′

Continuation of Main Trail

▼ 0.0   Continue to the southwest.
5.9 ▲   SO   Cattle guard and Volunteer Gate; then well-used track on left is alternate exit to Baker. Zero trip meter.
GPS: N35°09.48′ W116°01.65′

▼ 0.3   SO   Start to cross Soda Lake bed.
5.6 ▲   SO   Leave Soda Lake bed.
GPS: N35°08.87′ W116°03.67′

▼ 2.9   SO   Cross through channel.
3.0 ▲   SO   Cross through channel.
GPS: N35°08.54′ W116°04.35′

▼ 3.1   SO   Cross through channel.

2.8 ▲   SO   Cross through channel.
GPS: N35°08.45′ W116°04.52′

▼ 3.4   SO   Cross through channel.
2.5 ▲   SO   Cross through channel.
▼ 4.3   SO   Travelers or Government Cairn—large cairn in the middle of Soda Lake. Zzyzx Spring can be seen surrounded by palm trees behind the monument to the north.
1.6 ▲   SO   Travelers or Government Cairn—large cairn in the middle of Soda Lake. Zzyzx Spring can be seen surrounded by palm trees behind the monument to the north.
GPS: N35°07.85′ W116°05.67′

▼ 5.6   BR   Bear right at The Granites.
0.3 ▲   BL   Bear left at The Granites and proceed across the lakebed.
GPS: N35°07.12′ W116°06.66′

▼ 5.9   SO   Track on right goes toward Zzyzx but does not go through to connect to I-15. Track on left is the Tonopah & Tidewater Railroad grade. Exit Soda Lake. Zero trip meter.
0.0 ▲   Continue to the east.
GPS: N35°07.24′ W116°06.87′

▼ 0.0   Continue to the southwest.
1.8 ▲   BR   Track on left goes toward Zzyzx but does not go through to I-15. Track on right is the Tonopah & Tidewater Railroad grade. Zero trip meter and start to cross Soda Lake bed.
▼ 0.9   BL   Entering Rasor OHV Area at sign; then track on right. Many small tracks on right and left for the next 10.9 miles; only major ones are mentioned. Remain on main trail.
0.9 ▲   SO   Track on left; then leaving Rasor OHV Area at sign.
GPS: N35°06.85′ W116°07.60′

▼ 1.8   SO   Cross over graded dirt Rasor Road and zero trip meter. I-15 is 5.1 miles to the right. There is gas at the freeway exit.
0.0 ▲   Continue to the northeast.
GPS: N35°06.52′ W116°08.57′

▼ 0.0   Continue to the southwest.

10.0 ▲   SO   Cross over graded dirt Rasor Road and zero trip meter. I-15 is 5.1 miles to the left. There is gas at the freeway exit.

▼ 2.1   SO   Cross through wash.

7.9 ▲   SO   Cross through wash.

▼ 2.3   SO   Shaw Pass.

7.7 ▲   SO   Shaw Pass.

      GPS: N35°05.61' W116°10.65'

▼ 2.4   SO   Start to cross Mojave River floodplain.

7.6 ▲   SO   Exit Mojave River floodplain.

▼ 2.5   TL   4-way intersection. Turn left, keeping cairns on your right.

7.5 ▲   TR   4-way intersection. Turn right, keeping cairns on your left.

      GPS: N35°05.43' W116°10.87'

▼ 3.3   SO   Entering extremely soft, loose sand.

6.7 ▲   SO   Exiting the worst of the soft sand.

▼ 3.5   SO   Track on left and track on right. Continue to the southwest, keeping cairns on your right.

6.5 ▲   SO   Track on left and track on right. Continue to the northeast, keeping cairns on your left.

      GPS: N35°04.58' W116°10.78'

▼ 3.8   SO   Track on left.

6.2 ▲   BL   Track on right.

      GPS: N35°04.51' W116°11.11'

▼ 8.6   SO   Track on left.

1.4 ▲   SO   Track on right.

      GPS: N35°03.92' W116°16.03'

▼ 10.0   SO   Trail crosses graded dirt Basin Road. I-15 is 3.6 miles to the right. Continue straight ahead and zero trip meter. Leaving Rasor OHV Area. Intersection is marked by cairns.

0.0 ▲   Continue to the east and enter Rasor OHV Area. Many small tracks on right and left for the next 10.9 miles. Keep cairns on left and remain on main trail.

      GPS: N35°03.10' W116°17.17'

▼ 0.0   Continue to the west.

6.7 ▲   SO   Trail crosses graded dirt Basin Road. I-

      15 is 3.6 miles to the left. Continue straight ahead and zero trip meter. Intersection is marked by cairns.

▼ 0.2   SO   Ford through the Mojave River.

6.5 ▲   SO   Ford through the Mojave River.

      GPS: N35°03.09' W116°17.34'

▼ 0.6   SO   Track on right to mine remains.

6.1 ▲   SO   Track on left to mine remains.

      GPS: N35°02.92' W116°17.76'

▼ 0.9   SO   Track on right to mine. Mining remains on right.

5.8 ▲   BR   Track on left to mine. Mining remains on left.

      GPS: N35°02.78' W116°18.09'

▼ 1.0   TR   Ford through Mojave River; then turn right.

5.7 ▲   TL   Turn left; then ford through the Mojave River.

▼ 1.2   SO   Ford through Mojave River.

5.5 ▲   SO   Ford through Mojave River.

▼ 1.5   SO   Track on left and track on right. Ford through the Mojave River; then pass under railroad bridge and enter the start of Afton Canyon. The route is marked by BLM open route markers past this point.

5.2 ▲   SO   Pass under railroad bridge and exit Afton Canyon. Ford through the Mojave River; then track on left and track on right.

      GPS: N35°02.55' W116°18.50'

▼ 1.6   SO   Track on left and track on right.

5.1 ▲   SO   Track on left and track on right.

▼ 2.1   SO   Canyon walls start to narrow. Many crossings of the Mojave River channel for the next 4.6 miles.

4.6 ▲   SO   Canyon starts to widen. End of the many crossings of the Mojave River channel.

▼ 4.9   SO   Track on left.

1.8 ▲   SO   Track on right.

▼ 5.0   TL   T-intersection with track alongside rail line. Turn left along rail line.

1.7 ▲   TR   Turn right away from rail line.

      GPS: N35°01.56' W116°21.55'

▼ 5.4 SO Pull-in on left. Trail is now directly alongside rail line.

1.3 ▲ SO Pull-in on right.

▼ 5.6 SO Ford through the Mojave River. This ford can often be quite deep. The Caves are a 0.5-mile hike to the left. If the growth is low, The Caves can be seen from the road on the northern side of the curve.

1.1 ▲ SO Ford through the Mojave River. This ford can often be quite deep. The Caves are a 0.5-mile hike to the right. If the growth is low, The Caves can be seen from the road on the northern side of the curve.

GPS: N35°01.88' W116°21.98'

▼ 6.5 BR Bear right away from rail line. Site of Afton Station.

0.2 ▲ SO Join rail line. Site of Afton Station.

▼ 6.6 SO Ford through the Mojave River. This crossing can be quite deep.

0.1 ▲ SO Ford through the Mojave River. This crossing can be quite deep.

▼ 6.7 SO Afton Canyon BLM Campground on right—fee charged. Zero trip meter. Exit Afton Canyon.

0.0 ▲ Continue to the east alongside railroad line and enter Afton Canyon. Many crossings of the Mojave River channel for the next 4.6 miles.

GPS: N35°02.27' W116°23.00'

▼ 0.0 Continue to the west along graded road.

8.0 ▲ SO Afton Canyon BLM Campground on left—fee charged. Zero trip meter.

▼ 0.3 SO Track on left.

7.7 ▲ SO Track on right.

▼ 0.5 SO Afton Canyon NPS Group Camping Area on left.

7.5 ▲ SO Afton Canyon NPS Group Camping Area on right.

GPS: N35°02.46' W116°23.38'

▼ 0.7 TL Turn sharp left onto smaller, graded dirt road, following sign for Mojave Road.

7.3 ▲ TR Turn right and join the wide graded dirt road, following sign for Afton Canyon.

GPS: N35°02.49' W116°23.58'

▼ 0.8 SO Pass under rail line. Track on right and track on left along rail line; then pass through gate into wildlife viewing area. Enter Mojave River wash.

7.2 ▲ SO Pass through gate, exiting the Mojave River wash and wildlife viewing area. Track on right and track on left along rail line; then pass under rail line.

▼ 7.1 SO Track on left.

0.9 ▲ SO Track on right.

GPS: N34°59.79' W116°28.47'

▼ 8.0 SO Track on right is spur to the Triangle Intaglios. Intersection is marked by a cairn with a railroad sleeper placed vertically in the middle of it. Zero trip meter.

0.0 ▲ Continue to the northeast.

GPS: N34°59.13' W116°28.78'

Spur to Triangle Intaglios

▼ 0.0 Proceed to the west.

▼ 0.2 SO Track on left and track on right.

▼ 0.3 UT Turning circle. Park here and hike to the top of the mesa above the Mojave River wash, up the small gully to the southeast of the parking area. The intaglios are protected by a barrier on top of the mesa. There are approximately 20 intaglios. The largest are 10 feet long and 6 feet wide. All are triangular in shape.

GPS: N34°59.23' W116°29.08'

Continuation of Main Trail

▼ 0.0 Continue to the southwest.

7.5 ▲ SO Track on left is spur to the Triangle Intaglios. Intersection is marked by a cairn with a railroad sleeper placed vertically in the middle of it. Zero trip meter.

GPS: N34°59.13' W116°28.78'

▼ 3.9 BR Track swings west up Manix Wash, leaving the Mojave River wash.

3.6 ▲ BL Track swings northeast down Mojave River wash, leaving Manix Wash.

EDWARD FITZGERALD BEALE

Regarded as "Mr. California," Edward Beale played many successful roles throughout his life. Born in 1822, he had a variety of professions, ranging from naval officer and prominent explorer to bureaucrat and politician. Those who knew him described him as a thin, wiry man whose outspoken thoughts were often very frank. Status, wealth, and a thirst for adventure seemed to drive E. F. Beale in his many exploits.

Edward Fitzgerald Beale

Beale first gained prominence in the Mexican War of 1846–48. He and Kit Carson slipped through enemy lines at San Pasqual and fetched relief for the embattled American troops. Over the course of that war, he made many transcontinental journeys with dispatches to Washington. On one of those trips, he carried the first sample of California gold to President Polk, helping to inspire the gold rush of 1849.

Beale left military service in 1851 after a promotion to lieutenant. The following year he entered politics as California's first superintendent of Indian affairs. He used the post to promote humanitarian solutions in disputes between whites and Indians, but also connived to purchase some Indian lands for himself at a greatly reduced price. In 1856, he resigned the position to become brigadier general of the California state militia. He proposed the formation of a camel corps to better supply forts across the dry deserts of the Southwest. In 1857, he accepted a job as superintendent for a transcontinental wagon road, which led to the creation of the Beale Wagon Road and the introduction of camels in the American Southwest. When the State Department sold the animals, Beale relocated them to his ranch near Bakersfield. He spent the Civil War in the West as surveyor general of California and Nevada.

Beale stayed in politics through his later years. He was active in the Pennsylvania movement for African-American suffrage. During the 1870s, he climbed the Republican political ladder and soon became one of President Ulysses S. Grant's personal friends, serving a year as ambassador to Austria-Hungary. He died April 21, 1893, at the age of 71.

	GPS: N34°58.46′ W116°32.32′	
▼ 4.6	SO	Track on right.
2.9 ▲	SO	Track on left.
▼ 5.4	SO	Track on left and track on right. Pass under power lines.
2.1 ▲	SO	Track on left and track on right. Pass under power lines.
	GPS: N34°59.21′ W116°33.54′	
▼ 5.9	SO	Exit Manix Wash.
1.6 ▲	SO	Enter down Manix Wash.
▼ 6.0	SO	Pass through wire gate.
1.5 ▲	SO	Pass through wire gate.
	GPS: N34°59.40′ W116°34.16′	

▼ 6.1	BR	Track on left.
1.4 ▲	SO	Track on right.
▼ 6.3	SO	Track on left.
1.2 ▲	BL	Track on right.
▼ 7.1	SO	Track on right along rail line. Continue along rail line.
0.4 ▲	BR	Track continues along rail line. Bear right, leaving the rail line.
	GPS: N34°59.04′ W116°35.31′	
▼ 7.4	TR	4-way intersection with graded dirt Alvord Mountain Road. Turn right and cross over rail line. This is Manix.
0.1 ▲	TL	Cross over rail line and immediately turn left, running alongside the rail line. This is Manix.

GPS: N34°58.90' W116°35°62'

| ▼ 7.5 | TL | T-intersection with paved Yermo Road. Zero trip meter. |
| 0.0 ▲ | | Continue to the southeast. |

GPS: N34°58.93' W116°35.65'

▼ 0.0		Continue to the southwest, remaining on paved road.
3.1 ▲	TR	Turn right onto graded dirt Alvord Mountain Road and zero trip meter.
▼ 3.1		Trail ends at intersection of Yermo Road and Harvard Road, on the south side of I-15 at the Harvard Road exit.
0.0 ▲		Trail commences at the Harvard Road exit of I-15, 24 miles east of Barstow. Proceed to the south side of the freeway at the intersection of Harvard Road and Yermo Road. Zero trip meter and proceed northeast on paved Yermo Road. Remain on paved road.

GPS: N34°57.64' W116°38.63'

DESERT #14

East Lanfair Valley Trail

STARTING POINT: Route 66 at Goffs
FINISHING POINT: Nevada 164, 1.1 miles west of intersection with US 95 in Searchlight, NV
TOTAL MILEAGE: 49.1 miles
UNPAVED MILEAGE: 48.3 miles
DRIVING TIME: 5.5 hours
ELEVATION RANGE: 2,600–4,500 feet
USUALLY OPEN: Year-round
BEST TIME TO TRAVEL: September to May
DIFFICULTY RATING: 4
SCENIC RATING: 9
REMOTENESS RATING: +1

Special Attractions

■ Extensive remains of the Leiser Ray Mine.
■ Remote, lightly traveled trail within the Mojave National Preserve.
■ Piute Gorge.
■ Intersects with historic Desert #13: Mojave Road.

History

Many nineteenth-century opportunists who pushed west through the much-avoided desert regions were mining prospectors. Travelers had no real intention of settling the harsh deserts and were wary of the problems associated with Indians who frequented the regions.

Searchlight, Nevada, at the northern end of this trail, was an important camp during the early development of this region. Mineral deposits were promising. Summit Springs, located 3.5 miles east of Searchlight, was the district name and location marker for claims in the area. The earliest working mines here were the Red Iron Claim and the Bowland Tunnels. In 1896 and 1897, John C. Swickard located and claimed the Golden Treasure and Copper King Mines, which were to become part of the Quartette Mining Company, the largest gold producer in Searchlight. On January 4, 1898, Mr. Colton and A. E. Moore located the Searchlight Claim, after which the mining district and camp were eventually named. The district produced gold, silver, copper, and lead. At the Quartette Mine, just south of this trail in Searchlight, ore values averaged $3.80 per ton for the first 100 feet. However, down at 700 feet, some ore assayed at $1,335.00 per ton. The Quartette's shaft went to 1,167 feet, and the length of the workings totaled 5.5 miles. Lumber and stone supports were used throughout.

The greatest mining activity in Searchlight took place between 1902 and 1916. There were more than 300 mining claims in 1906. A brief boom occurred in the early 1930s with a high-grade strike at the Cyrus Noble Mine. From 1902 to 1959, 246,997 ounces of gold were extracted from lode mines and 26 ounces from placer mines.

In 1902, the Quartette built a 20-stamp mill on the Colorado River with a 12-mile narrow gauge railroad connecting it to the mine site. The railroad also carried passengers from the mine to steamboats on the Colorado River. In 1906, the mill was moved to the mine site and the rails were sold. In the Searchlight District, water flooded the shafts around the 250-foot depth, which provided ample water for on-site processing. During a down time in 1904, the Duplex alone accumulated 350,000 gallons of water in its shaft. After 1906, the Quartette had enough water to operate a 40-stamp mill at the mine. It was one of the first mills in Nevada to use cyanide processing. The Quartette Mill burned down in 1913.

Searchlight became more connected with the outside world in 1907. Trains were already operating from Goffs to Barnwell when the Atchison, Topeka & Santa Fe linked Barnwell and Searchlight in April 1907. At its peak, daily railroad services operated from Goffs, north up Lanfair Valley, to Barnwell. From there trains continued to Searchlight every day except Sundays. This line operated until 1924.

Searchlight's other main industry was cattle ranching. Two roundups a year took place—one in spring to get new calves for branding and the other in fall to separate animals for sale. In the 1920s, the Kennedy family's ranching endeavors extended from Hole-in-the-Wall in the eastern Mojave Desert to the Newberry Mountains and Cottonwood Island.

Goffs was one of several locations used as a military training camp during World War II. Military units spent three months here before other units arrived for training. General Patton thought this vast region accommodated the need for realistic maneuvers. Goffs was a hive of activity during the war years. Troops and vehicles obliterated almost everything in their paths. Only lines of stones were visible between tents and roadways, some of which remain to this day. A visit to the restored Goffs Schoolhouse, with its unusual architecture and its information on life in the California desert over the centuries, will answer almost any question that may occur to travelers along this trail.

The Lanfair Valley was named in 1910 for Ernest Lanfair, a merchant from Searchlight who used his real estate connections to exploit the valley. He constructed a windmill to pump water in this seemingly dry valley and

Mill foundations at the Leiser Ray Mine

sold many acres to hopeful homesteaders. Whether he added water when would-be buyers appeared is debatable. However, the impression was that the land held water not far below the surface and thus the land sold.

Description

East Lanfair Valley Trail crosses the Mojave National Preserve in a south to north direction, intersecting with Desert #13: Mojave Road, which travels east to west. The small formed trail is well defined for most of its length as it travels from Goffs, California, to Searchlight, Nevada.

The trail begins in Goffs and immediately passes the historic Goffs Schoolhouse, recently renovated and open to the public on occasion. Once the trail enters the Mojave National Preserve, it turns off onto a small, sandy trail that travels north toward the prominent Signal Hill.

One interesting feature along the trail is the remains of the Leiser Ray Mine. Several diggings, concrete foundations, and stone walls remain. The trail north of the mine is lightly used. Many travelers swing east at this point, but the trail described here continues north, following wash lines and ridges to intersect with Desert #13: Mojave Road. The two trails follow the same route for 0.5 miles before Mojave Road continues west and East Lanfair Valley Trail continues north.

The Piute Range is now the dominant feature on the eastern side. A short spur leads 0.6 miles to the western end of the Fort Piute/Piute Spring Hiking Corridor. This hiking trail connects with Fort Piute on the eastern side of the ridge. It is a moderately strenuous but rewarding hike. The vehicle turnaround at the end of the spur offers a panoramic view of the Piute Range and the vast Lanfair Valley.

The main trail continues north and skirts Piute Gorge. There are some excellent campsites on the rim of the gorge, but they have no shade and no windbreaks. However, the view more than makes up for the exposure.

Past the gorge, the trail is lightly used as it winds through abundant vegetation. Tight twists and turns make for slow travel.

The trail emerges onto a small graded road at the southern end of the New York Mountains. It then turns east, following the formed trail through the Castle Mountains into Nevada. The trail here is well defined but rocky and eroded in places; it is the 4-rated section of the trail. The remainder of the trail is rated 2 to 3 for difficulty. The latter part of the trail meanders along washes and among large boulders past some of the most spectacular scenery along its length.

The trail crosses into Nevada at Stray Cow Well. The state line is marked by a white post, but no sign. From here, it follows a variety of rough trails down the bajada toward Searchlight. The final section follows the old railroad grade. Sections along this part of the trail are very moguled; wheel articulation and side tilt angles will be tested along this stretch.

Current Road Information

National Park Service
Mojave National Preserve
2701 Barstow Road
Barstow, CA 92311
(760) 252-6100

Map References

BLM   Amboy, Ivanpah, Davis Dam
USGS 1:24,000   Goffs, Signal Hill, East of Grotto Hills, Hart Peak, Tenmile Well, Hopps Well, Searchlight (NV) 1:100,000 Amboy, Ivanpah, Davis Dam
Maptech CD-ROM: San Bernardino County/Mojave
Southern & Central California Atlas & Gazetteer, pp. 86, 72
Nevada Atlas & Gazetteer, p. 72
California Road & Recreation Atlas, pp. 98, 107
Trails Illustrated, Mojave National Preserve (256)

Route Directions

▼ 0.0   From National Trails Highway (Route 66) at the north side of the railroad crossing in Goffs, turn north on paved Lanfair Road and zero trip meter.

DESERT #14: EAST LANFAIR VALLEY TRAIL

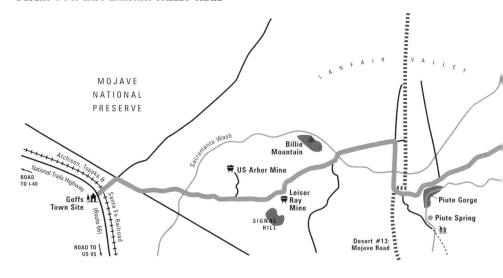

3.3 ▲   Trail ends on National Trails Highway (Route 66) in Goffs. Turn left for US 95 and Needles; turn right for Fenner and I-40.
GPS: N34º55.18' W115º03.89'

▼ 0.1   SO   Goffs Schoolhouse on left.
3.2 ▲   SO   Goffs Schoolhouse on right.
▼ 0.4   SO   Cattle guard.
2.9 ▲   SO   Cattle guard.
▼ 0.7   SO   Entering Mojave National Preserve.
2.6 ▲   SO   Leaving Mojave National Preserve.
GPS: N34º55.74' W115º04.20'
▼ 0.8   TR   Turn right off paved road onto small formed trail. There is a track opposite to the left. Immediately track on right.
2.5 ▲   TL   Track on left; then turn left and join paved Lanfair Road. There is a track straight ahead.
GPS: N34º55.77' W115º04.22'
▼ 1.7   TL   Turn left onto formed trail. There is a cairn at the intersection. Track continues ahead.
1.6 ▲   TR   T-intersection. Turn right onto formed trail. There is a cairn at the intersection.
GPS: N34º56.41' W115º03.54'

▼ 2.8   SO   Small track on right.
0.5 ▲   SO   Small track on left.

▼ 3.3   SO   Track on right and track on left under power lines. Zero trip meter and continue straight ahead on formed trail.
0.0 ▲   Continue to the south.
GPS: N34º57.71' W115º03.21'

▼ 0.0   Continue to the north.
4.7 ▲   SO   Track on right and track on left under power lines. Zero trip meter and continue straight ahead on formed trail.
▼ 0.5   SO   Cross through wash.
4.2 ▲   SO   Cross through wash.
▼ 0.6   SO   Cross through Sacramento Wash.
4.1 ▲   SO   Cross through Sacramento Wash.
▼ 0.7   SO   Cross through wash.
4.0 ▲   SO   Cross through wash.
▼ 2.6   SO   Track on left to US Arbor Mine.
2.1 ▲   SO   Track on right to US Arbor Mine.
GPS: N34º59.81' W115º02.19'

▼ 2.8   SO   Small track on left.
1.9 ▲   SO   Small track on right.
▼ 3.5   SO   Small track on left.
1.2 ▲   SO   Small track on right.
▼ 3.6   SO   Small track on right.
1.1 ▲   SO   Small track on left.
▼ 3.7   SO   Track on left.
1.0 ▲   SO   Track on right.
▼ 3.9   SO   Track on right; then cross through wash.
0.8 ▲   SO   Cross through wash; then track on left.

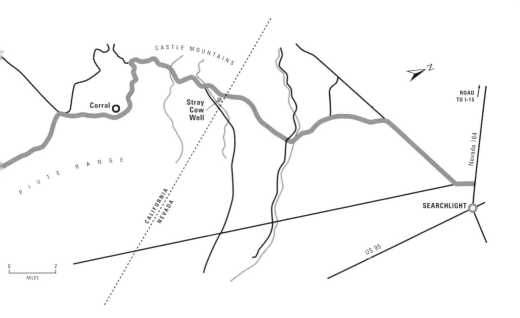

GPS: N35°00.99′ W115°01.89′

▼ 4.1 SO Cross through wash.
0.6 ▲ SO Cross through wash.
▼ 4.4 BL Bear left up wash.
0.3 ▲ BR Bear right out of wash.
▼ 4.6 SO Track on right into Leiser Ray Mine. Concrete foundations and diggings on right; then track on left and track on right.
0.1 ▲ SO Track on left and track on right; then track on left into Leiser Ray Mine. Concrete foundations and diggings on left.
GPS: N35°01.52′ W115°02.03′

▼ 4.7 TL T-intersection in front of second set of concrete foundations. Track on right into mine. Zero trip meter.
0.0 ▲ Continue to the southwest.
GPS: N35°01.63′ W115°02.00′

▼ 0.0 Continue to the northwest past track on left.
5.6 ▲ TR Track on right; then turn right in front of concrete foundations of the Leiser Ray Mine. Track straight ahead goes into mine. Zero trip meter.
▼ 0.1 SO Track on right; then enter wash.
5.5 ▲ SO Exit wash; then track on left.

▼ 0.2 SO Well-used track on right out of wash marked by cairn. Remain in wash.
5.4 ▲ SO Well-used track on left out of wash marked by cairn. Remain in wash.
GPS: N35°01.75′ W115°02.05′

▼ 0.7 SO Exit wash.
4.9 ▲ SO Enter down wash.
▼ 0.9 SO Track on right to diggings.
4.7 ▲ SO Track on left to diggings.
GPS: N35°02.19′ W115°02.55′

▼ 1.7 SO Small track on right.
3.9 ▲ SO Small track on left.
▼ 1.8 SO Track on right to diggings. Billie Mountain is on the left.
3.8 ▲ SO Track on left to diggings. Billie Mountain is on the right.
GPS: N35°02.89′ W115°02.76′

▼ 2.0 SO Track on left at diggings.
3.6 ▲ SO Track on right at diggings.
▼ 2.1 SO Track on right.
3.5 ▲ BR Track on left.
▼ 2.3 SO Cross through wash.
3.3 ▲ SO Cross through wash.
▼ 2.4 SO Track on left.
3.2 ▲ SO Track on right.
▼ 2.8 SO Track on right.
2.8 ▲ SO Track on left.

GPS: N35°03.76' W115°02.85'

▼ 3.1 SO Cross through wide Sacramento Wash.
2.5 ▲ SO Cross through wide Sacramento Wash.
GPS: N35°03.99' W115°03.09'

▼ 3.4 SO Water tank on left.
2.2 ▲ SO Water tank on right.
GPS: N35°04.22' W115°03.18'

▼ 4.7 SO Cattle guard.
0.9 ▲ SO Cattle guard.
▼ 5.6 TR 4-way intersection with graded road. Zero trip meter.
0.0 ▲ Continue to the southeast.
GPS: N35°06.19' W115°03.06'

▼ 0.0 Continue to the northeast.
2.4 ▲ TL 4-way intersection. Zero trip meter and turn onto smaller, graded trail. Intersection is unmarked.
▼ 0.4 SO Cross through Sacramento Wash.
2.0 ▲ SO Cross through Sacramento Wash.

▼ 1.3 SO Cross through wash.
1.1 ▲ SO Cross through wash.
▼ 1.9 TL Intersection with Desert #13: Mojave Road, which is straight ahead over cattle guard and to the left. Turn left, joining Mojave Road.
0.5 ▲ TR T-intersection. Track on left over cattle guard is continuation of Desert #13: Mojave Road. Turn right, leaving Mojave Road.
GPS: N35°05.68' W115°01.11'

▼ 2.4 SO 4-way intersection. Track on right is a short spur that goes 0.6 miles to the top of Piute Hill and the start of Fort Piute/Piute Spring Hiking Corridor. Intersection is marked by stone cairns. Track on left is continuation of Desert #13: Mojave Road, which leaves East Lanfair Valley Trail at this point. Zero trip meter.
0.0 ▲ Continue to the south.
GPS: N35°05.98' W115°00.78'

The original Goffs Schoolhouse is now a regional museum

▼ 0.0   Continue to the north.
9.9 ▲ SO 4-way intersection. Track on left is a short spur that goes 0.6 miles to the top of Piute Hill and the Fort Piute/Piute Spring Hiking Corridor. Track on right is Desert #13: Mojave Road, which joins East Lanfair Valley Trail at this point. Intersection is marked by stone cairns. Zero trip meter.

▼ 0.3 SO Corral on left.
9.6 ▲ SO Corral on right.
▼ 0.6 BL Track on right on the edge of Piute Gorge.
9.3 ▲ SO Second entrance to track on left.
▼ 0.7 SO Second entrance to track on right.
9.2 ▲ BR Track on left on the edge of Piute Gorge.
      GPS: N35°06.55' W115°00.56'

▼ 0.9 SO Campsite on right on the edge of Piute Gorge. Viewpoint over gorge.
9.0 ▲ SO Campsite on left on the edge of Piute Gorge. Viewpoint over gorge.
▼ 1.4 SO Track on right.
8.5 ▲ SO Track on left.
▼ 1.9 SO Track on right.
8.0 ▲ SO Track on left.
▼ 2.0 BR Well-used track on left.
7.9 ▲ SO Well-used track on right.
      GPS: N35°07.49' W115°01.00'

▼ 2.9 SO Track on right.
7.0 ▲ SO Track on left.
▼ 3.0 SO Track on right.
6.9 ▲ SO Track on left.
▼ 3.2 SO Well-used track on right.
6.7 ▲ SO Well-used track on left.
      GPS: N35°08.52' W115°01.23'

▼ 5.3 SO Pass through wire gate.
4.6 ▲ SO Pass through wire gate.
      GPS: N35°10.29' W115°01.78'

▼ 8.1 BR Track on left. Bear right to pass alongside dam.
1.8 ▲ SO Track on right rejoins.
      GPS: N35°12.70' W115°02.28'

▼ 8.4 SO Track on left rejoins.
1.5 ▲ BL Track on right. Bear left to pass alongside dam.

▼ 9.9 TR 4-way intersection with well-used trail. Intersection is unmarked. Zero trip meter.
0.0 ▲   Continue to the southeast, entering Lanfair Valley.
      GPS: N35°13.72' W115°03.60'

▼ 0.0   Continue to the northeast, leaving Lanfair Valley.
5.2 ▲ TL 4-way intersection with well-used trail. Intersection is unmarked. Zero trip meter.
▼ 1.2 SO Pass through wire gate.
4.0 ▲ SO Pass through wire gate.
      GPS: N35°14.68' W115°03.21'

▼ 2.5 SO Corral on left.
2.7 ▲ SO Corral on right.
      GPS: N35°15.85' W115°02.82'

▼ 2.9 SO Cross through wash.
2.3 ▲ SO Cross through wash.
▼ 3.1 SO Track on right.
2.1 ▲ BR Track on left.
      GPS: N35°16.29' W115°03.08'

▼ 3.5 SO Cross through wash.
1.7 ▲ SO Cross through wash.
▼ 3.6 SO Cross through wash.
1.6 ▲ SO Cross through wash.
▼ 5.2 TR T-intersection with well-used track. Intersection is unmarked. Zero trip meter. There is no access to the left through the large open pit mine of the Viceroy Company. Some of the old Hart mines are accessible from this point. No vehicle access onto tracks running northwest up the Castle Mountain ridge.
0.0 ▲   Continue to the northeast.
      GPS: N35°16.68' W115°05.02'

▼ 0.0   Continue to the north.
5.2 ▲ TL Turn left onto unmarked, small formed trail and zero trip meter. There is no access straight ahead through the large open pit mine of the Viceroy Company. Some of the old Hart mines are accessible from this point. No vehicle access onto the tracks running

northwest up the Castle Mountain
ridge.

▼ 0.3   SO   Track on left.
4.9 ▲   SO   Track on right.
▼ 1.9   SO   Track on left.
3.3 ▲   SO   Track on right.
        GPS: N35°18.00′ W115°04.33′

▼ 2.0   SO   Cross through wash.
3.2 ▲   SO   Cross through wash.
▼ 2.4   BL   Track on right.
2.8 ▲   BR   Track on left.
        GPS: N35°18.17′ W115°03.85′

▼ 2.6   TL   T-intersection with track in wash.
2.6 ▲   TR   Turn right out of wash. Track continues
             down wash.
        GPS: N35°18.16′ W115°03.65′

▼ 3.0   SO   Exit line of wash.
2.2 ▲   SO   Enter down line of wash.
▼ 3.4   SO   Enter down line of wash.
1.8 ▲   SO   Exit line of wash.
▼ 4.6   BL   Bear left out of wash.
0.6 ▲   BR   Bear right and enter line of wash.
▼ 4.7   SO   Pass through wire gate; then cross
             through wash.
0.5 ▲   SO   Cross through wash; then pass
             through wire gate.
        GPS: N35°19.55′ W115°02.70′

▼ 4.8   BR   Bear right down wash.
0.4 ▲   BL   Bear left out of wash.
▼ 4.9   BL   Bear left up second wash. Track on
             right down wash.
0.3 ▲   BR   Bear right up second wash. Track on
             left down wash.
        GPS: N35°19.63′ W115°02.58′

▼ 5.0   SO   Exit wash.
0.2 ▲   SO   Enter wash.
▼ 5.2   SO   Cross through wash; then Stray Cow
             Well on right. Crossing from California
             into Clark County, NV. State line is
             marked by a white post. Zero trip
             meter at well.
0.0 ▲   Continue to the southeast.
        GPS: N35°19.88′ W115°02.60′

▼ 0.0   Continue to the north past track on left.

▼ 5.6 ▲   SO   Track on right; then Stray Cow Well on
               left. Zero trip meter at well. Crossing
               from Nevada into California. State line
               is marked by a white post.
▼ 0.1   SO   Cross through wash; then track on left.
5.5 ▲   BL   Track on right; then cross through wash.
▼ 0.2   SO   Enter wash.
5.4 ▲   SO   Exit wash.
▼ 0.4   TL   Turn left and bear right up embank-
             ment. Track on left up side wash goes
             to Kennedy Well. Exit wash.
5.2 ▲   TR   Descend embankment. Track on right
             up side wash goes to Kennedy Well;
             then turn right and enter up wash.
        GPS: N35°20.18′ W115°02.40′

▼ 0.5   SO   Track on left.
5.1 ▲   SO   Track on right.
▼ 0.6   SO   Cross through wash; then track on right.
5.0 ▲   SO   Track on left; then cross through wash.
▼ 0.9   SO   Track on left.
4.7 ▲   SO   Track on right.
        GPS: N35°20.47′ W115°02.32′

▼ 1.2   SO   Enter wash.
4.4 ▲   SO   Exit wash.
▼ 1.5   SO   Entering Limited Use Area at sign. Trail
             is marked a designated route.
4.1 ▲   SO   Exiting Limited Use Area at sign.
        GPS: N35°20.70′ W115°01.75′

▼ 1.7   SO   Track on left to game tank.
3.9 ▲   SO   Track on right to game tank.
▼ 1.8   SO   Track on left to game tank.
3.8 ▲   SO   Track on right to game tank.
▼ 1.9   BL   Track on right is designated route.
3.7 ▲   BR   Track on left is designated route.
        GPS: N35°20.77′ W115°01.24′

▼ 2.0   SO   Cross through wide wash.
3.6 ▲   SO   Cross through wide wash.
▼ 2.4   SO   Cross through wide wash.
3.2 ▲   SO   Cross through wide wash.
▼ 3.1   SO   Cross through wide wash. Designated
             route on right and left up and down wash.
2.5 ▲   SO   Cross through wide wash. Designated
             route on left and right up and down wash.
        GPS: N35°21.49′ W115°00.29′

▼ 3.3   SO   Cross through wash.

2.3 ▲   SO Cross through wash.

▼ 3.4   SO Track on left is designated route.

2.2 ▲   SO Track on right is designated route.

▼ 3.9   SO Cross through wash; then track on left.

1.7 ▲   SO Track on right; then cross through wash.

▼ 4.0   SO Track on right is designated route.

1.6 ▲   SO Track on left is designated route.

        GPS: N35°21.99′ W114°59.90′

▼ 4.5   SO Track on left to game tank.

1.1 ▲   SO Second track on right to game tank.

▼ 4.6   SO Second track on left to game tank.

1.0 ▲   SO Track on right to game tank.

▼ 4.7   SO Track on left is designated route.

0.9 ▲   SO Track on right is designated route.

▼ 5.6   SO Well-used track on left around edge of deep wash is designated route. Zero trip meter.

0.0 ▲   Continue to the south.

        GPS: N35°23.38′ W115°00.56′

▼ 0.0   Continue to the north.

2.6 ▲   SO Second entrance to well-used track on right around edge of deep wash is designated route. Zero trip meter.

▼ 0.1   SO Second entrance to track on left.

2.5 ▲   BL Track on right.

▼ 0.4   SO Cross through wash. Cross through many washes for the next 2.2 miles.

2.2 ▲   SO Cross through wash. End of wash crossings.

▼ 2.6   TR T-intersection. Cross cattle guard and zero trip meter. End of wash crossings. Track is now following the old Barnwell & Searchlight Railroad embankment.

0.0 ▲   Continue to the southeast.

Piute Gorge

▼ 0.0   Continue to the northeast.

4.6 ▲ TL Cattle guard. Designated route continues ahead, following the old Barnwell & Searchlight Railroad embankment. Zero trip meter. Many wash crossings for the next 2.2 miles.

▼ 0.4 SO Cross through wash. Many wash crossings for the next 3.5 miles.

4.2 ▲ SO Cross through wash. End of wash crossings.

▼ 0.8 BL Cross through wash; then track on right goes to well.

3.8 ▲ SO Track on left goes to well; then cross through wash.

GPS: N35°26.01' W114°59.06'

▼ 1.0 SO Track on left and track on right at wash.

3.6 ▲ SO Track on left and track on right at wash.

▼ 1.2 SO Cattle guard.

3.4 ▲ SO Cattle guard.

▼ 3.0 SO Track on left.

1.6 ▲ SO Track on right.

▼ 3.9 TL 5-way intersection under power lines. Turn second left onto graded road under power lines. Old railroad embankment continues straight ahead, but is not used as a roadway past this point. End of wash crossings.

0.7 ▲ TR 5-way intersection. Turn second right onto formed trail that runs along old Barnwell & Searchlight Railroad embankment. Old railroad embankment continues to the left but is not used as a roadway. Many wash crossings for the next 3.5 miles.

GPS: N35°27.62' W114°56.33'

▼ 4.3 SO Track on left. Track on right is pipeline road. Continue straight ahead and cross cattle guard; then track on right and track on left.

0.3 ▲ BR Track on right and track on left; then cattle guard; then road splits three ways. Bear slightly right, taking the middle trail and keeping the power lines on your right.

GPS: N35°27.98' W114°56.26'

▼ 4.6 Track on left and right; then trail ends at intersection with paved Nevada 164. Turn right for Searchlight; turn left for Nipton, CA, and I-15.

0.0 ▲ Trail commences on paved Nevada 164, 1.1 miles west of intersection with US 95 in Searchlight. Zero trip meter and turn south on graded dirt road immediately before power lines. Immediately track on left and track on right.

GPS: N35°28.19' W114°56.24'

DESERT #15

New York Mountains Trail

STARTING POINT: Nevada 164, 6.9 miles west of Searchlight, NV

FINISHING POINT: Black Canyon Road, 0.2 miles south of the turn to Hole-in-the-Wall Visitor Center

TOTAL MILEAGE: 62.1 miles

UNPAVED MILEAGE: 62.1 miles

DRIVING TIME: 5 hours

ELEVATION RANGE: 4,000–5,600 feet

USUALLY OPEN: Year-round

BEST TIME TO TRAVEL: September to May

DIFFICULTY RATING: 2

SCENIC RATING: 9

REMOTENESS RATING: +0

Special Attractions

■ Town site of Hart.

■ Joshua tree forest in the Mojave National Preserve.

■ Access to hiking trails through oak forest in the New York Mountains, a rarity in the Mojave Desert.

■ Camp Rock Spring and Government Holes on Desert #13: Mojave Road.

History

Barnwell, formerly known as Manvel, was founded in 1893 at the foot of the New York Mountains. The Nevada Southern Railway Company was expected to construct a line north from Goffs. With this in mind, speculators moved in and established Manvel; six months later the railroad showed up. The new town was named after Allen Manvel, president of the Santa Fe Railroad. It became an important staging terminal for goods headed to Eldorado, Goodsprings, and the Ivanpah district. By the late 1890s freight teams were busy hauling goods from the railroad terminal at Manvel to Searchlight, Nevada.

Manvel supported two stores, a blacksmith, a butcher shop, saloons, and a small school. By 1902 the railroad company, which was now named California Eastern, had extended the line north to Ivanpah. This extension somewhat reduced the need for Manvel as a terminal. However, Searchlight continued to boom and stages and freight wagons kept Manvel thriving as a shipping depot.

The town's name was changed to Barnwell in 1907. By 1908, the need for improved transportation in and out of Searchlight brought about the construction of the Barnwell & Searchlight Railroad, and the decline of Barnwell.

The Santa Fe Railroad engaged the services of the only doctor in this region and appointed him to Barnwell. Although Dr. Haenszel lived in Searchlight, where most of his patients were, his appointment was to the smaller town of Barnwell because he was licensed to practice in California. In fact, the doctor covered a large area of desert, about 40 to 50 miles in radius, tending to miners and ranchers. No one complained that Nevada did not recognize his California license. Dr. Haenszel accepted this position because his own ill health forced him to live

Ox Ranch tank

in a dry climate. He had been confined to bed for years with tuberculosis, but he managed to keep up to date with his evolving profession while his wife tended to his needs.

The railroad station at Searchlight was quite substantial for its time, with living quarters on the first floor for the agent and his family. During its peak period, trains ran to Goffs daily except Sundays. A cattle loading ramp and a turntable for the tall-stack locomotive were installed. By 1923 the Santa Fe Railroad abandoned the line. Today, nothing but the concrete foundations of a tank and the railroad berm remain at the Searchlight Station.

Searchlight has experienced three eras since its founding in the 1890s. Initially, the town catered to ranchers and miners, and, like many Wild West towns, faded with the dwindling minerals in the region. The town lost the railroad and most of its residents by the end of this period in the 1920s.

Searchlight was revived between 1933 and 1935 with the construction of the Hoover Dam. Entertainment venues that were shunned, both in Boulder City and Las Vegas, flourished in Searchlight. Most of the workers had automobiles, and roads were improved by this time. Searchlight became an escape from the construction site, and workers could spend their money with few questions asked. Bordellos became big business in Searchlight. Associated crime and unscrupulous characters were attracted to the town. It was not until the late 1950s that Clark County authorities managed to curtail illegal businesses. The eventual closure and burning of the most prominent premises, El Rey, signaled the end of the world's oldest profession in Searchlight. Most of the old street frontages from the town's mining days were lost to fires as time passed.

The completion of US 95 from Needles to Las Vegas in the 1950s brought the next wave of people to Searchlight. This time it was travelers and tourists. Filling stations appeared on the main road through town, with restaurants and motels following close be-

hind. The new main street developed perpendicular to the old one. Traffic en route to Cottonwood Landing, on the Colorado River, brought many tourists to Searchlight as well. Some passing travelers decided that the fine climate, elevation, access to the river, desert attractions, and proximity to Las Vegas were enough reason to remain. Retirees filled the new streets with their trailers, bringing more activity than had been seen in the town in decades. A casino in the town center started operating in the late 1970s and has been one of the town's major employers.

In December 1907, Jim Hart and the Hitt brothers, Bert and Clark, discovered gold-bearing ore of rich proportions in the Castle Mountains in California. Hart sprang to life east of Manvel and immediately boomed. By April of the following year, the town had a hotel, post office, and stores that supported a population of several hundred. A newspaper ran from 1908 to 1909. The town apparently had neither a church nor a school.

Three mine names stood out, the Oro Belle, Jumbo, and Big Chief. Ore was transported 3.5 miles northwest to Hitt Siding on the Barnwell & Searchlight Railroad for processing in Searchlight. The Big Chief Mine eventually had its own mill. Hart seemed to have everything but liquor, apparently because liquor licenses were unavailable. Within a number of months, the high-grade ore dwindled and the attraction of Hart receded. The post office remained until 1915.

Silence returned to the Castle Mountains until 1984, when the mines reopened to make a profit using modern techniques. More than half a million ounces of gold had been extracted by the Viceroy Company by the mid-1990s.

The Walking Box Ranch, at the start of this trail in Nevada, was owned by silent-movie actress Clara Bow and her actor husband, Rex Bell. The ranch became headquarters for the Viceroy's mining operations for several years. The ranch, one of the earliest in the eastern Mojave region, has been listed on the National Register of Historic Places and has been restored to its former 1930s glory.

Stone chimney at the town site of Hart

Description

This trail runs from Searchlight, Nevada, to Desert #13: Mojave Road, which it joins for a short distance before continuing south. The standard is much easier than Mojave Road, being predominantly rough, graded dirt road, with some sections of easy formed trail. Unlike Mojave Road, which requires a 4WD vehicle, New York Mountains Trail can be driven in a high-clearance 2WD in dry weather. In wet weather or snow, it is likely to be impassable.

The trail commences along Walking Box Ranch Road, passing the ranch once owned by Clara Bow and Rex Bell. It follows their wide, graded dirt access road through a Joshua tree forest on the north side of the Castle Mountains. This access road is not accurately represented on maps. A short dis-

tance before an open pit mine, a spur leads to the site of Hart. A historical marker marks the site, which is now in the shadow of the modern open pit mine. A large chimney and wooden headframe are all that remains of the town. The coordinates of Hart town site are GPS: N35º17.18' W115º06.53'.

The main trail swings around the open pit mine, following a roughly graded road along the Barnwell & Searchlight Railroad grade for a short distance. At the small settlement of Barnwell, the trail joins the wide, graded Ivanpah Road, traveling south into the Mojave National Preserve near the old grade of the Ivanpah to Goffs railroad. It then turns off onto the smaller New York Mountains Road at a corral and water tank that still bear the mark of the Ox Cattle Company, once the major ranching interest in this region.

Joshua trees grow in front of the Castle Mountains

New York Mountains Road winds along the face of the jumbled range. A spur leads a short distance north up Caruthers Canyon, past a balanced rock toward some mines high on the mountainside. The mountains offer excellent hiking opportunities through oak forests that are left over from a time when the whole region was lush with vegetation. This is a beautiful canyon and well worth the slight detour.

The trail runs along Cedar Canyon Road for a short distance, following the course of Mojave Road, before it turns south along Black Canyon Road. The trail follows around the scenic loop of Wild Horse Canyon Road. The blocky mountains and wide valleys along this section make for some of the best scenery in the preserve. The trail finishes at the developed Hole-in-the-Wall Campground and Visitor Center.

Current Road Information
National Park Service
Mojave National Preserve
2701 Barstow Road
Barstow, CA 92311
(760) 252-6100

Map References
BLM   Mesquite Lake, Ivanpah
USGS 1:24,000   Hopps Well, Hart Peak,
       Castle Peaks, Grotto Hills, Pinto
       Valley, Mid Hills, Columbia Mt.
       1:100,000 Mesquite Lake, Ivanpah
Maptech CD-ROM: San Bernardino
       County/Mojave
Southern & Central California Atlas &
       Gazetteer, pp. 71, 72
Nevada Atlas & Gazetteer, p. 72
California Road & Recreation Atlas, p. 98
Trails Illustrated, Mojave National Preserve
       (256)

Route Directions

▼ 0.0   From Nevada 164, 6.9 miles west of Searchlight, 0.4 miles west of mile marker 12, zero trip meter and turn south on graded dirt Walking Box Ranch Road at sign. The road is also marked as a BLM designated route.

7.5 ▲   Trail ends at T-intersection with Nevada 164. Turn right for Searchlight, NV; turn left for Nipton, CA.
       GPS: N35°30.02′ W115°02.12′

▼ 0.2 SO Designated route on left and right.
7.3 ▲ SO Designated route on left and right.
▼ 0.7 BR Entrance to Walking Box Ranch on left.
6.8 ▲ BL Entrance to Walking Box Ranch on right.
▼ 1.1 SO Track on left.
6.4 ▲ SO Track on right.
▼ 3.0 SO Track on right; then corral on left.
4.5 ▲ SO Corral on right; then track on left.
       GPS: N35°27.44′ W115°03.26′

▼ 5.0 SO Cross over wash.
2.5 ▲ SO Cross over wash.
▼ 7.5 SO Designated route on left, opposite corral on right. Zero trip meter.
0.0 ▲   Continue to the north.
       GPS: N35°23.84′ W115°05.08′

▼ 0.0   Continue to the south.
8.7 ▲ SO Designated route on right, opposite corral on left. Zero trip meter.
▼ 1.1 SO Designated route on left.
7.6 ▲ SO Designated route on right.
▼ 2.1 SO Small track on right; then cross through wash.
6.6 ▲ SO Cross through wash; then small track on left.
▼ 3.3 SO Track on left and track on right.
5.4 ▲ SO Track on left and track on right.
       GPS: N35°21.33′ W115°06.20′

▼ 3.8 SO Track on right.
4.9 ▲ SO Track on left.
▼ 3.9 SO Track on right and track on left.
4.8 ▲ SO Track on left and track on right.
▼ 4.1 SO Track on left.
4.6 ▲ SO Track on right.
▼ 4.7 SO Track on left.
4.0 ▲ SO Track on right.
▼ 5.5 SO Track on left.
3.2 ▲ SO Track on right.
▼ 6.0 SO Track on left.
2.7 ▲ SO Track on right.
▼ 6.1 SO Cattle guard.
2.6 ▲ SO Cattle guard.
       GPS: N35°19.08′ W115°06.54′

DESERT #15: NEW YORK MOUNTAINS TRAIL

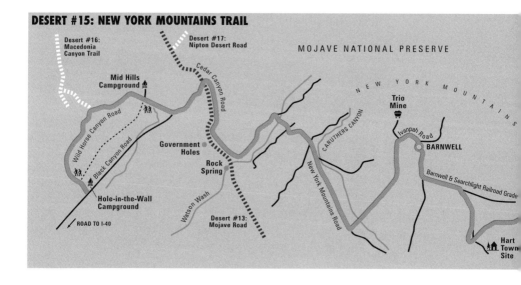

GPS: N35°16.66' W115°07.13'

▼ 7.5　SO　Track on right. Track on left goes past corral.

1.2 ▲　SO　Track on left. Track on right goes past corral.

GPS: N35°18.00' W115°07.33'

▼ 7.7　SO　Cattle guard.

1.0 ▲　SO　Cattle guard.

▼ 8.3　SO　Track on left.

0.4 ▲　SO　Track on right.

▼ 8.7　SO　Graded road on left and right. Intersection is unmarked, but there are stop signs on each side track. Zero trip meter. Road on left goes 1.2 miles to Hart town site.

0.0 ▲　　　Continue to the north.

GPS: N35°16.92' W115°07.14'

▼ 0.0　　　Continue to the southeast.

8.2 ▲　SO　Graded road on left and right. Intersection is unmarked, but there are stop signs on each side track. Zero trip meter. Road on right goes 1.2 miles to Hart town site.

▼ 0.3　TR　Turn sharp right onto graded road at water tank. Immediately small track on left. Workings of the open pit mine and buildings are visible ahead.

7.9 ▲　TL　Small track on right; then turn sharp left onto graded road at water tank. Workings of the open pit mine and buildings are visible ahead.

▼ 0.4　SO　Cross through wash.

7.8 ▲　SO　Cross through wash.

▼ 0.7　SO　Nursery on left provides native plants for revegetation of the mine.

7.5 ▲　SO　Nursery on right provides native plants for revegetation of the mine.

▼ 1.4　SO　Graded road on right; then cattle guard.

6.8 ▲　BR　Cattle guard; then graded road on left.

GPS: N35°17.37' W115°07.91'

▼ 1.5　SO　Track on right.

6.7 ▲　SO　Track on left.

▼ 1.8　SO　Track on right and well #15 on left.

6.4 ▲　SO　Track on left and well #15 on right.

▼ 2.1　SO　Track on right.

6.1 ▲　SO　Track on left.

▼ 2.2　SO　Track on right at well #24.

6.0 ▲　SO　Track on left at well #24.

▼ 2.6　SO　Track on right.

5.6 ▲　SO　Track on left.

▼ 3.1　SO　Track on right.

5.1 ▲　SO　Track on left.

GPS: N35°17.98' W115°09.60'

▼ 3.6　BL　Track on right is the Barnwell & Searchlight Railroad grade. Trail now joins the railroad grade.

4.6 ▲　BR　Track on left is continuation of railroad grade. Bear right away from the grade.

GPS: N35°17.95' W115°10.01'

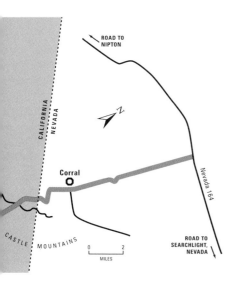

Barnwell. Private property on left and right.

▼ 0.1 SO Cross through wash.
7.0 ▲ SO Cross through wash.
▼ 0.9 SO Track on left.
6.2 ▲ SO Track on right.
▼ 1.2 SO Track on right goes to Trio Mine.
5.9 ▲ SO Track on left goes to Trio Mine.
   GPS: N35°16.79′ W115°14.81′

▼ 2.5 SO Cattle guard.
4.6 ▲ SO Cattle guard.
▼ 4.0 SO Cross through wash.
3.1 ▲ SO Cross through wash.
▼ 4.1 SO Railroad grade enters on left.
3.0 ▲ SO Railroad grade leaves on right.
▼ 4.3 SO Cross through wash; then track on right.
2.8 ▲ SO Track on left; then cross through wash.
▼ 4.6 SO Track on right.
2.5 ▲ SO Track on left.
▼ 5.1 SO Cross through wash.
2.0 ▲ SO Cross through wash.
▼ 5.3 SO Cross through wash.
1.8 ▲ SO Cross through wash.
▼ 5.7 SO Cross through wash.
1.4 ▲ SO Cross through wash.
▼ 6.6 SO Track on left.
0.5 ▲ SO Track on right.
▼ 6.8 SO Track on right.
0.3 ▲ SO Track on left.
▼ 7.1 TR Gate; then turn right onto the smaller, graded road marked New York Mountains Road. Zero trip meter. Turn is opposite a well and corral.
0.0 ▲ Continue to the northwest and pass through gate, following close to the old railroad grade.
   GPS: N35°12.18′ W115°12.11′

▼ 0.0 Continue to the west, leaving the railroad route, and pass through wire gate.
5.4 ▲ TL Wire gate; then turn left onto wider, graded road marked Ivanpah Road. Zero trip meter. Turn is opposite a well and corral.
▼ 0.9 SO Track on right.
4.5 ▲ SO Track on left.
▼ 3.0 SO Track on right and track on left. Crossing Ross Horse Pasture.

▼ 5.4 SO Track on right.
2.8 ▲ SO Track on left.
▼ 5.5 SO Cross through wash.
2.7 ▲ SO Cross through wash.
▼ 5.8 SO Track on left.
2.4 ▲ SO Track on right.
   GPS: N35°16.69′ W115°11.97′

▼ 6.1 SO Track on left.
2.1 ▲ SO Track on right.
▼ 7.5 SO Well and tank on left.
0.7 ▲ SO Well and tank on right.
   GPS: N35°17.34′ W115°13.44′

▼ 7.6 SO Track on right to corral and well.
0.6 ▲ SO Track on left to corral and well.
▼ 7.8 SO Well on left.
0.4 ▲ SO Well on right.
▼ 8.1 SO Cross through wash at Barnwell. Private property on left and right.
0.1 ▲ SO Leaving Barnwell. Cross through wash.
▼ 8.2 TL T-intersection with graded Ivanpah Road. Zero trip meter.
0.0 ▲ Continue to the southeast alongside the Barnwell & Searchlight Railroad grade.
   GPS: N35°17.56′ W115°14.15′

▼ 0.0 Continue to the southwest.
7.1 ▲ TR Turn right onto graded Hart Mine Road. Zero trip meter. This is the site of

2.4 ▲   SO Track on right and track on left.
             Crossing Ross Horse Pasture.
             GPS: N35°12.62' W115°15.32'

▼ 4.3   SO Cattle guard.
1.1 ▲   SO Cattle guard.
▼ 4.7   BL Well-used track on right.
0.7 ▲   BR Well-used track on left.
             GPS: N35°12.90' W115°17.07'

▼ 5.4   SO 4-way intersection. Track on right trav-
             els 2 miles toward Caruthers Canyon.
             Zero trip meter. Intersection is
             unmarked.
0.0 ▲   Continue to the northeast.
             GPS: N35°13.04' W115°17.82'

▼ 0.0   Continue to the southwest.
3.0 ▲   SO 4-way intersection. Track on left trav-
             els 2 miles toward Caruthers Canyon.
             Zero trip meter. Intersection is
             unmarked.
▼ 0.3   SO Track on left to mine.
2.7 ▲   SO Track on right to mine.
▼ 0.4   SO Track on right and track on left.
2.6 ▲   SO Track on right and track on left.
▼ 0.5   BL Track on right.
2.5 ▲   BR Track on left.
             GPS: N35°13.03' W115°18.36'

▼ 0.9   SO Track on right and track on left.
2.1 ▲   SO Track on right and track on left.
▼ 1.5   SO Track on left.
1.5 ▲   SO Track on right.
▼ 1.9   SO Well-used track on left and track
             on right.
1.1 ▲   SO Well-used track on right and track
             on left.
             GPS: N35°12.45' W115°19.33'

▼ 2.4   BL Track on right.
0.6 ▲   BR Track on left.
▼ 2.7   SO Track on left.
0.3 ▲   SO Track on right.
▼ 2.9   SO Cross through Watson Wash.
0.1 ▲   SO Cross through Watson Wash.
             GPS: N35°12.30' W115°20.40'

▼ 3.0   TL T-intersection. Track on right goes into
             Fourth of July Canyon. Zero trip meter.

0.0 ▲   Continue to the northeast.
             GPS: N35°12.30' W115°20.49'

▼ 0.0   Continue to the southeast.
3.5 ▲   TR Track straight ahead goes into Fourth
             of July Canyon. Zero trip meter.
▼ 0.1   SO Track on right.
3.4 ▲   BR Track on left.
▼ 0.6   SO Small track on left.
2.9 ▲   SO Small track on right.
▼ 1.1   SO Track on right through wire gate.
2.4 ▲   SO Track on left through wire gate.
▼ 1.3   SO Track on right; then Pinto Mountain
             on right.
2.2 ▲   SO Pinto Mountain on left; then track
             on left.
▼ 3.4   SO Cross through wash; then pipeline
             crosses track.
0.1 ▲   SO Pipeline crosses track; then cross
             through wash.
▼ 3.5   TR T-intersection with wide, graded Cedar
             Canyon Road. Trail briefly joins Desert
             #13: Mojave Road.
0.0 ▲   Continue to the north.
             GPS: N35°09.43' W115°19.90'

▼ 0.0   Continue to the west.
1.7 ▲   TL Turn left onto smaller graded road and
             bear slightly right. Trail leaves Desert
             #13: Mojave Road.
▼ 0.1   SO Track on left is Desert #13: Mojave
             Road, which leaves Cedar Canyon
             Road at this point.
1.6 ▲   SO Track on right is Desert #13: Mojave
             Road, which briefly joins Cedar Canyon
             Road at this point.
▼ 0.3   SO Track on left.
1.4 ▲   SO Track on right.
▼ 0.5   SO Track on right.
1.2 ▲   SO Track on left.
▼ 1.0   SO Track on right.
0.7 ▲   SO Track on left.
▼ 1.7   SO Track on left is Desert #13: Mojave
             Road, which rejoins New York
             Mountains Trail at this point. Zero trip
             meter.
0.0 ▲   Continue to the east.
             GPS: N35°09.18' W115°21.68'

▼ 0.0   Continue to the west.

3.3 ▲ BL Track on right is Desert #13: Mojave Road, which leaves New York Mountains Trail at this point. Zero trip meter.

▼ 0.1 SO Track on right.

3.2 ▲ SO Track on left.

▼ 0.3 SO Track on right; then cattle guard.

3.0 ▲ SO Cattle guard; then track on left.

▼ 0.7 SO Track on right.

2.6 ▲ SO Track on left.

▼ 1.7 SO Track on right; then cattle guard; then second track on right.

1.6 ▲ SO Track on left; then cattle guard; then second track on left.

▼ 2.4 SO Track on right.

0.9 ▲ SO Track on left.

▼ 3.3 TL Turn left onto graded dirt Black Canyon Road, following sign for Hole-in-the-Wall Campground and Mitchell Caverns. Zero trip meter. Desert #13: Mojave Road continues straight ahead at this point.

0.0 ▲ Continue to the northeast.

GPS: N35°10.45′ W115°24.65′

▼ 0.0 Continue to the southeast and cross through wash.

2.7 ▲ TR Cross through wash; then T-intersection with graded Cedar Canyon Road. Zero trip meter. Trail now follows Desert #13: Mojave Road for a short distance.

▼ 0.8 SO Track on left.

1.9 ▲ SO Track on right.

▼ 2.4 SO Track on right to Hollman Well.

0.3 ▲ SO Track on left to Hollman Well.

GPS: N35°08.43′ W115°24.10′

▼ 2.5 SO Corral and track on right.

0.2 ▲ SO Corral and track on left.

▼ 2.7 TR Turn right onto wide, graded dirt Wild Horse Canyon Road, following the sign to Mid Hills Campground. Zero trip meter.

0.0 ▲ Continue to the north.

GPS: N 35°08.19′ W115°24.10′

▼ 0.0 Continue to the west.

5.4 ▲ TL T-intersection with graded dirt Black Canyon Road. Zero trip meter and turn left, following the sign to Kelso Dunes.

▼ 1.5 SO Cross through wash.

3.9 ▲ SO Cross through wash.

▼ 1.9 SO Well on left. Hiking and horse trailhead for the Mid Hills to Hole-in-the-Wall Trail. Graded road on right goes into Mid Hills NPS Campground (fee charged).

3.5 ▲ SO Well on right. Hiking and horse trailhead for the Mid Hills to Hole-in-the-Wall Trail. Graded road on left goes into Mid Hills NPS Campground (fee charged).

GPS: N35°07.40′ W115°25.93′

▼ 2.6 SO Two tracks on right.

2.8 ▲ SO Two tracks on left.

▼ 2.7 SO Cattle guard.

2.7 ▲ SO Cattle guard.

▼ 3.8 SO Track on left.

1.6 ▲ SO Track on right.

▼ 5.4 SO Track on right is Desert #16: Macedonia Canyon Trail, marked by a post. Zero trip meter.

0.0 ▲ Continue to the north.

GPS: N35°04.73′ W115°27.35′

▼ 0.0 Continue to the south.

5.6 ▲ SO Track on left is Desert #16: Macedonia Canyon Trail, marked by a post. Zero trip meter.

▼ 0.9 SO Track on right to Willow Well; then cattle guard.

4.7 ▲ SO Cattle guard; then track on left to Willow Well.

▼ 1.5 SO Track on right and track on left.

4.1 ▲ SO Track on left and track on right.

▼ 2.5 SO Track on left.

3.1 ▲ SO Track on right.

▼ 4.6 SO Hiking and horse trailhead on left for Mid Hills to Hole-in-the-Wall Trail.

1.0 ▲ SO Hiking and horse trailhead on right for Mid Hills to Hole-in-the-Wall Trail.

GPS: N35°02.21′ W115°24.41′

▼ 5.0 SO Track on left; then cattle guard.

0.6 ▲ SO Cattle guard; then track on right.

▼ 5.1 SO Track on left.

0.5 ▲ SO Track on right.

▼ 5.5 SO Cross through wash.

0.1 ▲ SO Cross through wash.

▼ 5.6   Trail ends on paved Black Canyon
         Road, 0.2 miles south of the turn to
         Hole-in-the-Wall NPS Visitor Center
         and Campground (fee charged). Turn
         right for Mitchell Caverns and I-40;
         turn left to return to Cedar Canyon
         Road and Cima.

0.0 ▲   Trail commences on paved Black
         Canyon Road, 0.2 miles south of the
         turn to Hole -in-the-Wall NPS Visitor
         Center and Campground (fee charged),
         approximately 21 miles north of Essex
         Road exit of I-40. Zero trip meter and
         turn west on wide graded Wild Horse
         Canyon Road, marked with a post.
         GPS: N35°02.31′ W115°23.34′

DESERT #16

Macedonia Canyon Trail

STARTING POINT: Desert #15: New York
 Mountains Trail, 5.6 miles northwest
 of Hole-in-the-Wall Campground
FINISHING POINT: Kelso–Cima Road, 8 miles
 south of Cima
TOTAL MILEAGE: 8.1 miles, plus 1.9-mile spur
 to Columbia Mine
UNPAVED MILEAGE: 8.1 miles, plus 1.9-mile
 spur
DRIVING TIME: 1 hour
ELEVATION RANGE: 3,100–5,000 feet
USUALLY OPEN: Year-round
BEST TIME TO TRAVEL: September to June
DIFFICULTY RATING: 3
SCENIC RATING: 8
REMOTENESS RATING: +0

Special Attractions

■ Can be combined with Desert #15: New
 York Mountains Trail to exit to the west.
■ Long trail in a spectacular canyon.
■ Remains of the Columbia Mine.

History

The workings of the Columbia Mine include a shaft reaching a depth of 380 feet.
The mine was worked around the turn of
the twentieth century and a 5-stamp mill
operated on site. The gneiss vein followed
layers of dense, dark gray quartz and ortho-
clase. Records from the mid-1920s show the
Columbia ores yielded 35 ounces of silver
and 0.28 ounces of gold per ton.

Several copper mines were started in this
region with promising content at surface level. However, none paid well enough to continue digging beyond a few feet. Many of
these small excavations can be seen around
Columbia Mountain.

Description

Macedonia Canyon Trail is a sandy trail that
connects the southern end of Desert #15:
New York Mountains Trail with Kelso–Cima
Road. The trail is well marked at the start. It
immediately drops down into the loose, gravelly wash of Macedonia Canyon and descends steadily between the high walls of the
canyon, before spilling out onto the bajada
that leads down to Kelso Wash.

As the trail leaves Macedonia Canyon, a
spur leads 1.9 miles to the remains of the Columbia Mine that are scattered around the
hillside.

The trail officially ends by heading straight
out to Kelso–Cima Road. However this route
passes under the rail line at a point where there
is insufficient clearance for most vehicles: approximately 6 feet, 4 inches (this clearance may
change with build-up of sand). Taller vehicles
will need to bear north alongside the rail line to
exit at a point 2 miles farther north, where there
is greater clearance, approximately 7 feet, 4
inches. Whichever exit you chose, watch your
roofline carefully to avoid damage.

Current Road Information

National Park Service
Mojave National Preserve
2701 Barstow Road
Barstow, CA 92311
(760) 252-6100

Map References

BLM   Ivanpah
USGS 1:24,000   Columbia Mtn.,
       Hayden, Cima

1:100,000 Ivanpah
Maptech CD-ROM: San Bernardino
   County/Mojave
Southern & Central California Atlas &
   Gazetteer, p. 71
California Road & Recreation Atlas, p. 97
Trails Illustrated, Mojave National Preserve
   (256)

Route Directions

▼ 0.0   From graded dirt Wild Horse Canyon
   Road (part of Desert #15: New York
   Mountains Trail), 5.6 miles northwest
   of Hole-in-the-Wall Campground, zero
   trip meter and turn northwest onto
   formed Macedonia Canyon Trail and
   immediately pass through wire gate.

2.5 ▲   Trail ends at T-intersection with graded
   dirt Wild Horse Canyon Road (part of
   Desert #15: New York Mountains
   Trail). Turn right for Hole-in-the-Wall
   Campground; turn left to exit to Cedar
   Canyon Road.

GPS: N35°04.73' W115°27.35'

▼ 0.1   SO   Enter line of wash.
2.4 ▲   SO   Exit line of wash.
▼ 1.1   SO   Mine on left.
1.4 ▲   SO   Mine on right.
     GPS: N35°04.52' W115°28.39'

▼ 1.5   SO   Track on left. Exit Macedonia Canyon.
1.0 ▲   SO   Track on right. Enter Macedonia Canyon.
▼ 2.5   TR   T-intersection. Turn right and exit
   wash. Track on left is spur to Columbia
   Mine. Zero trip meter. There is a wood-
   en marker for Macedonia Canyon
   Wash Road at the intersection.
0.0 ▲   Continue to the northeast.
     GPS: N35°04.37' W115°29.88'

Spur to Columbia Mine

▼ 0.0   Proceed southeast.
▼ 0.1   SO   Track on right.
▼ 0.2   SO   Enter up wash. Track on right down wash.
▼ 0.6   BR   Track on left. Bear right in wash.

Remains of the Columbia Mine dugout

DESERT #16: MACEDONIA CANYON TRAIL

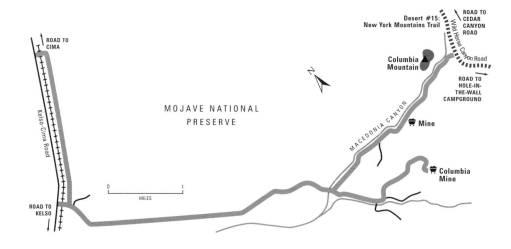

GPS: N35°03.95′ W115°29.46′

▼ 0.7 SO Track on right.
▼ 0.8 TL Turn left and exit wash. Track continues in wash.
      GPS: N35°03.89′ W115°29.32′

▼ 0.9 BR Bear right up wash.
▼ 1.0 SO Gate.
      GPS: N35°04.03′ W115°29.20′

▼ 1.6 SO Exit wash.
▼ 1.7 BL Track on right. Columbia Mine remains on left—concrete foundations, old machinery, and timber loading hoppers.
      GPS: N35°03.98′ W115°28.56′

▼ 1.8 SO Track on right rejoins; then dugout on left.
▼ 1.9 UT Spur ends at adit and remains of Columbia Mine.
      GPS: N35°03.88′ W115°28.57′

Continuation of Main Trail

▼ 0.0   Continue to the northwest.
3.6 ▲ TL Turn left and enter wash at wooden marker for Macedonia Canyon Wash Road. Track ahead is spur to Columbia Mine. Zero trip meter.
      GPS: N35°04.37′ W115°29.88′

▼ 3.5 SO Wire gate.
0.1 ▲ SO Wire gate. Trail is marked Macedonia Canyon.

▼ 3.6 TR Track on right; then pass under rail line to exit to paved Kelso–Cima Road. This underpass is very low, approximately 6′4″ in height. Tall vehicles should zero trip meter and turn right along unmarked small track alongside railroad.
0.0 ▲   Continue to the southeast.
      GPS: N35°06.05′ W115°32.97′

▼ 0.0   Continue to the northeast alongside rail line.
2.0 ▲ TL Turn left onto formed trail away from rail line. To the right is the exit to Kelso–Cima Road for shorter vehicles. Zero trip meter.

▼ 2.0   Turn left and pass under rail line. Trail finishes on paved Kelso-Cima Road. Turn right for Cima; turn left for Kelso.
0.0 ▲   Trail commences on Kelso–Cima Road, 8 miles south of Cima and 3.6 miles south of the intersection with Black Canyon Road. Zero trip meter and turn east. Pass under rail line; then immediately turn right (south) and follow alongside rail line on formed sandy trail.
      GPS: N35°07.60′ W115°32.04′

Nipton Desert Road

STARTING POINT: I-15 at Primm, NV
FINISHING POINT: Desert #13: Mojave Road, 2.8 miles southwest of intersection with Black Canyon Road
TOTAL MILEAGE: 41.4 miles, plus spurs
UNPAVED MILEAGE: 41.4 miles, plus spurs
DRIVING TIME: 4 hours
ELEVATION RANGE: 2,600–4,500 feet
USUALLY OPEN: Year-round
BEST TIME TO TRAVEL: September to June
DIFFICULTY RATING: 2
SCENIC RATING: 8
REMOTENESS RATING: +0

Special Attractions

- Old railroad sidings and the San Pedro, Los Angeles & Salt Lake Railroad.
- Long, easygoing Mojave Desert trail through dense Joshua tree forests.
- Remains of the Death Valley and Lucy Gray Mines.

History

During the Pleistocene period, the dry Ivanpah Lake and surrounding Ivanpah Valley were believed to have been under water. Paleo-Indians camped along the shoreline and surrounding hills, which supported juniper woodlands. As the region dried out, plant life receded to the mountain tops, and lake-dwelling toads, turtles, and pupfish lost their habitat.

Nipton Trading Post

The most northerly siding in California along this stretch of the Union Pacific Railroad gained its name like a lot of early borderline camps. Calada is a shortened version of California and Nevada. The Calada Railway Siding sits on the old Von Schmidt Boundary line of 1873.

Nipton, to the south along the railroad, was originally known as Nippeno Camp, a name taken from a local mine just over the Nevada state line. The settlement developed in the 1870s at the intersection of two trade routes where freight wagon drivers camped en route to nearby mines. The developing camp gained additional trade on February 9, 1905, when the first train arrived on the newly constructed San Pedro, Los Angeles & Salt Lake Railroad.

The name was changed to Nipton when the San Pedro, Los Angeles & Salt Lake merged with the Union Pacific around 1910. A regular stagecoach and freight service ran from the railroad to Searchlight, Nevada. Construction of the Hotel Nipton was completed by 1910, during the local mining boom. For many years, the depot was a cattle loading station for several local ranches, including one of the earliest, the Yates Ranch, whose headquarters were at Valley Wells on the west side of the Ivanpah Mountains. Other notable ranches included the Walking Box and Rock Springs Land and Cattle Company. The town became a supply center for the Clark Mining District. It was also a social center for the widely dispersed population of the region, supporting a school, post office, and several small businesses.

In the 1920s, the nearby Walking Box Ranch, just inside the Nevada border, was purchased by the famous Hollywood silent movie stars, Clara Bow and her husband, Rex Bell. They ran cattle on the ranch and herded them to the Nipton Siding when shipping them to market. Clara entertained a number of Hollywood guests, who availed themselves of the Nipton Hotel's hospitality. A car service dropped houseguests off at the stylish Walking Box Ranch headquarters en route to Searchlight, Nevada.

The small settlement of Nipton endured boom and bust times over the following decades and by the early 1950s, the railroad station was abandoned and Nipton became just another siding along the long desert railroad.

During the mid-1980s, large-scale mining at the nearby Old Hart, Morning Star, and Colosseum Mines brought life back to the Nipton Hotel and store, somewhat of a return to the boom of early Nippeno Camp. By the turn of the twenty-first century, Nipton was no longer totally reliant on fluctuating mining activities. The small settlement has established itself as a remote destination, where travelers can relax and sample the untamed desert.

The name Ivanpah comes from the Chemehuevi word *aavimpa,* which means white clay water, sometimes called sweet water. Ivanpah was the earliest settlement and boomtown in the eastern Mojave region as a result of mining activities in 1870. At its peak, the town's population approached 500, mainly miners. Though the camp came and went by the close of the nineteenth century, the name lingered and was attached to a nearby railroad station.

Thomas Place, near the southern end of the trail, gained its name from Lewis and his brother "Wimpy" Thomas, who used the cabin there.

Description
Nipton Desert Road follows what is now the Union Pacific Railroad for the majority of its length. Commencing next to the state line in Primm, Nevada, the trail heads out along the desert trails to the east. Once it reaches the railroad, the trail swings south, following the roughly graded road that parallels the rail line. It passes the sidings that once served trains along the old San Pedro, Los Angeles & Salt Lake Railroad. The sidings are now little more than names on the map.

The small settlement of Nipton, California, survives more than a century after it blossomed in this remote desert area. Nipton currently has a general store, hotel, and cantina. There is no gas available. Continuing south along the railroad into the Mojave National Preserve, the trail becomes formed and narrow before rejoining the graded road approaching Ivanpah Siding. This section of the trail offers stunning views of the New York Mountains, and passes through a dense forest of Joshua trees, yuccas, and other desert vegetation.

The remains of the Death Valley Mine are close to Cima. A spur trail leads 5.6 miles into the Mid Hills to some mining remains. Death Valley Mine is posted as no trespassing, but the trail passes the gate and offers a good view of the old buildings.

The main trail continues south on a small formed trail, passing the Thomas Place well and tank to finish on the graded dirt Cedar Canyon Road, part of Desert #13: Mojave Road.

Current Road Information
National Park Service
Mojave National Preserve
2701 Barstow Road
Barstow, CA 92311
(760) 252-6100

Map References
BLM   Mesquite Lake, Ivanpah
USGS 1:24,000   Ivanpah Lake, Desert,
        Nipton, Ivanpah, Joshua, Mid Hills
        1:100,000 Mesquite Lake, Ivanpah
Maptech CD-ROM: San Bernardino
        County/Mojave
Southern & Central California Atlas & Gazetteer, pp. 57, 71
California Road & Recreation Atlas, p. 98
Trails Illustrated, Mojave National Preserve (256)

Route Directions

▼ 0.0   Trail commences at Primm, NV, on the east side of I-15. Zero trip meter and continue east on the paved Underpass Road.
1.6 ▲   Trail ends in Primm, NV, on the east side of I-15.
          GPS: N35°36.75′ W115°23.23′

▼ 0.1   SO Stoplight.
1.5 ▲   SO Stoplight.

▼ 0.2   TR Turn right onto unmarked paved road immediately before RV park.
1.4 ▲   TL T-intersection with Underpass Road.
          GPS: N35°36.78′ W115°23.00′

▼ 0.3   TL Turn left at the end of the paved road onto graded dirt road under power lines.
1.3 ▲   TR Turn right onto paved road on the outskirts of Primm.
          GPS: N35°36.58′ W115°22.92′

▼ 0.7   TR 4-way intersection under power lines. Turn right and follow along fence line.
0.9 ▲   TL 4-way intersection under power lines.
          GPS: N35°36.72′ W115°22.74′

▼ 0.9   TL Turn left away from the fence line on well-used, formed trail.
0.7 ▲   TR T-intersection. Turn right along fence line.
          GPS: N35°36.51′ W115°22.73′

▼ 1.3   SO Track on left and track on right; then second track on left and track on right.
0.3 ▲   SO Track on left and track on right; then second track on left and track on right.

▼ 1.5   SO Track on left.
0.1 ▲   SO Track on right.

▼ 1.6   TR T-intersection with track alongside railroad. Zero trip meter.
0.0 ▲   Continue to the northwest. Immediately track on left.
          GPS: N35°36.12′ W115°22.13′

▼ 0.0   Continue to the south.
6.4 ▲   TL Turn left onto well-used trail away from railroad and zero trip meter.

▼ 0.3   SO Cross through wash.
6.1 ▲   SO Cross through wash.

▼ 0.4   SO Cattle guard.
6.0 ▲   SO Cattle guard.
          GPS: N35°35.76′ W115°22.20′

▼ 0.6   SO Cross through wash; then track on right; then California state line at cattle guard. Entering San Bernardino County, CA.
5.8 ▲   SO Cattle guard at the Nevada state line. Entering Clark County, NV. Track on left; then cross through wash.
          GPS: N35°35.50′ W115°22.24′

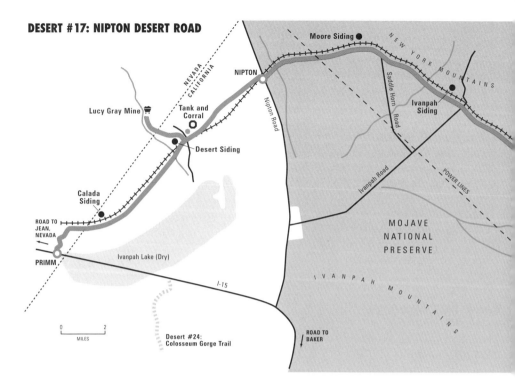

▼ 4.0   SO   Maintenance track on left.

▼ 1.0   SO   Cross through wash.
2.4 ▲   BL   Maintenance track on right.
5.4 ▲   SO   Cross through wash.
▼ 4.8   SO   Cross through wash.
▼ 1.6   SO   Site of Calada Railway Siding.
1.6 ▲   SO   Cross through wash.
4.8 ▲   SO   Site of Calada Railway Siding.
▼ 5.2   SO   Cross through wash.
         GPS: N35°34.69' W115°22.16'
1.2 ▲   SO   Cross through wash.
▼ 5.6   SO   Track on right.
▼ 1.8   SO   Cross through wash. Track on left up
0.8 ▲   SO   Track on left.
              wash under bridge.
▼ 5.7   SO   Cross through wash; then track on right.
4.6 ▲   SO   Cross through wash. Track on right up
0.7 ▲   SO   Track on left; then cross through wash.
              wash under bridge.
▼ 6.3   SO   Desert Siding. There is a private house
▼ 2.1   SO   Cross through wash.
              and a water tower.
4.3 ▲   SO   Cross through wash.
0.1 ▲   SO   Desert Siding. There is a private house
▼ 2.4   SO   Cross through wash; then track on right.
              and a water tower.
4.0 ▲   SO   Track on left; then cross through wash.
         GPS: N35°31.35' W115°18.94'
▼ 3.0   SO   Cross through wash.
3.4 ▲   SO   Cross through wash.
▼ 6.4   TL   Track on right is a dead end. Track
▼ 3.4   SO   Cross through wash.
              continues ahead on west side of rail-
3.0 ▲   SO   Cross through wash.
              road. Turn left and pass under rail line;
▼ 3.8   BR   Maintenance track on left.
              then turn immediately right and contin-
2.6 ▲   SO   Maintenance track on right.
              ue south on the east side of the line.
         GPS: N35°32.97' W115°20.88'
              Track on left. Track straight ahead is
              the spur to the Lucy Gray Mine. Zero
▼ 3.9   SO   Cross through wash.
              trip meter under rail line.
2.5 ▲   SO   Cross through wash.
0.0 ▲   Continue to the northwest.

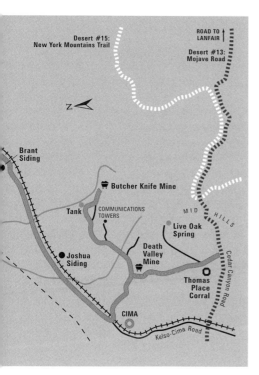

GPS: N35°31.28' W115°18.85'

Spur to Lucy Gray Mine

▼ 0.0   Continue to the northeast from the railroad bridge and cross cattle guard. Immediately track on right.

▼ 0.6   BR   Track on left.
               GPS: N35°31.70' W115°18.52'

▼ 1.1   SO   Enter up line of wash.

▼ 1.5   SO   Cross state line (unmarked) back into Nevada.
               GPS: N35°32.46' W115°18.08'

▼ 1.6   SO   Enter wash at mouth of canyon into Lucy Gray Mountains.

▼ 1.8   BR   Track on left.
               GPS: N35°32.64' W115°17.90'

▼ 2.1   BR   Mine on left; then bear right up wash past track on left.
               GPS: N35°32.68' W115°17.58'

▼ 2.2   Bear left out of wash. Small mines are

scattered around the hillside, including the Lucy Gray.
               GPS: N35°32.70' W115°17.43'

Continuation of Main Trail

▼ 0.0   Continue to the southeast. Road is now paved.

4.3 ▲   TR   Track on right is the spur to the Lucy Gray Mine. Track straight ahead. Turn left and pass under rail line. Zero trip meter. Turn second right on west side of rail line onto roughly graded road that remains below the railroad tracks. Track straight ahead is a dead end.
               GPS: N35°31.28' W115°18.85'

▼ 0.2   SO   Corral and tank on left.

4.1 ▲   SO   Corral and tank on right.

▼ 0.8   BL   Track on right. Remain on paved road and cross cattle guard. Railroad leaves on right.

3.5 ▲   BR   Cattle guard. Track on left. Remain on paved road. Trail runs alongside the Union Pacific Railroad.

▼ 3.0   SO   Cattle guard; then track on right.

1.3 ▲   SO   Track on left; then cattle guard.

▼ 3.2   SO   Track on right.

1.1 ▲   SO   Track on left.

▼ 3.3   SO   Track on left.

1.0 ▲   SO   Track on right.

▼ 3.7   SO   Track on right. Railroad rejoins on right.

0.6 ▲   SO   Track on left. Railroad leaves on left.

▼ 4.3   TR   Turn right onto paved Nipton Road at Nipton and cross over railroad. Zero trip meter.

0.0 ▲   Continue to the northwest.
               GPS: N35°28.03' W115°16.29'

▼ 0.0   Continue to the southeast.

5.5 ▲   TL   Cross over railroad and turn left onto small paved road, marked Nipton Desert Road. Zero trip meter.

▼ 0.1   TL   Turn left onto graded dirt road running on the west side of the railroad. The road is marked Nipton-Moore Road.

5.4 ▲   TR   Turn right onto the paved Nipton Road at Nipton.
               GPS: N35°28.00' W115°16.35'

▼ 0.4 SO Cross through wash.
5.1 ▲ SO Cross through wash.
▼ 0.8 SO Cross through wash.
4.7 ▲ SO Cross through wash.
▼ 1.2 SO Cross through wash.
4.3 ▲ SO Cross through wash.
▼ 1.6 SO Cross through wash.
3.9 ▲ SO Cross through wash.
▼ 2.2 SO Cross through wash. Track on left up
wash.
3.3 ▲ SO Cross through wash. Track on right up
wash.
GPS: N35°26.26′ W115°15.65′

▼ 2.6 SO Cross through wash; then track on
right along power lines.
2.9 ▲ SO Track on left along power lines; then
cross through wash.
▼ 3.1 SO Cross through wash.
2.4 ▲ SO Cross through wash.
▼ 3.4 SO Cross through wash.
2.1 ▲ SO Cross through wash.
▼ 3.7 SO Cross through wash.
1.8 ▲ SO Cross through wash.
▼ 4.1 SO Cross through wash.
1.4 ▲ SO Cross through wash.
▼ 4.4 SO Moore Siding on left.
1.1 ▲ SO Moore Siding on right.
GPS: N35°24.28′ W115°15.49′

▼ 4.5 SO Cross through wash.
1.0 ▲ SO Cross through wash.
▼ 5.5 BL Graded road on right over cattle guard
is Saddle Horn Road. Zero trip meter.
0.0 ▲ Continue to the northeast alongside
railroad.
GPS: N35°23.36′ W115°15.84′

▼ 0.0 Continue to the southwest alongside
railroad.
4.4 ▲ SO Graded road on left over cattle guard is
Saddle Horn Road. Zero trip meter.
▼ 0.1 SO Cross through wash.
4.3 ▲ SO Cross through wash.
▼ 0.6 SO Cross through wash.
3.8 ▲ SO Cross through wash.
▼ 1.4 SO Cross over wash.
3.0 ▲ SO Cross over wash.
▼ 2.5 BR Cross through wash. Track on left up
wash. Then track on left.

1.9 ▲ SO Track on right; then cross through
wash. Track on right up wash.
GPS: N35°21.63′ W115°17.59′

▼ 3.1 SO Cross through wash.
1.3 ▲ SO Cross through wash.
▼ 3.4 TR Turn right alongside railroad; maintenance track on left.
1.0 ▲ TL Turn left away from railroad; maintenance track straight ahead.
GPS: N35°21.01′ W115°18.13′

▼ 3.6 SO Track on left.
0.8 ▲ BL Track on right.
▼ 3.7 SO Cross through wash. Ivanpah Siding
on left.
0.7 ▲ SO Ivanpah Siding on right. Cross through
wash.
▼ 4.4 SO Cross over paved Ivanpah Road and
continue straight ahead on west side
of railroad. Zero trip meter.
0.0 ▲ Continue to the northeast.
GPS: N35°20.30′ W115°18.76′

▼ 0.0 Continue to the southwest.
4.5 ▲ SO Cross over paved Ivanpah Road and
continue straight ahead. Zero trip
meter.
▼ 0.1 SO Cross through wash.
4.4 ▲ SO Cross through wash.
▼ 0.6 BL Cattle guard; then track on right.
3.9 ▲ SO Track on left; then cattle guard.
▼ 1.3 SO Cross through wash.
3.2 ▲ SO Cross through wash.
▼ 2.0 SO Cross through wash.
2.5 ▲ SO Cross through wash.
▼ 2.4 SO Track on right.
2.1 ▲ SO Track on left.
▼ 2.8 BL Track on right is marked as Lawler Lane.
1.7 ▲ SO Track on left is marked as Lawler Lane.
GPS: N35°18.50′ W115°20.87′

▼ 3.3 SO Cross through wash.
1.2 ▲ SO Cross through wash.
▼ 4.4 SO Wire gate on left at the start of track
alongside railroad.
0.1 ▲ SO Wire gate on right at the start of track
alongside railroad.
GPS: N35°17.53′ W115°22.23′

▼ 4.5 BR Wire gate on left at the start of track alongside railroad. Leave railroad. Trail is now smaller and formed. This is Brant Siding. Zero trip meter.

0.0 ▲ Continue to the north.

GPS: N35°17.50′ W115°22.32′

▼ 0.0 Continue to the west.

6.5 ▲ BL Wire gate on right at the start of track alongside railroad. Bear left alongside railroad. Trail is now wider and roughly graded. This is Brant Siding. Zero trip meter.

▼ 0.2 SO Cross through wash.

6.3 ▲ SO Cross through wash.

▼ 0.4 SO Small track on left.

6.1 ▲ SO Small track on right.

▼ 0.9 SO Cross through wash.

5.6 ▲ SO Cross through wash.

▼ 1.2 SO Track on left; then cross through wash.

5.3 ▲ SO Cross through wash; then track on right.

▼ 1.5 SO Cross through wash.

5.0 ▲ SO Cross through wash.

▼ 2.1 SO Track on right.

4.4 ▲ BR Track on left.

GPS: N35°17.12′ W115°24.30′

▼ 2.6 SO Cross through wash.

3.9 ▲ SO Cross through wash.

▼ 3.5 SO Cross through wash.

3.0 ▲ SO Cross through wash.

▼ 4.2 SO Cross through wash; then Joshua Siding on left.

2.3 ▲ SO Joshua Siding on right; then cross through wash.

GPS: N35°16.47′ W115°26.51′

▼ 4.8 SO Cross through wash.

1.7 ▲ SO Cross through wash.

▼ 4.9 SO Cross through wash.

1.6 ▲ SO Cross through wash.

▼ 5.3 SO Cross through wash.

1.2 ▲ SO Cross through wash.

GPS: N35°16.01′ W115°27.58′

▼ 6.5 SO Pass through wire gate; then cross through wash; then pass through second wire gate onto road alongside railroad. Zero trip meter between gates.

0.0 ▲ Continue to the north.

GPS: N35°15.27′ W115°28.68′

▼ 0.0 Continue to the south.

1.6 ▲ BL Pass through wire gate; then cross through wash; then bear left and pass through second wire gate onto small formed trail. Gate on right continues alongside railroad. Zero trip meter between gates.

▼ 0.1 BR Bear right onto graded road below railroad.

1.5 ▲ SO Track on right.

▼ 0.6 SO Track on left; then cross through wash.

1.0 ▲ BL Cross through wash; then track on right.

▼ 1.6 TL Turn left and cross over railroad. Immediately road on right and track on left. Zero trip meter. Turning right at this point takes you immediately out to paved Kelso–Cima Road at Cima.

0.0 ▲ Continue to the northeast.

GPS: N35°14.26′ W115°29.86′

▼ 0.0 Continue to the southeast.

2.3 ▲ TR Road on left and track on right; then cross over railroad and turn right alongside railroad. Zero trip meter. Continuing straight at this point takes you immediately out to paved Kelso–Cima Road at Cima.

▼ 0.6 SO Cattle guard.

1.7 ▲ SO Cattle guard.

▼ 1.8 SO Cross through wash.

0.5 ▲ SO Cross through wash.

▼ 2.3 BR Bear right onto smaller trail. Track on left is spur to the Death Valley and Butcher Knife Mines. The mines are posted as private property. Zero trip meter.

0.0 ▲ Continue to the northwest.

GPS: N35°13.42′ W115°27.87′

Spur to Death Valley and Butcher Knife Mines

▼ 0.0 Continue to the east.

▼ 0.2 BL Death Valley Mine on right.

GPS: N35°13.33′ W115°27.71′

▼ 0.9 SO Track on right.

GPS: N35°13.50′ W115°26.90′

▼ 1.7 BL Track on right goes to communications towers.

▼ 1.9 SO Cross through wash; then track on right.

▼ 3.8 SO Corral and tank on left.
       GPS: N35°14.92′ W115°24.58′

▼ 4.5 TL Track continues straight ahead.
       GPS: N35°14.42′ W115°24.30′

▼ 5.1 SO Cross through wash.

▼ 5.3 TR Track continues straight ahead.
       GPS: N35°14.31′ W115°23.49′

▼ 5.6   Trail ends at the Butcher Knife Mine—timber-lined shaft and tailings.
       GPS: N35°14.26′ W115°23.45′

Continuation of Main Trail

▼ 0.0   Continue to the south.

3.2 ▲ SO Track on right is spur to Death Valley and Butcher Knife Mines. The mines are posted as private property. Zero trip meter.
       GPS: N35°13.42′ W115°27.87′

▼ 0.3 SO Cross through wash.

2.9 ▲ SO Cross through wash.

▼ 0.4 SO Mine workings on left.

2.8 ▲ SO Mine workings on right.
       GPS: N35°13.11′ W115°27.89′

▼ 0.7 SO Cross through wash.

2.5 ▲ SO Cross through wash.

▼ 1.5 SO Cross through wash.

1.7 ▲ SO Cross through wash.

▼ 1.9 SO Cross through wash.

1.3 ▲ SO Cross through wash.

▼ 2.2 SO Cross through two washes.

1.0 ▲ SO Cross through two washes.

▼ 3.2 BR 4-way intersection. Track on sharp left goes to Live Oak Spring. Zero trip meter and bear right toward the corral.

0.0 ▲   Continue to the northwest.
       GPS: N35°10.60′ W115°27.68′

▼ 0.0   Continue to the south.

1.1 ▲ BL 4-way intersection. Track straight ahead goes to Live Oak Spring. Zero

trip meter and bear left, rejoining main trail.

▼ 0.1 TL Turn left in front of Thomas Place corral, tank, and cabin.

1.0 ▲ TR Thomas Place corral, tank, and cabin ahead.
       GPS: N35°10.54′ W115°27.73′

▼ 0.2 TR Turn right to rejoin main trail.

0.9 ▲ TL Turn left toward corral and tank.

▼ 0.9 SO Track on left.

0.2 ▲ SO Track on right.

▼ 1.0 BR Track on left and track straight ahead.

0.1 ▲ BL Track on right and track straight ahead.

▼ 1.1   Trail ends at intersection with graded dirt Cedar Canyon Road, part of Desert #13: Mojave Road. Turn left to travel the road to Lanfair; turn right to exit to Cima and the Kelso–Cima Road.

0.0 ▲   Trail commences on graded dirt Cedar Canyon Road, part of Desert #13: Mojave Road, 2.8 miles southwest of intersection with Black Canyon Road and 2.9 miles southeast of intersection with Kelso–Cima Road. Zero trip meter and turn north on unmarked, well-used formed trail that runs alongside a fence line.
       GPS: N35°09.83′ W115°27.41′

Cima Dome Trail

STARTING POINT: Cima Road, 10 miles south of I-15, 1.2 miles northwest of the Teutonia Peak Hiking Trailhead

FINISHING POINT: Kelbaker Road, 19 miles southeast of Baker

TOTAL MILEAGE: 19.4 miles

UNPAVED MILEAGE: 19.4 miles

DRIVING TIME: 1.5 hours

ELEVATION RANGE: 3,200–5,100 feet

USUALLY OPEN: Year-round

BEST TIME TO TRAVEL: September to May

DIFFICULTY RATING: 2

SCENIC RATING: 8

REMOTENESS RATING: +1

Tall Joshua trees along Cima Road

Special Attractions

- Cima Dome and Cinder Cones.
- Views from Cima Dome over the Mojave Desert to the Kingston Range.
- Excellent example of a dense Joshua tree forest.

History

Cima Dome is an almost perfectly rounded landform consisting of quartz monzonite. Because of its immense size, its symmetrical shape is not always apparent at close range. A study of a topographical map shows how evenly the circular contour lines are spaced. Geologists describe this landform as a molten mass that stopped rising well before it reached the earth's surface, a feature referred to as a batholith. The massive dome rises as high as 1,500 feet above the surrounding desert area and supports one of the most striking Joshua tree forests in the Southwest. Cima (Spanish for "summit") Dome is approximately 10 miles in diameter and covers nearly 75 square miles. The name Cima was adopted by the nearby Union Pacific Railroad station in 1907.

Farther southwest along this trail are many small cinder cones. Some eruptions occurred 7 million years ago; the most recent was around 10,000 years ago. Lava spewed during violent eruptions cooled almost instantly, capturing bubbles of gas within. Eruptions continued for a long period of time, slowly developing the high cinder cones we see along the trail today. There are 53 vents and over 60 flows spread across this lava landscape.

The cinder cones near Black Tank Wash are the site of several cinder mines. The Valco cinder sites were discovered in 1954 and the nearby Red Beauty in 1955. Although a lot of mining activity occurred—screening plants were established on-site and roads were built to truck the material out—the mining claims were declared void by the BLM in the 1980s. The case was tied up in court for years before it was declared that the claims lacked marketability; they were not able to turn a profit when operating in the 1950s, and on these grounds should have been discontinued.

DESERT #18: CIMA DOME TRAIL

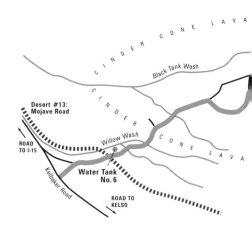

Description

The trail commences on Cima Road, a short distance from the popular hiking trailhead to Teutonia Peak in the Mojave National Preserve. Initially the trail is a graded dirt road that leads to the active Valley View Ranch. The trail passes through the middle of the ranch's yards, so be aware that there may be people and animals around. Past the ranch, the trail becomes a well-used, formed sandy trail. It runs high along the north face of Cima Dome. The elevation gives excellent views to the north over Shadow Valley toward the Clark Range and the distant Kingston Range.

The trail passes by a series of water tanks, corrals, and extensive Joshua tree forests. Desert #13: Mojave Road intersects this trail near Willow Wash, which provides an excellent example of the shapes lava may take as it cools. The trail then joins a roughly graded road and travels through the cinder pit of the Aikens Mine before descending the north slope to finish on paved Kelbaker Road.

Current Road Information

National Park Service
Mojave National Preserve
2701 Barstow Road
Barstow, CA 92311
(760) 252-6100

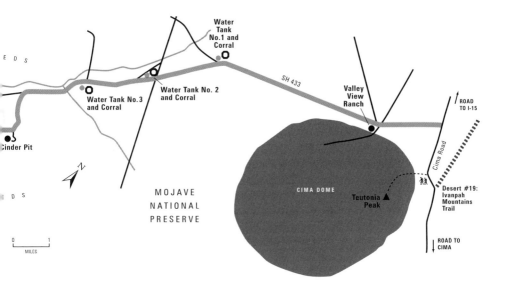

Map References

BLM   Ivanpah
USGS   1:24,000   Cima Dome, Cow Cave,
Marl Mtn., Indian Spring
1:100,000 Ivanpah
Maptech CD-ROM: San Bernardino
County/Mojave
*Southern & Central California Atlas &
Gazetteer,* pp. 71, 70
California Road & Recreation Atlas, p. 97
Trails Illustrated, Mojave National Preserve
(256)

Route Directions

▼ 0.0   From Cima Road, 10 miles south of I-
15 and 1.2 miles northwest of Teutonia
Peak Hiking Trailhead, zero trip meter
and turn southwest on small graded
dirt road. There is a sign for Valley
View Ranch at the intersection.
6.0 ▲   Trail ends at T-intersection with paved
Cima Road. Turn right for Cima; turn
left for I-15.
GPS: N35°20.01′ W115°33.50′

▼ 1.6   BL   Bear left of main shed. Track on right.
4.4 ▲   BR   Bear right of main shed; then track
on left.
GPS: N35°19.19′ W115°34.93′

▼ 1.7   SO   4-way intersection. Proceed through
the Valley View Ranch yard, leaving
the homestead on left. Track on right.
Proceed southwest and follow formed
trail, marked with BLM post SH 433 for
4WDs, ATVs, and motorbikes.
4.3 ▲   SO   Track on left; then 4-way intersection.
Continue straight, leaving homestead
on right. Proceed northeast through the
Valley View Ranch yard.
GPS: N35°19.16′ W115°34°98′

▼ 2.3   SO   Track on left.
3.7 ▲   BL   Track on right.

▼ 6.0   SO   Corral and tank on right, track on right.
Zero trip meter at corral. This is Water
Tank No. 1.
0.0 ▲   Continue to the northeast.
GPS: N35°18.09′ W115°39.67′

▼ 0.0   Continue to the southwest.
5.3 ▲   SO   Corral and tank on left, track on left.
Zero trip meter at corral. This is Water
Tank No. 1.

▼ 1.8   SO   Track on left and track on right along
power poles. Continue through gate,
keeping corral on your right. This is
Water Tank No. 2.
3.5 ▲   SO   Pass through gate, corral on left. This
is Water Tank No. 2. Track on left and
track on right along power poles.

Valley View Ranch in the winter

GPS: **N35°16.91' W115°40.94'**

▼ 2.2　SO　Well-used track on right.

3.1 ▲　BR　Well-used track on left.

GPS: **N35°16.57' W115°41.30'**

▼ 3.5　SO　Track on left.

1.8 ▲　SO　Track on right.

▼ 3.6　SO　Track on right, corral and well on left. This is Water Tank No. 3.

1.7 ▲　SO　Track on left, corral and well on right. This is Water Tank No. 3.

GPS: **N35°15.84' W115°42.54'**

▼ 4.2　SO　Cross through wash.

1.1 ▲　SO　Cross through wash.

▼ 5.3　SO　Track on right. Zero trip meter.

0.0 ▲　　　Continue to the northeast.

GPS: **N35°14.81' W115°43.82'**

▼ 0.0　　　Continue to the southwest.

6.7 ▲　SO　Track on left. Zero trip meter.

▼ 1.2　BR　Pass cinder pit works on left.

5.5 ▲　BL　Pass cinder pit works on right.

GPS: **N35°13.92' W115°43.51'**

▼ 1.3　SO　Cattle guard. Exit cinder pit area.

5.4 ▲　SO　Cattle guard. Enter cinder pit area.

▼ 2.2　SO　Track on right.

4.5 ▲　BR　Track on left.

▼ 3.5　BL　Well-used track on right.

3.2 ▲　SO　Well-used track on left.

JOSHUA TREE

The Joshua tree, the largest of the yuccas, is a member of the lily family. These picturesque, spike-leafed evergreens grow in dry soils on plains, slopes, and mesas, often in groves. They range from 15 to 40 feet in height with a diameter of 1 to 3 feet. Flowers are bell-shaped, 1 to 1 ½ inches long, with six creamy, yellow-green petal-like sepals. The flowers are crowded into 12- to 18-inch, many-branched clusters with an unpleasant odor; they blossom mostly in the spring. Not all trees flower annually. Joshua tree fruit is elliptical, green-brown, 2 to 4 inches long, and somewhat fleshy. It dries and falls soon after maturity in late spring, revealing many flat seeds. Joshua trees (and most other yuccas) rely on the female pronuba moth (also called the yucca moth) for pollination. No other animal visiting the blooms transfers the pollen from one flower to another. In fact, the female yucca moth has evolved special organs to collect and distribute the pollen onto the surface of the flower. She then lays her eggs in the flowers' ovaries, and when the larvae hatch, they feed on the yucca seeds. Without the moth's pollination, the Joshua tree could not reproduce, nor could the moth, whose larvae would have no seeds to eat. Although an old Joshua tree can sprout new plants from its roots, only the seeds produced in pollinated flowers can scatter far enough to establish a new stand.

Joshua Tree

Joshua trees can live 100 to 300 years. In Southern California, Joshua Tree National Park provides protection for this unique species. Early Mormon visitors to California named them. The outstretched branches of Joshua trees reminded the Mormon pioneers of a biblical Joshua reaching out to heaven.

▼ 3.8   SO   Well-used track on right.
2.9 ▲   BR   Well-used track on left.
▼ 4.2   SO   Track on right.
2.5 ▲   SO   Track on left.
▼ 4.6   SO   Cross through wash.
2.1 ▲   SO   Cross through wash.
▼ 5.2   SO   Track on right onto cinder cone.
1.5 ▲   SO   Track on left onto cinder cone.

GPS: N35°11.52' W115°45.98'

▼ 5.3   SO   Track on right.
1.4 ▲   SO   Track on left.
▼ 5.6   SO   Cross through Willow Wash.
1.1 ▲   SO   Cross through Willow Wash.
▼ 5.7   SO   Cross through wash.
1.0 ▲   SO   Cross through wash.
▼ 5.9   SO   Cross through wash.
0.8 ▲   SO   Cross through wash.
▼ 6.0   SO   Cross through wash.
0.7 ▲   SO   Cross through wash.
▼ 6.4   SO   Water Tank No. 6 on right.
0.3 ▲   SO   Water Tank No. 6 on left.
▼ 6.5   SO   Corral on right.
0.2 ▲   SO   Corral on left.
▼ 6.6   SO   Track on right to corral.
0.1 ▲   BR   Track on left to corral.
▼ 6.7   SO   Track on right and track on left is Desert #13: Mojave Road. Cairns mark the intersection. Zero trip meter.
0.0 ▲   Continue to the north.

GPS: N35°10.38' W115°46.61'

▼ 0.0   Continue to the south.
1.4 ▲   SO   Track on right and track on left is Desert #13: Mojave Road. Cairns mark the intersection. Zero trip meter.
▼ 0.9   SO   Track on right.
0.5 ▲   SO   Track on left.
▼ 1.4   Trail ends at intersection with paved Kelbaker Road. Turn left for Kelso; turn right for Baker and I-15.
0.0 ▲   Trail starts on paved Kelbaker Road, 19 miles southeast of Baker. Zero trip meter and turn north on graded dirt road. Old sign for Aikens Mine Road at intersection and a small track opposite.

GPS: N35°09.32' W115°47.38'

DESERT #19

Ivanpah Mountains Trail

STARTING POINT: I-15, Bailey Road exit at Mountain Pass
FINISHING POINT: Cima Road, 11.7 miles south of I-15
TOTAL MILEAGE: 12.8 miles, plus 1.5-mile spur to Riley's Camp
UNPAVED MILEAGE: 12 miles, plus 1.5-mile spur
DRIVING TIME: 3 hours
ELEVATION RANGE: 4,500–5,400 feet
USUALLY OPEN: Year-round
BEST TIME TO TRAVEL: September to May
DIFFICULTY RATING: 3
SCENIC RATING: 9
REMOTENESS RATING: +0

Special Attractions

■ Dinosaur trackway.
■ Remains of Evening Star Mine and Riley's Camp.
■ Lightly traveled Mojave Desert trail.

History

The Mountain Pass Rare Earth Mine, which was established in 1949, was originally thought to have been a uranium find. Tests by the U.S. Bureau of Mines proved it to be rare earth bastnaesite. The site was abandoned by the prospectors who had found it with a Geiger counter because the ore was useless at the time. Molycorp soon took an interest in the site and set about finding a market for its ore. Though it took 20 years to attract a market, the metals are now sought after for use in glass manufacturing, television tubes, microwave ovens, and as a coloring agent to control the index of glass refraction.

The northern end of this trail climbs slowly around the Mescal Range south of I-15. The southern face of this range contains a unit of cross-bedded arenitic sandstone, possibly reaching to a depth of more than 600 feet. Imprinted in the sandstone are the only dinosaur tracks to have yet been discovered in California. The prints, made when dinosaurs walked the soft mud and sediments that are now hardened rock, measure 2 to 4 inches in diameter and are difficult to find. Guided tours can be arranged through the Needles BLM Field Office.

Riley's Camp was a mining camp worked by John Riley Bembery, whose grave can be found a short distance from the site. Bembery spent many years prospecting in the Mojave Desert. On his death in 1984, the camp was ceded to the government and is now preserved by Bembery's friends.

Description

Ivanpah Mountains Trail takes a winding route through the rugged Ivanpah Mountains, which sit between I-15 and the Mojave National Preserve. The trail heads south from I-15, traveling along a small, roughly graded dirt road into the Mescal Range. It climbs steadily to a saddle before descending along the southern side into Piute Valley.

A prominent peak to the southwest is Kokoweef Peak, which is actively mined. The trail skirts the edge of the Dinosaur Trackway Area of Critical Environmental Concern, where dinosaur prints in the sandstone are preserved for posterity.

Continuing into Piute Valley, the trail passes through many Joshua trees near the remains of the Silverado and Evening Star Mines. The Evening Star has a large timber structure, part of a headframe, and part of a loading hopper still standing. There are three graves alongside the trail, one of which is John Riley Bembery's. His camp is a short distance away, on the rise overlooking the graves. It can be reached by a spur from the main trail. A timber cabin and various mining remains can be seen at the camp.

The trail ends on paved Cima Road, opposite Teutonia Peak, a short distance south of the hiking trailhead to the peak.

Current Road Information

National Park Service
Mojave National Preserve
2701 Barstow Road
Barstow, CA 92311
(760) 252-6100

Map References

BLM   Ivanpah
USGS 1:24,000   Mescal Range, Cima Dome
       1:100,000 Ivanpah
Maptech CD-ROM: San Bernardino County/Mojave
Southern & Central California Atlas & Gazetteer, p. 71
California Road & Recreation Atlas, p. 97
Trails Illustrated, Mojave National Preserve (256)

Route Directions

▼ 0.0   From I-15 at the Bailey Road exit (also called Mountain Pass), 14.8 miles west of Primm, NV, proceed to the south side of the freeway and zero trip meter at cattle guard. Immediately turn left on paved road and head east alongside the freeway.

3.7 ▲   Turn right and proceed north to I-15 at the Bailey Road exit (also called Mountain Pass).
         GPS: N35°28.02′ W115°31.66′

▼ 0.8   SO   Road turns to graded dirt and swings away from freeway. Cross through wash; then track on left and track on right.

2.9 ▲   SO   Track on left and track on right; then cross through wash. Road is now paved and runs alongside the freeway.

▼ 1.0   SO   Track on left.
2.7 ▲   SO   Track on right.
▼ 1.2   SO   Corral on right; then two tracks on right.
2.5 ▲   SO   Two tracks on left; then corral on left.
         GPS: N35°27.63′ W115°30.97′

▼ 1.4   SO   Track on right.
2.3 ▲   SO   Track on left.
▼ 1.6   SO   Track on left.
2.1 ▲   SO   Track on right.
▼ 1.9   SO   Two tracks on right.
1.8 ▲   SO   Two tracks on left.
▼ 2.7   SO   Track on left; then track on right.
1.0 ▲   SO   Track on left; then track on right.
         GPS: N35°26.69′ W115°30.11′

▼ 2.9 BR Bear right past graded road on left; then track on right.

0.8 ▲ SO Track on left; then graded road on right.

GPS: N35°26.53' W115°30.29'

▼ 3.7 BR Track on right; then graded road on left goes 1 mile to an active mine on Kokoweef Peak. Track on right. Bear right on graded road and zero trip meter.

0.0 ▲ Continue to the north past track on left.

GPS: N35°26.00' W115°30.78'

▼ 0.0 Continue to the south.

5.2 ▲ SO Graded road on right goes 1 mile to an active mine on Kokoweef Peak. Track on left. Zero trip meter.

▼ 0.5 BL Graded road on right goes to Iron Horse Mine and Blue Buzzard Mine.

4.7 ▲ BR Graded road on left goes to Iron Horse Mine and Blue Buzzard Mine.

GPS: N35°25.56' W115°31.06'

▼ 0.7 SO Tank on left.

4.5 ▲ SO Tank on right.

▼ 0.8 SO Cross over runway.

4.4 ▲ SO Cross over runway.

▼ 0.9 BR Track on left.

4.3 ▲ BL Track on right.

▼ 1.3 TL 4-way intersection. Tank ahead. Graded road on right and track straight ahead. Turn left on formed trail.

3.9 ▲ TR 4-way intersection. Tank on left. Track straight ahead and track on left. Turn right on graded road.

GPS: N35°24.96' W115°31.16'

▼ 1.6 SO Track on left.

3.6 ▲ SO Track on right.

▼ 2.1 SO Track on left and track on right.

3.1 ▲ SO Track on left and track on right.

▼ 2.5 SO Track on left.

2.7 ▲ SO Track on right.

▼ 2.8 BL Track on right.

2.4 ▲ BR Track on left.

▼ 3.3 SO Track on left.

1.9 ▲ SO Track on right.

▼ 3.5 SO Track on right to Silverado Mine.

1.7 ▲ SO Track on left to Silverado Mine.

GPS: N35°23.14' W115°31.27'

▼ 3.9 SO Track on left goes to Standard Mine No. 1.

1.3 ▲ SO Track on right goes to Standard Mine No. 1.

GPS: N35°22.88' W115°31.54'

Evening Star Mill truck now located along I-15 at Halloran Summit

▼ 4.1 SO Track on left goes to Standard Mine No. 1.

1.1 ▲ BL Track on right goes to Standard Mine No. 1.

▼ 4.4 SO Track on right.

0.8 ▲ SO Track on left.

▼ 4.6 SO Small cemetery on left.

0.6 ▲ SO Small cemetery on right.

GPS: N35°22.41' W115°31.99'

▼ 4.9 SO Track on left.

0.3 ▲ SO Track on right.

▼ 5.2 SO 4-way intersection. Graded road on right and left; to the left is the spur to Riley's Camp. Zero trip meter and continue straight ahead on formed trail.

0.0 ▲ Continue to the northeast.

GPS: N35°21.98' W115°32.38'

Spur to Riley's Camp

▼ 0.0 Proceed to the east.

▼ 0.2 SO Track on left and track on right.

GPS: N35°21.95' W115°32.15'

▼ 0.4 SO Track on right.

▼ 0.7 SO Track on right.

▼ 1.2 BR Track on left.

GPS: N35°21.77' W115°31.06'

▼ 1.5 UT Spur ends at Riley's Camp.

GPS: N35°21.62' W115°30.92'

Continuation of Main Trail

▼ 0.0 Continue to the southwest.

0.4 ▲ SO 4-way intersection. Graded road on right and left; to the right is the spur to Riley's Camp. Zero trip meter and continue straight ahead on formed trail.

GPS: N35°21.98' W115°32.38'

▼ 0.1 SO Track on left and track on right.

0.3 ▲ SO Track on left and track on right.

▼ 0.3 TL Track on right; then track on left.

0.1 ▲ BR Track on right; then track on left.

GPS: N35°21.82' W115°32.58'

▼ 0.4 SO Track on left goes 0.8 miles to remains of the Evening Star Mine. Zero trip meter.

DESERT #19: IVANPAH MOUNTAINS TRAIL

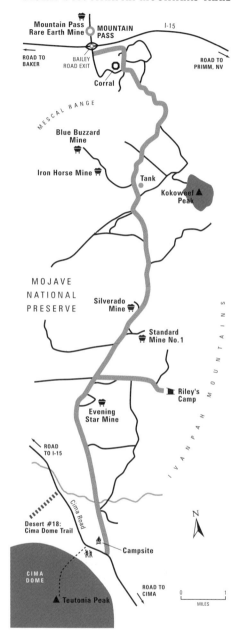

0.0 ▲ Continue to the northeast.

GPS: N35°21.71' W115°32.68'

▼ 0.0 Continue to the southwest.

3.5 ▲ SO Track on right goes 0.8 miles to remains of the Evening Star Mine. Zero trip meter.

▼ 0.3	SO	Cross through wash; then track on left.
3.2 ▲	SO	Track on right; then cross through wash.
▼ 0.8	SO	Track on left.
2.7 ▲	SO	Track on right.
▼ 1.1	SO	Track on left.
2.4 ▲	SO	Track on right.
▼ 1.7	SO	Cross through wash.
1.8 ▲	SO	Cross through wash.
▼ 2.3	SO	Cross through wash. Track on left up wash.
1.2 ▲	SO	Cross through wash. Track on right up wash.

GPS: N35°19.72′ W115°32.70′

| ▼ 2.5 | SO | Track on left. |
| 1.0 ▲ | BL | Track on right. |

GPS: N35°19.55′ W115°32.66′

| ▼ 3.1 | SO | Campsite on right in shelter of large granite boulders. |
| 0.4 ▲ | SO | Campsite on left in shelter of large granite boulders. |

GPS: N35°19.00′ W115°32.61′

| ▼ 3.5 | | Trail ends on paved Cima Road, opposite Teutonia Peak. Turn right for I-15; turn left for Cima. |
| 0.0 ▲ | | Trail commences on paved Cima Road, 11.7 miles south of I-15. Zero trip meter and turn northwest on formed dirt trail. Intersection is unmarked, but it is opposite Teutonia Peak and 0.6 miles south of Teutonia Peak Hiking Trailhead. |

GPS: N35°18.67′ W115°32.58′

DESERT #20

Starbright Trail

STARTING POINT: Irwin Road, 9.5 miles northeast of Barstow
FINISHING POINT: Goldstone Road (C332), 28.5 miles north of Barstow
TOTAL MILEAGE: 29.1 miles
UNPAVED MILEAGE: 29.1 miles
DRIVING TIME: 3 hours
ELEVATION RANGE: 2,300–3,900 feet

USUALLY OPEN: Year-round
BEST TIME TO TRAVEL: September to May
DIFFICULTY RATING: 3
SCENIC RATING: 8
REMOTENESS RATING: +1

Special Attractions

- Remains of the Starbright Mine.
- Views of the Superior Valley.
- Trail ends close to the site of Goldstone.
- Can be combined with Desert #21: Black Canyon Road to form a loop from Barstow.

History

Rainbow Basin lies east of this trail in the unattractive sounding Mud Hills. This area provides a fossil link to the mammals that once roamed this region about 15 million years ago, when the surrounding landscape was more lush and a shallow lake provided ample water. Giant pigs, camels, and bears frequented the region during the middle Miocene time and their bones have been found here. Sedimentary rocks of many colors, such as green, brown, red, and white, are present in the basin, hence the name. The rocks within Rainbow Basin have been folded and faulted over the years. The area was designated a national landmark in 1972.

Goldstone, near the northern end of this trail, was a hive of mining activity in 1881. Goldstone had been quiet for many decades when in 1958, it was chosen by the U.S. Army Ordnance Corps, Jet Propulsion Laboratory division, as the site for a ground-based, deep-space communication station. The reason behind Goldstone's selection was that it had no radio reception, or, as officials put it, it was an environment as free from radio noise as possible. NASA currently leases this quiet part of the Mojave Desert from the U.S. Army. The area is part of NASA's Deep Space Network (DSN). This network supports interplanetary spacecraft missions and a select number of earth orbiting missions. The network currently consists of three listening locations around the world. The other two facilities are not quite as quiet as old Goldstone.

They are in Madrid, Spain, and Canberra, Australia.

In 1826, fur trapper Jedediah Smith may have been the first American to have met the Indians living in this region of the Mojave Desert. Many others followed, traveling the Old Spanish Trail between Santa Fe and the pueblo of Los Angeles. The old trail passed east of the Starbright Trail, close to the southeast boundary of the Fort Irwin Military Reservation. Bitter Spring, located just inside the boundary, was a popular camping spot along the trail. Kit Carson and Captain John C. Frémont traveled the Fort Irwin region in 1844 and established an official camp at Bitter Spring. Despite difficulties with Indians, the camp developed into a trading center as settlers and prospectors moved into the region. The camp was situated along the main Los Angeles to Salt Lake City route and trading boomed. The army constructed a stone fort above Bitter Spring in 1846, in an effort to gain control of the Fort Irwin region during the Indian Wars.

In the late 1880s, mining as far away as Death Valley contributed to the development of this crossroads settlement, resulting in the establishment of the nearby town of Barstow. By 1940 the Mojave Anti-Aircraft Range was established, encompassing old Fort Irwin. This military reservation covered an area of approximately 1,000 square miles and has had several roles over the years. Though deactivated at times and placed on basic maintenance status, the Fort Irwin National Training Center continues to serve as a major training center. To that end, it is safest to remain outside the reservation and not attempt to visit any of the historical locations mentioned that are within the range.

China Lake, to the north of this trail, became a research, development, test, and evaluation (RDT&E) site in 1943. By 1967, it was classed as a Naval Weapons Center. The site covers an area of more than one million acres and is used for the development and testing of air weapons and associated aircraft systems. Everything from air to surface mis-

This small stone cabin sits in a wash

siles used in the Gulf War to demonstrating the technology of the Lunar Soft Landing Vehicle has occurred on the site. Again, for safety and security reasons, do not enter this site.

Description

This trail takes a circuitous route through the mountains and hills north of Barstow, twisting through the hills to finish near the boundary of the military reservation. Along the way, the trail travels past mining remains, along dry washes, on ridge tops that offer panoramic views of the sweeping Superior Valley, and past the dry beds of Coyote and Superior Lakes.

Navigation is very difficult along the trail. The trails are typically small, formed, and unmarked. Intersections are often confusing. A GPS unit will be invaluable here. A short time putting the route coordinates in will make navigation through the maze of unmarked trails much easier.

The trail commences on paved Irwin Road, which leads northeast from Barstow. There is also a Fort Irwin Road that intersects with Irwin Road; the two roads should not be confused. Initially, the trail follows a graded dirt road before peeling off into the network of small trails. Many of the trails in this region are dead ends that branch into the mountains and either stop at a mining claim or just peter out.

The trail crosses the northern end of the Calico Mountains before swinging north to pass the remains of the Starbright Mine. There is a cabin at the site, as well as the wooden remains of an old loading hopper, numerous diggings, shafts, and tailings heaps.

The trail swings north, running through the sandy, creosote covered flats to intersect with Goldstone Road at the end of the trail. The site of Goldstone is a short distance to the north. The military reservation is located north of the finishing point. From the end of the trail, there are excellent views north and west into Superior Valley and the smooth surface of Superior Lake's bed.

Current Road Information

Bureau of Land Management
Needles Field Office

DESERT #20: STARBRIGHT TRAIL

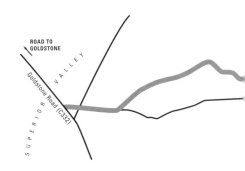

1303 South US Highway 95
Needles, CA 92363
(760) 326-7000

Map References

BLM   Soda Mtns.
USGS 1:24,000 Nebo, Lane Mtn.,
      Williams Well, Goldstone
      1:100,000 Soda Mtns.
Maptech CD-ROM: San Bernardino
      County/Mojave
*Southern & Central California Atlas &
      Gazetteer*, p. 68
California Road & Recreation Atlas,
      pp. 95, 105

Route Directions

▼ 0.0   From Irwin Road, 9.5 miles northeast
           of Barstow, zero trip meter and turn
           northwest on unmarked, formed dirt
           trail. Turn is 0.4 miles west of the
           major intersection of Irwin Road and
           Fort Irwin Road and is opposite the
           marked, paved road—Kolath Place.
6.3 ▲   Trail ends on Irwin Road. Turn right for
           Barstow.
           GPS: N34°59.97' W116°56.15'

▼ 0.6   SO Track on left.
5.7 ▲   SO Track on right.
▼ 1.0   SO Track on left.
5.3 ▲   SO Track on right.
▼ 1.3   SO Track on right.
5.0 ▲   SO Track on left.

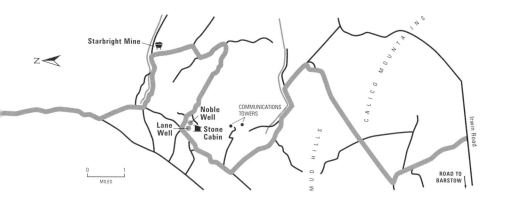

▼ 1.6	BR	Track on left.	
4.7 ▲	SO	Track on right.	

GPS: N35º01.18' W116º57.01'

▼ 1.8	SO	Track on left.

4.5 ▲	BL	Track on right.
▼ 1.9	SO	Well-used track on right.
4.4 ▲	BR	Well-used track on left.

GPS: N35º01.43' W116º57.15'

The rolling Mud Hills

▼ 2.1   SO Track on right; then track on left.
4.2 ▲   SO Track on right; then track on left.
▼ 2.3   SO Track on left.
4.0 ▲   SO Track on right.
▼ 2.4   TR Turn sharp right before power lines; then track on left. Many tracks on left to transmission pylons ahead.
3.9 ▲   TL Track on right; then turn sharp left before reaching power lines.
      GPS: N35°01.59' W116°57.57'

▼ 2.5   SO Track on right.
3.8 ▲   SO Track on left.
▼ 3.7   BR Well-used track on left.
2.6 ▲   SO Well-used track on right.
      GPS: N35°02.39' W116°56.50'

▼ 3.8   SO Graded road on right and left.
2.5 ▲   SO Graded road on right and left.
      GPS: N35°02.45' W116°56.44'

▼ 4.5   SO Track on left.
1.8 ▲   SO Track on right.
▼ 5.0   SO Stone enclosure on right.
1.3 ▲   SO Stone enclosure on left.
      GPS: N35°03.13' W116°55.46'

▼ 5.2   SO Track on left.
1.1 ▲   SO Track on right.
▼ 6.0   SO Track on left; then track on right.
0.3 ▲   SO Track on left; then track on right.
      GPS: N35°03.60' W116°54.65'

▼ 6.3   TL T-intersection with road along small power lines. Zero trip meter.
0.0 ▲   Continue to the southwest. Many dead-end tracks to pylons ahead.
      GPS: N35°03.83' W116°54.47'

▼ 0.0   Continue to the northwest and cross through many deep washes for the next 0.9 miles.
4.1 ▲   TR End of wash crossings. Track continues straight ahead. Turn away from the small power lines and zero trip meter.
▼ 0.3   SO Track on left and faint track on right.
3.8 ▲   SO Track on left and faint track on right.
▼ 0.9   TL T-intersection with track in wash under small power line. Proceed up the wash.
3.2 ▲   TR Turn right out of wash. Cross through

many deep washes for the next 0.9 miles.
      GPS: N35°04.31' W116°55.18'

▼ 1.5   SO Track on left.
2.6 ▲   SO Track on right.
▼ 1.6   SO Track on left.
2.5 ▲   SO Track on right.
▼ 1.8   TL Track on left and track on right. Turn away from the power lines up side wash.
2.3 ▲   TR Track on left and track on right. Follow along power lines down main wash.
      GPS: N35°04.35' W116°55.96'

▼ 2.1   BR Small track on left.
2.0 ▲   BL Small track on right.
▼ 2.4   BR Fork in wash.
1.7 ▲   BL Fork in wash.
      GPS: N35°04.44' W116°56.60'

▼ 2.7   SO Small track on right.
1.4 ▲   SO Small track on left.
▼ 2.9   SO Exit wash.
1.2 ▲   SO Enter wash.
▼ 3.0   SO Saddle. Track on right and track on left at saddle.
1.1 ▲   SO Saddle. Track on right and track on left at saddle.
      GPS: N35°04.84' W116°56.99'

▼ 3.4   SO Track on left and track on right.
0.7 ▲   SO Track on right and track on left.
▼ 3.9   TR T-intersection with well-used formed trail.
0.2 ▲   TL Turn left onto well-used formed trail.
      GPS: N35°05.39' W116°57.61'

▼ 4.0   SO Road is now small, single-lane paved.
0.1 ▲   SO Road is now formed dirt.
▼ 4.1   BL Bear left onto formed dirt trail. Paved road continues to the right to communication towers, but is blocked by a locked gate. Zero trip meter.
0.0 ▲   Continue to the south.
      GPS: N35°05.56' W116°57.47'

▼ 0.0   Continue to the north.
2.1 ▲   SO Continue on small, single-lane paved road. Paved road on left continues to communications towers, but is blocked by a locked gate. Zero trip meter.

▼ 0.3 BL Track on right.
1.8 ▲ BR Track on left.
   GPS: N35°05.80' W116°57.31'

▼ 0.4 BR Track on left.
1.7 ▲ BL Track on right.
▼ 0.7 BR Track on left.
1.4 ▲ BL Track on right.
▼ 0.9 SO Track on right and track on left.
1.2 ▲ SO Track on right and track on left.
   GPS: N35°06.22' W116°57.07'

▼ 1.3 SO Track on left.
0.8 ▲ BL Track on right.
   GPS: N35°06.46' W116°56.74'

▼ 1.6 TR 4-way intersection.
0.5 ▲ TL 4-way intersection.
   GPS: N35°06.59' W116°56.54'

▼ 1.7 SO Track on left. Remain in line of wash.
0.4 ▲ SO Track on right. Remain in line of wash.
▼ 1.8 SO Track on left.
0.3 ▲ SO Track on right.
▼ 1.9 SO Lane Well behind fence on right.
0.2 ▲ SO Lane Well behind fence on left.
   GPS: N35°06.51' W116°56.23'

▼ 2.0 SO Mine shaft behind fence on left; then track on left; then track on right; then concrete tank on right.
0.1 ▲ BL Concrete tank on left; then track on left; then track on right; then mine shaft behind fence on right.
   GPS: N35°06.49' W116°56.18'

▼ 2.1 BL Track on right goes 0.2 miles to stone cabin at Noble Well. Zero trip meter.
0.0 ▲ Continue to the northwest.
   GPS: N35°06.42' W116°56.15'

▼ 0.0 Continue to the east and start to head down canyon.
2.2 ▲ BR Track on left goes 0.2 miles to stone cabin at Noble Well. Exit canyon. Zero trip meter.
▼ 1.0 SO Track on left.
1.2 ▲ SO Track on right.
▼ 1.3 SO Track on left.
0.9 ▲ SO Track on right.

▼ 1.8 SO Track on left and track on right. Exit canyon.
0.4 ▲ SO Track on left and track on right. Enter canyon.
   GPS: N35°05.83' W116°54.51'

▼ 2.0 SO Faint track on left.
0.2 ▲ SO Faint track on right.
▼ 2.2 TL T-intersection. Zero trip meter. Track on right continues down wash.
0.0 ▲ Continue to the west.
   GPS: N35°05.76' W116°54.03'

▼ 0.0 Continue to the northwest.
1.2 ▲ TR Turn right out of wash and zero trip meter. Track on left continues down wash.
▼ 0.1 BR Track on left. Exit line of wash.
1.1 ▲ SO Track on right. Enter line of wash.
▼ 0.4 SO Concrete foundations on right.
0.8 ▲ SO Concrete foundations on left.
   GPS: N35°06.02' W116°54.24'

▼ 0.8 BR Track on left.
0.4 ▲ BL Track on right.
   GPS: N35°06.31' W116°54.56'

▼ 1.2 TL Well-used track on right. Zero trip meter.
0.0 ▲ Continue to the southwest.
   GPS: N35°06.49' W116°54.24'

▼ 0.0 Continue to the northwest.
2.9 ▲ TR Well-used track on left. Zero trip meter.
▼ 0.5 SO Exit wash. Track on left to mine.
2.4 ▲ SO Track on right to mine. Enter wash.
   GPS: N35°06.90' W116°54.42'

▼ 0.6 SO Enter wash.
2.3 ▲ SO Exit wash.
▼ 0.8 SO Exit wash.
2.1 ▲ SO Enter wash.
▼ 1.0 SO Small track on left.
1.9 ▲ SO Small track on right.
▼ 1.2 SO 4-way intersection. Cabin ruin on left. Continue past mine hopper of the Starbright Mine.
1.7 ▲ SO Pass mine hopper of the Starbright Mine; then 4-way intersection. Cabin ruin on right.
   GPS: N35°07.39' W116°54.51'

▼ 1.3   TL   T-intersection with track in wash.
                Turn left up wash.
1.6 ▲   TR   Track continues straight ahead. Turn
                right out of wash.
                GPS: N35°07.45' W116°54.51'

▼ 1.7   BL   Track on right up side wash.
1.2 ▲   SO   Track on left up side wash.
                GPS: N35°07.36' W116°55.01'

▼ 1.8   SO   Track on left.
1.1 ▲   SO   Track on right.
▼ 2.2   BR   Track on left up side wash.
0.7 ▲   BL   Track on right up side wash.
                GPS: N35°07.31' W116°55.44'

▼ 2.4   SO   Track on left.
0.5 ▲   SO   Track on right.
▼ 2.8   SO   Track on left into diggings.
0.1 ▲   SO   Track on right into diggings.
▼ 2.9   TR   4-way intersection. Track on left and
                track on right. Exit wash. Zero trip
                meter.
0.0 ▲   Continue to the east.
                GPS: N35°07.55' W116°56.03'

▼ 0.0   Continue to the northeast.
5.2 ▲   TL   4-way intersection. Track on right and
                track on left. Enter wash. Zero trip
                meter.
▼ 0.2   SO   Track on right and track on left.
5.0 ▲   SO   Track on right and track on left.
▼ 0.6   SO   Track on left and track on right.
4.6 ▲   SO   Track on left and track on right.
▼ 0.7   SO   Track on left.
4.5 ▲   SO   Track on right.
▼ 0.9   SO   Track on left; then track on right.
4.3 ▲   SO   Track on left; then track on right.
▼ 1.2   TR   Track on right; then turn right at sec-
                ond track on right.
4.0 ▲   TL   Track continues ahead; then second
                track on left.
                GPS: N35°08.49' W116°56.42'

▼ 1.3   SO   Track on left.
3.9 ▲   BL   Track on right.
                GPS: N35°08.58' W116°56.41'

▼ 1.6   BL   Well-used track on right.

3.6 ▲   SO   Well-used track on left.
▼ 1.7   SO   Track on right.
3.5 ▲   SO   Track on left.
▼ 2.1   SO   Enter wash. Track on right down wash.
3.1 ▲   SO   Track on left down wash. Exit wash.
                GPS: N35°09.14' W116°56.25'

▼ 2.5   SO   Track on right.
2.7 ▲   SO   Track on left.
▼ 4.2   SO   Exit out top of wash.
1.0 ▲   SO   Enter wash.
▼ 4.8   BR   Well-used track on left.
0.4 ▲   SO   Well-used track on right.
                GPS: N35°11.53' W116°56.73'

▼ 5.2   TL   4-way intersection. Zero trip meter.
0.0 ▲   Continue to the southwest.
                GPS: N35°11.67' W116°56.38'

▼ 0.0   Continue to the north.
5.1 ▲   TR   4-way intersection. Zero trip meter.
▼ 0.1   SO   Track on right.
5.0 ▲   SO   Track on left.
▼ 1.5   SO   Track on right.
3.6 ▲   SO   Track on left.
                GPS: N35°12.93' W116°56.16'

▼ 3.8   TR   Well-used track on left.
1.4 ▲   BL   Well-used track on right.
                GPS: N35°14.65' 116°57.45'

▼ 4.7   SO   Track on left and track on right.
                Concrete foundations on left.
0.4 ▲   SO   Track on left and track on right.
                Concrete foundations on right.
▼ 4.8   SO   Track on left and track on right.
0.3 ▲   SO   Track on left and track on right.
                GPS: N35°15.55' W116°57.45'

▼ 5.1   Trail ends at T-intersection with graded
                dirt Goldstone Road (C332), on the
                edge of Superior Valley. Turn left to
                return to Barstow, passing the start of
                Desert #21: Black Canyon Road after
                2.9 miles.
0.0 ▲   Trail starts on graded dirt Goldstone
                Road (C332), 22.4 miles north of the
                intersection of Copper City Road
                (Goldstone Road turns into Copper City
                Road to the south) and Irwin Road, 2.9

miles northeast of the intersection of Goldstone Road and Desert #21: Black Canyon Road. Zero trip meter and turn south on formed trail. Intersection is unmarked.

GPS: N35°15.92′ W116°57.45′

Black Canyon Road

STARTING POINT: Goldstone Road (C332), 2.9 miles southwest of the northern end of Desert #20: Starbright Trail

FINISHING POINT: California 58 at Hinkley, 7 miles west of Barstow

TOTAL MILEAGE: 35.4 miles

UNPAVED MILEAGE: 34 miles

DRIVING TIME: 2.5 hours

ELEVATION RANGE: 2,000–3,100 feet

USUALLY OPEN: Year-round

BEST TIME TO TRAVEL: September to May (dry weather only)

DIFFICULTY RATING: 3

SCENIC RATING: 10

REMOTENESS RATING: +1

Special Attractions

- Land sailing on the dry bed of Superior Lake.
- Numerous petroglyphs in Inscription Canyon and Black Canyon.
- Rockhounding for opal and jasper at Opal Mountain.
- Can be combined with Desert #20: Starbright Trail to form a loop from Barstow.
- Birding at Harper Lake.

History

The northern end of this trail crosses the wide expanse of the dry Superior Lake. The lake depression is along the route to the old mining settlement of Copper City, which was active around the turn of the twentieth century. The town is approximately 7 miles inside the boundary of China Lake Naval Weapons Center.

By 1904, there were several mining claims in operation around Copper City, part of the Morrow Mining District. The state mineralogist reports that the Union Development Company (out of Boston) owned the Juanita Mine and 141 surrounding claims. Some shafts were more than 200 feet deep. By 1917, updated maps showed Copper City as ruins. Lower levels of mining activity prevailed at some of the claims until the early 1920s.

Long before the establishment of Copper City, generations of Indians camped in the region. The remains of regular camps can be seen in Black Canyon, where hundreds of petroglyphs adorn the volcanic canyon walls. Pot shards show that campfires blackened some of the already heavily patinaed rocks. Another campsite lies farther north along the trail. Inscription Canyon has thousands of petroglyphs that can set the imagination on fire. Paleo-Indians spent an enormous amount of time here, recording events, sightings, and beliefs on the surrounding landscape. Though no dates are available to tell us when these rock engravings were made, people are thought to have inhabited the California desert as early as 10,000 to 12,000 years ago.

In 1906, the first law was introduced to protect the artifacts of our ancestors. Since then, many improved laws have been passed to stem the removal of cultural items from their original locations, where they have the most relevant meaning and offer the greatest insight on how people lived in an earlier landscape.

The silver boom of 1873 in the Panamint Range led to the development of many roads through the region. Wells Fargo, the major stage company of the time, refused to travel to Panamint City because of its general lawlessness and the risk of holdups. So mine owners there banded together and formed their own company. They shaped their silver into 500-pound half balls that were too heavy to carry off on horseback. The route they took traveled down Black Canyon, where a stage station was set up as an overnight stopping point with wells used for water. Aaron Lane, a trader on the Mojave River, was responsible for pushing the route through Black Canyon.

The initials found partway down the canyon, low on the boulders, are those of A. Tillman, a teamster who regularly traveled the Black Canyon route. His signature can be found at other places within the region as well.

Scouts Cove is located in a side canyon between the main trail down Black Canyon and Opal Mountain. It was the site of an opal mining camp in the early 1900s. Miners carved their homes in the tufa rock at the site of the mines, which were financed by the Tiffany Company of New York.

J. W. Robinson chose the eastern side of Harper Lake as the spot for his camp in 1869. Recent rains had enhanced the pastures, and he thought the area would be good to ranch. Another early settler, J. D. Harper, left his name permanently attached to the lake. By 1872, Harper's homesteading work was improved upon to develop the first real known ranch in the region. C. S. Black arrived and constructed an adobe home that catered to stagecoach passengers. He made improvements to the ranch when time permitted. Black's ranch and stage station became known as Grant's Station, a valued service in this remote locality.

Around the same time, Anglo pioneers were settling near the Mojave River in the Barstow region to the southeast and prospectors were venturing into the mountain ranges to the north. The Searles brothers discovered borax at their namesake lake in 1863, though mining activity did not get under way for about 10 years. The Death Valley borax sites were established by the mid-1870s. Ed Stiles established a route for his mule teams from the Eagle Borax Works in Death Valley, over Wingate Pass, south via Granite Wells and Black's Ranch, and on to Daggett.

Harper Lake has long been an important refuge for birds migrating through this arid region. The lake's wetlands have diminished over the last century, yet the remaining marshes continue to attract waterfowl, wetland birds, shorebirds, and birds of prey. Animals such as jack rabbits, coyotes, and bobcats live well in this environment. The desert horned lizard and the zebratail can also be seen here. Measures have been taken to retain the disappearing water supply in order to help maintain the marshland and associated wildlife. In the late 1990s, the BLM installed a well with an irrigation system to provide an ongoing water source for this desert oasis.

Many birders come to the lake to try to spot the many species that can be seen here. Virginia rails, short-eared owls, and American bitterns can be found in the marshes. Great blue herons, white pelicans, snowy egrets, and ibises can also be seen. Killdeer, snowy and mountain plover, and American avocets can be found on the mud flats. The general area also supports a large population of raptors

South of Harper Lake lies the settlement of Hinkley (originally spelled Hinckley). The town was named after the son of D. C. Henderson (of Barstow) when the railroad was constructed in 1882. Hinkley was the setting for the movie *Erin Brockovitch* (2000), starring Julia Roberts. The movie is based on a real-life story of the battle against a large corporation that was contaminating local water supplies and causing cancers and other related illnesses in the people of the town.

Description

Black Canyon Road has a number of interesting features spread along its length. It can be combined with Desert #20: Starbright Trail to create a full day's excursion from Barstow. The graded dirt Indian Spring Road can be used as a fast entry point to the northern end of the trail.

The trail leaves Goldstone Road and heads west, crossing the dry lakebed of Superior Lake. The lake is often used for land yachts. Its perfectly flat, smooth surface makes for ideal conditions when dry. Land yachting is not exactly new to the desert; it has been enjoyed since the turn of the twentieth century. In wet weather, the lakebed quickly turns to mire and should be avoided. The trail leads across the lake, intersecting with other trails in the middle. Please remain on the main route and travel in a straight line from shore to shore. Motorized vehicle use off the designated trail line is not permitted.

Inscription Canyon petroglyph

The trail is faint, so it helps to set the coordinates of the exit point into your GPS unit to use as a GoTo point.

Once away from Superior Lake, the trail joins graded Copper City Road for a short distance before entering the Black Canyon Area of Critical Environmental Concern (ACEC). The entrance to the short, shallow Inscription Canyon is passed next. Park at the barrier and take the short hike into the canyon to see some excellent petroglyphs scattered on the dark lava boulders within the canyon. A few faint red-ochre pictographs can be seen if you look carefully.

The vehicle trail continues alongside a lava flow for the next mile. There are many more petroglyphs to be seen, including the well-known Birdman Petroglyph.

The trail then enters into the sandy Black Canyon wash. A well-used but rough trail leads east to the popular rockhounding area of Opal Mountain, where it is still possible to find opal and jasper. This trail also leads to the location of the old opal camp of Scouts Cove. Past this turn the trail enters the twisting Black Canyon, traveling in a sandy wash. The canyon is a good place to view wildflowers in spring. More petroglyphs can be found in the canyon, as well as one of the Tillman signatures (low on the rock wall). This particular one says, "A. Tillman S.F. July 1874."

Once out of the canyon, the trail swings south toward the flat, dry Harper Lake. A keen eye may be able to spot some white-colored chalcedony on the flats north of the lake. The section of trail that crosses Harper Lake should definitely be avoided when wet. The soft lakebed can quickly turn to quagmire, and it is extremely easy for a vehicle to bog down. The trail across the lake is hard to follow, being faint in places and covered with sagebrush. Keep a close eye on the trail so you don't inadvertently stray from the correct route.

South of the lake, the trail is sandy as it passes beside the well at Black's Ranch. It continues to the south over sandy, undulating ground to finish in Hinkley.

There is some good primitive camping to be found at the northern end of the trail, though it is very exposed with no shelter from wind or sun. Alternatively, the developed BLM campground at Owl Canyon is a short distance from the southern end of the trail.

Current Road Information

Bureau of Land Management
Ridgecrest Field Office
300 South Richmond Road
Ridgecrest, CA 93555
(760) 384-5400

Map References

BLM   Cuddeback Lake, Soda Mtns.
USGS 1:24,000 Superior Lake, Opal
       Mtn., Bird Spring, Lockhart, Water
       Valley, Hinkley
       1:100,000 Cuddeback Lake,
       Soda Mtns.
Maptech CD-ROM: Barstow/San
       Bernardino County; San
       Bernardino County/Mojave
Southern & Central California Atlas &
       Gazetteer, pp. 67, 81
California Road & Recreation Atlas,
       pp. 95, 104

Route Directions

▼ 0.0   From Goldstone Road, 19.5 miles north of the intersection of Copper City Road (Goldstone Road turns into Copper City Road to the south) and Irwin Road, 2.9 miles southwest of the intersection of Goldstone Road and Desert #20: Starbright Trail, zero trip meter and turn southwest at unmarked intersection on the edge of Superior Lake (dry). There is a brown BLM marker post at the intersection, but no trail number.

4.4 ▲   Trail ends at intersection with Goldstone Road. Turn sharp right for Barstow; turn left to continue to Desert #20: Starbright Trail.

      GPS: N35°14.81' W117°00.12'

▼ 0.2 SO Track on left and track on right. Start to cross Superior Lake.

4.2 ▲ SO Track on left and track on right. Exit Superior Lake.

▼ 1.1   SO   Track on left and track on right.

3.3 ▲   SO   Track on left and track on right.

          GPS: N35°14.42′ W117°01.31′

▼ 1.6   SO   Well-used track on left is Indian Springs Road.

2.8 ▲   SO   Well-used track on right is Indian Springs Road.

          GPS: N35°14.29′ W117°01.75′

▼ 2.5   SO   Exit lakebed. There is a brown BLM marker post at the exit.

1.9 ▲   SO   Start to cross Superior Lake. There is a brown BLM marker post at this point.

          GPS: N35°14.16′ W117°02.66′

▼ 2.6   SO   Start to cross small dry lake.

1.8 ▲   SO   Exit lake.

▼ 2.7   SO   Track on left.

1.7 ▲   SO   Track on right.

▼ 2.8   SO   Exit lake.

1.6 ▲   SO   Start to cross small dry lake.

▼ 4.0   TL   Turn left onto graded dirt Old Copper City Road (C2617). Stone foundations opposite are Curtis Well. Small track to well.

0.4 ▲   TR   Turn right onto formed trail C332, marked for 4WDs, ATVs, and motorbikes. Stone foundations opposite are Curtis Well.

          GPS: N35°13.09′ W117°03.65′

▼ 4.4   TR   Turn right onto graded dirt Copper City Road (EF 373) and zero trip meter. Copper City Road also continues to the left. Small track straight ahead.

0.0 ▲   Continue to the northwest.

          GPS: N35°12.84′ W117°03.42′

▼ 0.0   Continue to the west.

7.8 ▲   TL   Turn left onto graded dirt Old Copper City Road (C2617) and zero trip meter. Copper City Road continues straight ahead. Small track on right.

▼ 0.3   SO   Track on left.

7.5 ▲   SO   Track on right.

Expansive view north over Superior Lake

A strong wind whips up dust on the edge of Harper Lake

▼ 0.4   SO   Track on right.
7.4 ▲   SO   Track on left.
▼ 1.4   SO   Graded road continues on right. Track on left and track straight ahead. Continue straight ahead on smaller trail.
6.4 ▲   SO   Graded road on left and track straight ahead. Track on right. Continue straight ahead, joining graded road.
     GPS: N35°12.85′ W117°04.79′

▼ 1.8   SO   Track on left and track on right.
6.0 ▲   SO   Track on left and track on right.
▼ 2.6   SO   Track on left and track on right.
5.2 ▲   SO   Track on left and track on right.
     GPS: N35°12.86′ W117°06.21′

▼ 4.4   SO   Track on left.
3.4 ▲   SO   Track on right.
▼ 4.7   SO   Track on right.
3.1 ▲   BR   Track on left.
     GPS: N35°12.98′ W117°08.45′

▼ 6.1   SO   Track on left.
1.7 ▲   SO   Track on right.

▼ 6.3   SO   Enter Black Mountains ACEC at sign.
1.5 ▲   SO   Exit Black Mountains ACEC at sign.
     GPS: N35°12.30′ W117°09.95′

▼ 7.0   BL   Track on right.
0.8 ▲   SO   Track on left.
     GPS: N35°12.21′ W117°10.71′

▼ 7.5   SO   Track on left.
0.3 ▲   SO   Track on right.
▼ 7.8   TR   T-intersection in front of wooden barrier at Inscription Canyon petroglyphs. Zero trip meter.
0.0 ▲   Continue to the east.
     GPS: N35°11.91′ W117°11.55′

▼ 0.0   Continue to the north. There are petroglyphs on the boulders to the left for the next mile.
3.5 ▲   TL   Turn left in front of wooden barrier at Inscription Canyon petroglyphs. Zero trip meter. Track continues straight ahead.
▼ 0.2   BL   Track on right.

3.3 ▲	SO	Track on left.
▼ 0.7	SO	Track on right.
2.8 ▲	BR	Track on left.
		GPS: N35°12.41′ W117°11.96′

▼ 0.8	SO	Two tracks on right.
2.7 ▲	SO	Two tracks on left. There are petro-glyphs on the boulders to the right for most of the next mile.
▼ 1.6	SO	Track on left.
1.9 ▲	SO	Track on right.
▼ 1.9	SO	Track on right.
1.6 ▲	SO	Track on left.
▼ 2.3	SO	4-way intersection. Small caves on right. Trail forks a few times but all rejoin quickly. Enter line of wash.
1.2 ▲	SO	4-way intersection. Small caves on left. Exit line of wash.
		GPS: N35°11.52′ W117°13.07′

▼ 2.7	SO	Well-used track on right.
0.8 ▲	BR	Well-used track on left.
		GPS: N35°11.22′ W117°13.31′

▼ 2.8	BR	Bear right to pass mine adit.
0.7 ▲	SO	Rejoin main trail.
▼ 2.9	SO	Track on left rejoins and is marked EF 373.
0.6 ▲	BL	Track on right is marked EF 373. Bear left past mine adit on C283.
		GPS: N35°11.03′ W117°13.31′

▼ 3.2	SO	Track on left to mine.
0.3 ▲	BL	Track on right to mine.
▼ 3.5	SO	Track on left goes approximately 4 miles to Opal Mountain rockhounding area and Scouts Cove. Zero trip meter.
0.0 ▲		Continue to the north. Trail forks a few times but all rejoin quickly.
		GPS: N35°10.57′ W117°13.29′

▼ 0.0		Continue to the south.
5.2 ▲	SO	Track on right goes approximately 4 miles to Opal Mountain rockhounding area and Scouts Cove. Zero trip meter.
▼ 0.9	SO	Stone tank and well on right. Entering Black Canyon.
4.3 ▲	SO	Stone tank and well on left. Exiting Black Canyon.
		GPS: N35°10.00′ W117°13.87′

▼ 1.7	SO	Track on right.
3.5 ▲	SO	Track on left.
▼ 2.5	SO	Site of Black Canyon Stage Station—little remains.
2.7 ▲	SO	Site of Black Canyon Stage Station—little remains.
		GPS: N35°09.50′ W117°14.89′

▼ 3.2	SO	Track on right.
2.0 ▲	SO	Track on left.
		GPS: N35°08.66′ W117°15.56′

▼ 4.9	SO	Petroglyphs and Tillman signature on right. There are also petroglyphs on the left, marked by a sign.
0.3 ▲	SO	Petroglyphs on right, marked by a sign; then petroglyphs and Tillman signature on left.
		GPS: N35°07.35′ W117°15.30′

▼ 5.2	TL	Trail exits canyon. Turn left at unmarked intersection in wash. Harper Lake can be seen on the left. Track continues straight ahead.
0.0 ▲		Continue to the northeast.
		GPS: N35°07.22′ W117°15.33′

▼ 0.0		Continue to the south.
2.5 ▲	TR	Turn right at T-intersection in wash and enter Black Canyon.
▼ 0.5	SO	Exit line of wash.
2.0 ▲	SO	Enter line of wash.
▼ 1.0	SO	Exit Black Mountains ACEC at sign.
1.5 ▲	SO	Enter Black Mountains ACEC at sign.
		GPS: N35°06.37′ W117°15.12′

▼ 2.5	SO	Well-used track on left and right is EF 401. Intersection is unmarked. Zero trip meter.
0.0 ▲		Continue to the northwest.
		GPS: N35°04.98′ W117°14.80′

▼ 0.0		Continue to the southeast.
4.8 ▲	SO	Well-used track on right and left is EF 401. Intersection is unmarked. Zero trip meter.
▼ 1.0	SO	Track on left and track on right.
3.8 ▲	SO	Track on left and track on right.
▼ 1.5	SO	Track on left and track on right.
3.3 ▲	SO	Track on left and track on right.

DESERT #21: BLACK CANYON ROAD

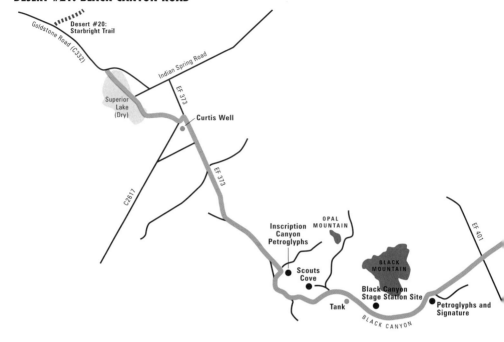

GPS: N35°03.63' W117°14.49'

▼ 1.8 SO Unmarked track on left is C034.
3.0 ▲ SO Unmarked track on right is C034.
GPS: N35°03.35' W117°14.34'

▼ 2.2 SO Start to cross edge of Harper Lake.
2.6 ▲ SO Exiting Harper Lake.
GPS: N35°03.05' W117°14.24'

▼ 4.5 SO Exiting Harper Lake
0.3 ▲ SO Start to cross edge of Harper Lake.
GPS: N35°01.30' W117°13.80'

▼ 4.7 SO Track on right; then track on left.
0.1 ▲ BR Track on right; then track on left.
GPS: N35°01.09' W117°13.71'

▼ 4.8 SO Pass through wire gate. Well on right at Black's Ranch. Zero trip meter at gate.
0.0 ▲ Continue to the north.
GPS: N35°01.04' W117°13.68'

▼ 0.0 Continue to the south. Track on right through fence.

7.2 ▲ SO Track on left; then well on left at Black's Ranch. Pass through wire gate and zero trip meter.
▼ 0.3 SO Track on right.
6.9 ▲ BR Track on left.
▼ 1.0 SO Cattle guard; then track on right along fence line.
6.2 ▲ SO Track on left along fence line; then cattle guard.
▼ 1.5 TL T-intersection with formed dirt road along power lines, immediately west of cattle guard.
5.7 ▲ TR Cattle guard; then immediately turn right on unmarked, small formed trail and leave power lines.
GPS: N34°59.72' W117°13.42'

▼ 1.6 TR Turn right onto small formed trail and leave power lines. Small track opposite.
5.6 ▲ TL T-intersection with formed dirt road along power lines. Small track straight ahead.
GPS: N34°59.71' W117°13.35'

▼ 2.5 SO Track on left.

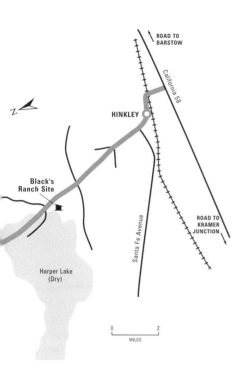

4.7 ▲	SO	Track on right.
▼ 3.0	SO	Track on left.
4.2 ▲	SO	Track on right.
▼ 3.3	SO	Track on left and track on right.
3.9 ▲	SO	Track on left and track on right.

GPS: N34°58.27′ W117°12.87′

▼ 3.8	SO	Track on right; then track on left.
3.4 ▲	SO	Track on right; then track on left.
▼ 3.9	BR	Track on left.
3.3 ▲	SO	Track on right.
▼ 4.1	SO	Track on right.
3.1 ▲	SO	Track on left.

GPS: N34°57.59′ W117°12.60′

▼ 4.4	SO	Track on right.
2.8 ▲	BR	Track on left.
▼ 4.7	SO	Track on left and track on right; then track on left.
2.5 ▲	SO	Track on right; then track on left and track on right.
▼ 5.1	SO	Track on left and track on right.
2.1 ▲	SO	Track on left and track on right.

PELICANS

California is one of the few states in which one can view pelicans. Two species of this distinctive water bird winter in Southern California. American white pelicans, the largest birds in the state with a length of about 5 feet, visit the inland lakes of the region, including the Salton Sea; smaller, but more colorful, brown pelicans can be seen in coastal areas. American white pelicans are mostly white with a long, flat orange bill. Brown pelicans are brown with a yellow head and black underbody. Unlike brown pelicans, which dive from great heights to capture fish, American white

Brown pelican

pelicans cooperate to surround fish in shallow water where they can be easily scooped up. The population of brown pelicans fell dramatically because of agricultural runoff containing DDT, but recent years have seen some reversal of the decline.

White pelican

▼ 5.2 TL Track on left; then T-intersection with wide graded Santa Fe Avenue. Intersection is unmarked. Then graded road on left.

2.0 ▲ TR Graded road on right; then immediately turn right on unmarked formed trail on left-hand bend. Proceed northwest. Intersection is unmarked. Immediately track on right.

GPS: N34°56.60' W117°12.28'

▼ 5.6 SO Graded road on left and right.
1.6 ▲ SO Graded road on left and right.
▼ 5.7 SO Track on right.
1.5 ▲ SO Track on left.
▼ 5.8 SO Road on right is Almeda Street. Continue on Santa Fe Avenue alongside railroad. Road is now paved.
1.4 ▲ SO Road on left is Almeda Street. Road bears away from the railroad and turns to graded dirt.

GPS: N34°56.15' W117°11.97'

▼ 6.4 TR Turn right onto Hinkley Road and cross over railroad.
0.8 ▲ TL Cross over railroad and immediately turn left on Santa Fe Avenue.

GPS: N34°56.00' W117°11.30'

▼ 7.2 Trail ends on California 58, 7 miles west of Barstow. Turn left for Barstow; turn right for Kramer Junction.
0.0 ▲ Trail commences on California 58 at Hinkley, 7 miles west of Barstow. Zero trip meter and turn north on paved Hinkley Road, following sign for Hinkley.

GPS: N34°55.32' W117°11.29'

DESERT #22

Grass Valley Trail

STARTING POINT: Trona Road, 1.3 miles north of intersection with US 395 at Johannesburg
FINISHING POINT: US 395, 13.4 miles north of Kramer Junction

TOTAL MILEAGE: 50.6 miles
UNPAVED MILEAGE: 50.6 miles
DRIVING TIME: 3.5 hours
ELEVATION RANGE: 2,300–3,800 feet
USUALLY OPEN: Year-round
BEST TIME TO TRAVEL: Year-round
DIFFICULTY RATING: 3
SCENIC RATING: 9
REMOTENESS RATING: +1

Special Attractions

- Steam Well Petroglyphs.
- Remote and rugged high desert scenery along a seldom traveled trail.
- Trail travels a vehicle corridor through the Grass Valley Wilderness.

History

The dry Cuddeback Lake lies in a shallow depression south of Almond Mountain along the northern end of this quiet trail. The lake's name comes from a local prospector named John Cuddeback, who hauled ore in team wagons from the mines at Randsburg south to the railroad siding at Kramer Junction. The famed 20-mule teams were a familiar sight in the east-west direction across the dusty depression of Cuddeback Lake. The teams (which actually consisted of 18 mules and 2 horses) pulled up to 30-ton loads in gigantic wagons. Two of these wagons generally carried ore plus an additional 500-gallon water tank. It was no easy task for man or beast to trek across the long straight stretch to Mojave, nearly 50 miles to the southeast. Blackwater Well was a welcome sight to teamsters returning northeast to the borax mines in Death Valley. From the well the route went through the Black Hills to Granite Wells (nowadays on the edge of the China Lake Naval Weapons Center Mojave Range B), then heading north around the Granite Mountains to Owl Hole Springs, before dropping into Death Valley.

Recently, Cuddeback Lake was the background scenery for the movie *Desert Son (1999)*. Car manufacturers Buick, Mazda, and Cadillac have promoted their vehicles at the dry lake with rugged mountains in the distance.

Fremont Peak, a landmark known to many travelers in the northern Mojave region, was named for the famed explorer John C. Frémont. The name was also given to the railroad siding just west of the peak, along the railroad extension from Four Corners (Kramer Junction) to Johannesburg. Construction of the railroad was prompted by the discovery of huge gold deposits at the Yellow Aster Mine on what became known as Rand Mountain. The Randsburg and Johannesburg region boomed; some thought it would be another Comstock. Machinery needed to be installed at the mines, ore needed to be transported out to the mill, and the railroad was up and running by January 1898.

By June of the same year, Barstow had a 50-stamp mill and was receiving ore from the Yellow Aster Mine via the Randsburg Railroad, as it was called. The Barstow mill closed in 1901 because two mills with a total of 130 stamps were operating at Randsburg. Water was piped from Garlock to keep the mills running. By 1904 there were more than 10 miles of tunnels in the Yellow Aster Mine. By 1905 Atolia was producing tungsten, and the mill in Barstow was revived and converted to process the mine's ore.

Silver was the next boom for this desert community. Kelly Silver Mine at the base of Red Mountain (near the northern end of this trail) was discovered in 1919. The claim owner had recently passed away so his son sold out for $15,000. The mine went on to produce more than $7 million worth of silver in its first four years of operation.

Description

This long easygoing trail would be suitable for high-clearance 2WD vehicles in dry weather if it wasn't for a rough, uneven section through the Gravel Hills. A high-clearance 2WD, or even a carefully driven passenger vehicle, can access the Steam Well Petroglyphs from Trona Road in dry weather. Beyond the petroglyphs, 4WD is preferred.

The long trail leaves Trona Road a short distance north of US 395 and Johannesburg. Initially it passes alongside Red Mountain, following the well-used, formed

Motorbike memorial to three men who frequented and loved this region

trail. After 3.9 miles, a sign on the north side of the trail marks the start of a short hiking trail to the Steam Well Petroglyphs. Park your vehicle beside the sign and head approximately 0.4 miles along the old vehicle trail before bearing left to visit the petroglyphs. Unfortunately, the images have been extensively vandalized; people have removed parts of the rock face to get them out. However, they are still worth a visit. The coordinates of the petroglyphs are GPS: N35°23.38' W117°32.42'.

Past Steam Well the trail is marked on some maps as Granite Well Road. To the south, the wide dry expanse of Cuddeback Lake can be seen. The trail crosses through a 2-mile swath of an air force gunnery range impact area. This is not marked on the ground, and it might be wise to exercise some caution.

The trail turns sharply to the south near Blackwater Well and travels through a vehicle corridor that traverses the Grass Valley Wilderness. This is one of the most scenic sections of the trail, with rugged hills rising up from wide valley vistas. Cuddeback Lake can be seen lower down to the west at this point.

One poignant feature along the trail is the motorbike memorial, found to the south of the wilderness area. An old motorbike stands partially buried in the desert next to memorial markers for three friends, all avid desert rats.

The next major scenic area is the Granite Hills. This is the roughest section of the trail as it passes along a wash and through tight canyons in the low granitic hills. Much of this area is posted as private property. Please respect the landowners' rights and remain on the main trail.

The circuitous route joins the roughly graded Lockhart Road for a short distance before swinging west again to pass along the southern face of Fremont Peak. This section of the route can be slightly brushy. The road widens again for the final straight shot that crosses the old Randsburg Railroad embankment at Fremont Siding, before joining US 395 north of Kramer Junction.

Current Road Information

Bureau of Land Management
Ridgecrest Field Office
300 South Richmond Road
Ridgecrest, CA 93555
(760) 384-5400

Map References

BLM   Cuddeback Lake
USGS 1:24,000   Klinker Mtn., Red Mtn.,
      Cuddeback Lake, Blackwater Well,
      Bird Spring, Fremont Peak, Boron NE
      1:100,000 Cuddeback Lake
Maptech CD-ROM: Barstow/San
      Bernardino County
Southern & Central California Atlas & Gazetteer, pp. 66, 67
California Road & Recreation Atlas, p. 95

Route Directions

▼ 0.0   From Trona Road, 1.3 miles north of intersection with US 395 at Johannesburg, zero trip meter and turn northeast onto formed trail RM 1444 for 4WDs, ATVs, and motorbikes. There is a brown marker post slightly after the turn.

3.9 ▲   Trail ends on Trona Road. Turn right for Trona; turn left for US 395 and Johannesburg.
         GPS: N35°22.94' W117°36.45'

▼ 0.2   SO Track on right.
3.7 ▲   SO Track on left.
▼ 0.4   SO Pipeline track on right and left; then second track on left. Red Mountain is on the right.
3.5 ▲   SO Track on right; then pipeline track on left and right. Red Mountain is on the left.
▼ 0.6   SO Track on right.
3.3 ▲   SO Track on left.
▼ 0.7   SO Track on right.
3.2 ▲   SO Track on left.
▼ 1.5   SO Track on left.
2.4 ▲   SO Track on right.
▼ 1.6   SO Two tracks on left.
2.3 ▲   SO Two tracks on right.
         GPS: N35°23.31' W117°34.69'

▼ 1.7 BL Bear left, remaining on RM 1444, past two tracks on right.

2.2 ▲ SO Track on left; then second track on left. Remain on RM 1444.

▼ 1.9 SO Track on right and track on left.

2.0 ▲ SO Track on left and track on right.

▼ 2.1 BL Track on right.

1.8 ▲ SO Track on left.

GPS: N35°23.21' W117°34.16'

▼ 2.2 SO Track on left and track on right.

1.7 ▲ SO Track on left and track on right.

▼ 2.4 SO Two tracks on right.

1.5 ▲ SO Two tracks on left.

▼ 2.6 SO Track on right into mine workings and track on left.

1.3 ▲ SO Track on left into mine workings and track on right.

GPS: N35°23.23' W117°33.69'

▼ 3.9 SO Pull-in on left and sign for Steam Well Archaeological District and Golden Valley Wilderness. Zero trip meter.

0.0 ▲ Continue to the northwest.

GPS: N35°22.82' W117°32.36'

▼ 0.0 Continue to the southeast.

5.8 ▲ SO Pull-in on right and sign for Steam Well Archaeological District and Golden Valley Wilderness. Zero trip meter.

▼ 1.7 SO Track on right.

4.1 ▲ SO Track on left.

GPS: N35°21.57' W117°31.40'

Steam Well Petroglyphs high above Cuddeback Lake

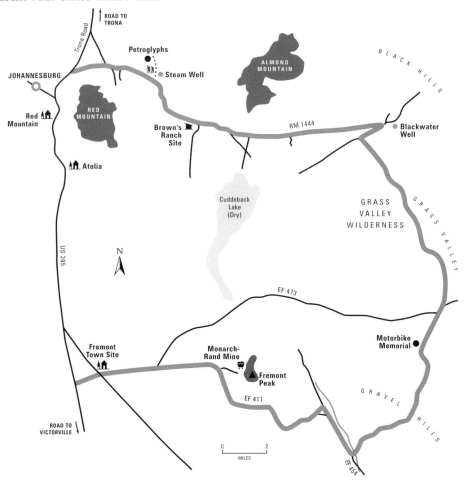

▼ 5.2 SO Track on right.
0.6 ▲ SO Track on left.
▼ 5.8 SO Track on right; then cattle guard underneath old ranch entrance. Zero trip meter.
0.0 ▲ Continue to the southwest.
        GPS: N35°20.74' W117°27.15'

▼ 2.7 SO Track on right.
3.1 ▲ SO Track on left.
▼ 3.0 SO Track on right in large cleared area in creosote with concrete foundations at the intersection. This is the site of Brown's Ranch.
2.8 ▲ SO Track on left in large cleared area in creosote with concrete foundations at the intersection. This is the site of Brown's Ranch. Remain on marked RM 1444.
        GPS: N35°21.22' W117°30.07'

▼ 0.0 Continue to the northeast.
5.5 ▲ SO Cattle guard underneath old ranch entrance; then track on left. Zero trip meter.
▼ 0.7 SO Track on left.
4.8 ▲ SO Track on right.
▼ 1.3 SO Track on right to tanks.
4.2 ▲ SO Track on left to tanks.

▼ 4.2 BL Track on right.
1.6 ▲ SO Track on left.

▼ 1.7   SO   Track on left.

3.8 ▲   SO   Track on right.

▼ 1.9   SO   Small track on right.

3.6 ▲   SO   Small track on left.

▼ 2.4   SO   Track on left and track on right.

3.1 ▲   SO   Track on left and track on right. Remain on marked RM 1444.

▼ 5.5   TR   Turn sharp right in front of gate. Track on left and track straight ahead through gate. Zero trip meter.

0.0 ▲   Continue to the west.

GPS: N35°21.37' W117°21.16'

▼ 0.0   Continue to the southwest.

1.3 ▲   TL   Turn sharp left in front of gate. Track straight ahead and track on right through gate. Zero trip meter.

▼ 1.3   TL   Turn left on unmarked, well-used trail and enter vehicle corridor through Grass Valley Wilderness. Track continues straight ahead. Zero trip meter.

0.0 ▲   Continue to the northeast.

GPS: N35°20.86' W117°22.39'

▼ 0.0   Continue to the southeast past Grass Valley Wilderness sign.

8.9 ▲   TR   T-intersection. Exit vehicle corridor through Grass Valley Wilderness. Zero trip meter.

▼ 3.2   SO   Pass through wire gate.

5.7 ▲   SO   Pass through wire gate.

GPS: N35°18.89' W117°20.23'

▼ 5.5   SO   Track on left and track on right. Pass through wire gate.

3.4 ▲   SO   Pass through wire gate. Track on left and track on right.

GPS: N35°17.06' W117°19.18'

▼ 8.9   TR   T-intersection with EF 473. Exit vehicle corridor through Grass Valley Wilderness. Zero trip meter.

0.0 ▲   Continue to the north.

GPS: N35°14.55' W117°17.98'

▼ 0.0   Continue to the southwest.

9.2 ▲   TL   Turn left onto well-used trail and enter vehicle corridor through the Grass Valley Wilderness. Zero trip meter. There is a sign at the intersection for Grass Valley Wilderness.

▼ 0.3   SO   Two tracks on left into mine workings.

8.9 ▲   SO   Two tracks on right into mine workings.

▼ 0.4   SO   Track on left.

8.8 ▲   BL   Track on right.

▼ 0.6   TL   Turn left onto unmarked, well-used trail. There is a large Joshua tree and a sign for the Grass Valley Wilderness at the intersection.

8.6 ▲   TR   T-intersection with EF 473. There is a large Joshua tree and a sign for the Grass Valley Wilderness at the intersection.

GPS: N35°14.18' W117°18.37'

▼ 2.0   BR   Trail forks. Track on left.

7.2 ▲   SO   Track on right rejoins.

▼ 2.1   TL   Motorbike memorial. Turn left at the motorbike. Track straight ahead and track on right.

7.1 ▲   TR   Motorbike memorial. Turn right at the motorbike. Track straight ahead and track on left.

GPS: N35°12.95' W117°18.99'

▼ 2.2   SO   Track on left rejoins.

7.0 ▲   BL   Track on right.

▼ 2.4   SO   Enter down line of wash.

6.8 ▲   SO   Exit line of wash.

▼ 9.1   BL   Cross through wash, bearing slightly left down the wash; then immediately exit wash to the right.

0.1 ▲   BR   Cross through wash, bearing slightly left up the wash; then almost immediately bear right on small, unmarked formed trail up side wash. There is a private property warning at the start of the trail. Remain on main trail through restricted area.

GPS: N35°08.67' W117°22.18'

▼ 9.2   TR   Cross over old graded Lockhart Road; then turn right onto unmarked, roughly graded Lockhart Road (EF 454). Zero trip meter.

0.0 ▲   Continue to the northeast up side wash.

GPS: N35°08.65' W117°22.22'

▼ 0.0   Continue to the northwest.

2.4 ▲ TL Turn left off graded road onto small unmarked trail. Cross old graded Lockhart Road; then bear left up wash. Zero trip meter.

▼ 1.0 SO Track on right. Road is now roughly formed.

1.4 ▲ SO Track on left.

▼ 2.0 SO Track on left.

0.4 ▲ SO Track on right.

▼ 2.4 TL Turn sharp left onto well-used formed trail marked 411. Zero trip meter.

0.0 ▲ Continue to the southeast.

GPS: N35°10.55′ W117°23.63′

▼ 0.0   Continue to the south.

6.8 ▲ TL Turn sharp right onto unmarked, well-used trail. There is a marker for the trail you are leaving (411) at the intersection. Zero trip meter.

▼ 0.5 BR Well-used track on left joins.

6.3 ▲ BL Track on right.

GPS: N35°10.25′ W117°23.93′

▼ 1.5 BL Track on right.

5.3 ▲ BR Track on left.

GPS: N35°09.85′ W117°24.84′

▼ 3.2 SO Cross through wash. Tracks on left and right up and down wash.

3.6 ▲ SO Cross through wash. Tracks on left and right up and down wash.

GPS: N35°10.33′ W117°26.06′

▼ 3.3 TL T-intersection.

3.5 ▲ TR Track continues straight ahead.

GPS: N35°10.39′ W117°26.11′

▼ 4.3 SO Track on left.

2.5 ▲ SO Track on right.

GPS: N35°10.49′ W117°27.22′

▼ 6.8 TL T-intersection with formed trail. Zero trip meter. To the right goes 1 mile to the Monarch-Rand Mine. There is a marker for EF 411 at the intersection pointing back the way you came.

0.0 ▲ Continue to the south.

GPS: N35°11.86′ W117°28.68′

▼ 0.0   Continue to the west.

6.8 ▲ TR Turn right onto formed trail marked EF 411. Track ahead goes 1 mile to the Monarch-Rand Mine. Zero trip meter.

▼ 0.4 BL Track on right.

6.4 ▲ SO Track on left.

GPS: N35°11.97′ W117°29.07′

▼ 0.6 SO Two tracks on right.

6.2 ▲ BR Two tracks on left.

▼ 1.6 SO Track on left and track on right.

5.2 ▲ SO Track on right and track on left.

▼ 2.6 SO Track on left and track on right.

4.2 ▲ SO Track on left and track on right.

GPS: N35°11.81′ W117°31.41′

▼ 3.0 SO Join larger graded Cuddeback Road (EF 473).

3.8 ▲ BR Bear right onto smaller formed road EF 411, marked by brown marker post.

GPS: N35°11.78′ W117°31.76′

▼ 3.8 SO Track on left.

3.0 ▲ SO Track on right.

▼ 5.2 SO Track on left.

1.6 ▲ SO Track on right.

▼ 5.5 SO Track on left and track on right; then second track on left and track on right. This is the site of Fremont on the old Randsburg Railroad grade.

1.3 ▲ SO Track on left and track on right; then second track on left and track on right. This is the site of Fremont on the old Randsburg Railroad grade.

GPS: N35°11.50′ W117°34.57′

▼ 6.8   Trail ends at T-intersection with paved US 395. Turn left for Victorville; turn right for Randsburg.

0.0 ▲ Trail commences on US 395, 13.4 miles north of Kramer Junction. Zero trip meter and turn northeast on graded dirt road. Immediately cross over pipeline road; then track on left. Continue straight ahead, following the brown marker post for Fremont Road (EF 411).

GPS: N35°11.08′ W117°35.65′

Trona Pinnacles Trail

STARTING POINT: California 178, 1.8 miles south of Trona

FINISHING POINT: Trona Road, 6 miles south of the intersection with Searles Station Cut Off Road

TOTAL MILEAGE: 24.6 miles

UNPAVED MILEAGE: 24.6 miles

DRIVING TIME: 2 hours

ELEVATION RANGE: 1,600–3,900 feet

USUALLY OPEN: Year-round

BEST TIME TO TRAVEL: October to May

DIFFICULTY RATING: 3

SCENIC RATING: 9

REMOTENESS RATING: +0

Special Attractions

■ Trona Pinnacles.

■ Spangler Hills OHV Area.

History

The Trona Pinnacles are enormous tufa (calcium carbonate) towers, deposited by algal precipitation near carbonate-enriched springs on the lake floor of Searles Lake between 130,000 and 35,000 years ago. The lake reached depths approaching 600 feet at times and spilled into Panamint Valley through the Slate Range to the east. The land was lush and tropical at that stage. Some sections of the early shoreline are visible as horizontal bands to the northwest of the pinnacles. There are more than 500 tufa spires over an area of approximately 13 square miles. Some reach as high as 140 feet above the surrounding lakebed. The formations were known as Cathedral City to early travelers.

The Trona Pinnacles were designated as a National Natural Landmark in 1986. The dramatic scenery has been used as the backdrop for many movies, including *Star Trek V: The Final Frontier (1989), Dinosaur (2000),* and *Pitch Black (2000).* The 2001 remake of *Planet of the Apes* was also filmed here.

Planet of the Apes movie set at the Trona Pinnacles

Trona Pinnacles

John and Dennis Searles discovered borax at their namesake lake in 1863 and saline production began about 10 years later. The once tropical lake is now a mix of mud and sand to the northeast of this trail. The 12-square-mile area contains disseminated salt crystals to an average depth of 70 feet. Salts exist at lesser depths over a broad area around the lakebed. Potassium salt, boric acid, borax, lithium carbonate, bromine, and phosphoric acid are in near pure form, requiring little processing at the on-site plant. The town name Trona refers to a mineral consisting of sodium carbonate and bicarbonate.

Two different wagon routes were used by the Searles brothers to haul the borax they produced to the railroad at Mojave. The southern route passed west of the Trona Pinnacles to Searles freight station at Garden City. This is now the route of the current railroad. The western route traveled through Salt Wells Canyon (Poison Canyon, part of today's California 178) to a dry station 1 mile from the head of the canyon, to Garden City where the routes joined. It then continued through Garlock to Mojave.

The American Trona Corporation was formed in 1913 and found that the local mule haulage company, Rinaldi and Clark, cost too much money and took too much time. A more efficient transportation method was needed. The corporation struggled to finance its own railroad that stretched more than 30 miles up Teagle Wash to reach the Southern Pacific line. The trains were running by 1916 and still run to this day.

The Spangler brothers, Tony and Rea, worked a small, low-paying gold mine just west of the military road near Teagle Wash. Their house, close to the tamarisks growing near the railroad, was also the site of the Spangler water tower used by the old Trona Railroad steam engines.

Description

As you approach the Trona Pinnacles, you may find that they look familiar. This surreal landscape of gray spires and rocky pinnacles has been used as the setting for the alien planetscape in many science fiction films.

The well-marked graded road heads off from California 178, south of the borax town of Trona. The road is dusty as it leads directly toward the pinnacles, which are visible a few miles away. There is a network of small tracks around the pinnacles that lead off from the main trail. The entire pinnacles area is best avoided when wet, because it can turn into a quagmire that will impound the most capable of vehicles. There are no official campgrounds here, but primitive camping is permitted.

The trail continues past the pinnacles as a well-used formed trail. Several miles southwest of the pinnacles, you will cross a paved road. This road is part of the China Lake Naval Weapons Center; there is no public access along this road! You are permitted to cross the road, remaining on RM 143, but not to exit along this road.

The trail follows the roughly graded RM 143 for a short distance before turning off onto the smaller 7A trail. This trail has very loose, deep sand as it climbs along the wash through scattered Joshua trees in the Summit Range.

The final section of the trail runs alongside the Spangler Hills OHV Area, where there are many trails and open areas suitable for a wide variety of off-road vehicles. To the south is the Golden Valley Wilderness, encompassing the rugged Lava Mountains. This area is more suited to remote hiking and horseback riding. The trail exits the mountains to finish on Trona Road, north of Red Mountain.

Current Road Information

Bureau of Land Management
Ridgecrest Field Office
300 South Richmond Road
Ridgecrest, CA 93555
(760) 384-5400

Map References

BLM   Ridgecrest, Cuddeback Lake
USGS   1:24,000   Westend, Spangler Hills
       East, West of Black Hills, Klinker Mtn.
       1:100,000 Ridgecrest, Cuddeback
       Lake
Maptech CD-ROM: Barstow/San
       Bernardino County
*Southern & Central California Atlas &
       Gazetteer*, pp. 53, 52, 66
California Road & Recreation Atlas, p. 95

Route Directions

▼ 0.0   From California 178, 1.8 miles south of
           Trona, zero trip meter and turn south-
           east on graded dirt road at the sign for
           Trona Pinnacles. The road is marked
           RM 143, suitable for 4WDs, ATVs, and
           motorbikes.
4.1 ▲   Trail ends on California 178. Turn right
           for Trona; turn left for Ridgecrest.
           GPS: N35°40.89' W117°23.44'

▼ 0.5 SO Track on right; then cross through wash.
3.6 ▲ SO Cross through wash; then track on left.
▼ 0.6 BR Graded road on left. Follow sign for
           RM 143; then track on right.
3.5 ▲ SO Track on left; then graded road on
           right. Follow sign for RM 143.
           GPS: N35°40.68' W117°22.92'

▼ 1.1 SO Track on right.
3.0 ▲ SO Track on left.
▼ 1.2 SO Track on right; then cross over railroad.
2.9 ▲ SO Cross over railroad; then track on left.
           GPS: N35°40.12' W117°22.75'

▼ 3.3 SO Track on right.
0.8 ▲ SO Track on left.
▼ 3.9 SO Track on right.
0.2 ▲ SO Track on left.
▼ 4.0 SO Track on right; then entering the

DESERT #22: TRONA PINNACLES TRAIL

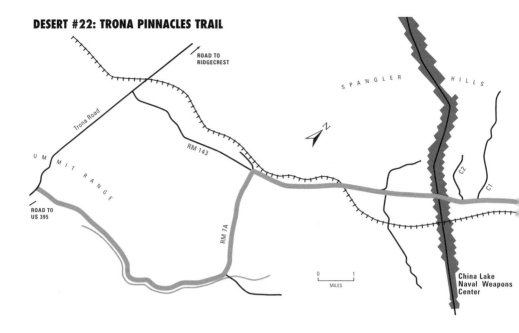

Trona Pinnacles at sign.

0.1 ▲   SO   Leaving the Trona Pinnacles; then track on left.

GPS: N35°37.70′ W117°22.69′

▼ 4.1   SO   Well-used track on left goes into the pinnacles. Zero trip meter.

0.0 ▲   Continue to the north.

GPS: N35°37.56′ W117°22.70′

▼ 0.0   Continue to the south and immediately second track on left into pinnacles. Remain on RM 143.

1.1 ▲   SO   Track on right into the pinnacles; then second track on right after rise. Zero trip meter at second track on right.

▼ 0.6   SO   Track on left.

0.5 ▲   SO   Track on right.

▼ 1.0   SO   Track on left.

0.1 ▲   SO   Track on right.

▼ 1.1   BR   Graded road on left into pinnacles. Zero trip meter.

0.0 ▲   Continue to the northwest.

GPS: N35°36.65′ W117°22.55′

▼ 0.0   Continue to the south.

4.7 ▲   BL   Graded road on right into pinnacles. Zero trip meter.

▼ 0.2   SO   Cross over railroad track.

4.5 ▲   SO   Cross over railroad track.

▼ 0.4   SO   Track on left.

4.3 ▲   SO   Track on right.

▼ 0.5   SO   Track on left.

4.2 ▲   SO   Track on right.

▼ 0.8   SO   Track on left.

3.9 ▲   SO   Track on right.

▼ 1.4   BL   Trail forks. Well-used track on right.

3.3 ▲   SO   Well-used track on left.

GPS: N35°35.97′ W117°23.59′

▼ 2.0   SO   Faint track on left.

2.7 ▲   SO   Faint track on right.

▼ 2.1   SO   Track on right.

2.6 ▲   BR   Track on left.

▼ 3.6   SO   Track on right is marked C1.

1.1 ▲   SO   Track on left is marked C1.

GPS: N35°34.89′ W117°25.57′

▼ 4.1   SO   Track on right.

0.6 ▲   SO   Track on left.

▼ 4.2   SO   Track on right is marked C2.

0.5 ▲   SO   Track on left is marked C2.

GPS: N35°34.44′ W117°26.09′

▼ 4.7   SO   Track on right; then trail crosses paved road, which is government property—

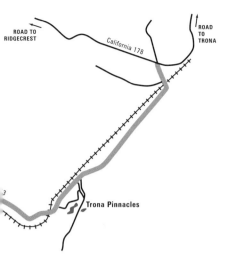

ROAD TO
RIDGECREST

California 178

ROAD
TO
TRONA

Trona Pinnacles

▼ 2.7   SO Track on right; then cross over railroad and zero trip meter.

0.0 ▲   Continue to the northeast past track on left.

GPS: N35°32.74' W117°28.75'

▼ 0.0   Continue to the southwest. Track on left and track on right.

2.5 ▲   SO Track on left and track on right; then cross over railroad. Zero trip meter.

▼ 1.0   SO Cross through wash.

1.5 ▲   SO Cross through wash.

▼ 1.2   SO Track on right and track on left.

1.3 ▲   SO Track on right and track on left.

GPS: N35°31.94' W117°29.71'

▼ 1.3   SO Track on left. Remain on RM 143.

1.2 ▲   BL Track on right. Remain on RM 143.

▼ 1.8   SO Track on right and small track on left.

0.7 ▲   SO Track on left and small track on right.

▼ 2.5   TL 4-way intersection. Unmarked track on right, track on left is RM 7A, and RM 143 continues straight ahead. Zero trip meter and turn onto RM 7A at the marker post.

0.0 ▲   Continue to the northeast.

GPS: N35°31.45' W117°30.95'

---

no public vehicles allowed. Zero trip meter and continue on RM 143.

0.0 ▲   Continue to the northeast, following sign to the Trona Pinnacles; then track on left.

GPS: N35°34.22' W117°26.52'

▼ 0.0   Continue to the southwest.

2.7 ▲   SO Trail crosses paved road, which is government property—no public vehicles allowed. Zero trip meter and continue on RM 143.

▼ 0.2   SO Cross through wash.

2.5 ▲   SO Cross through wash.

▼ 0.7   SO Track on left and track on right.

2.0 ▲   SO Track on left and track on right.

▼ 1.0   SO Cross through wash.

1.7 ▲   SO Cross through wash.

▼ 1.4   SO Small track on left and small track on right.

1.3 ▲   SO Small track on left and small track on right.

▼ 1.7   SO Small track on left and small track on right.

1.0 ▲   SO Small track on left and small track on right.

▼ 1.9   SO Track on right.

0.8 ▲   SO Track on left.

▼ 0.0   Continue to the southeast. Trail is marked as both RM 7 and RM 7A.

3.0 ▲   TR 4-way intersection. RM 143 on left and on right and track straight ahead. Zero trip meter and turn right onto RM 143 at the marker post. Trail is marked as suitable for 4WDs, ATVs, and motorbikes.

▼ 0.5   SO Track on left.

2.5 ▲   SO Track on right.

▼ 1.5   BL Track on right.

1.5 ▲   SO Track on left.

▼ 1.6   SO Track on left and track on right. Remain on RM 7A.

1.4 ▲   SO Track on left and track on right. Remain on RM 7A.

GPS: N35°30.20' W117°30.19'

▼ 1.9   SO Faint track on left and faint track on right.

1.1 ▲   SO Faint track on left and faint track on right.

▼ 2.0   SO Motorbike trail crosses on left and right.

1.0 ▲   SO Motorbike trail crosses on left and right.

▼ 3.0   TR   Turn right into wash, remaining on RM
             7A. Track on left down wash and track
             straight ahead. Zero trip meter.
0.0 ▲   Continue to the northwest.
             GPS: N35°29.17′ W117°29.35′

▼ 0.0   Continue to the south.
6.5 ▲   TL   Turn left out of wash at the marker,
             remaining on RM 7A. Track on right
             and track straight ahead in wash.
             Zero trip meter.
▼ 1.3   BL   Track on right; then second track on
             right is marked RM 1127.
5.2 ▲   SO   Track on left is marked RM 1127; then
             second entrance to track on left.
             GPS: N35°28.20′ W117°30.07′

▼ 2.7   SO   Second entrance to track on right.
3.8 ▲   SO   Track on left.
             GPS: N35°27.53′ W117°31.23′

▼ 3.6   SO   Small track on right.
2.9 ▲   SO   Small track on left.
▼ 4.3   SO   Track on right.
2.2 ▲   SO   Track on left.
▼ 4.5   SO   Top of rise. Trail exits wash. Track
             on right.
2.0 ▲   SO   Top of rise. Track on left. Trail ahead is
             now marked RM 7A for 4WDs, ATVs,
             and motorbikes. Trail enters down
             wash.
             GPS: N35°27.73′ W117°33.07′

▼ 4.9   SO   Track on right.
1.6 ▲   SO   Track on left.
▼ 5.1   SO   Trail enters line of wash. Track on right.
1.4 ▲   BR   Track on left. Trail leaves line of wash.
▼ 5.2   SO   Track on right.
1.3 ▲   SO   Track on left.
▼ 5.8   SO   Track on left; then track on right.
0.7 ▲   SO   Track on left; then track on right.
▼ 5.9   SO   Track on right is C2.
0.6 ▲   BR   Track on left is C2.
▼ 6.2   SO   Track on left and track on right follow
             pipelines.
0.3 ▲   SO   Track on right and track on left follow
             pipeline.
▼ 6.5   Trail finishes at Trona Road. Turn right
             for Ridgecrest; turn left for Red
             Mountain and US 395.

0.0 ▲   From Trona Road, 4.5 miles south of
             the railroad and 6 miles south of the
             intersection with Searles Station Cut
             Off Road, zero trip meter and turn
             northeast on formed trail that travels
             up a wide, sandy wash. There is a
             small track opposite and a sign for
             BLM Limited Use Area, but no sign-
             posts. Track is called Savoy Road on
             some maps. Immediately, track on left
             is marked C2 and main trail is marked
             C2. Proceed straight ahead in wash
             on C2.
             GPS: N35°27.28′ W117°35.08′

Colosseum Gorge Trail

STARTING POINT: I-15 at Yates Well Road exit,
    5 miles southwest of Primm, NV
FINISHING POINT: Kingston Road, 6.5 miles
    north of I-15
TOTAL MILEAGE: 18.4 miles
UNPAVED MILEAGE: 18.4 miles
DRIVING TIME: 2.5 hours
ELEVATION RANGE: 2,800–5,500 feet
USUALLY OPEN: Year-round
BEST TIME TO TRAVEL: September to June
DIFFICULTY RATING: 3
SCENIC RATING: 8
REMOTENESS RATING: +0

Special Attractions
■ Dry Ivanpah Lake, popular place for land
  yachting.
■ Clark Mountain Range and Mojave
  Desert scenery within the Mojave National
  Preserve.

History
The Chemehuevi, Mojave, and Paiute frequented the Clark Mountain region for
many generations. Evidence of their
turquoise mining was reported as early as
1898. Pottery shards, tools, and thousands of
petroglyphs were found for quite some distance around the mines.

Clark Mountain is a notable landmark from afar; it is the highest mountain in the eastern Mojave region. The peak, which is to the south of this trail, reaches 7,929 feet. The mountain was formed from a series of thrust faults, and it was named after an early day miner, Senator William A. Clark, the copper king of Montana.

With the end of the war with Mexico and the ceding of these lands to the United States in 1848, there was a slow influx of surveyors, prospectors, and settlers in the region. Mineral deposits looked promising and the Clark Mining District was established in 1865. In 1869, the Paiute Company of California found silver deposits in the Clark Mountains (which may have been originally spelled Clarke). The first town in this remote region, old Ivanpah on the eastern side of Clark Mountain, had a popula-

The large open pit of the Colosseum Mine

tion of about 500 people who were mainly workers at the mines. A supply route from the mines, through Crescent Springs in Nevada, to a steamboat landing at Cottonwood Island on the Colorado River developed. Though some activity occurred at the Colosseum Mine in the 1860s, no major development occurred until the 1930s, when gold, silver, copper, and lead were extracted. This minor boom lasted until the World War II years. There was little activity until 1986, when an Australian company built a mill and began serious mining. Nearly 7,000 ounces of gold were produced each month until 1993. Since its closing in the 1990s, millions of dollars of reclamation work has been undertaken at the site.

The Yates Ranch was one of the earliest cattle grazing ventures to work this eastern Mojave region in the 1880s. The name is remembered at the eastern end of this trail in the form of Yates Well Road. The well is now used by the Primm Valley Golf Club for irrigation. The Yates Ranch headquarters were on the western side of Clark Mountain

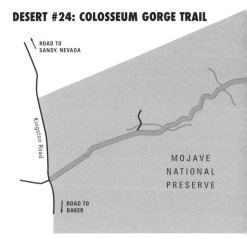

DESERT #24: COLOSSEUM GORGE TRAIL

at Valley Wells, which is to the north of Valley Wells Rest Area on present-day I-15.

Midway along the trail is old Greene's Cabin. The timber cabin was owned by the Greene family from 1900 to 1920. It was divided into a couple distinct areas. Mr. and Mrs. Greene used the western end of the cabin as their quarters; the middle section

Old timber cabin in Colosseum Gorge

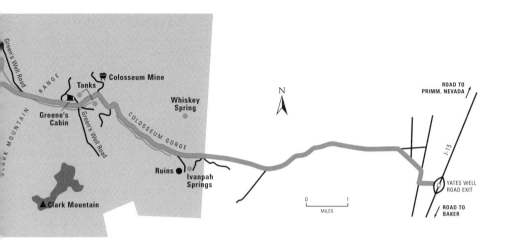

was the kitchen where Mrs. Greene cooked for miners who worked at the Greenes' gold mines to the north of the old cabin.

Description

Colosseum Gorge runs up the eastern side of the Clark Mountain Range from I-15, southwest of the casino town of Primm, Nevada. The trail turns off the paved road at the Primm Valley Golf Club, and travels along a graded dirt road up the gently sloping bajada toward the bulk of Clark Mountain. The bajada is vegetated with creosote bush, Mojave yuccas, chollas, and sagebrush. The trail enters Colosseum Gorge and climbs a wide, rough shelf road along the side of the gorge. The road used to serve the Colosseum open pit mine at the top of the saddle, so it was once wide enough for mining trucks, but it is now eroding and somewhat rough. At the top of the gorge is the open pit mine, which is currently not in use. It is posted and there is no access. Mining works in the area are being revegetated.

The trail descends the far side of the gorge on Green's Well Road along a smaller trail, running in or alongside the wash for the first 1.9 miles. Greene's Cabin can be found beside the wash.

The trail then swings out of the wash to follow a smaller formed trail that winds over the undulating slopes of the Clark Mountain Range, through a variety of vegetation, which

on the west side of the range includes Joshua trees.

The trail finishes far below on paved Kingston Road.

Current Road Information

National Park Service
Mojave National Preserve
2701 Barstow Road
Barstow, CA 92311
(760) 252-6100

Map References

BLM   Mesquite Lake
USGS   1:24,000   Ivanpah Lake, Clark
        Mtn., Pachalka Spring
        1:100,000 Mesquite Lake
Maptech CD-ROM: San Bernardino
        County/Mojave
Southern & Central California Atlas & Gazeteer, pp. 56, 57
California Road & Recreation Atlas, p. 97

Route Directions

▼ 0.0   From I-15 at the Yates Well Road exit, 5 miles southwest of Primm and the Nevada state line, proceed to the west side of the freeway and zero trip meter. Proceed west on paved road.

1.0 ▲   Trail finishes at I-15. Proceed east for Primm, NV, west for Baker.

GPS: N35°32.46' W115°25.25'

▼ 0.4 TR Turn right at T-intersection onto paved road, following sign for Primm Valley Golf Club.

0.6 ▲ TL Turn left onto unmarked paved road.

▼ 0.7 TL Turn left on paved road. Road straight ahead goes into Primm Valley Golf Club.

0.3 ▲ TR Turn right on paved road. Road on left goes into Primm Valley Golf Club.
GPS: N35°32.75′ W115°25.64′

▼ 1.0 BL Bear left onto graded dirt road. Two paved roads on right. Intersection is unmarked. Zero trip meter.

0.0 ▲ Continue to the south on paved road.
GPS: N35°32.90′ W115°25.91′

▼ 0.0 Continue to the north on graded dirt road.

8.3 ▲ BR Bear right onto paved road. Two paved roads on left. Intersection is unmarked. Zero trip meter.

▼ 0.4 BL Bear left along power lines. Graded road on right.

7.9 ▲ BR Bear right leaving power lines. Graded road on left.
GPS: N35°33.16′ W115°26.22′

▼ 0.9 SO Track on left at pump on left.

7.4 ▲ SO Track on right at pump on right.

▼ 1.4 SO Track on right and track on left along power lines. Leave power lines.

6.9 ▲ SO Track on right and track on left along power lines. Continue alongside power lines.

▼ 3.7 SO Well-used track on left.

4.6 ▲ SO Well-used track on right.
GPS: N35°32.55′ W115°29.60′

▼ 5.0 BR Two tracks on left, second of which goes to Ivanpah Springs; then enter Mojave National Preserve. The preserve has no sign, just a marker.

3.3 ▲ SO Exit Mojave National Preserve. There is no sign, just a marker at the boundary. Two tracks on right, first of which goes to Ivanpah Springs.
GPS: N35°32.69′ W115°31.07′

▼ 5.1 SO Cross through wash. Track on right at

wash goes toward Whiskey Spring, and track on left up wash. Trail gradually starts to ascend Colosseum Gorge.

3.2 ▲ SO Track on right up wash. Cross through wash. Track on left at wash goes toward Whiskey Spring. Trail levels out.

▼ 5.5 SO Cross through wash.

2.8 ▲ SO Cross through wash.

▼ 5.7 SO Memorial marker on right.

2.6 ▲ SO Memorial marker on left.
GPS: N35°32.77′ W115°31.87′

▼ 5.8 SO Track on left toward stone ruins.

2.5 ▲ SO Track on right toward stone ruins.
GPS: N35°32.78′ W115°31.93′

▼ 6.2 SO Track on left goes into wash. Trail starts to climb wide shelf road up Colosseum Gorge.

2.1 ▲ SO Track on right goes into wash. End of shelf road.

▼ 7.8 SO Cross over Colosseum Gorge Wash.

0.5 ▲ SO Cross over Colosseum Gorge Wash.

▼ 7.9 SO Well-used track on left goes into area of old mine workings.

0.4 ▲ SO Well-used track on right goes into area of old mine workings.
GPS: N35°33.55′ W115°33.62′

▼ 8.1 SO Tank on right.

0.2 ▲ SO Tank on left.

▼ 8.3 TL Turn left onto well-used, smaller trail. Track on right goes 0.4 miles to Colosseum Mine. Zero trip meter.

0.0 ▲ Continue to the east.
GPS: N35°33.86′ W115°34.01′

▼ 0.0 Continue to the southwest and enter line of wash.

0.6 ▲ TR Turn right and exit line of wash onto larger, roughly graded road. Track on left goes 0.4 miles to Colosseum Mine. Zero trip meter.

▼ 0.2 SO Tank on left and two tracks on right.

0.4 ▲ SO Tank on right and two tracks on left.
GPS: N35°33.76′ W115°34.22′

▼ 0.5 SO Small tank on right.

0.1 ▲ SO Small tank on left.

▼ 0.6　SO　5-way intersection. Two tracks on left and track on right. Second track on left is Green's Well Road, Public Bypass Route. Zero trip meter.

0.0 ▲　　Continue to the north.

GPS: N35°33.55' W115°34.48'

▼ 0.0　　Continue to the southwest.

1.3 ▲　SO　5-way intersection. Two tracks on right and track on left. First track on right is marked Green's Well Road, Public Bypass Route. Zero trip meter.

▼ 0.1　SO　Concrete footings on right.

1.2 ▲　SO　Concrete footings on left.

▼ 0.4　SO　Greene's Cabin on right.

0.9 ▲　SO　Greene's Cabin on left.

GPS: N35°33.60' W115°34.82'

▼ 0.5　SO　Track on right.

0.8 ▲　SO　Track on left.

▼ 0.6　SO　Track on left.

0.7 ▲　SO　Track on right.

▼ 1.3　BL　Bear left out of wash on well-used track. Green's Well Road continues ahead in wash. Intersection is unmarked but there is a metal post opposite the turn. Zero trip meter.

0.0 ▲　　Continue to the east.

GPS: N35°33.74' W115°35.78'

▼ 0.0　　Continue to the west on smaller formed trail.

7.2 ▲　BR　Bear right up wash, joining Green's Well Road, which also continues to the left down wash. Intersection is unmarked but there is a metal post opposite the turn.

▼ 0.1　BR　Well-used track on left.

7.1 ▲　SO　Well-used track on right.

▼ 1.7　SO　Cross through wash.

5.5 ▲　SO　Cross through wash.

▼ 1.8　SO　Cross through wash.

5.4 ▲　SO　Cross through wash.

▼ 2.2　SO　Wire gate.

5.0 ▲　SO　Wire gate.

GPS: N35°33.66' W115°38.06'

▼ 2.5　SO　Cross through wash.

4.7 ▲　SO　Cross through wash.

▼ 2.8　SO　Cross through wash.

4.4 ▲　SO　Cross through wash.

▼ 3.3　SO　Cross through wash.

3.9 ▲　SO　Cross through wash.

▼ 3.7　SO　Cross through wash.

3.5 ▲　SO　Cross through wash.

▼ 3.9　SO　Cross through wash.

3.3 ▲　SO　Cross through wash.

▼ 4.1　SO　Cross through wash.

3.1 ▲　SO　Cross through wash.

▼ 4.5　SO　Cross through wash.

2.7 ▲　SO　Cross through wash.

▼ 5.4　SO　Track on right.

1.8 ▲　BR　Track on left.

GPS: N35°32.54' W115°40.64'

▼ 6.1　SO　Track on right.

1.1 ▲　SO　Track on left.

▼ 7.2　　Trail ends at intersection with paved Kingston Road. Turn left for I-15 and Baker; turn right for Sandy, NV. There is a small track opposite.

0.0 ▲　　Trail commences on Kingston Road, 6.5 miles north of the Excelsior Mine Road exit on I-15, 5.7 miles south of the intersection of Kingston Road and Excelsior Mine Road. Zero trip meter and turn northeast on well-used formed trail, which leads straight toward the Clark Mountain Range. Intersection is unmarked but there is a small track opposite.

GPS: N35°31.63' W115°42.27'

DESERT #25

Kingston Wash Trail

STARTING POINT: Excelsior Mine Road, 8.6 miles north of the intersection with Kingston Road

FINISHING POINT: California 127, opposite the site of Renoville

TOTAL MILEAGE: 30 miles, plus 6.1-mile spur to Crusty Bunny Ranch

UNPAVED MILEAGE: 30 miles, plus 6.1-mile spur

DRIVING TIME: 4 hours (including spur)
ELEVATION RANGE: 700–3,600
USUALLY OPEN: Year-round
BEST TIME TO TRAVEL: September to June
DIFFICULTY RATING: 3
SCENIC RATING: 8
REMOTENESS RATING: +1

Special Attractions

■ Long, remote desert wash trail that travels a vehicle corridor in the Kingston Range Wilderness.
■ The Crusty Bunny Ranch cabin.

History

The settlement of Kingston, located just inside the California border, was homesteaded in the early 1920s. Dry farming was attempted throughout the valley, but the short growing season made efforts unprofitable. A post office was opened in 1924, and a school was established as well. Vineyards were ambitiously planted and bootlegging took place during Prohibition. Homesteaders had little choice during the Depression but to try and survive on their Kingston properties. A community hall was erected, a small library was established, and one store catered to the small settlement. When options opened up after the Depression, homesteaders slowly left their lands. The post office's closure in 1938 signaled the end of Kingston.

Kingston Wash formed part of a trail that was used by Indians, and later Spanish and American travelers. The Kingston Range was a welcome relief from the Mojave Desert for all who passed this way. Horsethief Spring, to the north of Kingston Peak, was a reliable watering point for herds of horses being traded along the Old Spanish Trail, which ran north of the mountains. The spring was also used to hide stolen horses.

At the western end of the trail lies the remote site of Valjean, a small settlement along the Tonopah & Tidewater Railroad. The railroad was constructed between 1905 and 1907, stretching from Ludlow, California, to Beatty, Nevada. This section of railroad operated on a schedule that was meant to prevent two trains from colliding. Yet in

August 1929, two men were killed in a 15-car train accident south of Valjean. Nothing had been spotted on the line ahead and it seemed the train had simply crashed for no reason, killing the engineer and fireman. Like most railroads, this route was monitored regularly for line damage. However, there had been no foot patrol of the particular 2.5-mile-long section where the accident occurred. An official inquiry concluded that a rainstorm in the Silurian Hills to the south of this trail caused a localized flash flood that eroded a section of bridge. The damage was most likely undetectable from the engine car. Even if the displaced rail lines had been noticed by the engineer, it was doubtful the train could have stopped in time.

The Silurian Hills gained their name from the Silurian (Paleozoic) rocks found within.

Operating a railroad through such a harsh environment combined with a fluctuating freight market ultimately proved unprofitable. An application to close the route was lodged in 1938. The last train traveled the scenic route some time in 1940.

Description

Kingston Wash Trail is a recognized OHV access route through the remote Kingston Range Wilderness. It is lightly traveled and offers a remote, high desert experience for vehicle-based travelers.

The trail commences on Excelsior Mine Road, some 27 miles southeast of Tecopa via Tecopa Pass. The BLM has marked the trail with route markers. However, they are sporadic in places and should not be relied upon.

The trail travels along the southern edge of the Kingston Range, undulating across the bajada before entering a small wash line that gradually descends to join the wide channel of Kingston Wash. Within Kingston Wash, the trail can be difficult to see. Vehicles often take different routes. The constant rearrangement of boulders and vegetation within the wash makes it difficult to give precise directions. As long as you remain within the main wash channel it is unlikely that you will go wrong. You may need a bit of scouting to find the best route for your vehicle. Outside the wash channel is the Kingston Range Wilderness, where vehicle travel is prohibited.

The trail passes two springs. The first, Coyote Holes, is in the main wash channel. The second, Kingston Spring, is found after the trail has left the main wash.

A well-used spur trail goes 6.1 miles to the Crusty Bunny Ranch, where an old cabin is available on a first-come first-served basis to passing travelers. It is furnished and in generally good order. If you use the cabin, make sure you leave it in better condition than you found it. As always, when entering old premises be aware of the danger of hantavirus (see page 13).

From the Crusty Bunny Ranch spur the trail runs along the open Valjean Valley, crossing the old Tonopah & Tidewater Railroad grade and passing the site of Valjean. Nothing remains at the site except a few piles of rusty cans. The trail ends at the intersection with California 127, opposite the unmarked site of Renoville.

The route is marked as D171 on some maps, but not on the marker posts along the route.

Current Road Information

Bureau of Land Management
Needles Field Office
1303 South US Highway 95
Needles, CA 92363
(760) 326-7000

Map References

BLM   Mesquite Lake, Owlshead Mtns.
USGS 1:24,000   East of Kingston Peak,
      Kingston Peak, Kingston Spring,
      Silurian Hills, Silurian Lake
      1:100,000 Mesquite Lake,
      Owlshead Mtns.
Maptech CD-ROM: Barstow/San
      Bernardino County; San
      Bernardino County/Mojave
*Southern & Central California Atlas &
      Gazetteer,* pp. 55, 56
California Road & Recreation Atlas, p. 97

Kingston Spring

Route Directions

▼ 0.0   From Excelsior Mine Road, 8.6 miles north of the intersection with Kingston Road, zero trip meter and turn west on well-used, formed trail. A marker post at the start gives the name of the trail and indicates its suitability for 4WDs, ATVs, and motorbikes.

6.5 ▲   Trail ends at intersection with paved Excelsior Mine Road. Turn left for Tecopa; turn right for I-15 and Baker.
       GPS: N35°43.00' W115°48.25'

▼ 1.5   SO   Cross through wash.
5.0 ▲   SO   Cross through wash.
▼ 2.1   SO   Pass through wire gate.
4.4 ▲   SO   Pass through wire gate.
       GPS: N35°41.31' W115°49.17'

▼ 2.3   SO   Enter line of wash.
4.2 ▲   SO   Exit line of wash.
▼ 2.4   BR   Bear right down main wash.
4.1 ▲   BL   Bear left out of main wash.
▼ 6.5   BR   Bear right and enter main channel of Kingston Wash. Zero trip meter. There is no vehicle travel to the left up Kingston Wash.
0.0 ▲   Continue to the north up side wash.
       GPS: N35°38.31' W115°51.84'

▼ 0.0   Continue to the west down Kingston Wash.
5.3 ▲   BL   Bear left out of main channel of Kingston Wash, following directional marker into a smaller side wash. Vehicles cannot continue in the main Kingston Wash past this point. Zero trip meter.
▼ 5.3   SO   Old wire corral on right. Rock pile and visitor's book contained in a box on the right is marked Box 2. Zero trip meter.
0.0 ▲   Continue to the northeast.
       GPS: N35°38.48' W115°57.30'

▼ 0.0   Continue to the southwest.
2.2 ▲   SO   Old wire corral on left. Rock pile and visitor's book contained in a box on the left is marked Box 2. Zero trip meter.

▼ 0.2   SO   Coyote Holes on right.
2.0 ▲   SO   Coyote Holes on left.
       GPS: N35°38.45' W115°57.50'

▼ 0.8   SO   Adit on left in high embankment.
1.4 ▲   SO   Adit on right in high embankment.
       GPS: N35°38.20' W115°58.13'

▼ 2.2   BL   Follow directional marker out of main Kingston Wash into a smaller side wash. Vehicles cannot continue in Kingston Wash past this point. Zero trip meter.
0.0 ▲   Continue to the northeast up Kingston Wash.
       GPS: N35°37.73' W115°59.44'

▼ 0.0   Continue to the east up smaller side wash.
6.9 ▲   BR   Bear right up main Kingston Wash and zero trip meter. Vehicles cannot travel down the wash to left.
▼ 1.4   SO   Leave main wash and bear right.
5.5 ▲   SO   Bear left into wash.
▼ 1.8   SO   Bear right out of line of wash.
5.1 ▲   SO   Bear left and enter line of wash.
▼ 1.9   BR   Kingston Spring on right.
5.0 ▲   BL   Bear left and pass Kingston Spring on left.
       GPS: N35°37.22' W115°57.73'

▼ 2.0   SO   Cross through wash.
4.9 ▲   SO   Cross through wash.
▼ 2.5   SO   Enter wash.
4.4 ▲   SO   Exit wash.
▼ 3.5   BL   Bear left out of wash following directional marker.
3.4 ▲   BR   Bear right up wash.
       GPS: N35°36.94' W115°59.23'

▼ 3.7   SO   Cross through wide wash.
3.2 ▲   SO   Cross through wide wash.
▼ 4.1   SO   Cross through wash. Trail crosses many small washes for the next 2.8 miles.
2.8 ▲   SO   Cross through wash. End of wash crossings.
▼ 6.9   SO   Well-used track on left is spur to Crusty Bunny Ranch cabin. Zero trip meter and follow marker to Hwy 127.

0.0 ▲		Continue to the northeast. Trail crosses many small washes for the next 2.8 miles.
		GPS: N35°35.45' W116°02.18'

Spur to the Crusty Bunny Ranch Cabin

▼ 0.0		Bear east on well-used, formed trail.
▼ 0.5	SO	Cross through wash. Many small wash crossings for next 0.4 miles.
▼ 0.9	SO	End of wash crossings.
▼ 4.3	SO	Enter wash.
▼ 6.1	UT	Mine workings of the Eastern Star Mine on right; then Crusty Bunny Ranch cabin.
		GPS: N35°33.97' W115°56.11'

Continuation of Main Trail

▼ 0.0		Continue to the west into Valjean Valley.
9.1 ▲	BL	Well-used track on right is spur to Crusty Bunny Ranch cabin. Zero trip meter.
		GPS: N35°35.45' W116°02.18'

▼ 0.5	SO	Enter line of wash.
8.6 ▲	SO	Exit line of wash.
▼ 4.8	SO	Cross over old Tonopah & Tidewater Railroad grade. Track on left and right along railroad corridor is for vehicle use through the wilderness. Site of Valjean is immediately past intersection on right—nothing remains. Trail exits line of wash and crosses bajada.
4.3 ▲	SO	Trail enters line of wash. Site of Valjean on left—nothing remains. Then cross over old Tonopah & Tidewater Railroad grade. Track on left and right along railroad corridor is for vehicle use through the wilderness.
		GPS: N35°35.14' W116°07.37'

▼ 8.8	SO	Track on left.
0.3 ▲	SO	Track on right.
		GPS: N35°33.40' W118°11.10'

▼ 8.9	SO	Cross through Salt Creek.
0.2 ▲	SO	Cross through Salt Creek.
▼ 9.1		Trail ends at T-intersection with California 127, opposite the unmarked site of Renoville. Turn left for Baker; turn right for Tecopa.

DESERT #25: KINGSTON WASH TRAIL

0.0 ▲		Trail commences on California 127, opposite the unmarked site of Renoville, 23 miles north of Baker. Zero trip meter and turn north at unmarked intersection onto wide formed trail. The turn is 0.1 miles southeast of mile marker 21.5 and 0.6 miles southeast of an emergency phone.
		GPS: N35°33.20' W116°11.32'

Sperry Wash Route

STARTING POINT: California 127, at the entrance to the Dumont Dunes
FINISHING POINT: Furnace Creek Road, 9 miles southeast of Tecopa
TOTAL MILEAGE: 18.6 miles
UNPAVED MILEAGE: 15.8 miles
DRIVING TIME: 2.5 hours
ELEVATION RANGE: 500–2,300 feet
USUALLY OPEN: Year-round
BEST TIME TO TRAVEL: September to May
DIFFICULTY RATING: 4
SCENIC RATING: 9
REMOTENESS RATING: +0

Special Attractions
■ Dumont Dunes OHV Area.
■ Historic Sperry town site.
■ Many crossings of the Amargosa River.

History
The Dumont Dunes were created approximately 18,000 years ago by the drying of Lake Manly, in Death Valley, and Lake Dumont, in Silurian Valley. Sand was blown around and deposited here by local prevailing winds. The main dune area is 4 miles long, 1 mile wide, with a high point about 450 feet above the desert floor. The total volume of sand is estimated at 7 billion cubic feet. Studies of aerial photographs taken in the summer of 1953 compared to similar photos taken in 1978 indicate that the Dumont Dunes had advanced a distance of 1.8 miles to the northeast. This translates into an expansion of approximately 40-odd feet per year over the 25-year period. The dunes crossed and almost obliterated the old Tonopah & Tidewater Railroad easement.

The Tonopah & Tidewater Railroad was constructed through the Amargosa Desert from 1905 to 1907. Much of the roadbed was built up with tailings from the borax mill in Death Valley, which gave the grade a white appearance as it snaked its way up the Amargosa River. Trestles as long as 500 feet and deep cuts were necessary to enter the canyon. Tent camps were erected in the wide wash to house and feed the railroad construction gang. Heat drove many of the workers away; some would spray others with water as they worked in the stifling heat. They would then switch to take a turn at the pick and shovel. Lack of materials, a dwindling workforce, and temperatures reportedly reaching as high as 140 degrees Fahrenheit forced the abandonment of further construction during the summer of 1906. Construction of the railroad had been estimated at $3 million. However, the Amargosa River section pushed the project way over budget. Later calculations show that construction of the railroad up the Amargosa River cost more than $40,000 per mile! The first train service between Ludlow and Sperry ran in February 1907. Originally, the line was planned to stretch from the shipping port near Los Angeles to Tonopah, Nevada, but only the middle section was ever completed. Hence, the line was referred to as "the railroad with no beginning and no end."

Even after completion, the railroad was seldom out of the red. Flash floods commonly required major repairs. The last train ran in 1940, and the track was carefully dismantled two years later and shipped to Egypt for use in World War II.

The eastern end of the trail finishes at the intersection with Furnace Creek Road at what was once called Lower Noonday Camp, close to the Western Talc Mine. The foundations of the camp can still be seen near the edge of the creek. An old graveyard is on the north side of Furnace Creek at Tecopa Pass. The pass marks the southern end of the Nopah Range. The Tonopah & Tidewater Railroad ran a branch to this spot to service the mines surrounding old Tecopa.

One of the prominent mines in the area was the Gunsight Mine, located about 3 miles north of the small graveyard. The Gunsight Mine was part of the Tecopa property renowned for its lead. Exploration work at the Gunsight Mine found the lead-rich ledge had pinched out. This brought great concerns to investors. However, in late August 1908, a sigh of relief was heard in the lead-mining industry when the rich ledge was found to resume at a depth of 600 feet.

At that stage, 50 men were employed and 50 tons of ore a day were being hauled to the Tecopa Siding for shipment to the smelter at Salt Lake City. Early in 1909, plans were under way to construct a large concentrating plant. That same year, work began on a private railroad between Tecopa Station and the mine heads at Gunsight and Noonday. An impressive tramway was built up to the second level of the Gunsight Mine. Trains came

Dumont Dunes

Old Tonopah & Tidewater Railroad embankment alongside the trail

close to the mine, where they were loaded under the large ore bin that, in turn, was loaded by ore carts traveling along narrow tracks to an elevated position above the bin.

Closer to the graveyard, the Noonday Mine lay over a faulted offset of the same ore body as the Gunsight Mine. Closer still, the War Eagle Mine, which developed after World War II, also worked the same ledge.

Description

Sperry Wash Route is a well-known OHV route that leads away from the open OHV area of Dumont Dunes. It follows part of the route of the Tonopah & Tidewater Railroad grade, as well as passing through the site of Sperry.

The trail leaves California 127 and travels the graded road to Dumont Dunes OHV Area. The OHV area is open for use by ATVs, motorbikes, sand rails, and 4WD vehicles. The tall dunes have many varying faces for vehicle play. There is a large open area that is suitable for RVs and tent camping, although it can be extremely windy.

The start of the wash route is well marked by an overhead sign. The formed trail leads down to the Amargosa River and follows alongside the river in the main channel for the first few miles. There are many fords through the main river; these are normally shallow and easy to negotiate. The raised grade of the Tonopah & Tidewater Railroad is visible in places on the east side of the wash.

At the town site of Sperry, the trail leaves the Amargosa River and travels up the smaller, rockier Sperry Wash between the Sperry and Dumont Hills. The narrow canyon twists its way up the range before running over the Sperry Hills and down to the graded Western Talc Road at the Western Talc Mine.

The trail is marked along its length by cairns with a large paw print on the face. Navigation is relatively easy.

The trail ends by passing the remains of various talc mines. The Old Tecopa Cemetery is located 0.1 miles west of the eastern end of the trail along Furnace Creek Road. A few graves, marked by piles of stone and small crosses, sit on a rise overlooking the wash. The coordinates of the cemetery are N35º48.13' W116º05.99'.

Current Road Information
Bureau of Land Management
Needles Field Office
1303 South US Highway 95
Needles, CA 92363
(760) 326-7000

Map References
BLM   Owlshead Mtns.
USGS 1:24,000   Saddle Peak Hills,
        Dumont Dunes, Tecopa, Tecopa
        Pass
        1:100,000 Owlshead Mtns.
Maptech CD-ROM: Barstow/San
        Bernardino County
Southern & Central California Atlas &
        Gazetteer, pp. 55, 56
California Road & Recreation Atlas,
        pp. 96, 97

Route Directions

▼ 0.0   Trail commences on California 127, 23
             miles south of Shoshone. Zero trip
             meter and turn northeast on graded
             dirt road at the sign for Dumont Dunes.
             Dunes are visible directly ahead after
             the turn.
3.7 ▲   Trail ends at T-intersection with
             California 127. Turn right for Shoshone;
             turn left for Baker.
             GPS: N35º41.53' W116º18.11'

▼ 3.7   BL   Bear left onto smaller trail and pass
             under entrance marking the Sperry
             Wash Route. Graded road continues
             0.5 miles to the right into the Dumont
             Dunes OHV Area. Zero trip meter.
0.0 ▲   Continue to the west.
             GPS: N35º41.92' W116º15.16'

▼ 0.0   Continue to the east.
3.2 ▲   SO   Join graded dirt road from Dumont
             Dunes. Road on left goes 0.5 miles into
             the Dumont Dunes OHV Area. Zero trip
             meter.

▼ 0.3   SO   Follow alongside Amargosa River in
             main line of wash.
2.9 ▲   SO   Leave Amargosa River Wash.
▼ 0.7   BR   Bear right and ford through Amargosa
             River.
2.5 ▲   BL   Ford through Amargosa River.
             GPS: N35º42.21' W116º14.47'

▼ 0.9   SO   Track on right.
2.3 ▲   SO   Track on left.
▼ 1.3   SO   Track on left.
1.9 ▲   SO   Track on right.
             GPS: N35º42.54' W116º14.10'

▼ 1.4   SO   Track on right; then ford through
             Amargosa River.
1.8 ▲   SO   Ford through Amargosa River; then
             track on left.
             GPS: N35º42.65' W116º14.06'

▼ 1.6   BL   Ford through Amargosa River; then
             bear left.
1.6 ▲   BR   Bear right; then ford through Amargosa
             River.
▼ 2.1   SO   Track on right.
1.1 ▲   BR   Track on left.
▼ 2.2   SO   Track on right.
1.0 ▲   SO   Track on left.
▼ 2.3   SO   Track on right.
0.9 ▲   BR   Track on left.
▼ 2.4   SO   Ford river twice.
0.8 ▲   SO   Ford river twice.
▼ 2.6   SO   Track on right.
0.6 ▲   SO   Track on left.
▼ 2.7   SO   Track on right up wash.
0.5 ▲   SO   Track on left up wash.
▼ 3.0   SO   Track on right.
0.2 ▲   SO   Track on left.
▼ 3.1   SO   Ford through Amargosa River.
0.1 ▲   SO   Ford through Amargosa River.
             GPS: N35º43.80' W116º13.21'

▼ 3.2   SO   Entering Kingston Range Wilderness
             corridor at sign. Zero trip meter.
0.0 ▲   Continue to the south.
             GPS: N35º43.87' W116º13.22'

▼ 0.0   Continue to the north.
1.1 ▲   SO   Leaving wilderness corridor at sign.
             Zero trip meter.

DESERT #26: SPERRY WASH ROUTE

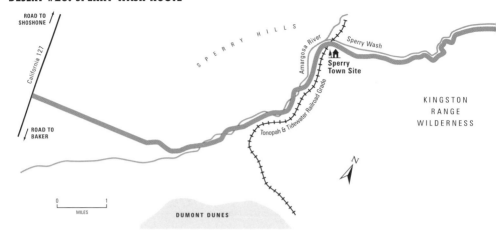

▼ 0.1 BL Ford through river; then bear left along-
           side old Tonopah & Tidewater Railroad
           embankment. Track on right.

1.0 ▲ BR Track on left; then bear right and ford
           through river, leaving railroad embank-
           ment.

▼ 0.7 SO Entering Amargosa Canyon ACEC—
           wildlife habitat.

0.4 ▲ SO Leaving Amargosa Canyon ACEC—
           wildlife habitat.
           GPS: N35°44.46′ W116°13.24′

▼ 1.1 BR Bear right up Sperry Canyon. This is
           Sperry town site. Follow sign to
           Tecopa and Furnace Creek Road. Zero
           trip meter.

0.0 ▲   Continue to the south.
           GPS: N35°44.77′ W116°13.22′

▼ 0.0   Continue to the northeast.

4.2 ▲ BL Leave Sperry Canyon and bear left
           down Amargosa River Wash. This is
           Sperry town site. Zero trip meter.

▼ 3.6 BR Bear right out of canyon and wash.

0.6 ▲ BL Bear left into wash and enter canyon.
           GPS: N35°46.21′ W116°10.77′

▼ 4.0 SO Cross through wash.

0.2 ▲ SO Cross through wash.

▼ 4.2 SO Leaving wilderness corridor at sign.
           Zero trip meter.

0.0 ▲   Continue to the southwest.
           GPS: N35°46.48′ W116°10.24′

▼ 0.0   Continue to the northeast.

2.0 ▲ SO Entering Kingston Range Wilderness
           corridor at sign. Zero trip meter.

▼ 0.4 SO Enter line of wash.

1.6 ▲ SO Exit line of wash.

▼ 1.9 BR Track on left; bear right at cairn. Exit
           line of wash.

0.1 ▲ BL Enter line of wash. Track on right; bear
           left at cairn.
           GPS: N35°46.54′ W116°08.28′

▼ 2.0 TL T-intersection. Intersection is unmarked.
           Zero trip meter. Track on right is Desert
           #27: Alexander Hills Trail.

0.0 ▲   Continue to the west.
           GPS: N35°46.54′ W116°08.20′

▼ 0.0   Continue to the northwest.

0.8 ▲ TR Turn right onto well-used trail. Track
           ahead is Desert #27: Alexander Hills
           Trail. Intersection is unmarked. Zero
           trip meter.

▼ 0.1 SO Cross through wash.

0.7 ▲ SO Cross through wash.

▼ 0.6 SO Track on right.

0.2 ▲ BR Track on left.

▼ 0.7 SO Track on right into talc mine.

0.1 ▲ SO Track on left into talc mine.

▼ 0.8 SO Pass under Sperry Wash Route sign
           and bear left onto Western Talc Road.
           Road on right goes into Western Talc
           Mine. Zero trip meter.

0.0 ▲   Continue to the southeast.

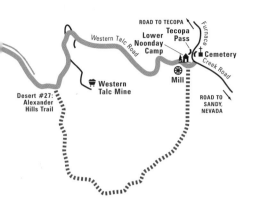

2.5 ▲ SO Track on left.
▼ 1.4 SO Track on right.
2.2 ▲ SO Track on left.
▼ 2.8 SO Track on left.
0.8 ▲ SO Track on right.
▼ 3.4 SO Track on right; then second track on right before mill; then track on left.
0.2 ▲ SO Track on right; then track on left after mill; then second track on left.
▼ 3.5 SO Remains of mill on right. Track on right is Desert #27: Alexander Hills Trail.
0.1 ▲ SO Remains of mill on left. Track on left is Desert #27: Alexander Hills Trail.

GPS: N35°47.98' W116°05.95'

▼ 3.6 Trail ends at T-intersection with paved Furnace Creek Road. Turn left for Tecopa; turn right for Sandy.
0.0 ▲ From Furnace Creek Road, 9 miles southeast of Tecopa, zero trip meter and turn south on graded dirt road marked Western Talc Road and cross through wash on concrete ford. Past the wash on the right is the first trail marker for Sperry Wash Route—a small cairn bears the imprint of a large paw print.

GPS: N35°48.07' W116°05.84'

Alexander Hills Trail

STARTING POINT: Desert #26: Sperry Wash Route, 0.1 miles southwest of Furnace Creek Road
FINISHING POINT: Desert #26: Sperry Wash Route, 3.6 miles southwest of Furnace Creek Road
TOTAL MILEAGE: 6.4 miles
UNPAVED MILEAGE: 6.4 miles
DRIVING TIME: 1 hour
ELEVATION RANGE: 2,100–3,000 feet
USUALLY OPEN: Year-round
BEST TIME TO TRAVEL: September to June
DIFFICULTY RATING: 4
SCENIC RATING: 8
REMOTENESS RATING: +0

GPS: N35°47.10' W116°08.33'

▼ 0.0 Continue to the northwest.
3.6 ▲ BR Road on left goes into Western Talc Mine. Bear right and pass under Sperry Wash Route sign. Zero trip meter.
▼ 0.2 SO Track on right and track on left.
3.4 ▲ SO Track on right and track on left.
▼ 0.3 SO Track on left and track on right into mine workings.
3.3 ▲ SO Track on right and track on left into mine workings.
▼ 0.4 SO Track on left and track on right; then track on right goes to overlook over open cut mine.
3.2 ▲ SO Track on left goes to overlook over open cut mine; then track on right and track on left.
▼ 0.5 BR Two tracks on left.
3.1 ▲ BL Two tracks on right.
▼ 0.6 BR Track on left.
3.0 ▲ BL Track on right.
▼ 0.7 SO Track on right.
2.9 ▲ SO Track on left.
▼ 0.8 BL Paved road on right is blocked. Bear left and join paved road.
2.8 ▲ BR Paved road continues on left but is blocked. Bear right onto graded dirt road.

GPS: N35°47.43' W116°08.27'

▼ 1.1 SO Track on right.

Adit lined with branches and timbers

Special Attractions
- Remains of many talc mines.
- Narrow shelf road provides panoramic views of Valjean Valley and the Ibex Hills.
- Can be combined with Desert #26: Sperry Wash Route to make a longer, 4-rated trail.

Description
This short, moderate trail can be combined with Desert #26: Sperry Wash Route to provide an alternate exit to Furnace Creek Road that maintains a 4 difficulty rating. The trail leaves alongside the mill site at the northern end of Western Talc Road. It climbs a ridge, and not until you are on top do you see the trail stretching into the distance.

The formed trail follows a wash line for some distance. The most spectacular section of trail is along a very narrow shelf road, which winds around the southern end of the Alexander Hills. Panoramic views of Valjean Valley spread out to the southwest. This section of road is a very narrow single-track with extremely limited passing places. If you en-

counter an oncoming vehicle along this stretch, be prepared to back up for quite some distance.

A spur off the main trail leads 0.5 miles to a viewpoint over Valjean Valley and the Ibex Hills. It terminates in a loop that travels past a large adit. Other adits and mining remains can be found in the vicinity.

The main trail continues down the wash, passing the Acme Mine. Trails within the mine area lead to several viewpoints. The trail rejoins Desert #26: Sperry Wash Route, 3.6 miles from the northern end. Vehicles can exit via Western Talc Road back to Furnace Creek Road, or they can travel Sperry Wash Route to the Dumont Dunes.

Current Road Information
Bureau of Land Management
Needles Field Office
1303 South US Highway 95
Needles, CA 92363
(760) 326-7000

DESERT #27: ALEXANDER HILLS TRAIL

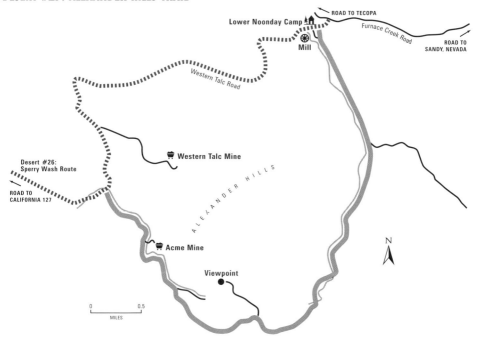

Map References

BLM   Owlshead Mts.
USGS 1:24,000   Tecopa Pass, Tecopa
      1:100,000 Owlshead Mts.
Maptech CD-ROM: Barstow/San
      Bernardino County
Southern & Central California Atlas &
      Gazetteer, pp. 55, 56
California Road & Recreation Atlas, p. 97

Route Directions

▼ 0.0   From Desert #26: Sperry Wash Route,
         0.1 miles from its northern end at
         Furnace Creek Road, zero trip meter
         and turn south on unmarked formed
         trail that climbs ridge toward an old
         water tank, keeping mill remains on
         the right.
3.9 ▲   Mill remains on left; then trail finishes
         back on Desert #26: Sperry Wash
         Route, immediately south of Furnace
         Creek Road. Turn left to travel Sperry
         Wash Route to Dumont Dunes; turn
         right for Furnace Creek Road.

GPS: N35°47.98' W116°05.95'

▼ 0.1   BL Track on right returns to Sperry Wash
            Route. Bear left on formed trail leading
            away from mill.
3.8 ▲ BR Track on left leads down to Sperry
            Wash Route.

GPS: N35°47.91' W116°05.95'

▼ 0.6 SO Pass through wire gate.
3.3 ▲ SO Pass through wire gate.

GPS: N35°47.52' W116°05.67'

▼ 1.2 BR Track on left.
2.7 ▲ SO Track on right.

GPS: N35°47.05' W116°05.39'

▼ 2.9 SO Enter line of wash.
1.0 ▲ BL Bear left away from line of wash.
▼ 3.0 BR Exit line of wash. Faint track on left.
0.9 ▲ BL Enter line of wash. Faint track on right.
▼ 3.1 SO Cross through wash.
0.8 ▲ SO Cross through wash.
▼ 3.3 SO Cross through wash.
0.6 ▲ SO Cross through wash.

▼ 3.5　SO　Start of shelf road. Views southwest to Valjean Valley.

0.4 ▲　SO　Shelf road ends. Views southwest to Valjean Valley.

▼ 3.9　SO　Well-used track on right goes 0.5 miles to viewpoint. Zero trip meter.

0.0 ▲　　　Continue to the northeast.

GPS: N35°45.49′ W116°06.53′

▼ 0.0　　　Continue to the southwest.

2.5 ▲　SO　Well-used track on left goes 0.5 miles to viewpoint. Zero trip meter.

▼ 0.3　SO　Cross saddle. End of shelf road.

2.2 ▲　SO　Cross saddle. Start of shelf road.

▼ 0.5　SO　Enter down line of wash.

2.0 ▲　SO　Exit line of wash.

▼ 1.1　SO　Small track on right.

1.4 ▲　BR　Small track on left.

GPS: N35°45.72′ W116°07.43′

▼ 1.8　SO　Two tracks on right. Both lead up to the Acme Mine and loop through the mine.

0.7 ▲　BR　Two tracks on left. Both lead up to the Acme Mine and loop through the mine.

GPS: N35°46.17′ W116°07.77′

▼ 2.4　SO　Exit line of wash.

0.1 ▲　SO　Enter line of wash.

▼ 2.5　　　Trail ends at intersection with Desert #26: Sperry Wash Route. Turn left to continue along Sperry Wash; turn right to exit back to Western Talc Road.

0.0 ▲　　　Trail starts on Desert #26: Sperry Wash Route, 3.6 miles from the northern end at Furnace Creek Road. Zero trip meter and turn southeast on unmarked formed trail. Sperry Wash Route turns to the west at this point.

GPS: N35°46.54′ W116°08.19′

DESERT #28

Harry Wade Exit Route

STARTING POINT: California 127 at Ashford Junction

FINISHING POINT: California 127, 27 miles south of Shoshone

TOTAL MILEAGE: 30.5 miles

UNPAVED MILEAGE: 30.5 miles

DRIVING TIME: 1.5 hours

ELEVATION RANGE: 0–500 feet

USUALLY OPEN: Year-round

BEST TIME TO TRAVEL: September to June

DIFFICULTY RATING: 2

SCENIC RATING: 8

REMOTENESS RATING: +0

Special Attractions

■ Easy graded trail through the southern end of Death Valley.

■ Trail follows the approximate route used by Harry Wade and party to escape Death Valley in 1849.

History

The Harry Wade Exit Route is thought to have been the southerly exit from Death Valley used by the Wade family in 1849. Most of the family was born in England and had come to America in search of opportunity out West. They were the only members of the lost wagon train of 1849 to escape with their wagons intact. Other members of the group, including the Jayhawkers and the Bennett-Arcane party, either abandoned or burned their wagons. Their wagon train had attempted to follow a shortcut to the California goldfields. All of the members experienced starvation and extreme hardships trying to cope with the impossible terrain and extreme weather. Their oxen could barely pull the wagons because they were malnourished and dehydrated as well. It became a situation in which every man had to fend for himself. The wagon train split up near Furnace Creek, where it was confronted with the insurmountable Panamint Range dead ahead. The Wade party bore south, initially following an old Indian trail. They remained with their wagons, unlike some who had burned theirs to cook and smoke ox meat. Fortunately, the family managed to negotiate its way through Death Valley, and on to civilization.

The Confidence Mine is in the Black Mountains approximately 7 miles northeast of the Confidence Mill site. Mary Scott discovered what she thought was a silver vein in the early 1890s and moved on. Just a few years later, George Montgomery bought the claim for $36,000, once he realized that the vein contained gold. The mine was worked extensively, but the Confidence Mining Co. faced exorbitant haulage costs to ship ore out of Death Valley and to have supplies shipped in. As a result, Montgomery sought financial partners. The Confidence Mill was constructed late in 1895 in the valley below this trail. More than 20 men were employed by the company at the time. A well was dug nearby, which unfortunately produced very salty water that required additional treat-

ment to render it useful. Despite such investments, the mill only ran for a few months because it was unable to sufficiently reduce the ore. Funds had run out and employees walked off the job because of nonpayment, leaving the mine and mill idle.

By 1897, Montgomery managed to sell out for more than $80,000 to a partner named Cannon. Cannon tried unsuccessfully to sell the mine to outsiders. Two separate investors failed to make the mine profitable, one in 1911 and the other in 1913. By the mid-1920s, the mill was dismantled and the mine was quiet. A rumored reopening in the 1940s was the last mention of the old mine.

Harry Wade Exit Route passes through the southern end of Death Valley

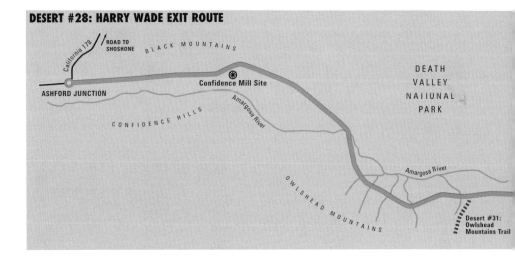

Description

Harry Wade Exit Route leaves the southern end of Death Valley, traveling through the sandy valley floor to intersect with California 127. The trail leaves from Ashford Junction, turning off the paved road to run south along the wide valley. The valley is framed by the Owlshead Mountains to the west and the Black Mountains to the east.

The road is suitable for high-clearance vehicles for its entire length. Soft sandy sections, particularly around the Amargosa River Wash, make it unsuitable for passenger vehicles. The road is often very washboardy. It is likely to be impassable after rain, when deep powder-fine sand traps turn to a sticky morass.

The trail intersects with the Desert #31: Owlshead Mountains Trail and Desert #29: Ibex Dunes Trail before it finishes on California 127.

Current Road Information

Death Valley National Park
PO Box 579
Death Valley, CA 92328-0579
(760) 786-3200

Map References

BLM   Owlshead Mtns.
USGS 1:24,000   Shore Line Butte,
      Epaulet Peak, Confidence Hills
      East, East of Owl Lake, Old Ibex
      Pass, Saddle Peak Hills
      1:100,000 Owlshead Mtns.

Maptech CD-ROM: Barstow/San
   Bernardino County
*Southern & Central California Atlas &
   Gazetteer,* pp. 54, 55
California Road & Recreation Atlas, p. 96

Route Directions

▼ 0.0   From California 178 at Ashford
          Junction, 25 miles west of the inter-
          section with California 127, zero trip
          meter and turn southeast on graded
          dirt road, following sign to Baker.
18.3 ▲   Trail ends on paved California 178.
          Turn right for Shoshone; turn left for
          Furnace Creek.
          GPS: N35°53.99' W116°39.35'

▼ 6.5 SO Confidence Mill site on right—nothing
           remains. The site is unmarked.
11.8 ▲ SO Confidence Mill site on left—nothing
           remains. The site is unmarked.
           GPS: N35°50.59' W116°33.65'

▼ 11.8 SO Start to cross wide Amargosa River
            Wash.
6.6 ▲   SO Exit Amargosa River Wash.
            GPS: N35°46.11' W116°31.62'

▼ 12.5 SO Exit Amargosa River Wash.
5.8 ▲   SO Start to cross wide Amargosa River
            Wash.
▼ 14.1 SO Cross through wash.

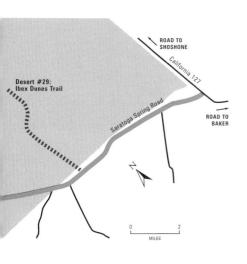

ROAD TO
SHOSHONE

California 127

Desert #29:
Ibex Dunes Trail

Saratoga Spring Road

ROAD TO
BAKER

N

0   2
MILES

4.2 ▲		SO	Cross through wash.
▼ 15.9		SO	Cross through wash.
2.4 ▲		SO	Cross through wash.
▼ 16.0		SO	Cross through wash.
2.3 ▲		SO	Cross through wash.
▼ 17.5		SO	Cross through wash.
0.8 ▲		SO	Cross through wash.
▼ 18.3		SO	Graded road on right is Desert #31: Owlshead Mountains Trail. Zero trip meter.
0.0 ▲			Continue to the northwest.

GPS: N35°41.57′ W116°29.42′

▼ 0.0			Continue to the southeast.
6.4 ▲		BR	Graded road on left is Desert #31: Owlshead Mountains Trail. Zero trip

Looking across the wide Amargosa River Wash

meter and follow sign to Furnace Creek.

▼ 4.9   SO Track on right.
1.5 ▲   SO Track on left.
         GPS: N35°39.09′ W116°24.93′

▼ 5.1   SO Leaving Death Valley National Park.
1.3 ▲   SO Entering Death Valley National Park.
▼ 5.8   SO Track on right.
0.6 ▲   SO Track on left.
         GPS: N35°38.82′ W116°24.18′

▼ 6.4   SO Track on left is Desert #29: Ibex
             Dunes Trail, sign-posted to Saratoga
             Spring. Zero trip meter.
0.0 ▲   Continue to the west.
         GPS: N35°38.80′ W116°23.47′

▼ 0.0   Continue to the east.
5.8 ▲   SO Track on right is Desert #29: Ibex
             Dunes Trail, sign-posted to Saratoga
             Spring. Zero trip meter.
▼ 4.0   SO Track on right.
1.8 ▲   SO Track on left.
         GPS: N35°38.56′ W116°19.19′

▼ 5.8   Trail ends at T-intersection with
             California 127, 27 miles south of
             Shoshone. Turn right for Shoshone;
             turn left for Baker.
0.0 ▲   Trail commences on California 127,
             27 miles south of Shoshone. Zero trip
             meter and turn west on graded dirt
             road. There is a historical marker at the
             start of the trail for Harry Wade Exit
             Route, but otherwise the trail is
             unmarked. Start of the road is called
             Saratoga Spring Road on some maps.
         GPS: N35°37.99′ W116°17.40′

DESERT #29

Ibex Dunes Trail

STARTING POINT: California 127, 16 miles
  south of Shoshone
FINISHING POINT: Desert #28: Harry Wade
  Exit Route, 5.8 miles west of California
  127

TOTAL MILEAGE: 11.1 miles
UNPAVED MILEAGE: 11.1 miles
DRIVING TIME: 1 hour
ELEVATION RANGE: 200–1,600 feet
USUALLY OPEN: Year-round
BEST TIME TO TRAVEL: October to May
DIFFICULTY RATING: 3
SCENIC RATING: 9
REMOTENESS RATING: +0

Special Attractions

■ Ibex Sand Dunes.
■ Saratoga Spring.
■ Bird-watching and photography
  opportunities.

History

Saratoga Spring is one of the largest fresh-water springs in the northern Mojave Desert. The Southern Paiute are thought to have had regular camps at Saratoga Spring, then known as Muta, before Euro-American arrivals. In a region of low rainfall and extreme weather conditions, these waters were essential for Indians, prospectors, and teamsters in the southern end of Death Valley. The spring was named by G. K. Gilbert during a mapping survey in 1871.

When the price of borax fell in the mid-1880s, William Tell Coleman of the Amargosa Borax Works had to find ways to reduce the cost of freighting borax to the railroad at Mojave. When his contract with hauler Charles Bennett was up, Coleman developed his own freighting business with the assistance of his foreman, John Perry. They constructed massive wagons capable of carrying 10 tons of borax each. The wagons were then towed by 20-mule teams. This was the beginning of what was to become the Pacific Coast Borax Company's trademark, "20 Mule Team Borax."

Although the company claimed that it never lost a single animal on these death-defying, record-breaking trips, it did lose one teamster at Saratoga Spring in 1886. In a San Bernardino court hearing, Sterling Wassam, the swamper who operated the brakes on the wagon, claimed that he was attacked by teamster Al Bryson while lunching at the spring. He said he hit Bryson in self-defense with the nearest item at hand—a shovel. The teamster did not live to argue the point and Bryson was acquitted.

In 1905, prospector W. A. Kelly found rock salt near Saratoga Spring and formed a company with partner Jonas Osborne. The pair was unable to finance the freight costs out of Death Valley and the mining venture did not pay off. In 1912, Kelly sold out to millionaire William Kerckhoff. With the proper financing available, things looked promising; a railroad was planned and sample shafts were dug. Kerckhoff acquired nearby gypsum mines also but none paid well enough to warrant further investment.

In 1909, the Pacific Nitrate Company began to explore for minerals. The company enlarged the small Saratoga Spring to serve as a water source for its processing plant. The nitrate deposits were never worked because they were too poor in quality, but the enlarged pools remained. In the 1930s, the Saratoga Water Company bottled the water as a health cure. A resort was built around the pools, where people could "take the waters."

Description

The Ibex Dunes sit at the southern tip of Death Valley, in the small valley between the Saddle Peak Hills and the Ibex Hills. This trail runs along the western side of the dunes, far enough away that deep sand is not too much of a problem and near enough that photographers and others who appreciate the shape and form of the dunes can see them clearly.

Initially the trail leaves California 127 and runs down a sandy wash, descending steadily to Ibex Valley. Out of the wash, the trail forks, with the trail to Ibex ghost town and spring leaving to the northwest. Ibex Dunes

Saratoga Spring

DESERT #29: IBEX DUNES TRAIL

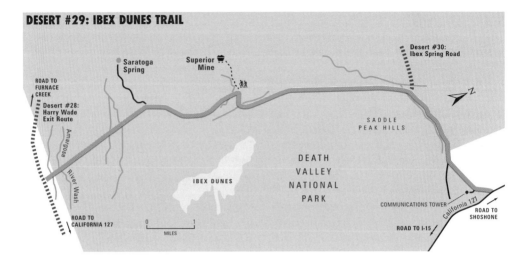

Trail follows around the edge of the valley, passing the warning sign for deep sand. The sandy patches are deep enough that 4WD is preferred, especially in the reverse direction, when you tackle them heading uphill. However, they are short and interspersed with firmer ground.

The trail joins the graded road that leads to Saratoga Spring. The very beautiful reed-fringed pools support vast bird and animal populations, as well as the Saratoga Springs pupfish found nowhere else in the world. Late afternoon is a good time to visit the spring, when the low afternoon light brings out the colors of the surrounding rocks. No camping is permitted at the spring, and because of the unique wildlife populations, access is limited. An excellent view can be obtained by climbing the small ridge from the parking area.

Current Road Information

Death Valley National Park
PO Box 579
Death Valley, CA 92328-0579
(760) 786-3200

Map References

BLM Owlshead Mtns.
USGS 1:24,000 Ibex Pass, Old Ibex Pass,
       Ibex Spring
       1:100,000 Owlshead Mtns.
Maptech CD-ROM: Barstow/San

Bernardino County
Southern & Central California Atlas & Gazeteer, p. 55
California Road & Recreation Atlas, p. 96
Trails Illustrated, Death Valley National Park (221)

Route Directions

▼ 0.0   From California 127, 16 miles south of Shoshone, zero trip meter and turn southwest on unmarked graded dirt road. The road initially leads toward a communications tower.
2.7 ▲   Trail ends on California 127. Turn left for Shoshone; turn right for Baker and I-15.
        GPS: N35°46.33' W116°19.49'

▼ 0.3   BR Track on left to communications tower.
2.4 ▲   BL Track on right to communications tower.
▼ 0.6   SO Cross through wash.
2.1 ▲   SO Cross through wash.
▼ 1.1   SO Track on left.
1.6 ▲   BL Track on right.
▼ 1.2   SO Entering Death Valley National Park at sign.
1.5 ▲   SO Leaving Death Valley National Park at sign.
        GPS: N35°45.84' W116°20.52'

▼ 1.6   SO Enter line of wash.
1.1 ▲   SO Exit line of wash.

▼ 2.7 BL Road forks. Track on right at warning sign for deep sand is Desert #30: Ibex Spring Trail. Zero trip meter.

0.0 ▲ Continue to the northeast.

GPS: N35°45.62' W116°22.17'

▼ 0.0 Continue to the southwest.

5.8 ▲ SO Track on left is Desert #30: Ibex Spring Trail. Zero trip meter.

▼ 3.1 SO Enter wash.

2.7 ▲ SO Exit wash.

GPS: N35°42.96' W116°23.25'

▼ 3.3 SO Exit wash.

2.5 ▲ SO Enter wash.

▼ 3.8 BL Old vehicle trail (now a hiking trail) on right leads to Superior Mine.

2.0 ▲ BR Old vehicle trail (now a hiking trail) on left leads to Superior Mine.

GPS: N35°42.71' W116°23.63'

▼ 3.9 SO Cross through wash.

1.9 ▲ SO Cross through wash.

▼ 5.8 BL Join larger graded road on bend. Zero trip meter. Road on right goes 1.2 miles to Saratoga Spring.

0.0 ▲ Continue to the north

GPS: N35°41.09' W116°24.11'

▼ 0.0 Continue to the south.

2.6 ▲ BR Bear right onto smaller, formed track. Intersection is unmarked, but is on a left-hand curve. There is a deep sand warning sign at the start of the track. Graded road continues on left for 1.2 miles to Saratoga Spring. Zero trip meter.

▼ 0.7 SO Cross through wash.

1.9 ▲ SO Cross through wash.

▼ 1.7 SO Cross through wash.

0.9 ▲ SO Cross through wash.

▼ 2.1 SO Cross through wash.

0.5 ▲ SO Cross through wash.

▼ 2.2 SO Cross through Amargosa River Wash.

Ibex Dunes

20-MULE TEAMS

Around 1880, a prospector named Aaron Winters was living in Death Valley when he noticed a certain type of rock covering the desert floor. By chance, he met another roaming prospector named Henry Spiller, who told Winters about a mineral that was quickly climbing in value. Winters realized the rocks he noticed could be the mineral that Spiller had described.

20-Mule Team

Camping that night with his wife, Winters tested some of the rocks using the method Spiller described and was delighted when it began to turn green. The prospector knew then he had discovered a rich deposit of borax, a mineral used in the manufacture of glass and ceramics. The discovery sparked a period of intense borax mining in Death Valley.

Mining companies soon found that it was quite difficult to transport the mineral out of Death Valley. The only viable method was to use mule-drawn wagons. From 1883 to about 1907, 20-mule teams (actually two horses and 18 mules) carried some 2.5 million pounds of borax a year from the mines to a railroad depot in Mojave. Each specially constructed, 16-foot wagon traveled 165 miles across harsh desert with a load of up to 36 ½ tons. The trip over the Panamint Mountains and back took 20 days. It took a team of three men to drive the wagons and direct the mule teams over the rugged terrain.

Eventually trucks replaced the mule teams, but their mystique survived. Ronald Reagan hosted a television series dramatizing their treks. Members of the Boron Chamber of Commerce opened the Twenty Mule Museum, where visitors today can see exhibits about the mule teams and the mines they helped support.

0.4 ▲	SO	Cross through Amargosa River Wash.
		GPS: N35°39.11' W116°23.56'

▼ 2.3	SO	Leaving Death Valley National Park at sign.
0.3 ▲	SO	Entering Death Valley National Park at sign.
		GPS: N35°39.03' W116°23.54'

▼ 2.4	SO	Cross through wash.
0.2 ▲	SO	Cross through wash.
▼ 2.6		Trail ends at T-intersection with Desert #28: Harry Wade Exit Route. Turn left for Tecopa; turn right to continue along Harry Wade Exit Route toward Furnace Creek.
0.0 ▲		Trail commences on Desert #28: Harry Wade Exit Route, 5.8 miles west of California 127. Zero trip meter and turn north on graded dirt road at sign for Saratoga Spring.
		GPS: N35°38.81' W116°23.47'

DESERT #30

Ibex Spring Road

STARTING POINT: Desert #29: Ibex Dunes Trail, 2.7 miles west of California 127
FINISHING POINT: Ibex Mine
TOTAL MILEAGE: 7.8 miles (one-way)
UNPAVED MILEAGE: 7.8 miles
DRIVING TIME: 1 hour (one-way)
ELEVATION RANGE: 200–500 feet
USUALLY OPEN: Year-round
BEST TIME TO TRAVEL: October to May
DIFFICULTY RATING: 3
SCENIC RATING: 9
REMOTENESS RATING: +1

Special Attractions
■ Ibex ghost town.
■ Several well-preserved talc mines.
■ Sand dunes in Buckwheat Wash Valley.

History
Ibex Spring and nearby Saratoga Spring are small yet valuable oases in this desert region.

They are both noted for their abundance of arrowheads. Some low stone structures against the hills near Ibex Spring were thought to have housed miners before the Lost Buthane Mining Company established a mining town.

The Ibex Mine was first opened in 1882. The silver- and lead-bearing ore looked promising and a dry-roasting mill was constructed the following year. As was often the case in this region, the remote location worked against the mine. The overwhelming heat, lack of water, and hefty freight costs into this part of Death Valley proved too much for the mine's survival.

In 1906, new prospectors were reworking the Ibex and Rusty Pick Mines, both in Buckwheat Wash. But again, the returns could not make up for the expenses of operating mines in this remote location. A low level of activity continued at the mines throughout the years. One family moved to the other climatic extreme in Alaska in an effort to make a financial comeback. Several more unsuccessful attempts at working the mines were undertaken in the following decades, with prospecting continuing in the area into the 1970s.

A different kind of mining occurred in the mid-twentieth century. The Ibex Spring talc claims were established by Charles Moorehouse in the 1930s. Moorehouse successfully operated his mines into the 1940s, when he then leased them to the Sierra Talc Company. Massive quantities of talc were removed from the Moorehouse region up until the 1960s. The Monarch Talc Mines took off in the late 1930s and the nearby Pleasanton Talc Mines did the same in the early 1940s. These mines, all leased by the Sierra Talc Company, were on the eastern side of the Ibex Hills. The late 1960s brought a close to activity in the region. Many mining structures have succumbed to time and weather over the decades since.

Description
This short spur trail leads away from Desert #29: Ibex Dunes Trail and passes several historic points of interest along its length. The

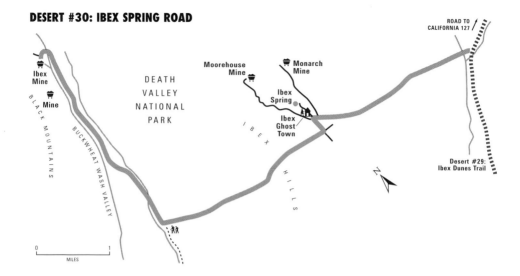

formed trail is well used and is easy to follow as far as Ibex ghost town. Erosion is a constant problem along the way; several deep gully washouts have to be negotiated or bypassed.

At Ibex, easily spotted from a distance by the large palm trees at the spring, the trail branches in four directions. Continuing straight ahead leads into the center of the camp, where the Mojave River Valley Museum of Barstow (which has adopted the site) has placed a marker and visitors book. Many of the old houses and structures around Ibex are still standing. These date from the days of the talc mining operations in the 1930s. Past Ibex, the trail continues for 0.9 miles to the Moorehouse Talc Mine, where you can see extensive remains of the wooden loading chutes and tramway. Photographers will find some excellent viewpoints from this location. Bearing right at the 4-way intersection and remaining in the wash takes you to Ibex Spring itself, which is surrounded by palm trees.

The main trail turns to the southeast at the 4-way intersection, and travels along the wash for a short distance. Route finding is tricky along this section. The trail is lightly used and can be hard to follow, especially in the washes. It comes out of the first wash and turns west along the original road. Although this road seems to lead back to the main trail, a major washout has rendered it impassable.

The route winds west through the Ibex

Hills, following a wash into the wide Buckwheat Wash Valley. On the far side of the valley (the southern end of the Black Mountains), sand has collected against the eastern face. These spectacular sand dunes are especially attractive in the low light of afternoon. The trail turns north up the wash and heads toward the most challenging section to navigate. Set your GPS to guide you to the exit point so that you don't miss it.

The trail leaves the wash and finishes at the Ibex Mine. An old corrugated iron cabin sits out of the wash here. You can spend some time exploring the rusting hulks of mine machinery scattered around the hill.

Exit the trail the way you came in. You have the choice of returning to California 127 or exiting via the equally pretty Desert #29: Ibex Dunes Trail. Past Ibex Spring, the trail is only marked on the *Southern & Central California Atlas & Gazetteer.*

Current Road Information

Death Valley National Park
PO Box 579
Death Valley, CA 92328-0579
(760) 786-3200

Map References

BLM   Owlshead Mtns.
USGS 1:24,000   Ibex Pass, Ibex Spring

Sand-covered hills along Buckwheat Wash

Ibex ghost town

1:100,000 Owlshead Mtns.
Maptech CD-ROM: Barstow/San
    Bernardino County
*Southern & Central California Atlas &
    Gazetteer*, p. 55
California Road & Recreation Atlas, p. 96
Trails Illustrated, Death Valley National
    Park (221)

Route Directions

▼ 0.0   From Desert #29: Ibex Dunes Trail, 2.7
         miles west of California 127, zero trip
         meter and turn west on unmarked
         formed trail. There is a sign for deep
         sand ahead on the Ibex Dunes Trail,
         but otherwise the intersection is
         unmarked.
         GPS: N35°45.62' W116°22.17'

▼ 0.1   SO   Cross through wash.
▼ 0.4   SO   Cross through deep washout.
▼ 1.1   SO   Cross through deep washout.
▼ 2.2   SO   Track on right goes 0.5 miles to
              remains of the Monarch Talc Mine.
▼ 2.3   TL   Turn first left down small wash. Track
              straight ahead goes 0.9 miles to the
              Moorehouse Mine and the historical
              marker at Ibex ghost town. Track on
              right continues in the wash for 0.3
              miles to Ibex Spring. Zero trip meter.
              GPS: N35°46.14' W116°24.51'

▼ 0.0   Continue to the southeast.
▼ 0.1   SO   Old cans and remains of vehicle on right.
▼ 0.2   TR   4-way intersection.
              GPS: N35°45.92' W116°24.49'

▼ 0.6   SO   Small washout in trail.
▼ 1.1   SO   Small track on right.
▼ 1.3   SO   Enter wash.
▼ 2.2   SO   Exit wash and start to cross alluvial
              fan toward Buckwheat Wash.
▼ 2.8   BR   Old track on left was once the mule
              team trail (now a hiking trail) to
              Saratoga Spring. Trail bears right up
              wash.
              GPS: N35°46.26' W116°27.01'

▼ 3.8   SO   Trail dips down to enter wash.

GPS: N35°47.16' W116°27.19'

▼ 4.9   SO   Mine on left.
              GPS: N35°48.18' W116°27.11'

▼ 5.1   BL   Bear left at fork in wash.
              GPS: N35°48.30' W116°27.04'

▼ 5.3   TL   Turn left onto formed trail out of wash.
              GPS: N35°48.47' W116°27.04'

▼ 5.4   BL   Fork in trail. Bear left toward the mine
              at the edge of mine diggings.
▼ 5.5   Trail ends at the Ibex Mine cabin.
              GPS: N35°48.52' W116°27.17'

DESERT #31

Owlshead Mountains Trail

STARTING POINT: Desert #28: Harry Wade Exit
    Route, 12.2 miles north of California 127
FINISHING POINT: Communications tower
    within the Owlshead Mountains
TOTAL MILEAGE: 28.7 miles, plus 4.8-mile spur
    to Black Magic Mine
UNPAVED MILEAGE: 28.7 miles, plus 4.8-mile
    spur
DRIVING TIME: 2 hours (one-way)
ELEVATION RANGE: 50–1,200 feet
USUALLY OPEN: Year-round
BEST TIME TO TRAVEL: September to June
DIFFICULTY RATING: 2
SCENIC RATING: 8
REMOTENESS RATING: +1

Special Attractions

■ Very remote desert experience, partially
  within Death Valley National Park.
■ Panoramic views from the end of the trail.
■ Backcountry camping.

History

This trail traces part of the old borax road
from Mojave to Tecopa that was used by
Charles Bennett's 20-mule teams. Today's
trail runs along the section from the Amargosa River to the edge of the China Lake

Overlooking the alluvial wash of Lost Lake from the end of the trail.

Naval Weapons Center. The mule trail followed part of the Walker cutoff from Saratoga Spring to Granite Wells. Freight teams traveled from the Amargosa Borax Works, past Saratoga Spring, to cross the Amargosa River Wash in the southern end of Death Valley. From there, the trail slowly climbed the alluvial fan toward Owl Hole Springs and continued southwest into today's China Lake Naval Weapons Center, where this vehicle trail bears northwest. Wagons skirted the Leach Lake depression, past Leach Spring and Granite Wells, before traversing the long straight stretch across the Mojave Desert to the railroad at Mojave.

The New Deal and Black Magic Mines, on the spur from this trail, extracted manganese from a series of open cuts. The latter produced a high-grade ore used in the production of steel. Pyrolusite, which is black metallic manganese oxide, can be seen in large quantities around the open cuts. Red-brown hematite (iron oxide) can also be seen around the mine. Owl Hole Springs was the camp location and mill site for the mines that produced military hardware during the 1910s, '40s, and '50s. Some mining activity lasted as late as 1991.

The Epsom Salt Works, located on a hiking trail near the end of this trail, began operations in 1921. An ingenious monorail was constructed to transport the ore to Trona. The 20-mile route traveled west over Wingate Pass, across Panamint Valley, over the Slate Range, and across the southern end of Searles Lake into Trona. A single rail was laid on top of timbers that were suspended 4 feet above the ground by A-frames set 10 feet apart. Dodge engines powered the locomotive, which was a double-flanged, two-wheel, in-line model built for this project. It was guided and balanced by rollers running along a timber guide that was attached to the A-frames approximately one foot above the ground. This form of transportation required very little grading and appropriate inclines were chosen when setting up the A-frames. By 1925, the mine was deemed too expensive for the grade of ore extracted when compared to new mines being discovered. Sinking problems on Searles Lake associated with a replacement heavy-duty train combined to bring the Epsom Salt Works to a close. Some remnants of the unusual monorail supposedly lie within the boundaries of China Lake Naval Weapons Center.

Description

Owlshead Mountains Trail is a long spur that leads from Desert #28: Harry Wade Exit Route into the Owlshead Mountains. The trail crosses a mixture of BLM land and the southernmost part of Death Valley National Park. It also skirts the north end of Fort Irwin Military Reservation. The road is roughly graded for its entire length. It is maintained to service the communications tower at the end of the trail. However, because generators have been replaced with solar panels, the tower needs fewer service visits and the trail consequently receives less maintenance, so it can be rough and eroded in places. The trail is also lightly traveled. There are some very quiet backcountry campsites for those wanting to avoid the better-known trails in Death Valley.

A spur leads from the main trail to the remains of the New Deal and Black Magic Mines, which are set above the main trail in the Owlshead Mountains. This rough spur is 3-rated for difficulty, but offers a wonderful panoramic view of the area.

At the western extreme of the trail, a remote hiking trail leads to the site of the old Epsom Salt Works. The faint trail runs close to the China Lake Naval Weapons Center

The rough spur trail offers panoramic views over the Owlshead Mountains

and care must be taken not to enter the naval area for safety and security reasons. The main trail terminates a short distance past the hiking trailhead at a communications tower. At the trail's end, there are panoramic views over the dry pan of Lost Lake as well as the Owlshead Mountains, Death Valley, Black Mountains, and Quail Mountains.

Current Road Information
Death Valley National Park
PO Box 579
Death Valley, CA 92328-0579
(760) 786-3200

Map References
BLM   Owlshead Mtns.
USGS 1:24,000   Old Ibex Pass, East of
     Owl Lake, Owl Lake, Quail Spring,
     Hidden Spring
     1:100,000 Owlshead Mtns.
Maptech CD-ROM: Barstow/San
     Bernardino County
Southern & Central California Atlas &
     Gazetteer, pp. 54, 55
California Road & Recreation Atlas, p. 96

Route Directions

▼ 0.0   From Desert #28: Harry Wade Exit
    Route, 12.2 miles north of California
    127, zero trip meter and turn west on
    graded dirt road. Harry Wade Exit
    Route continues to the northwest at
    this point and is sign-posted to
    Furnace Creek. Owlshead Mountains
    Trail is unmarked.
    GPS: N35°41.57' W116°29.42'

▼ 0.7   SO   Cross through wash.
▼ 5.8   SO   Leaving Death Valley National Park and
        entering BLM land. Boundary is not
        clearly marked.
        GPS: N35°38.96' W116°34.92'

▼ 9.4   SO   Track on right to diggings.
        GPS: N35°38.28' W116°38.67'

▼ 9.5   BL   Track on right is the spur to Black

DESERT #31: OWLSHEAD MOUNTAINS TRAIL

Magic Mine. Zero trip meter. Owl Hole Springs on right at intersection.
GPS: N35°38.33' W116°38.81'

Spur to Black Magic Mine

▼ 0.0   From Owl Hole Springs, zero trip meter
     and turn northwest.
▼ 0.9   SO   Track on right to New Deal diggings.
▼ 1.6   SO   Entering Death Valley National Park
        at sign.
        GPS: N35°38.78' W116°40.43'

▼ 2.8   SO   Track on left.
▼ 2.9   SO   Track on left.
▼ 3.2   SO   Tailings on right.
▼ 3.8   SO   Loading hopper on left; then track on
        left at saddle goes 0.2 miles to dig-
        gings and view over the dry Owl Lake.
        Zero trip meter.
        GPS: N35°40.18' W116°40.79'

▼ 0.0   Continue to the northeast.
▼ 0.2   SO   Track on left.
▼ 1.0   UT   Spur ends at workings of the Black
        Magic Mine.
        GPS: N35°39.81' W116°40.08'

Continuation of Main Trail

▼ 0.0   Continue to the southwest.
▼ 0.3   SO   Track on left.

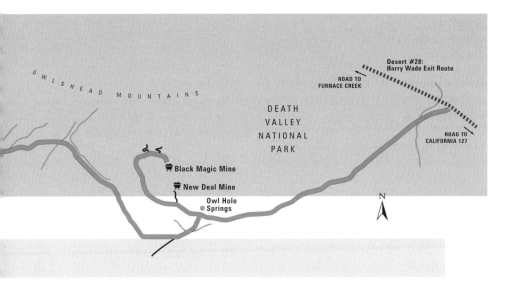

▼ 0.5   SO   Cross through wash.

▼ 1.2   BR   Graded road on left enters Fort Irwin Military Reservation—no unauthorized entry. Bear right onto smaller, graded dirt road.
     GPS: N35°37.64′ W116°39.66′

▼ 1.5   SO   Track on right.
▼ 1.6   SO   Track on right.
▼ 1.8   SO   Track on right.
▼ 3.9   SO   Entering Death Valley National Park at sign. Zero trip meter.
     GPS: N35°38.81′ W116°41.91′

▼ 0.0   Continue to the north.
▼ 0.6   BL   Track on right.
     GPS: N35°39.21′ W116°42.19′

▼ 1.1   SO   Enter line of wash.
▼ 2.7   SO   Exit line of wash. Dry bed of Owl Lake is visible on the right in the valley.
▼ 3.0   SO   Cross through wash.
▼ 4.1   SO   Cross through wide wash.
▼ 4.8   SO   Cross through wash.
     GPS: N35°40.23′ W116°46.12′

▼ 5.5   SO   Cross through wash.
     GPS: N35°40.12′ W116°46.86′

▼ 5.9   SO   Cross through wash.
▼ 6.5   SO   Cross through wash.
▼ 8.0   SO   The dry bed of Lost Lake is visible to the right.

▼ 9.4   SO   Cross through wash.
     GPS: N35°41.12′ W116°50.85′

▼ 10.3   SO   Cross through wash.
▼ 11.1   SO   Cross through wash.
▼ 13.0   BR   Closed vehicle track on left is now hiking trail to Epsom Salt Works. Zero trip meter.
     GPS: N35°41.45′ W116°54.40′

▼ 0.0   Continue to the north.
▼ 1.6   SO   Cross through wash.
▼ 2.3   Trail ends at communications tower on a peak in the Owlshead Mountains.
     GPS: N35°42.59′ W116°53.24′

DESERT #32

Death Valley West Side Road

STARTING POINT: California 178, 40 miles south of Furnace Creek Visitor Center, 28 miles west of Shoshone

FINISHING POINT: California 178, 6 miles south of Furnace Creek Visitor Center

TOTAL MILEAGE: 34.2 miles

UNPAVED MILEAGE: 34.2 miles

DRIVING TIME: 2 hours
ELEVATION RANGE: -80–0 feet
USUALLY OPEN: Year-round
BEST TIME TO TRAVEL: October to May
DIFFICULTY RATING: 1
SCENIC RATING: 8
REMOTENESS RATING: +0

Special Attractions
- Trail crosses the dried-up, prehistoric bed of Lake Manly.
- Historic sites, graves, and points of interest.
- Access to three 4WD spur trails that travel up canyons into the Panamint Range.

History
This trail runs around the ancient bed of Lake Manly, a Pleistocene lake formed indirectly by glaciation during the last ice age. Twenty thousand years ago, Lake Manly was 90 miles long, an average of 8 miles wide, and up to 600 feet deep. As glaciers in the Sierra Nevada melted, the water drained to the south, eventually reaching Death Valley. Although it is currently subject to seasonal flooding, Lake Manly has been predominantly dry for more than 10,000 years.

The site of the Eagle Borax works can be found along this trail. The works, which ran for two years, only managed to refine 150 tons of low-grade borax. It closed in 1884 because of the inefficient refining process and the long distance to the railroad. Borax had to be carted across 160 miles of desert to the railroad at Mojave.

A historical marker along the trail commemorates the site of Bennett's Long Camp. On its way west to the California goldfields, the Bennett-Arcane group of Death Valley forty-niners became stranded for a month. The group was saved when two of its members, William Lewis Manly and John Rogers, crossed the mountains on foot and made their way to Mission San Fernando Rey de España near Los Angeles. The rugged individuals returned with supplies, and the party eventually made its way to safety.

The graves of two good friends can also be found alongside the trail. Jim Dayton died in 1899 and was buried in this remote Death Valley spot. His friend Shorty Harris died in 1934. It was Shorty's wish to be buried beside his friend in the valley that they both loved.

Description
The main paved highway, California 178, travels along the east side of Death Valley near the foot of the Amargosa Range. On the west side of the valley, the graded dirt West Side Road travels an alternate route, closer to the Panamint Range, that crosses the prehistoric bed of Lake Manly. Along the 40-mile route to Furnace Creek, the road passes many historic points of interest as well as accessing three 4WD trails that penetrate west into the Panamint Range.

The road is graded dirt for its entire length and is suitable for passenger vehicles in dry weather. However, the surface can be extremely washboardy and slow going. There is a 25 mph speed limit. In wet weather, the crossing of the Amargosa River can be impassable, and the road may be closed by the National Park Service.

The trail passes the site of the Eagle Borax works, the graves of Jim Dayton and Shorty Harris, and several springs that were important water sources for early travelers through this harsh landscape.

The far end of the trail crosses Salt Creek in the middle of Death Valley where the road is slightly elevated above the salt plains. The uneven texture and ridges of the salt-encrusted ground are known as frost heaves, which are the result of evaporation and cold weather on the salt plains.

Current Road Information
Death Valley National Park
PO Box 579
Death Valley, CA 92328-0579
(760) 786-3200

Map References
BLM   Owlshead Mtns., Death Valley Junction
USGS 1:24,000 Mormon Point, Badwater, Hanaupah Canyon, Devils Speedway, Devils Golf Course, Shore Line Butte, Anvil

Spring Canyon East
1:100,000 Owlshead Mtns., Death
Valley Junction
Maptech CD-ROM: Barstow/San
Bernardino County; Kings Canyon/Death
Valley
*Southern & Central California Atlas &
Gazetteer,* pp. 54, 42
California Road & Recreation Atlas, p. 88
Trails Illustrated, Death Valley National
Park (221)
Other: Free NPS Death Valley map

Route Directions

▼ 0.0   From California 178, 40 miles south of
Furnace Creek Visitor Center and 28
miles west of Shoshone, zero trip

meter and turn southwest on wide
graded dirt road, signposted West
Side Road, and pass through gates.
The intersection is 1.7 miles north of
Ashford Mill on California 178.

2.8 ▲   Trail ends on California 178. Turn left to
return to Furnace Creek; turn right for
Shoshone.

GPS: N35°56.27′ W116°42.23′

▼ 0.7   SO Cross through Amargosa River Wash.
Crossing is impassable after rain.

2.1 ▲   SO Cross through Amargosa River Wash.
Crossing is impassable after rain.

▼ 2.8   SO Graded road on left is Desert #33:
Mengel Pass Trail, sign-posted to Butte
Valley. Zero trip meter and follow the
sign to Furnace Creek.

Salt-encrusted shapes along the Devils Golf Course

Graves of Shorty Harris and Jim Dayton

0.0 ▲		Continue to the southeast.
		GPS: N35°57.25′ W116°44.75′

▼ 0.0		Continue to the northwest through gate.
6.9 ▲	SO	Gate; then graded road on right is Desert #33: Mengel Pass Trail, sign-posted to Butte Valley. Zero trip meter and follow the sign to Shoshone.
▼ 6.9	SO	Tank on right opposite track on left is Salt Well. Zero trip meter.
0.0 ▲		Continue to the southeast.
		GPS: N36°01.80′ W116°49.70′

▼ 0.0		Continue to the northwest.
4.7 ▲	SO	Tank on left opposite track on right is Salt Well. Zero trip meter.
▼ 0.1	SO	Track on left travels toward Galena Canyon.
4.6 ▲	SO	Track on right travels toward Galena Canyon.
		GPS: N36°01.92′ W116°49.81

▼ 4.7	SO	Desert #36: Johnson Canyon Trail on left. Zero trip meter.
0.0 ▲		Continue to the south.
		GPS: N36°05.89′ W116°50.67′

▼ 0.0		Continue to the north.
7.7 ▲	SO	Desert #36: Johnson Canyon Trail on right. Zero trip meter.
▼ 4.6	SO	Historical marker on right for Bennett's Long Camp.
3.1 ▲	SO	Historical marker on left for Bennett's Long Camp.

DESERT #32: DEATH VALLEY WEST SIDE ROAD

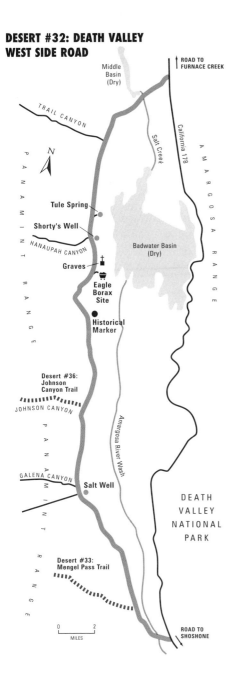

GPS: N36°09.81' W116°51.74'

▼ 7.7   SO Track on right goes 0.1 miles into
            Eagle Borax works site. Zero trip
            meter.
0.0 ▲   Continue to the south.
            GPS: N36°12.01' W116°52.18'

▼ 0.0   Continue to the north.
1.9 ▲   SO Track on left goes 0.1 miles into Eagle
            Borax works site. Zero trip meter.
▼ 0.5   SO Jim Dayton and Shorty (Frank) Harris
            graves on right, set back from the
            road.
1.4 ▲   SO Jim Dayton and Shorty (Frank) Harris
            graves on left, set back from the road.
            GPS: N36°12.45' W116°52.20'

▼ 1.9   SO 4-way intersection. Track on left is
            Hanaupah Canyon Trail, track on right
            goes 0.1 miles to Shortys Well. Zero
            trip meter.
0.0 ▲   Continue to the southeast.
            GPS: N36°13.55' W116°52.83'

▼ 0.0   Continue to the northwest.
1.1 ▲   SO 4-way intersection. Track on right is
            Hanaupah Canyon Trail, track on left
            goes 0.1 miles to Shortys Well. Zero
            trip meter.
▼ 1.1   SO Track on right goes 0.2 miles to Tule
            Spring. Zero trip meter.
0.0 ▲   Continue to the south.
            GPS: N36°14.56' W116°53.03'

▼ 0.0   Continue to the north.
4.0 ▲   SO Track on left goes 0.2 miles to Tule
            Spring. Zero trip meter.
▼ 4.0   SO Track on left travels up Trail Canyon.
            Zero trip meter.
0.0 ▲   Continue to the south.
            GPS: N36°18.18' W116°53.38'

▼ 0.0   Continue to the north.
5.1 ▲   SO Track on right travels up Trail Canyon.
            Zero trip meter.
▼ 3.3   SO Cross over Salt Creek.
1.8 ▲   SO Cross over Salt Creek.
▼ 5.1   Trail ends at T-intersection with
            California 178. Turn left for Furnace
            Creek; turn right for Shoshone.
0.0 ▲   Trail commences on California 178, 6
            miles south of Furnace Creek Visitor
            Center. Zero trip meter and turn south
            on graded dirt road, following sign for
            West Side Road.
            GPS: N36°21.95' W116°50.64'

Mengel Pass Trail

STARTING POINT: Panamint Valley Road
(California 178), at the turn to Ballarat,
21.5 miles north of Trona
FINISHING POINT: Desert #32: Death Valley
West Side Road, 2.8 miles from the
southern end
TOTAL MILEAGE: 50.1 miles, plus 0.6-mile spur
to Barker Ranch House
UNPAVED MILEAGE: 50.1 miles, plus 0.6-mile
spur
DRIVING TIME: 5.5 hours
ELEVATION RANGE: 0–4,400 feet
USUALLY OPEN: Year-round
BEST TIME TO TRAVEL: October to May
DIFFICULTY RATING: 4
SCENIC RATING: 10
REMOTENESS RATING: +1

Special Attractions

■ Site of the police capture of Charles Manson.
■ Many old mining remains and historic
cabins.
■ Beautiful scenery and panoramic vistas
within Death Valley National Park.
■ Warm Springs natural mineral springs.

History

Ballarat, at the western end of this trail, is
named after an Australian gold town of the
same name. Between 1897 and 1917, the
small settlement served the many mining
camps scattered throughout the Panamint
Range. Between them, these mines produced
nearly a million dollars worth of gold. Ballarat housed many of the miners who worked
in the Radcliff Mine in Pleasant Canyon. The
miners traveled to work up the canyon each
day. Little remains of Ballarat now. However,
you can still see a few adobe remains, the jail,
and the graveyard. A small general store continues to operate.

In more recent years, the Barker Ranch in
Goler Wash made headlines when one of
America's most notorious killers, Charles

Manson, and his followers were captured in
1969, following an apparent tip-off by a
BLM officer. The officer became suspicious
during a routine visit when he saw what
seemed like too many vehicles at the remote
ranch. Suspecting a possible vehicle theft
ring, he notified police, who in turn made a
multiagency raid on the ranch. The so-called
Manson Family was taken into custody and
initially charged with arson and grand theft
auto. However, it was quickly established
that they were homicide suspects as well.
Manson himself was not found right away.
He was hiding in a bathroom cupboard and
was found in due course. The cupboard has
since been removed from the house.

Mengel Pass is named after prospector
Carl Mengel, who had a number of small
claims in the area. Born in San Bernardino in
1868, Carl constructed a 3-stamp mill near
Redlands Canyon in 1898. Some of the red
and green timbers Carl used in the construction of the mill are said to have been salvaged
timbers carted all the way from Los Angeles.
However, controversy does exist regarding
their actual origin. The words "Baker Iron
Works — Los Angeles" were stamped into
some of the stamp casings.

In 1912, Carl bought the Oro Fino Mine
in Goler Wash and discovered an even more
promising mine farther down the wash. Sadly most of his claims played out too quickly
and Carl managed only a meager living during his life in the Panamints. The stone cabin at Greater View Spring was his home; its
builder is uncertain. A rock shelter nearby is
thought to have been used by Native Americans. Carl is buried on top of Mengel Pass
(4,328 feet) just outside the boundary of the
old Death Valley National Monument. He
died in 1944.

Striped Butte, on the east side of the pass
in Butte Valley, was originally named Curious
Butte by Hugh McCormack, who passed
through the region in the 1860s. The sedimentary outcropping is unusual in this area;
most of the surrounding rock is granitic.

Prospectors are thought to have made
claims in the Anvil Springs region as early as
the 1850s. Mormon prospectors were among

the first to find riches within Butte Valley. However, the mines changed hands many times because the potential for great wealth was always thwarted by the inaccessibility of the valley. The name Anvil dates from 1866, when a party of prospectors from San Bernardino worked this region under the leadership of Joseph Clews. Disillusioned after just three months, they threw a large anvil into the spring near their camp and left.

Asa Merton Russell, also known as "Panamint Russ," is said to have discovered and then lost the location of a very high-grade claim while prospecting in Butte Valley in 1925. He is credited with building what is known as the Geologist's Cabin in 1930. He also lined Anvil Spring with rocks and built a cistern with a wooden trap door. Big Blue #1 Mine is just one of the mines worked by

Panamint Russ. By 1962, Stella and Clinton Anderson were manually working the mines within the Greater View Springs claim, having been granted them by Panamint Russ. They chose to live on the remote property without electricity, phone service, or plumbing. Clinton died in 1973, but Stella remained until the late 1970s, when she moved to Trona.

Warm Spring Canyon leads out of the eastern end of Butte Valley. Warm Spring, known to the Panamint Shoshone as Pabuna, was a winter camp for the native people. During the 1880s, "Panamint Tom" ran a ranch and orchard in Warm Spring Canyon until a flash flood wiped out his crops and 150 fruit trees in July 1887. Because water was available from the springs, a mill was set up in 1932 to recover gold from the ore

This old arrastra was part of the Gold Hill Mill in Warm Spring Canyon

This well-constructed swimming pool stands next to old cabins at Warm Spring

mined at Gold Hill, somewhat farther up the canyon on the north side. The remains of the mill can still be seen between the camp and the current trail. The hot-shot diesel engine, Blake jaw crusher, cylindrical ball-mill, cone crusher, ore bin, and stone arrastra are relatively intact and offer an exceptional example of a gold-processing site.

Forty-niners William Lewis Manly and John Rogers traveled up Warm Spring Canyon during their epic journey out of Death Valley. They returned a month later with supplies and led the Bennett and Arcane families, who were stranded at Bennett Spring, to safety. They took a shorter route just north of Warm Spring. Their harsh trek proceeded up Galena Canyon, joining Warm Spring Canyon just before it enters Butte Valley. From there they headed slightly north to refresh at Arrastre Spring. Continuing southwest through Butte Valley, they passed Striped Butte on the north side and exited the valley to the west via Redlands Canyon. Exhausted, they made their next camp deep in the canyon at Redlands Spring. From there, the families exited into Panamint Valley and traveled over the Slate Range to the west.

Arrastre Spring seems to have been popular with Paleo-Indians who frequented this region; their early history can be seen near the spring in the form of petroglyphs. Native Americans also labored at the nearby Gold Hill mines during the 1800s transporting ore to an arrastra at the spring for reduction.

The name Manly appears throughout this region in honor of William Manly's heroic efforts to save members of his party. Geologist's Cabin sits at the eastern foot of Manly Peak. The vehicle trail up Redlands Canyon stops at the edge of Manly Peak Wilderness Area, and Manly Fall was a spectacular dry-fall located at Redlands Canyon's exit into Panamint Valley. This fall was later excavated by the Briggs gold mine.

Almost a century after the Bennett and Arcane families passed through Warm Spring Canyon, Louise Grantham and Ernest Huhn found a wealth of talc near Warm Spring. The demand for talc was run-

ning high for use in such products as paint, wall tiles, and insulators. Initial operations were sporadic, but by the late 1930s, large underground talc mines were developed. The ore-bearing rock was transported by truck to Dunn Siding, located west of Barstow on Desert #13: Mojave Road. World War II increased the demand for talc, particularly for use in paint. Massive quantities of paint were needed for naval vessels, and this region became one of the biggest suppliers in the western states. A talc-mining camp operated here at various levels of activity from the late 1930s to 1988.

The talc miners had quite a community based around the warm spring; it was regarded as one of the finest camps in Death Valley. Reports from the 1950s list a dormitory, two small houses, a mess hall, Mrs. Grantham's house, generator buildings, and a large swimming pool fed by the warm spring. Some of its structures remain today. In 1974, open pit mines were developed. They can still be seen today in Warm Spring Canyon. The talc-mining claims changed hands many times over the decades. Health and safety requirements improved some and closed others. The last claim holder, a man named Pfizer, donated the site to a conservation fund for eventual transfer to the National Park Service.

Description

Mengel Pass Trail is one of the few trails to traverse the Panamint Range, a rugged and barren range on the western edge of Death Valley National Park. The trail leaves from Ballarat, which has an operating general store. The store's hours of service are limited and there is no fuel.

The trail swings south from Ballarat, following Wingate Road, and hugs the western face of the Panamint Range, which rises abruptly from the sage-covered valley floor. Initially, the road is extremely smooth and well graded because it serves as the access road for trucks going to the active Briggs Open Cut Mine. The road drops in standard past the mine, and although graded, it receives considerably less maintenance and can be dusty, very washboardy, and slow going.

Mine adit at Warm Spring

There are views along the face of the Panamint Range, as well as to the west over the Panamint Valley to the Slate Range.

The trail turns east and enters the range along the narrow and steep-sided Goler Wash. It immediately drops in standard to become a narrow, loose-surfaced trail that travels up the wash. This spectacular section of the trail climbs steadily into the Panamint Range, passing between high rock walls studded with cotton top cactus. Wild burros and bighorn sheep can sometimes be spotted in the canyon. A well-preserved cabin, which is the headquarters of the Newman Mine, sits in the wash a few yards from the trail.

Immediately past the entrance to Death Valley National Park, there is a major fork in

the trail. The right-hand fork is a worthwhile detour that travels a short distance to the well-preserved Barker Ranch house. This cabin, now operated by the National Park Service, is available for public use. It is sparsely furnished, but very picturesque in its canyon setting. The park service has posted warnings for users to beware of hantavirus, a rare but deadly disease spread by contact with rodent droppings. Warnings about this disease are currently posted at all the cabins along this trail. For more information on hantavirus, see page 13.

A short distance past the Barker Ranch house is the Meyer Ranch, which is posted as private property.

The main trail becomes rocky as it approaches Mengel Pass; the surface is uneven and some large embedded rocks require careful wheel placement. Large vehicles will need to take extra care because of the tight clearance between some rocks. This 4-rated section extends over both sides of Mengel Pass, the highest point of the trail.

From Mengel Pass, the trail drops into the wide-open Butte Valley, passing the small stone cabin known as Geologist's Cabin for one of its original occupants. Like the Barker Ranch house, this cabin is available for use on a first-come, first-served basis. It is situated above Anvil Spring. Past the spring, the trail passes beside the distinctive Striped Butte, which rises 900 feet above the valley floor.

The trail continues along the open valley before dropping farther down Warm Spring Canyon. There are extensive mining remains at the site of Warm Spring. A well-preserved cabin as well as a tiled, concrete-lined swimming pool that used to tap the warm mineral waters can still be seen. The swimming pool was full as recently as 1999. The natural warm spring is a short distance up the hillside behind the cabin. There are two small natural pools where the water comes out of the rock. Each pool can fit one or two people for a shallow soak. The water temperature is tepid to warm. The park service has created two small picnic/camping areas next to the cabins, which are also available for use. Watch out for cheeky coyotes and kit foxes that will steal your food and trash given the chance.

Past Warm Spring, the trail continues in the line of the wash and heads out to descend into Death Valley. The trail ends on Desert #32: Death Valley West Side Road.

Current Road Information

Death Valley National Park
PO Box 579
Death Valley, CA 92328-0579
(760) 786-3200

Bureau of Land Management
Ridgecrest Field Office
300 South Richmond Road
Ridgecrest, CA 93555
(760) 384-5400

Map References

BLM   Darwin Hills, Ridgecrest, Owlshead Mts.
USGS 1:24,000   Maturango Peak SE, Ballarat, Manly Fall, Copper Queen Canyon, Sourdough Spring, Manly Peak, Anvil Spring Canyon West, Anvil Spring Canyon
      1:100,000 Darwin Hills, Ridgecrest, Owlshead Mts.
Maptech CD-ROM: Kings Canyon/Death Valley; Barstow/ San Bernardino County
Southern & Central California Atlas & Gazetteer, pp. 41, 53, 54
California Road & Recreation Atlas, pp. 88, 95
Trails Illustrated, Death Valley National Park (221)
Other: Free NPS Death Valley map

Route Directions

▼ 0.0   From Panamint Valley Road (California 178, also shown as Trona Wildrose Road on some maps), 21.5 miles north of Trona, zero trip meter and turn northeast on Ballarat Road, following the sign to Ballarat. There is a historical marker at the intersection.

3.5 ▲   Trail ends on Panamint Valley Road (California 178). Turn left for Trona; turn right for Panamint Springs.
          GPS: N36°02.02′ W117°16.84′

▼ 0.7 SO Track on left.
2.8 ▲ SO Track on right.

▼ 3.3 SO Graded road on right cuts across to Wingate Road. Road enters ghost town of Ballarat.

0.2 ▲ SO Graded road on left returns to Wingate Road. Leaving Ballarat.

▼ 3.4 SO Track on left is Indian Road.
0.1 ▲ SO Track on right is Indian Road.

▼ 3.5 TR 4-way intersection at Ballarat General Store. Turn right onto Wingate Road and zero trip meter. Road on left is Indian Ranch Road to Surprise Canyon. Road ahead is Desert #35: Pleasant Canyon Loop Trail.

DESERT #33: MENGEL PASS TRAIL

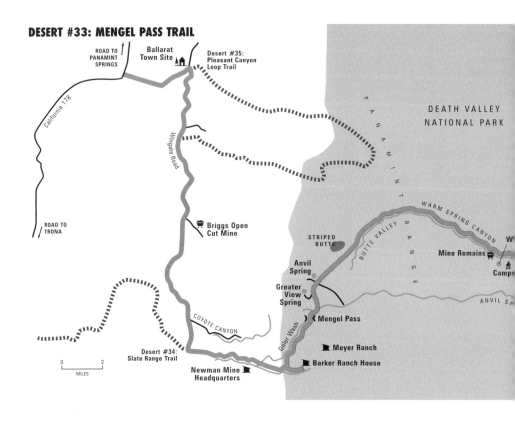

0.0 ▲		Continue to the southwest on Ballarat Road.
		GPS: N36°02.86' W117°13.40'

▼ 0.0		Continue to the southeast on Wingate Road.
3.7 ▲	TL	4-way intersection at Ballarat General Store. Turn left onto Ballarat Road and zero trip meter. Road straight ahead is Indian Ranch Road to Surprise Canyon. Road on right is Desert #35: Pleasant Canyon Loop Trail.
▼ 0.1	SO	Road on right cuts across to Ballarat Road.
3.6 ▲	BR	Road on left cuts across to Ballarat Road.
▼ 1.3	BR	Road on left.
2.4 ▲	BL	Road on right.
▼ 3.1	SO	Track on left.
0.6 ▲	SO	Track on right.
		GPS: N36°00.51' W117°13.17'

▼ 3.7	SO	Unmarked track on left is Desert #35: Pleasant Canyon Loop Trail. Zero trip meter.
0.0 ▲		Continue to the north.

		GPS: N36°00.01' W117°13.17'

▼ 0.0		Continue to the south.
3.7 ▲	SO	Unmarked track on right is Desert #35: Pleasant Canyon Loop Trail. Zero trip meter.
▼ 1.7	SO	Track on left.
2.0 ▲	SO	Track on right.
▼ 2.1	SO	Track on left.
1.6 ▲	SO	Track on right.
▼ 2.4	SO	Track on left.
1.3 ▲	SO	Track on right.
▼ 3.7	BR	Road on left goes into Briggs Open Pit Mine. Mine is active, so do not enter. Zero trip meter.
0.0 ▲		Continue to the north.
		GPS: N35°57.11' W117°12.13'

▼ 0.0		Continue to the south.
7.0 ▲	SO	Road on right goes into Briggs Open Pit Mine. Mine is active, so do not enter. Zero trip meter.
▼ 5.0	SO	Faint track on left.
2.0 ▲	SO	Faint track on right.

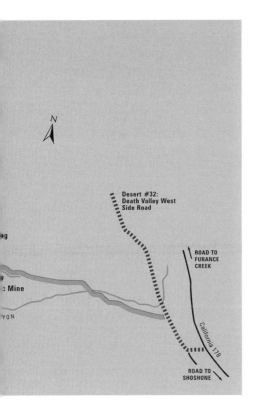

▼ 1.4　BL　Bear left and enter Goler Wash.
2.2 ▲　BR　Bear right and exit Goler Wash.
　　　　GPS: N35°51.55' W117°09.24'

▼ 2.9　SO　Loading hopper on right. Aerial tramway crosses to the workings high on the cliffs to the left.
0.7 ▲　SO　Loading hopper on left. Aerial tramway crosses to the workings high on the cliffs to the right.
　　　　GPS: N35°51.78' W117°08.25'

▼ 3.3　SO　Aerial tramway anchors on left.
0.3 ▲　SO　Aerial tramway anchors on right.
　　　　GPS: N35°51.60' W117°07.91'

▼ 3.6　BL　Trail forks in wash. Track on right goes to old cabin of Newman Mine Headquarters. Zero trip meter.
0.0 ▲　　　Continue to the south.
　　　　GPS: N35°51.71' W117°07.62'

▼ 0.0　　　Continue to the north.
2.0 ▲　SO　Track on sharp left goes to old cabin of Newman Mine Headquarters. Zero trip meter.
▼ 0.1　SO　Old cabin on right of trail is Newman Mine Headquarters.
1.9 ▲　SO　Old cabin on left of trail is Newman Mine Headquarters.
　　　　GPS: N35°51.73' W117°07.55'

▼ 0.7　SO　Track on right into mining activities.
1.3 ▲　SO　Track on left into mining activities.
　　　　GPS: N35°51.64' W117°07.01'

▼ 1.2　SO　Track on right; then stone ruin on right.
0.8 ▲　SO　Stone ruin on left; then track on left.
　　　　GPS: N35°51.58' W118°06.57'

▼ 1.8　BL　Track on right in wash, which peters out after short distance.
0.2 ▲　BR　Track on left in wash, which peters out after short distance.
　　　　GPS: N35°51.52' W117°05.90'

▼ 1.9　SO　Entering Death Valley National Park.
0.1 ▲　SO　Leaving Death Valley National Park.

▼ 5.4　SO　Track on left travels up Coyote Canyon.
1.6 ▲　SO　Track on right travels up Coyote Canyon.
　　　　GPS: N35°52.93' W117°10.98'

▼ 6.1　SO　Track on left.
0.9 ▲　SO　Track on right.
▼ 6.2　SO　Small track on left.
0.8 ▲　SO　Small track on right.
▼ 7.0　TL　Turn left, following marker for P52, suitable for 4WDs, ATVs, and motor-bikes. Track straight ahead marked P70 is Desert #34: Slate Range Trail. Zero trip meter.
0.0 ▲　　　Continue to the northwest.
　　　　GPS: N35°51.55' W117°10.74'

▼ 0.0　　　Continue to the east and travel up the alluvial fan.
3.6 ▲　TR　Turn right at T-intersection, following marker for P52. Track on left marked P70 is Desert #34: Slate Range Trail. Zero trip meter.
▼ 1.3　SO　Track on left to mine.
2.3 ▲　SO　Track on right to mine.

CHARLES MANSON AND HIS FAMILY

Charles Manson, October 1969

The story of Charles Mills Manson and his followers is well known to many people. It all began on November 12, 1934 in Cincinnati, Ohio, when Manson was born an illegitimate child to sixteen-year-old, Kathleen Maddox. Growing up, he was bounced from home to home. At various times he lived with his grandmother and aunt when his mother disappeared or served time in jail.

At the age of nine he was caught stealing for the first time and from this time through the rest of his life he was in and out of reform schools and prison. Between periods of institutionalization, he supported himself mainly through theft.

Although he protested to prison officials that he was not fit to be released back into society after serving an 8-year stint in prison, he was paroled on March 21, 1967, and given transportation to San Francisco. There he began recruiting his first followers. In the spring of 1968 he left San Francisco in his old, black school bus. He continued collecting more followers who were mostly social misfits. He indoctrinated them into his satanic beliefs and setting himself up as their leader. Many of his followers were young women, a number of whom subsequently bore his children, often with Manson as their only midwife. The group existed on the fringes of society, scavenging from supermarket trashcans; the women often traded sexual favors for rent and goods. They were heavy drug users and practiced many black magic rituals led by Manson.

Before moving to the Barker Ranch, the "family" lived in Canoga Park in the San Fernando Valley, an old movie set called Spahn Ranch in Chatsworth, and many other abandoned premises. Manson's personal belief was that a racial war was imminent. He embraced this idea with fervor and used it to incite his followers to commit several brutal murders.

To escape attention, Manson moved his group to the high desert. Some time was spent hiding out at the southern end of the Owens Valley in the Olancha area. Eventually, they ended up at the Barker Ranch. Manson had apparently spent time in the Death Valley region before, painting his name on rocks and old structures in the region, including high in the range at Panamint City.

Manson attempted to affiliate his group with a biker club called The Straight Satans, hoping that this would scare the public away from his ranch. One of its members stayed at the ranch, receiving special attention from the women in exchange for his mechanical services. The rest of the club disliked and distrusted Manson. When the bikers paid a group visit to the ranch to retrieve their friend, they threatened to kill the entire family if the man didn't leave with them. Manson apparently offered his own life to spare the others, but the biker group left without causing any harm.

Manson and four of his followers were convicted of multiple homicide in 1971. They were given death sentences that were later commuted to life in prison. To date, all attempts at parole have failed. Manson has acquired a cult status among many people. Public horror and fascination with Manson continue in almost equal measures to this day.

GPS: N35°51.60′ W117°05.81′

▼ 2.0　SO　Track on right is spur to Barker Ranch House. Zero trip meter.

0.0 ▲　　Continue to the southwest.

GPS: N35°51.64′ W117°05.75′

Spur to Barker Ranch House

▼ 0.0　　0.1 miles north of the boundary of Death Valley National Park, zero trip meter and turn southeast on unmarked, well-used trail.

▼ 0.3　SO　Track on left goes to mine dump and mine workings.

▼ 0.6　UT　Track on left to Barker Ranch House. Meyer Ranch is 0.2 miles farther and is posted as private property.

GPS: N35°51.54′ W117°05.25′

Continuation of Main Trail

▼ 0.0　　Continue to the northeast.

3.2 ▲　SO　Track on left is spur to Barker Ranch House. Zero trip meter.

GPS: N35°51.64′ W117°05.75′

▼ 0.2　SO　Track on right.

3.0 ▲　SO　Track on left.

▼ 0.5　BL　Bear left out of Goler Wash.

2.7 ▲　SO　Enter Goler Wash.

▼ 0.7　BR　Trail forks and rejoins almost immediately.

2.5 ▲　BL　Trail forks and rejoins almost immediately.

▼ 1.1　SO　Enter line of wash, rising gradually toward Mengel Pass.

2.1 ▲　SO　Exit line of wash.

▼ 2.3　SO　Trail forks and rejoins almost immediately.

0.9 ▲　SO　Trail forks and rejoins almost immediately.

▼ 2.7　SO　Cross through rocky wash.

0.5 ▲　SO　Cross through rocky wash.

GPS: N35°53.65′ W117°04.97′

▼ 3.2　SO　Mengel Pass. Cairn on left is Carl Mengel's grave. Track on right. Zero trip meter.

0.0 ▲　　Continue to the south.

GPS: N35°54.00′ W117°04.88′

▼ 0.0　　Continue to the north.

1.7 ▲　SO　Mengel Pass. Cairn on right is Carl

Mengel's grave. Track on left.
Zero trip meter.

▼ 1.3　SO　Track on left goes toward cabin at Greater View Spring.

0.4 ▲　SO　Second entrance to cabin.

GPS: N35°54.86′ W117°04.90′

▼ 1.4　SO　Second entrance to cabin.

0.3 ▲　BL　Track on right goes toward cabin at Greater View Spring.

▼ 1.6　SO　Track on left.

0.1 ▲　BL　Track on right.

▼ 1.7　BR　Track on left goes to small stone cabin at Anvil Spring. Zero trip meter.

0.0 ▲　　Continue to the south.

GPS: N35°55.26′ W117°04.99′

▼ 0.0　　Continue to the northeast.

6.9 ▲　SO　Track on right goes to small stone cabin at Anvil Spring. Zero trip meter.

▼ 0.2　SO　4-way intersection. Track on left goes to Anvil Spring and cabin, track on right goes to Anvil Spring Canyon Hiking Trail.

6.7 ▲　SO　4-way intersection. Track on right goes to Anvil Spring and cabin, track on left goes to Anvil Spring Canyon Hiking Trail.

GPS: N35°55.42′ W117°04.90′

▼ 2.0　SO　Track on left. Striped Butte is directly on the left.

4.9 ▲　SO　Track on right. Striped Butte is directly on the right.

GPS: N35°56.69′ W117°03.71′

▼ 6.8　SO　Enter line of wash.

0.1 ▲　SO　Exit line of wash.

GPS: N35°59.11′ W117°00.05′

▼ 6.9　SO　Well-used track on left marked with small stone cairn. Zero trip meter.

0.0 ▲　　Continue to the west.

GPS: N35°59.13′ W116°59.97′

▼ 0.0　　Continue to the east.

4.4 ▲　SO　Well-used track on right marked with small stone cairn. Zero trip meter.

▼ 2.0　SO　Mine on left.

2.4 ▲　SO　Mine on right.

GPS: N35°58.57′ W116°58.08′

▼ 2.6   SO   Small track on right and small track on left.

1.8 ▲   SO   Small track on left and small track on right.

▼ 4.3   SO   Old mining remains and cabin at Warm Spring on right.

0.1 ▲   SO   Old mining remains and cabin at Warm Spring on left.

     GPS: N35°58.13′ W116°55.83′

▼ 4.4   SO   Track on right to large mine adit. Adit is visible immediately to the right. Zero trip meter.

0.0 ▲   Continue to the northwest.

     GPS: N35°58.14′ W116°55.71′

▼ 0.0   Continue to the northeast.

1.8 ▲   SO   Track on left to large mine adit. Adit is visible immediately to the left. Zero trip meter.

▼ 0.1   SO   Track on right leads into Warm Spring area.

1.7 ▲   BR   Track on left leads into Warm Spring area.

▼ 0.4   SO   Faint track on right.

1.4 ▲   SO   Faint track on left.

▼ 1.2   SO   Open cut talc mine on right.

0.6 ▲   SO   Open cut talc mine on left.

     GPS: N35°57.92′ W116°54.46′

▼ 1.3   SO   Track on right.

0.5 ▲   BR   Track on left.

▼ 1.7   SO   Track on right into loading hopper.

0.1 ▲   SO   Track on left into loading hopper.

▼ 1.8   SO   Track on right leads into talc mine. Zero trip meter.

0.0 ▲   Continue to the west.

     GPS: N35°57.73′ W116°53.83′

▼ 0.0   Continue to the east.

8.6 ▲   SO   Track on left leads into talc mine. Zero trip meter.

▼ 1.6   SO   Exit line of wash.

7.0 ▲   SO   Enter line of wash.

▼ 1.7   SO   Graded road on right.

6.9 ▲   BR   Graded road on left.

     GPS: N35°57.61′ W116°52.01′

▼ 4.4   SO   Start to cross wide wash.

4.2 ▲   SO   Exit wash crossing.

▼ 4.7   SO   Exit wash crossing.

3.9 ▲   SO   Start to cross wide wash.

     GPS: N35°57.71′ W116°48.89′

▼ 4.8   SO   Cross through wash.

3.8 ▲   SO   Cross through wash.

▼ 4.9   SO   Track on right.

3.7 ▲   SO   Track on left.

▼ 5.4   SO   Cross through wash.

3.2 ▲   SO   Cross through wash.

▼ 8.6   Trail ends at T-intersection with Desert #32: Death Valley West Side Road. Turn left to continue along the trail; turn right to exit to California 178.

0.0 ▲   Trail commences on Desert #32: Death Valley West Side Road, 2.8 miles from the south end. Zero trip meter and turn west on graded dirt road, sign-posted to Butte Valley. Turn is immediately in front of gates. A sign after the intersection says High Clearance 4x4 Recommended.

     GPS: N35°57.25′ W116°44.75′

     DESERT #34

Slate Range Trail

STARTING POINT: California 178, 7.5 miles north of the railroad crossing in Trona

FINISHING POINT: Desert #33: Mengel Pass Trail, 14.4 miles south of Ballarat

TOTAL MILEAGE: 13.9 miles

UNPAVED MILEAGE: 13.9 miles

DRIVING TIME: 2 hours

ELEVATION RANGE: 1,100–3,100 feet

USUALLY OPEN: Year-round

BEST TIME TO TRAVEL: September to June

DIFFICULTY RATING: 3

SCENIC RATING: 8

REMOTENESS RATING: +1

Special Attractions

■ Trail travels part of the historic Forty-niner's Escape Trail from Death Valley.

■ Ridge top trail with fantastic views over the Panamint and Searles Valleys.

■ Silent Sepulchre.

History

The eastern end of Slate Range Trail commences at Valley Wells, which was a depot for the Rinaldi and Clark freight teams. The freight company delivered passengers and supplies to the Panamint mines on trails that were often worse than this particular one.

The forty-niner families, the Bennetts and Arcanes, who managed to escape death in Death Valley, crossed the Slate Range from the Panamint Valley on part of their long and painful journey to the West Coast. They passed through Fish Canyon on the east side of the range. Their quest for better times in the West saw them abandon their wagons in Death Valley and continue on foot with the assistance of William Lewis Manly and John Rogers. An earlier section of their escape route, where they descended into Panamint Valley near today's open cut Briggs Mine, is discussed in Desert #33: Mengel Pass Trail. Some weeks earlier, Manly and Rogers had made it on foot to Mission San Fernando Rey de España to purchase supplies for the families left behind in Death Valley. They returned to the stranded party with the supplies and retraced their steps, escorting the Bennetts and Arcanes to safety. The journey of approximately 250 miles was difficult for all concerned. Swollen joints, blistered feet, sick children, and extremely limited fresh water were all compounded by the extreme desert heat.

From Panamint Valley, they crossed the southern end of the valley to camp in Fish Canyon in the Slate Range. Just a month earlier, another forty-niner named Father Fish died here in an attempt to escape Death Valley. Fish had been a friend of Manly's, so respects were paid before they departed up the canyon.

Reverend Brier, who was Fish's travel companion, referred to the tight canyon as "a silent sepulchre of dismal appearance." He noticed Indians observing them from

Looking northeast into Panamint Valley

above on the canyon rims and he was concerned about the possibility of an ambush. Sickness and death were constant companions of forty-niners heading west through the harsh environment. The Bennetts and Arcanes were surprised to find Fish's body intact under some light sage bushes when they camped here on February 15, 1850. Fish Canyon is named after him and his grave is a short distance north of the Silent Sepulchre.

From here the party scaled its way up to what became known as Manly Pass. They then descended to the west down the middle fork of Isham Canyon, just north of the path of this trail. Isham was another forty-niner who had taken the supposed shortcut and died en route. Both oxen and humans had great difficulty in crossing the sharp rocks of the Slate Range. Cattle were given leather boots to protect against the rocks, but the makeshift gear quickly wore through, and progress was slow. Once over

Silent Sepulchre sign

the Slate Range, Manly and Rogers led the party across Searles Lake toward Indian Joe Spring, passing close to where Isham was buried.

Description

Slate Range Trail provides a scenic and historic alternate entry into the Panamint Valley from Trona that avoids a long loop of paved highway. It is the shortest, although not necessarily the quickest, access point to Desert #33: Mengel Pass Trail and Desert #35: Pleasant Canyon Loop Trail.

The trail leaves California 178, 7.5 miles north of Trona, along a graded dirt road that also serves as the access road for a gravel pit. The trail diverges from this road and turns onto a smaller, formed trail that climbs up stony Goff Canyon into the Slate Range. The trail is small, but well used and easy to follow. There are a few turns that might be slightly confusing. Sections of the canyon are rugged and rocky, with a mixture of embedded rock and loose material that provides poor traction at times.

The trail makes its way up to a saddle and starts the long descent into the Panamint Valley. This ridge top section is the most spectacular part of the trail. Views extend 2,000 feet down into the Panamint Valley with the Panamint Range on the far side. The trail surface is loose and scrabbly in places.

As you descend into Fish Canyon, a keen eye will spot the marker placed there by the Death Valley Escape Trail Conference, which details part of the route taken by the forty-niners out of Death Valley. A side trail leads 1.1 miles up Fish Canyon to the rocky grotto of the Silent Sepulchre. The grave of Father Fish is a short distance farther up the hillside. This short trail is very narrow and rough, involves slow rock crawling for most of the way, and is rated a 5 for difficulty.

The main trail slowly descends Fish Canyon to spill out into the Panamint Valley. The road here is initially rough, but it becomes smooth as it travels around the edge of the Panamint Valley near the foot of the Slate Range. The trail finishes at the intersection of

DESERT #34: SLATE RANGE TRAIL

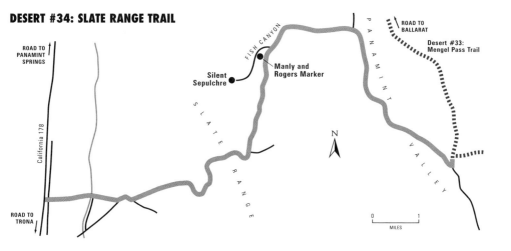

Desert #33: Mengel Pass Trail at the base of Goler Wash, 14.4 miles south of Ballarat.

The trail is absent from or poorly marked on topographical maps of the region. The trail is sporadically marked with BLM route markers. A GPS unit is extremely useful for route finding along this trail.

Current Road Information

Bureau of Land Management
Ridgecrest Field Office
300 South Richmond Road
Ridgecrest, CA 93555
(760) 384-5400

Map References

BLM   Ridgecrest
USGS 1:24,000   Trona East, Slate Range
      Crossing, Manly Fall, Copper
      Queen Canyon
      1:100,000 Ridgecrest
Maptech CD-ROM: Barstow/San
      Bernardino County
*Southern & Central California Atlas &
      Gazetteer,* p. 53
California Road & Recreation Atlas, p. 95

Route Directions

▼ 0.0   From California 178, 7.5 miles north of
         the railroad crossing in Trona, zero trip
         meter and turn east on graded dirt
         road. The road is marked as #82 by a

BLM marker. It is also the entrance for Valley Sand and Gravel.

1.9 ▲   Trail ends on California 178. Turn left
         for Trona; turn right for Panamint
         Springs.
         GPS: N35°50.70′ W117°20.13′

▼ 0.1   SO Graded road on right and left along
             power lines.
1.8 ▲   SO Graded road on right and left along
             power lines.
▼ 0.9   SO Track on left.
1.0 ▲   SO Track on right.
▼ 1.0   SO Track on left; then cross through wash.
             Track on right down wash.
0.9 ▲   SO Cross through wash. Track on left
             down wash; then track on right.
▼ 1.1   SO Track on left and track on right.
0.8 ▲   SO Track on left and track on right.
▼ 1.6   BL Graded road on right. Follow brown
             BLM route marker.
0.3 ▲   BR Graded road on left. Follow brown
             BLM route marker.
         GPS: N35°50.73′ W117°18.37′

▼ 1.7   SO Cross through wash. Track on left
             in wash.
0.2 ▲   SO Cross through wash. Track on right
             in wash.
         GPS: N35°50.75′ W117°18.31′

▼ 1.9   BL Bear left onto smaller, formed trail
             marked P 168, suitable for 4WDs,

ATVs, and motorbikes, and zero trip
meter. Graded road straight ahead
enters a quarry.

0.0 ▲ Continue to the west.
GPS: N35°50.74' W117°18.10'

▼ 0.0 Continue to the northeast.
3.4 ▲ BR Bear right, joining larger, graded road.
A quarry entrance is on the left. Zero
trip meter.
▼ 0.5 SO Cross through wash.
2.9 ▲ SO Cross through wash.
▼ 0.9 SO Enter line of wash.
2.5 ▲ SO Exit line of wash.
▼ 1.4 SO Track on right exits wash.
2.0 ▲ SO Track on left exits wash.
GPS: N35°50.95' W117°16.67'

▼ 1.6 BL Bear left into a side wash. Track continues in main wash.
1.8 ▲ BR Bear right into main wash. Track on
left up wash.
GPS: N35°50.83' W117°16.49'

▼ 2.3 BL Bear left out of wash up ridge.
1.1 ▲ BR Drop down from ridge and enter wash.
▼ 2.4 SO Well-used track on left.
1.0 ▲ SO Well-used track on right.
▼ 2.6 SO Enter wash.
0.8 ▲ SO Exit wash.
▼ 3.1 SO Exit wash.
0.3 ▲ SO Enter wash.
▼ 3.3 SO Track on right; cross through wash.
0.1 ▲ BR Cross through wash; track on left.
GPS: N35°51.63' W117°15.41'

▼ 3.4 SO Saddle in the Slate Range. The
Panamint Valley and Panamint Range
are visible to the north. Well-used
track on right. Zero trip meter.
0.0 ▲ Continue to the south.
GPS: N35°51.67' W117°15.39'

▼ 0.0 Continue to the north.
2.4 ▲ SO Saddle in the Slate Range. Trail now
leaves the Panamint Valley and starts
to descend toward Searles Valley.
Well-used track on left. Zero trip meter.
▼ 0.2 SO Well-used track on left; then cross
through wash.

2.2 ▲ SO Cross through wash; then well-used
track on right.
▼ 0.4 SO Cross through wash.
2.0 ▲ SO Cross through wash.
▼ 2.3 SO Marker on left commemorates Manly
and Rogers. Trail now enters Fish
Canyon wash.
0.1 ▲ BL Bear left and exit Fish Canyon up
ridge. Marker on right commemorates
Manly and Rogers.
GPS: N35°53.44' W117°15.04'

▼ 2.4 SO Track on left up wash goes 1.1 miles
to the Silent Sepulchre. Zero trip meter.
0.0 ▲ Continue to the southwest.
GPS: N35°53.54' W117°14.95'

▼ 0.0 Continue to the northeast.
2.1 ▲ BL Track on right up wash goes 1.1 miles
to the Silent Sepulchre. Zero trip meter.
▼ 0.5 SO Exit Fish Canyon wash and Fish Canyon.
1.6 ▲ SO Enter Fish Canyon wash and Fish Canyon.
GPS: N35°53.85' W117°14.65'

▼ 0.9 SO Cross through wash.
1.2 ▲ SO Cross through wash.
▼ 1.6 SO Cross through wash.
0.5 ▲ SO Cross through wash.
▼ 2.1 TR Well-used, formed track on left and
right is P 170. Small trail straight
ahead. Zero trip meter and turn right
onto P 170.
0.0 ▲ Continue to the southwest.
GPS: N35°53.89' 117°13.04'

▼ 0.0 Continue to the southeast.
4.1 ▲ TL Well-used, formed track on left is P
168. P 170 continues straight ahead
and small track on right. Zero trip
meter and turn left onto P 168.
▼ 1.3 BL Track on right.
2.8 ▲ BR Track on left.
GPS: N35°52.82' W117°12.76'

▼ 3.9 SO Cross through wash.
0.2 ▲ SO Cross through wash.
▼ 4.0 TL T-intersection. Turn left following sign
for P 70.
0.1 ▲ TR Turn right following sign for P 70.
Track straight ahead.

▼ 4.1   Trail finishes at intersection with
           Desert #33: Mengel Pass Trail (P 52).
           Turn right to continue over Mengel
           Pass; turn left to exit to Ballarat and
           California 178.

0.0 ▲   Trail commences on Desert #33:
           Mengel Pass Trail, 14.4 miles south of
           Ballarat, in the Panamint Valley. Zero
           trip meter and proceed south on
           P 70 at the trail marker. Mengel Pass
           Trail (P 52) swings due east at this
           point into Goler Wash.
           GPS: N35°51.55' W117°10.74'

DESERT #35

Pleasant Canyon Loop Trail

STARTING POINT: Desert #33: Mengel Pass
   Trail, 3.7 miles south of Ballarat
FINISHING POINT: Desert #33: Mengel Pass
   Trail in Ballarat
TOTAL MILEAGE: 23.5 miles
UNPAVED MILEAGE: 23.5 miles
DRIVING TIME: 6.5 hours
ELEVATION RANGE: 300–7,400 feet
USUALLY OPEN: Year-round
BEST TIME TO TRAVEL: Spring and fall
DIFFICULTY RATING: 7
SCENIC RATING: 10
REMOTENESS RATING: +2

Special Attractions

■ Long loop trail suitable for experienced
drivers in high-clearance 4WD vehicles.
■ Many mining remains, including the
Briggs Mine Cabin.
■ Unparalleled views into Death Valley
from the ridge top.

History

Mining prospectors entered Pleasant Canyon
in the early 1890s, and by 1896, Henry C.
Ratcliff's Never Give Up claim was one of the

early payers. With time, it became known as
the Ratcliff Mine. Some early maps and publications spell the mine's name as Radcliff and
others as Radcliffe.

Late in 1896, Bob and George Montgomery's World Beater Mine was successfully operating and the labor force in the
canyon grew to 200 men. The only problem
was the lack of suitable places to house
workers. In 1897, the makeshift camp
moved to the floor of Panamint Valley at the
mouth of Pleasant Canyon, where miners
established a town that would fulfill their
needs.

The new town needed a name and the
townsfolk gathered to hear suggestions. A
young Australian named George Riggins suggested that they look for a name associated
with other rich gold discoveries throughout
the world. He suggested Ballarat, after the
rich Ballarat goldfields in Victoria, Australia.
Many people already knew the name; the
Australian Ballarat had attracted many gold-seeking Californians, and the name was
adopted for the new Death Valley settlement.
It was hoped that the well-known name
would bring investors to the Panamint Valley.

Ballarat's population grew to almost 500.
It supported two stores, several saloons, a
Wells Fargo station, and the Calloway Hotel.
By 1899, Ballarat had a small school and a
jail. By 1900, seven mills were busy stamping
away in the area. A mass exodus occurred in
1901 when large strikes at Tonopah, Nevada,
drew miners away.

However, the World Beater Mine got its
second wind, and combined with other
smaller claims, it kept the town relatively active until 1905. By 1906, Skidoo was attracting most of the workforce away from Ballarat. The Montgomery brothers found
further mining success at Skidoo. Because of
Ballarat's location in the Panamint Valley, the
town continued to operate as a supply center
for the region's mining settlements. By 1917,
the post office shut down and the last saloon
closed its doors. A few people stayed on in
the town. Seldom Seen Slim, referred to as
the last resident of early Ballarat, was buried
in 1968.

Mining continued to some degree in the following decades. A reworking of the Ratcliff Mine tailings brought profitable rewards to the Clair family. The family name remains in Pleasant Canyon at Clair Camp. The impressive 10-stamp mill that was attached to the World Beater Mine was burned down in the late 1980s, supposedly by thrill seekers.

In March 1908, a car competing in the world's longest race, from New York to Paris, passed through Ballarat. The car, a Thomas Flyer, won the race by traveling the 13,341-mile route in a total of 169 days. Today, Ballarat has a small general store with few residents or none at all.

Ingenuity has always played a major role in establishing mines and conquering the odds to survive in Death Valley. One of the more cheerful tales of such determination is about a cook in Pleasant Canyon. The enormous Panamint Range did not deter a Chinese migrant from getting food to his hungry miners. He reportedly placed dinners on an aerial tramway for delivery to men in the mine. The food was then passed along the mountain crest and down to workers in the narrows of South Park Canyon.

Thorndike Mine, sometimes referred to as Honolulu Mine, was established by John Thorndike in 1907, on the south side of South Park Canyon. Ore from the mine was lowered to the canyon floor via an aerial tramway; mules then hauled the ore out of the canyon along a long and dangerous route. It was not until 1924 that Thorndike managed to construct a narrow shelf road down South Park Canyon. The hand-built stone embankments of this twisting road are still visible today. The mine was last worked in the early 1940s. Thorndike's name is still attached to the old cabin alongside Briggs Mine Cabin. Both are now part of the Adopt-A-Cabin program.

Briggs Mine Cabin in South Park Canyon takes its name from Harry Briggs. In the early 1930s, Briggs took over the operation of a mill and cyanide plant below Manly Fall. This remarkable ancient dry fall was named after William Lewis Manly, who along with John Rogers led the stranded and starving Bennett and Arcane families to safety through the Death Valley region. Their escape route descended through Redlands Canyon and passed just south of these falls. This same dry fall, located near the mouth of Redlands Canyon, was destroyed by the expanding open cut mine and mill just a few miles south of the southern approach to this trail.

In 1850, Manly and Rogers climbed to the highest point on this trail (over 7,000 feet above Death Valley floor) in their attempts to exit Death Valley. It seems they did not actually cross the range here; their climb was an effort to get their bearings for the best possible route over the Panamint Range. The semblance of an old burro trail leads down to Arrastre Spring in Butte Valley, where the rest of the Bennett and Arcane group made camp while awaiting directions from the duo. This ascent was just the start of their arduous 250-mile trek to the safety of California's coastal mountains.

Modern Native Americans are believed to have frequented the upper reaches of Pleasant Canyon in order to escape the unpleasant summer heat of Panamint Valley. The remainder of a stone corral is visible near a water source about a mile and a half below Rita's Cabin. Apparently, this was where they penned their livestock while off gathering food. Farther down Pleasant Canyon is the World Beater Mine, which installed a well near the stone corral. The pipe that supplied the mine with water can still be seen in places.

Description

This long loop road is slow and rough at times. However, for a high-clearance 4WD with an experienced driver, this is one of the more rewarding trails within Death Valley National Park. This challenging drive takes you from 300 to 7,400 feet in elevation and back offers plenty of history as it climbs through the picturesque Panamint Range.

The trail leaves Desert #33: Mengel Pass Trail, 3.7 miles south of Ballarat. The start of the trail is well used, but has no markers of any kind. Those with a GPS unit will have no

Stunning views over Striped Butte Valley and Mengel Pass

problem; the trail starts exactly along the 36-degree latitude line. Almost immediately, it starts a slow climb toward South Park Canyon. The shelf road is narrow and loose-surfaced, climbing steadily and steeply. Four-wheel drive is needed to maintain traction on the loose surface.

The trail dips down slightly as it enters South Park Canyon, before resuming the steady climb. South Park Canyon is very narrow in places, with towering rock walls on either side of the stony wash. The trail surface here is rough, alternating between uneven stony surface with some large embedded rocks and softer powdery sand that makes it easy to spin an opposing wheel. Sections within the canyon have some very large, embedded rocks that must be negotiated. Take special care with wheel placement. These sections make the trail unsuitable for vehicles with sidesteps, low-hanging skirts, or low-

slung bull bars. Vehicles with roof racks will need to take care on some sections with overhanging canyon walls. Large tires and a suspension lift are an advantage; longer vehicles may find sections potentially damaging.

The narrow shelf road to the Suitcase Mine is steep and loose. There are five extremely tight switchbacks on a steep shelf road that require nerves of steel. Drivers of long wheelbase vehicles may prefer to reverse up a couple of them rather than turn, but this also has its dangers. It is best to make sure that there are no oncoming vehicles at each section between passing points. The spectacular endpoint above the mine has a wide turning area. The mine has collapsed shafts and the remains of a cable tramway.

A short distance past the turn to the Suitcase Mine, you will reach three cabins on the edge of the canyon. The cabins are maintained by the Briggs and Thorndike Volun-

Old boiler at Clair Camp

teers under the Adopt-A-Cabin program. The first, Stone Cabin, is built of rock and corrugated iron and is sandwiched between a large boulder and the canyon wall. The old workshop next door is badly burned. The second and larger of the two is Briggs Mine Cabin. These cabins are a credit to the volunteers who maintain and enjoy them. Both are habitable. They have running hot water, a refrigerator, and a cooker, all powered by gas. All need to be activated carefully with the appropriate fuel. Although they are comfortable, the cabins are not suited for travelers expecting a luxury setting. There are shaded outdoor eating areas with barbecues, large bunk beds, and even an intercom between the two cabins. On our visit, the cabins were spotlessly clean with no sign of the rodent activity that can make using many of these idyllic backcountry cabins a dangerous business. It seems each visitor contributes to further enhance the historic and practical qualities of the cabins.

All are welcome to use the cabins on a first- come, first-served basis. However, you must be aware of the dangers of hantavirus (see page 13). Leave the cabins tidy, preferably in better order than you found them. Let us hope that these cabins remain in similar condition so those who venture this way can enjoy this historic and scenic region for years to come.

Immediately past the cabins is one of the narrowest sections of shelf road along the trail. It snakes precariously around an edge of the canyon wall, and because of the tight twists, it is not recommended for extra long or wide vehicles. The weight limit on the shelf bridge is 3 tons. It is recommended that you walk ahead for the short distance involved before committing your vehicle. Most SUVs will be fine if driven with care. The log bridge crossing part of the fallen shelf road is similarly narrow. This section of shelf road was blown out sometime in the late 1980s. The perpetrator and motive is unknown, but they succeeded in closing the trail until the log bridge was constructed by the same volunteers who maintain the cabin.

Other sections of this very narrow shelf road are rocky and rough, with an extremely low margin for error. Past the shelf road, the trail continues to climb steadily, entering Death Valley National Park past Coulter Spring. The waters from the spring flow down the track at this point. In winter this can ice up and make it difficult or impossible to gain enough traction to climb the somewhat steep grade.

The trail exits South Park Canyon into South Park and becomes easygoing and smooth as it runs through sagebrush. There is a major fork in the trail in South Park. Those wanting to explore farther can drive a slightly longer loop that travels for a longer time along the ridge tops before rejoining this trail.

Additional miners' cabins and mining remains are passed before the trail drops from a saddle and enters Middle Park. Again, the road is smooth and easygoing, a pleasant change from the rock crawling in the

canyon. It climbs out of Middle Park to the ridge top, where it undulates steeply through pinyons and junipers to Rogers Pass, which is marked by a historical marker. There are unparalleled views over Striped Butte Valley, Mengel Pass, and Death Valley from this section of the trail.

From Rogers Pass, the trail descends toward Pleasant Canyon, passing Rita's Cabin. The cabin is not in as good order as the Briggs Mine Cabin, but there are picnic tables under some small trees, and it makes a pleasant place for a picnic or overnight camp.

The trail within Pleasant Canyon is generally smoother and easier than in South Park Canyon. However, in the lower sections there are a couple of very tricky sections that maintain the overall 7 difficulty rating of the trail. In addition, flowing springs turn the lower section of the canyon into a creek bed. When temperatures are low enough in winter and early spring, this section turns to a slick sheet of ice and can become totally impassable.

Inside the old mill at Clair Camp

The abundance of water from the spring means that long sections of lower Pleasant Canyon are moderately brushy. The trail finishes at Ballarat. There is no fuel available in Ballarat.

In winter, the ridge-top sections of the trail can have snow on them. Although this trail is often passable all year, high summer temperatures make it unpleasant and hard on vehicles at lower elevations. The optimum travel times are spring and fall, although snow melt in early spring may make sections of trail around the springs extremely boggy.

Current Road Information

Death Valley National Park
PO Box 579
Death Valley, CA 92328-0579
(760) 786-3200

Bureau of Land Management
Ridgecrest Field Office
300 South Richmond Road
Ridgecrest, CA 93555
(760) 384-5400

Map References

BLM   Ridgecrest, Darwin Hills
USGS 1:24,000   Manly Fall, Panamint,
       Ballarat
       1:100,000 Ridgecrest, Darwin Hills
Maptech CD-ROM: Barstow/San
       Bernardino County; Kings
       Canyon/Death Valley
Southern & Central California Atlas & Gazetteer, pp. 41, 53
California Road & Recreation Atlas, p. 88
Trails Illustrated, Death Valley National
       Park (221)
Other: Free NPS Death Valley map
       (does not show road on map)

Route Directions

▼ 0.0   From Desert #33: Mengel Pass Trail, 3.7 miles south of Ballarat and 0.4 miles north of mile marker 8, zero trip meter and turn east on unmarked, formed trail. There is no sign at the intersection.

DESERT #35: PLEASANT CANYON LOOP TRAIL

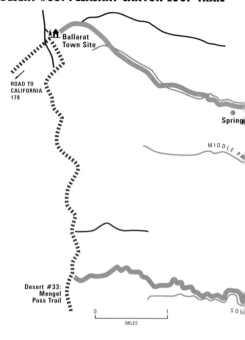

4.0 ▲   Trail finishes on Desert #33: Mengel Pass Trail in the Panamint Valley. Turn right for Ballarat; turn left to continue along Mengel Pass Trail.
        GPS: N36°00.01′ W117°13.17′

▼ 0.2   SO Start of shelf road.
3.8 ▲   SO End of shelf road.
▼ 1.9   SO Track on right is a shortcut up the ridge. This is very steep and loose and not recommended for travel uphill because the last section is extremely difficult. Proceed straight ahead to remain on main trail.
2.1 ▲   SO Track on left is end of steep shortcut.
        GPS: N35°59.85′ W117°11.73′

▼ 2.3   SO Shortcut up ridge rejoins on right.
1.7 ▲   BR Track on right is a very steep shortcut down the ridge. It is not recommended because of low traction.
▼ 2.6   SO Trail enters South Park Canyon.
1.4 ▲   SO Trails exits South Park Canyon.
▼ 2.7   SO Enter South Park Canyon wash. End of shelf road.

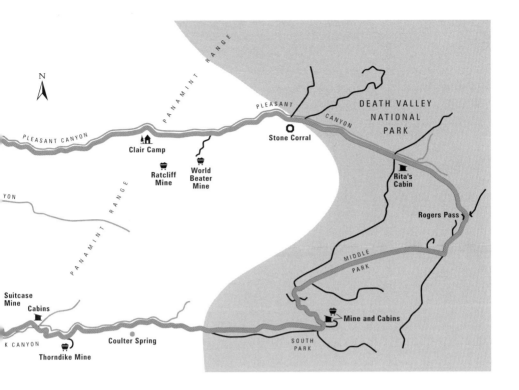

▼ 1.3 ▲	SO	Exit South Park Canyon wash. Start of shelf road.	

GPS: N35°59.70' W117°11.24'

▼ 3.5	SO	Track on left is old, washed-out mining road that rejoins almost immediately.
0.5 ▲	SO	Track on right is old, washed-out mining road that rejoins almost immediately.

GPS: N35°59.70' W117°10.66'

▼ 4.0	SO	Well-used track on left goes 1 mile to the Suitcase Mine. Zero trip meter.
0.0 ▲		Continue to the west down South Park Canyon.

GPS: N35°59.75' W117°10.42'

▼ 0.0		Continue to the east up South Park Canyon.
3.5 ▲	BL	Well-used track on right goes 1 mile to the Suitcase Mine. Zero trip meter.
▼ 0.7	BR	Two cabins on left. The first is Stone Cabin; the second is Briggs Mine Cabin. Track on left to cabins.
2.8 ▲	SO	Two cabins on right. The first is Briggs Mine Cabin; the second is Stone Cabin. Track on right to cabins.

GPS: N35°59.72' W117°09.83'

▼ 0.9	BR	Bear right out of wash. Start of narrow shelf road with no turnaround for 0.5 miles. Wide or long vehicles may wish to walk this section first.
2.6 ▲	BL	End of shelf road. Bear left down wash.

GPS: N35°59.63' W117°09.56'

▼ 1.2	SO	Narrow log bridge.
2.3 ▲	SO	Narrow log bridge.

GPS: N35°59.59' W117°09.50'

▼ 1.3	SO	End of shelf road. Enter wash.
2.2 ▲	SO	Exit wash. Start of narrow shelf road with no turnaround for 0.5 miles. Wide or long vehicles may wish to walk this section first.
▼ 1.4	SO	Track on right goes to the Thorndike Mine.
2.1 ▲	SO	Track on left goes to the Thorndike Mine.

GPS: N35°59.58' W117°09.28'

▼ 2.4	SO	Coulter Spring on right.
1.1 ▲	SO	Coulter Spring on left.

▼ 3.1 SO Exit line of wash.
0.4 ▲ SO Enter line of wash.
▼ 3.5 BL Trail forks. Well-used track on right. Zero trip meter. Entering South Park.
0.0 ▲   Continue to the west and start to descend into South Park Canyon.
           GPS: N35°59.55′ W117°07.27′

▼ 0.0   Continue to the northeast.
1.6 ▲ SO Well-used track on left. Continue out of South Park. Zero trip meter.
▼ 1.5 SO Track on right.
0.1 ▲ BR Track on left.
           GPS: N35°59.51′ W117°05.58′

▼ 1.6 SO Well-used track on right can be used to travel a longer loop within South Park. Continue toward mine and zero trip meter.
0.0 ▲   Continue to the west across South Park.
           GPS: N35°59.49′ W117°05.48′

▼ 0.0   Continue to the northeast past track on right.
3.0 ▲ BR Track on left; then well-used track on left is the end of the longer loop. Zero trip meter.
▼ 0.1 SO Pass two derelict cabins; then mine on right.
2.9 ▲ SO Mine on left; then pass two derelict cabins.
           GPS: N35°59.55′ W117°05.42′

▼ 0.2 SO Track on right into mine.
2.8 ▲ BR Track on left into mine.
▼ 0.6 SO 4-way intersection on saddle. Track on right to old mining truck and track on left. Descend to Middle Park.
2.4 ▲ SO 4-way intersection on saddle. Track on left to old mining truck and track on right. Descend to South Park.
           GPS: N35°59.84′ W117°05.81′

▼ 0.8 BR Two well-used tracks on left.
2.2 ▲ BL Two well-used tracks on right.
           GPS: N35°59.97′ W117°05.82′

▼ 1.0 SO Track on right.
2.0 ▲ SO Track on left.
▼ 2.0 SO Track on left.
1.0 ▲ SO Track on right.
▼ 2.9 SO Track on left.
0.1 ▲ SO Track on right.
           GPS: N36°00.33′ W117°03.64′

▼ 3.0 TL T-intersection at ridge top. Track on right is end of longer loop. Turn left and continue to climb ridge. Zero trip meter.
0.0 ▲   Continue to the west.
           GPS: N36°00.32′ W117°03.60′

▼ 0.0   Continue to the north.
0.6 ▲ TR Turn right onto well-used track and descend to Middle Park. Track ahead can be taken to travel a longer loop to South Park. Zero trip meter.
▼ 0.1 SO Track on left.
0.5 ▲ BL Track on right.
           GPS: N36°00.44′ W117°03.56′

▼ 0.5 SO Two tracks on left.
0.1 ▲ SO Two tracks on right.
▼ 0.6 TL Rogers Pass. There is a marker at the pass. Steep track straight ahead. Old, indistinct pack trail on right goes to Arrastre Spring. Zero trip meter at marker.
0.0 ▲   Continue to the southwest.
           GPS: N36°00.75′ W117°03.22′

▼ 0.0   Continue to the northwest.
4.2 ▲ TR Rogers Pass. There is a marker at the pass. Continue to climb steeply. Steep track on left. Old, indistinct pack trail straight ahead goes to Arrastre Spring. Zero trip meter at marker.
▼ 1.3 SO Track on left and Rita's Cabin on left. Entering Pleasant Canyon.
2.9 ▲ SO Track on right and Rita's Cabin on right. Exiting Pleasant Canyon.
           GPS: N36°01.48′ W117°04.19′

▼ 1.4 SO Well-used track on left is shorter, steeper route back into Middle Park that bypasses Rogers Pass.
2.8 ▲ BL Well-used track on right is shorter,

Log bridge along the narrow shelf road

steeper route into Middle Park that bypasses Rogers Pass.

▼ 1.5   SO   Track on right.
2.7 ▲   SO   Track on left.
▼ 1.6   BR   Track on left.
2.6 ▲   SO   Track on right.
▼ 2.0   BL   Track on right.
2.2 ▲   SO   Track on left.
         GPS: N36°01.83′ W117°04.85′

▼ 2.2   SO   Track on left rejoins. Trail enters line of wash.
2.0 ▲   BL   Track on right. Exit line of wash.
         GPS: N36°01.85′ W117°05.02′

▼ 2.8   SO   Well-used track on right.
1.4 ▲   BR   Well-used track on left.
         GPS: N36°02.00′ W117°05.66′

▼ 2.9   SO   Track on right and remains of stone corral on left. Leaving Death Valley National Park.
1.3 ▲   SO   Track on left and remains of stone corral on right. Entering Death Valley National Park.
         GPS: N36°02.02′ W117°05.77′

▼ 4.1   SO   Stone foundations on left and water tank on right.
0.1 ▲   SO   Stone foundations on right and water tank on left.
▼ 4.2   SO   Well-used track on left goes to the World Beater Mine. Zero trip meter
0.0 ▲   Continue to the east.
         GPS: N36°01.91′ W117°06.99′

▼ 0.0   Continue to the west.
6.6 ▲   SO   Well-used track on right goes to the World Beater Mine. Zero trip meter.
▼ 0.6   SO   Pass under aerial tramway cable.
6.0 ▲   SO   Pass under aerial tramway cable.
▼ 0.9   SO   Clair Camp—cabins and mining remains on right and left.
5.7 ▲   SO   Clair Camp—cabins and mining remains on left and right.
         GPS: N36°01.98′ W117°07.89′

▼ 1.0   SO   Gate. Leaving Clair Camp.
5.6 ▲   SO   Gate. Entering Clair Camp.
▼ 1.3   SO   Stone cabin on left.

5.3 ▲   SO   Stone cabin on right.
▼ 2.3   SO   Loading hopper on left and aerial tramway high on the canyon wall to the right.
4.3 ▲   SO   Loading hopper on right and aerial tramway high on the canyon wall to the left.
         GPS: N36°01.76′ W117°09.39′

▼ 2.6   SO   Mine on left.
4.0 ▲   SO   Mine on right.
▼ 2.9   SO   Pass under aerial tramway cable.
3.7 ▲   SO   Pass under aerial tramway cable.
▼ 3.0   SO   Spring.
3.6 ▲   SO   Spring.
         GPS: N36°01.90′ W117°10.50′

▼ 3.5   SO   Adit on left.
3.1 ▲   SO   Adit on right.
▼ 4.1   SO   Exit line of wash.
2.5 ▲   SO   Enter line of wash.
▼ 4.7   SO   Cross through wash; then track on left; then cross through wash.
1.9 ▲   SO   Cross through wash; then track on right; then cross through wash.
▼ 4.8   SO   Cross through wash.
1.8 ▲   SO   Cross through wash.
▼ 5.3   SO   Cross through wash.
1.3 ▲   SO   Cross through wash.
▼ 5.6   SO   Cross through wash. Exit Pleasant Canyon.
1.0 ▲   SO   Cross through wash. Enter Pleasant Canyon.
▼ 6.1   SO   Track on right.
0.5 ▲   BR   Track on left.
▼ 6.6   Trail ends in Ballarat. Continue straight ahead to exit to California 178; turn left to travel Desert #33: Mengel Pass Trail.
0.0 ▲   Trail commences in Ballarat in the Panamint Valley, along Desert #33: Mengel Pass Trail, 4 miles east of Trona Wildrose Road. Zero trip meter at the general store and proceed northeast on formed trail.
         GPS: N36°02.87′ W117°13.38′

Johnson Canyon Trail

STARTING POINT: Desert #32: Death Valley West Side Road, 14.4 miles from the south end
FINISHING POINT: Johnson Canyon
TOTAL MILEAGE: 10 miles (one-way)
UNPAVED MILEAGE: 10 miles
DRIVING TIME: 1.5 hours (one-way)
ELEVATION RANGE: -200–3,800 feet
USUALLY OPEN: Year-round
BEST TIME TO TRAVEL: October to May
DIFFICULTY RATING: 3
SCENIC RATING: 8
REMOTENESS RATING: +1

Special Attractions
- Rugged trail that penetrates the Panamint Range up Johnson Canyon.
- Hungry Bills Ranch site.

History
The Timbisha Shoshone have been associated with this area for many generations. Their ancestors roamed the land, using it in seasonal patterns. One seasonal dwelling area was in the canyon now referred to as Johnson Canyon. The Timbisha Shoshone valued the cooler temperatures of the canyon and the availability of springwater during the sweltering summer months.

The arrival of the forty-niners meant change for the native people's way of life. Word was spreading about the mineral

Traveling across an alluvial fan to Death Valley can be slow

A spring at the end of the vehicle trail marks the start of the hiking trail

wealth that could be found within this harsh landscape. Control of the intermittent water holes became an early source of conflict as whites arrived in search of mineral deposits. Native plants used for food by Indians were seen as fuel and construction materials by the new arrivals and hostilities quickly escalated into bloodshed. The Treaty of Ruby Valley, ratified by Congress in 1866, sought a peaceful solution to the situation. It granted new arrivals right of passage across Western Shoshone lands. However, miners were not easily placated and they continued to squeeze out the native Timbisha Shoshone.

With the influx of miners to the Panamints and, in particular, the boom at Panamint City in 1873, the demand for fresh fruit and vegetables far outweighed the available supply. Two Swiss men saw the opportunity for a fresh produce supply business and they began their market gardening operation in the upper reaches of Johnson Canyon, about 10 miles across the range from Panamint City. Having an obvious monopoly on the supply of fresh goods to the mining town, the entrepreneurs found they could charge phenomenal prices and still sell all they produced. Cabbage was reportedly fetching a price of approximately $1.20 a head, well above the average market price of 1875.

But when the boom times of Panamint City declined, so did the demand for fresh produce. The property was vacated and almost forgotten until a Shoshone named Hungry Bill stepped in to reclaim his family's land rights in the region. The aging ruins and orchard of Hungry Bills Ranch can be seen along the hiking trail from the end of the vehicle trail.

Description

This spur trail leaves Desert #32: Death Valley West Side Road to travel a slow and bumpy path up the rocky, barren bajada on the east side of the Panamint Range. The formed trail travels steadily for 6 miles up the alluvial fan, or bajada, following alongside Johnson Canyon Wash. The hardy creosote bush is the main plant that manages to survive in the open, windswept area.

After 6 miles, the trail descends to join Johnson Canyon Wash and the surface becomes slightly harder, rougher, and lumpier with some larger embedded rocks to negotiate. The canyon is fairly open. Its walls support sparse creosote bush and sagebrush.

Nearly 10 miles from the start, the vehicle trail finishes at a spring surrounded by large cottonwood trees and the site of an old corral. It is possible to hike past the spring to visit the remains of Hungry Bills Ranch. The well-prepared hiker can continue over Panamint Pass to the site of Panamint ghost town.

There is no camping for the first 2 miles of the trail from Desert #32: Death Valley West Side Road, and there are extremely limited choices after that.

Current Road Information

Death Valley National Park
PO Box 579
Death Valley, CA 92328-0579
(760) 786-3200

Map References

BLM   Death Valley Junction, Darwin Hills
USGS 1:24,000 Mormon Point, Galena
      Canyon, Panamint
      1:1,000,000 Death Valley
      Junction, Darwin Hills
Maptech CD-ROM: Kings Canyon/Death
      Valley

USGS bench mark at Deadman Pass

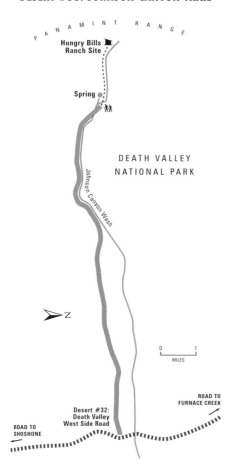

GPS: N36°05.17′ W116°57.12′

▼ 6.2   SO   Enter Johnson Canyon Wash.

▼ 9.9   SO   Cross through creek formed by flowing spring.

▼ 10.0   Trail ends at spring. Vehicle trail does not continue past this point. From here, hike up the canyon past the spring to reach Hungry Bills Ranch site.
      GPS: N36°05.33′ W117°00.33′

DESERT #37

Deadman Pass Trail

STARTING POINT: California 127, 7.1 miles south of Death Valley Junction
FINISHING POINT: Gold Valley
TOTAL MILEAGE: 27.5 miles
UNPAVED MILEAGE: 27.5 miles
DRIVING TIME: 1 hour for Deadman Pass section; 2.5 hours (one-way) for Gold Valley, including all 3 spurs
ELEVATION RANGE: 2,100–4,500 feet
USUALLY OPEN: Year-round
BEST TIME TO TRAVEL: September to June
DIFFICULTY RATING: 3
SCENIC RATING: 8
REMOTENESS RATING: +0

Special Attractions
■ Alternate entry/exit to Nevada from Death Valley.
■ Beautiful and varied Gold Valley.
■ Chance to see bighorn sheep around Willow Spring.

Southern & Central California Atlas & Gazetteer, p. 42
California Road & Recreation Atlas, p. 88
Trails Illustrated, Death Valley National Park (221)
Other: Free NPS Death Valley map

History
In February 1908, the nearby town of Greenwater was almost deserted because the population headed for Gold Valley in search of a lucky strike. Prospectors Harry Ramsey and O. P. Grover found promising ore and formed the Willow Creek Gold Mining Company, located in Gold Valley about 20 miles southwest of Greenwater. The initial ore from their seven claims was reported in the *Inyo Independent* as returning an average

Route Directions

▼ 0.0   From Desert #32: Death Valley West Side Road, 14.4 miles from the southern end of the trail, zero trip meter and turn west on formed dirt trail signposted to Johnson Canyon.
      GPS: N36°05.89′ W116°50.67′

▼ 6.0   SO   Trail descends toward Johnson Canyon Wash.

Looking back toward Nevada from Deadman Pass

of $148 to the ton. Ore from the nearby LeCry property was only returning an average of $37 to the ton. This was enough to cause a mild rush to Gold Valley. The Goldfield Review section of the *Inyo Independent* announced that Andy Kane had seven men working his claims. One had produced a sample of ore that assayed at 2,000 ounces silver; another produced copper ore at 40 to 60 percent. An assay office with a furnace was set up by Brockinghams of Boston. Bill Brong's auto line provided transportation to the new camp from the Tonopah & Tidewater Railroad's Death Valley Junction, located north of Deadman Pass.

The Willow Creek Gold Mining Company's ore could be handled by the stamp and plate process. Willow Creek's location near the claim, the farthest point on this trail, was noted as having enough water to run a 20-stamp mill without any further development. Transportation of

the ore—always a concern to Death Valley prospectors—seemed under control as the Tonopah & Tidewater Railroad was expected to complete a branch to nearby Greenwater. All the elements seemed in order for another booming mining region similar to the one at Rhyolite, Nevada. Unfortunately, like Greenwater, not much development came to Gold Valley, and prospectors moved on in their never-ending search for the big one.

Description

This trail is really two separate trails divided by Greenwater Valley Road. The Deadman Pass section can be driven alone as a way of accessing the southern end of Death Valley National Park. The Gold Valley section can be treated as a detour off the long north-south Greenwater Valley Road.

Deadman Pass Trail leaves California 127 south of Death Valley Junction. Initially, the

DESERT #37: DEADMAN PASS TRAIL

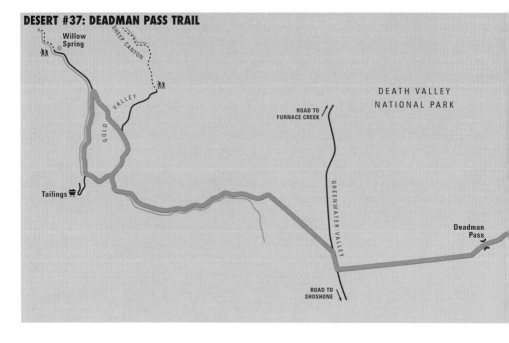

trail travels in a very loose, gravelly wash. This section can be slow and difficult, especially in hot weather. Leaving the wash, the trail climbs the gentle gradient to Deadman Pass, a wide pass in the Greenwater Range. There is a USGS bench mark at the pass but no sign. On the western side of the pass, the trail runs in a plumb line to join Greenwater Valley Road. The trail joins this road for 0.5 miles before turning west onto the Gold Valley section of the route.

Initially the trail is graded, but it quickly reverts to a well-used formed trail. Much of the trail's early section crosses an area of desert pavement. There are many faint tracks leading off on the right and left; remain on the main trail. As you approach Gold Valley, the trail becomes uneven and rougher, twisting up to a saddle with a view of the valley ahead and the Panamint Range beyond.

The trail follows a loop within Gold Valley, passing around the bowl of the valley through deep red rocks and pretty hills. There are three side trails that branch off from the loop. The first goes 0.6 miles south to some mine tailings. Two thirds of the way along this trail, it passes through a narrow crevice in the rocks, which will stop wider ve-

hicles. The second side trail leads 2.3 miles west down Willow Creek to a spring. The lush vegetation and reliable water supply make this creek a favorite spot for bighorn sheep and other animal and bird life. The third side trail meanders north through the hills toward Sheep Canyon and various mine tailings. The third side trail is the least used of the three.

When the loop is completed, you must exit back to Greenwater Valley Road. From here, you can travel south to Shoshone and the hot springs at Tecopa, north to Furnace Creek, or retrace your steps over Deadman Pass to Death Valley Junction.

Current Road Information

Death Valley National Park
PO Box 579
Death Valley, CA 92328-0579
(760) 786-3200

Map References

BLM   Death Valley Junction
USGS 1:24,000   West of Eagle Mtn.,
      Deadman Pass, Funeral Peak,
      Gold Valley
      1:100,000 Death Valley Junction

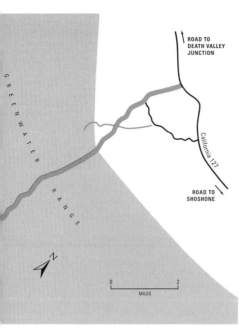

Maptech CD-ROM: Kings Canyon/Death
    Valley
Southern & Central California Atlas &
    Gazetteer, pp. 42, 43
California Road & Recreation Atlas, pp. 89, 88
Trails Illustrated, Death Valley National
    Park (221)
Other: Free NPS Death Valley map
    (trail is not marked)

Route Directions

▼ 0.0   From California 127, 7.3 miles south of
            Death Valley Junction, zero trip meter
            and turn south on unmarked, small
            formed trail. Trail is opposite the north
            end of Eagle Mountain and 0.1 miles
            west of the 2,000 feet elevation sign.
3.5 ▲   Trail ends at intersection with
            California 127. Turn left for Death
            Valley Junction; turn right for
            Shoshone.
            GPS: N36°12.60' W116°23.68'

▼ 0.1 BR Bear right into line of wash. Very
            loose, deep gravel for next 1.2 miles.
3.4 ▲ BL Bear left out of line of wash.
▼ 1.3 SO Track on right.

2.2 ▲ BR Track on left is alternate exit to
            California 127 that avoids a section of
            loose, deep gravel. Remain in wash.
            Very loose, deep gravel for next 1.2
            miles.
            GPS: N36°11.85' W116°24.26'

▼ 1.4 SO Track on left.
2.1 ▲ SO Track on right.
▼ 1.5 BL Track on right out of wash. Exit wash.
2.0 ▲ SO Enter wash. Track on left out of wash.
            GPS: N36°11.69' W116°24.38'

▼ 1.6 SO Cross through wash.
1.9 ▲ SO Cross through wash.
▼ 1.7 SO Cross through wash.
1.8 ▲ SO Cross through wash.
▼ 3.5 SO Entering Death Valley National Park
            at sign. Zero trip meter.
0.0 ▲   Continue to the north.
            GPS: N36°10.01' W116°24.65'

▼ 0.0   Continue to the south.
5.1 ▲ SO Leaving Death Valley National Park at
            sign. Zero trip meter.
▼ 5.1 SO Deadman Pass. Zero trip meter at the
            top. There is a USGS bench mark on
            the left at the pass but no other mark-
            er. Trail now gradually descends.
0.0 ▲   Continue to the north.
            GPS: N36°05.88' W116°26.68'

▼ 0.0   Continue to the south.
4.3 ▲ SO Deadman Pass. Zero trip meter at the
            top. There is a USGS bench mark on
            the right at the pass but no other
            marker. Trail now gradually descends.
▼ 1.9 SO Track on right.
2.4 ▲ SO Track on left.
▼ 4.3 TR T-intersection with roughly graded
            Greenwater Valley Road. Zero trip
            meter.
0.0 ▲   Continue to the northeast.
            GPS: N36°03.06' W116°29.97'

▼ 0.0   Continue to the northwest.
0.5 ▲ TL Turn left onto well-used, unmarked trail
            and zero trip meter.
▼ 0.5 TL Turn left onto unmarked, roughly grad-
            ed smaller trail. There is a metal post

opposite the intersection but no sign.
Zero trip meter. Trail is a spur from
this point.

0.0 ▲ Continue to the southeast.

GPS: N36°03.35' W116°30.39'

▼ 0.0 Continue to the west.
▼ 0.2 SO Cross through wash.
▼ 3.2 SO Enter line of wash.

GPS: N36°03.02' W116°33.75'

▼ 7.0 SO Trail exits line of wash.

GPS: N36°01.23' W116°36.93'

▼ 7.2 SO Pull-in on right.
▼ 7.7 BL Trail forks at the start of loop.
Zero trip meter.

GPS: N36°01.29' W116°37.31'

▼ 0.0 Continue to the west.
▼ 1.0 TR Track on left goes 0.6 miles to some
tailings piles and the wilderness
boundary. Zero trip meter.

GPS: N36°00.95' W116°38.09'

▼ 0.0 Continue to the northwest.
▼ 0.8 SO Enter line of wash.
▼ 2.4 TR Turn sharp right to continue around
loop and zero trip meter. Track on left
goes 1.7 miles to Willow Spring. A hiking trail continues down Willow Creek
from that point.

GPS: N36°02.74' W116°39.47'

▼ 0.0 Continue to the east.
▼ 1.5 SO Track on left goes 2.3 miles toward old
dugouts, mines, and hiking trail in
Sheep Canyon. Zero trip meter.

GPS: N36°02.36' W116°37.93'

▼ 0.0 Continue to the east.
▼ 1.5 End of loop. Continue straight ahead to
exit the way you came to Greenwater
Valley Road.

GPS: N36°01.29' W116°37.31'

Echo Canyon Trail

STARTING POINT: California 190, 2 miles east
of intersection with Death Valley Road
at Furnace Creek
FINISHING POINT: Inyo Mine
TOTAL MILEAGE: 9.1 miles (one-way)
UNPAVED MILEAGE: 9.1 miles
DRIVING TIME: 1 hour (one-way)
ELEVATION RANGE: 400–3,700 feet
USUALLY OPEN: Year-round
BEST TIME TO TRAVEL: October to May
DIFFICULTY RATING: 3
SCENIC RATING: 9
REMOTENESS RATING: +0

Special Attractions
■ Historic Travertine Hot Springs at the
start of the trail.
■ The natural rock window, Eye of the Needle.
■ The remains of the Inyo Mine camp.

History
Members of an 1849 wagon train camped at
Travertine Springs along their nightmare
"shortcut" route to the goldfields of the West.
The Brier family and the Mississippi Boys had
been forced to abandon their wagons in western Nevada when their weakened oxen could
no longer pull the weight of their possessions.
Crossing the Funeral Mountains had been an
arduous trip for all concerned, with no water
to be found along the way. They reached the
welcome waters of Travertine Springs on
Christmas Day and feasted on the only food
available—another ox. With malnourished
children in tow, the Bennett and Arcane families struggled over the mountains two days
later. They also camped and rested by the
warm Travertine Springs.
    Prior to this, local Indians had little inter-
action with new settlers. They used Death
Valley as a winter retreat and regularly
camped at the mouth of Furnace Creek (close
to where the inn is located today). Seeing the
emigrants' oxen as food, the Indians attacked
a beast with arrows. The forty-niners took

this to be an assault against them personally, and they moved on into Death Valley as quickly as they could gather the strength. Unfortunately, their problems in Death Valley had only begun! Nearly five weeks later, they would barely escape with their lives.

The earliest mining claims in the Echo Canyon region were made by Chet Leavitt and Maroni Hicks in 1905. Within months, the two prospectors were receiving offers to buy out their claims. Charles Schwab was among the first investors. He did not actually take up his earliest options, yet his name remains on the map to this day. Many such investors came and paid initial monies, but they did not follow up on their options. Within a year, two dozen claims were located along Echo Canyon.

Production at the Inyo Mine began in 1906 with a good deal of success. The Inyo Mining Company went public in 1907, but because of the economic panic of that year, it turned out to be a bad time to put the company stock up for sale. Mining investors were nowhere to be found and the Inyo Mining Company was forced to wind down its oper-

ations. Little happened at the mine for the next 30 years. The mines were sold and resold. The last serious attempt to work the mine ended in 1941.

At the mouth of Furnace Creek, Greenland Ranch was part of the growing borax empire of William Tell Coleman. Coleman's ranch was the largest and most profitable in Death Valley. It later became known as Furnace Creek Ranch. The impressive date grove at the ranch was planted in the 1920s by the Pacific Coast Borax Company. It began providing quality dates in the early 1930s. Date palms are not native to North America; these were imported from Algeria around the turn of the twentieth century. The ranch offered accommodations for visitors to Death Valley and housed the headquarters of Death Valley National Park. In 1927, the Pacific Coast Borax Company opened the Furnace Creek Inn, with attractions such as a golf course, tennis courts, swimming pool, and auto tours of Death Valley. By 1933, the Pacific Coast Borax Company expanded Furnace Creek Ranch into a resort, offering less expensive accommodation options.

Inyo Mine

Description

Echo Canyon Trail is a lightly traveled canyon trail within Death Valley National Park. Along the way, it passes some beautiful scenery as well as the remains of what was once a large mining camp.

At the start of the trail, a thicket of palms immediately to the west marks the Travertine Hot Springs. The waters are tapped and there is no pool for bathing. However, the small oasis is interesting and worth the short hike to view the cluster of palms. The spring is situated 0.3 miles northwest of the start of the trail on the north side of California 190.

The well-formed trail leaves California 190 and travels up the bajada to the mouth of Echo Canyon. No camping is permitted for the first 2 miles and no camping is permitted at the Inyo Mine. This is not a good trail for camping because the majority of it travels in a wash or canyon. Campers are better off selecting a site in one of the developed camp-grounds at Furnace Creek.

Within Echo Canyon, the trail winds along in the wash. There are a couple of rocky sections, but the main reason for the difficulty rating is the very deep, loose gravel in the wash. In warmer months, this can quickly cause a vehicle to overheat.

The Eye of the Needle is located 5.1 miles from the start of the trail. The small rock window, or natural arch, is easy to spot, and it is possible to scramble up to it. Shortly after the window, the canyon opens out to a wider valley. Desert #39: Funeral Range Trail leaves to the northeast. This difficult trail is an alternate exit from Echo Canyon to the Amargosa Valley. The Inyo Mine is a short distance past the intersection with the Funeral Range Trail. There are many old cabins and mining remains scattered over the hillside at the site. The trail ends at the wilderness boundary a short distance past the mine.

Current Road Information

Death Valley National Park
PO Box 579
Death Valley, CA 92328-0579
(760) 786-3200

Map References

BLM   Death Valley Junction
USGS 1:24,000   Furnace Creek, Echo Canyon
      1:100,000 Death Valley Junction
Maptech CD-ROM: Kings Canyon/Death Valley
Southern & Central California Atlas & Gazetteer, p. 42
California Road & Recreation Atlas, p. 88
Trails Illustrated, Death Valley National Park (221)
Other: Free NPS Death Valley map

Route Directions

▼ 0.0   From California 190, 2 miles southeast of the intersection with Death Valley Road at Furnace Creek, zero trip meter and turn northeast on formed trail. There is a small sign for Echo Canyon at the start. No camping for the first 2 miles. Trail travels up the alluvial fan.

8.6 ▲   Trail ends on California 190. Turn right for Furnace Creek; turn left for Death Valley Junction.
         GPS: N36°26.25' W116°49.40'

▼ 2.8   SO Entering Echo Canyon wash.
5.8 ▲   SO Exiting Echo Canyon wash. Trail now travels over alluvial fan.

▼ 3.3   SO Entering Echo Canyon.
5.3 ▲   SO Exiting Echo Canyon.
         GPS: N36°27.56' W116°46.26'

▼ 4.5   SO Eye of the Needle on right at top of cliff.
4.1 ▲   SO Eye of the Needle on left at top of cliff.
         GPS: N36°27.98' W116°45.52'

▼ 5.1   SO Small rock window directly ahead above tight gap.
3.5 ▲   SO Small rock window directly behind above tight gap.
         GPS: N36°28.19' W116°45.12'

▼ 5.2   SO Turnout on left. Leave narrow section of Echo Canyon.
3.4 ▲   SO Turnout on right. Enter narrow section of Echo Canyon.
         GPS: N36°28.28' W116°45.10'

In the wash of Echo Canyon

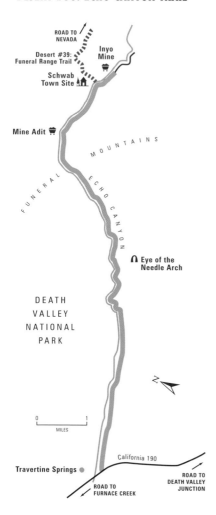

wilderness boundary. Retrace your steps to exit to California 190. Take Desert #39: Funeral Range Trail to continue into Nevada.

GPS: N36°29.61′ W116°42.18′

DESERT #39

Funeral Range Trail

STARTING POINT: Desert #38: Echo Canyon Trail, 8.6 miles northeast of California 190

FINISHING POINT: Nevada 373, 5 miles south of Amargosa Valley

TOTAL MILEAGE: 25.4 miles

UNPAVED MILEAGE: 14.0 miles

DRIVING TIME: 2 hours

ELEVATION RANGE: 2,300–4,900 feet

USUALLY OPEN: Year-round

BEST TIME TO TRAVEL: September to June

DIFFICULTY RATING: 6

SCENIC RATING: 9

REMOTENESS RATING: +2

Special Attractions
- Difficult trail through a variety of spectacular scenery.
- An alternate entry into Death Valley National Park from Nevada when coupled with Desert #38: Echo Canyon Trail.
- Site of historic Lees Camp.

History
It was through the harsh landscape of the Funeral Mountains in December 1849 that the Jayhawkers wagon party attempted to reach the goldfields of California by way of a supposed shortcut. Although four members of the party died in this region, the mountain range's name is thought to come from something else. It is attributed more to the natural black, cape-like lacing of basalt rock that sits above the light-colored rocks at the base, somewhat like mourning attire.

The town site of Schwab is near the junction of this trail and Desert #38: Echo Canyon Trail in the northern, or upper,

▼ 7.7   SO   Mine adit on left.
0.9 ▲   SO   Mine adit on right.
        GPS: N36°29.84′ W116°43.86′

▼ 8.6   SO   Track on left at small sign to Amargosa is the start of Desert #39: Funeral Range Trail. Zero trip meter.
0.0 ▲   Continue to the west.
        GPS: N36°29.78′ W116°42.59′

▼ 0.0   Continue to the east on dead end trail.
▼ 0.5   SO   Remains of the Inyo Mine. Trail continues for 0.8 miles past this point to

Rough, rocky section of the trail

branch of Echo Canyon. Named after Pennsylvania steel magnate Charles Schwab, the settlement served as a center for local miners during its brief existence. Founded in 1906, the town was deserted within a year. The remains in the area are remnants from the Inyo Mine, which operated on and off from 1906 to 1941.

Farther to the north along this trail is the town site of Echo. The Lee Golden Gate Mining Company located the town near the summit of the Funeral Range, expecting the mines in the region to invest in town property. It is doubtful if any allotments were actually sold because most of the surrounding mines were unsuccessful.

The site of Lees Camp is close to the Nevada border. A small mining camp existed here between 1906 and 1912. The settlement was founded to compete with another town named Lee just over the Nevada border. A good source of water enabled the California Lee to flourish while its rival floundered. Foundation walls and mine shafts mark the site.

Description

This difficult trail travels through the spectacular Funeral Mountains, part of the larger Amargosa Range that runs along the California-Nevada border. The trail commences on Desert #38: Echo Canyon Trail, 8.6 miles from the start. The turn is easy to spot, and there is a small sign for Amargosa at the intersection. Although this trail is rated a 6 overall, the majority of it is rated a 4. The 6 rating comes from three separate places where the trail climbs or descends some rocky waterfalls within the tight canyon. There is no alternate route around these places, which means that the trail is best driven by an excellent stock high-clearance 4WD with good tires. Additional clearance from larger tires

One of the many beautiful, tight canyons along this trail

and/or a suspension lift is an advantage. These sections will put vehicles with low hanging front or rear bars or side steps at a definite disadvantage; such vehicles risk body damage. The difficulty of these rock falls is not the steepness, rather it is the loose piles of boulders and unforgiving embedded rock and rock faces that makes any error of judgment potentially very costly. Take them slowly and plan your line of approach beforehand. Use a spotter to help with wheel placement and to ensure that you are not in danger of damaging the undercarriage of your vehicle.

The trail is well formed as it twists along the washes and ridge tops of the Funeral Mountains. There are some spectacular sections of canyon narrows; one in particular is the final canyon before the trail spills out into the Amargosa Valley. In addition, the ridge top sections provide long ranging views, particularly over the Amargosa Valley.

At the mouth of the canyon is the site of Lees Camp, once a booming mining camp. Little remains now except for some stone foundations and rusting piles of tin cans. Past the town site, the trail simultaneously exits California and Death Valley National Park and enters Nevada. There are no signs. From here it is an easy trail down the bajada to join paved Amargosa Farm Road, which takes you out to join Nevada 373.

Current Road Information

Death Valley National Park
PO Box 579
Death Valley, CA 92328-0579
(760) 786-3200

Map References

BLM   Death Valley Junction, Beatty
USGS 1:24,000   Echo Canyon, Lees Camp, Leeland, South of Amargosa Valley
          1:100,000 Death Valley Junction, Beatty
Maptech CD-ROM: Kings Canyon/Death Valley
Southern & Central California Atlas & Gazetteer, pp. 42, 30
Nevada Atlas & Gazetteer, p. 64

California Road & Recreation Atlas, pp. 88, 89
Trails Illustrated, Death Valley National Park (221)
Other: Free NPS Death Valley map (trail is not marked)

Route Directions

▼ 0.0   From Desert #38: Echo Canyon Trail, 8.6 miles northeast of California 190, zero trip meter and turn northeast on small formed trail following the sign to Amargosa.

3.6 ▲   Trail ends at intersection with Desert #38: Echo Canyon Trail. Turn left to visit the Inyo Mine; turn right to exit to California 190 via Echo Canyon.
          GPS: N36°29.78′ W116°42.59′

▼ 0.3 SO Track on right.
3.3 ▲ SO Track on left rejoins.
▼ 0.4 SO Enter wash.
3.2 ▲ SO Exit wash.
▼ 0.5 SO Track on right rejoins.
3.1 ▲ SO Track on left.
▼ 1.0 SO Enter canyon.
2.6 ▲ SO Exit canyon.
▼ 2.5 SO Track on right.
1.1 ▲ SO Track on left.
          GPS: N36°30.42′ W116°41.22′

▼ 2.8 SO Track on right out of wash to stone foundations.
0.8 ▲ SO Track on left out of wash to stone foundations.
          GPS: N36°30.65′ W116°41.10′

▼ 2.9 SO Narrow section of rough trail climbs small rock fall in a tight section of the canyon.
0.7 ▲ SO Narrow section of rough trail descends small rock fall in a tight section of the canyon.
          GPS: N36°30.64′ W116°40.99′

▼ 3.4 BL Faint track on left; then track on right; then well-used track on left. Track continues up narrow wash ahead. Bear left out of wash on well-used track.

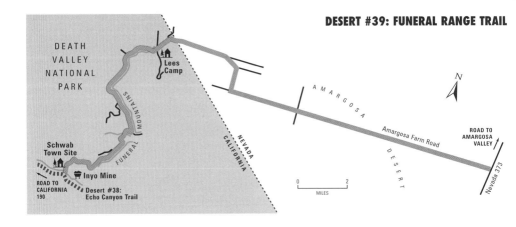

0.2 ▲   BR   Drop down and enter wash. Bear right in wash. Track on left up wash; then second track on left; then faint track on right.
GPS: N36°30.85' W116°40.68'

▼ 3.6   SO   4-way intersection on saddle. Well-used track on left and right on top of saddle. Zero trip meter.
0.0 ▲   Continue to the southwest.
GPS: N36°30.99' W116°40.66'

▼ 0.0   Continue to the northeast.
10.3 ▲   SO   4-way intersection on saddle. Well-used track on right and left on top of saddle. Zero trip meter.
▼ 0.1   SO   Track on left. Enter line of wash.
10.2 ▲   BL   Track on right. Bear left out of line of wash.
▼ 0.6   SO   Exit line of wash and crest ridge; then enter another wash line.
9.7 ▲   SO   Exit line of wash and crest ridge; then enter line of wash.
GPS: N36°31.39' W116°40.59'

▼ 0.8   TR   Well-used track on left leaves wash. Remain in smaller wash.
9.5 ▲   TL   Well-used track on right leaves wash. Join larger wash.
GPS: N36°31.42' W116°40.62'

▼ 1.0   SO   Exit line of wash.
9.3 ▲   SO   Enter line of wash.
▼ 1.3   SO   Cross through wash.
9.0 ▲   SO   Cross through wash.

▼ 1.5   SO   Saddle. Views ahead of the Amargosa Desert and Nevada.
8.8 ▲   SO   Saddle. Views behind of the Amargosa Desert and Nevada.
GPS: N36°31.80' W116°40.29'

▼ 1.7   TL   Turn left down line of wash. Track on right up wash is closed.
8.6 ▲   TR   Turn right out of wash. Track up wash ahead is closed.
GPS: N36°31.84' W116°40.12'

▼ 3.0   SO   Rocky waterfall. Choice of staying to the left and riding a pile of loose rubble or staying to the right and riding a large, water-smoothed boulder.
7.3 ▲   SO   Rocky waterfall. Choice of staying to the right and riding a pile of loose rubble or staying to the left and riding a large water-smoothed boulder.
GPS: N36°32.54' W116°40.84'

▼ 3.2   SO   Well-used track on left.
7.1 ▲   BL   Well-used track on right.
GPS: N36°32.71' W116°41.03'

▼ 3.9   BR   Bear right down canyon past track on left.
6.4 ▲   BL   Bear left up canyon past track on right. Track on right looks smoother and better used at this stage. Track on left appears lumpy and less used but it is the correct trail.
GPS: N36°32.96' W116°41.55'

▼ 5.2	SO	Exit canyon narrows.
5.1 ▲	SO	Enter canyon narrows.
▼ 5.4	TR	Turn right, heading down wash. Track on left goes up another wash.
4.9 ▲	TL	Turn left on well-used track. Track straight ahead goes up another wash.

GPS: N36°34.04' W116°41.35'

| ▼ 5.6 | BR | Well-used track on left out of wash. Remain in wash. |
| 4.7 ▲ | SO | Well-used track on right out of wash. Remain in wash. |

GPS: N36°34.25' W116°41.28'

| ▼ 6.7 | SO | Exit wash. |
| 3.6 ▲ | SO | Enter wash. |

GPS: N36°34.68' W116°40.29'

▼ 6.9	SO	Track on right at Lees Camp.
3.4 ▲	SO	Track on left at Lees Camp.
▼ 7.0	SO	Track on left and track on right.
3.3 ▲	SO	Track on left and track on right.
▼ 7.6	BR	Well-used track on left.
2.7 ▲	BL	Well-used track on right.

GPS: N36°35.28' W116°39.65'

| ▼ 8.0 | SO | Exiting Death Valley National Park and California into Nevada. State line is unmarked. |
| 2.3 ▲ | SO | Exiting Nevada into California and Death Valley National Park. State line is unmarked. |

GPS: N36°35.24' W116°39.26'

▼ 8.2	SO	Track on left.
2.1 ▲	SO	Track on right.
▼ 9.8	BR	Track on left. Remain on main graded road.
0.5 ▲	SO	Track on right. Remain on main graded road.
▼ 10.3	TL	Turn left onto larger graded road and zero trip meter.
0.0 ▲		Continue to the northwest.

GPS: N36°35.01' W116°36.71'

| ▼ 0.0 | | Continue to the east. |
| 11.5 ▲ | TR | Turn right onto smaller, roughly graded road. Turn is unmarked, but is opposite an orchard. Turn is hard to spot in this direction. Zero trip meter. |

| ▼ 0.1 | TR | Turn right onto paved Saddleback Drive at sign. Remain on paved road. |
| 11.4 ▲ | TL | Turn left onto graded dirt Frontier Drive at sign. |

GPS: N36°35.00' W116°36.56'

| ▼ 1.1 | TL | Turn left at T-intersection onto paved Amargosa Farm Road. Remain on this road, ignoring turns to the left and right. |
| 10.4 ▲ | TR | Turn right onto paved Saddleback Drive. |

GPS: N36°34.14' W116°36.56'

| ▼ 11.5 | | Trail ends at intersection with Nevada 373, 5 miles south of Amargosa Valley. Turn left for Amargosa Valley; turn right for Death Valley Junction. |
| 0.0 ▲ | | Trail commences on Nevada 373, 5 miles south of Amargosa Valley. Zero trip meter and turn northeast on paved road, marked Farm Road. Remain on this paved road, ignoring turns to the left and right for the next 10.4 miles. |

GPS: N36°34.13' W116°24.78'

Titus Canyon Trail

STARTING POINT: Nevada 374, 6 miles south-west of Beatty, NV
FINISHING POINT: North Highway, 15 miles north of the intersection with California 190
TOTAL MILEAGE: 25.4 miles
UNPAVED MILEAGE: 25.4 miles
DRIVING TIME: 2.5 hours
ELEVATION RANGE: 200–5,300 feet
USUALLY OPEN: October to May
BEST TIME TO TRAVEL: Dry weather
DIFFICULTY RATING: 2
SCENIC RATING: 10
REMOTENESS RATING: +0

Special Attractions
- Leadfield ghost town.
- Petroglyphs at Klare Spring.
- Popular, easy trail within Death Valley National Park.

History

In the summer of 1905, Titus Canyon was the scene of an incident that claimed two lives and gave the canyon its name. Edgar Morris Titus, Earle Weller, and their mining companion John Mullan had set out from Rhyolite, Nevada, to prospect in the Panamint Range. Sadly, they never made their destination. Although they were well provisioned and had a burro team in tow, they got lost in unfamiliar territory and missed an expected spring in the Grapevine Mountains. They made camp instead at a tiny seep. Titus continued down the canyon with several burros in an attempt to find a better water supply. He didn't return. His brother-in-law, Weller, went out after him the following morning, taking more burros. He didn't return. Although Titus and Weller found each other, they were too weak to travel farther. Both men died because of lack of water. Mullan was found about two weeks later, still at the seep and almost delirious. Yet he managed to survive the horrific ordeal.

In 1905, an attorney in Rhyolite named Clay Tollman produced worthwhile ores from the Titus Canyon region, but it wasn't until 1926 that Leadfield was established. Buildings left over from this mining boom can still be found along the trail. Although Leadfield sprang up very quickly, it was based on false advertising—there were no fortunes to be made from mining in Titus Canyon. Three hundred people came to Leadfield. A post office opened in 1926 but only lasted six months. Leadfield was listed on the National Register of Historic Places in June 1975.

Titanothere Canyon, close to the Nevada state line, contains many fossils, some dating back nearly 35 million years. In 1933, the fossilized skull of an enormous creature resembling a rhino, a *Titanothere*, was discovered. A replica of the skull is on display at the Furnace Creek Visitor Center. Titanothere Canyon is a popular day hike within the region.

Description

Titus Canyon is one of the most popular dirt roads within Death Valley National Park, and justly so. The meandering dirt road travels

Looking west from Red Pass over the site of Leadfield

The lower end of the Titus Canyon is tight with rock smoothed by flood waters

down a narrow canyon, passing the ghost town of Leadfield and the Klare Spring petroglyphs.

The trail can only be traveled from east to west, commencing southwest of Beatty in Nevada. The first few miles can be washboardy as the trail travels across the creosote- and sagebrush-covered flats toward the Amargosa Range. Entering Death Valley National Park, the trail first crosses the Von Schmidt Line, the original boundary between California and Nevada, and then the present-day state line into California. Neither is marked.

The trail winds into the Grapevine Mountains toward the aptly named Red Pass. The undulating trail, red-colored hills, and spectacular geology make this a trail best driven on a sunny day. On cloudy days, the colors of the rocks are muted.

The trail passes the ghost town of Leadfield, where there are several old cabins and remains, before entering the tight, narrow Titus Canyon. This canyon is one of the most spectacular within the Death Valley area, with high, tight canyon walls that have been smoothed by thousands of years of floodwaters. The trail surface is smooth and gravelly and is easygoing for the most part.

Palm trees at the oasis of Klare Spring provide a splash of green within the red and gray canyon. Human visitors have been coming to the spring for many years, as is evidenced by the petroglyphs on a large gray boulder alongside the spring. The water source is important to the bighorn sheep that frequent the canyon. They can often be seen high on the rocky cliffs around the spring.

Past the spring, the trail continues in the wash, before opening out abruptly into Death Valley. The final 2 miles of the trail are suitable for two-way traffic.

Titus Canyon floods easily, so it may be closed for a few days after rain or snow. It is closed to vehicular traffic during the hot summer months. Check with the park service for the latest road conditions.

Current Road Information
Death Valley National Park
PO Box 579
Death Valley, CA 92328-0579
(760) 786-3200

DESERT #40: TITUS CANYON TRAIL

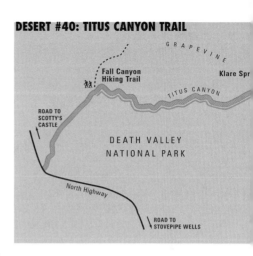

Bureau of Land Management
Bishop Field Office
351 Pacu Lane, Suite 100
Bishop, CA 93514
(760) 872-5000

Map References
BLM   Beatty, Saline Valley
USGS 1:24,000   Gold Center, Daylight
      Pass, Thimble Peak, Fall Canyon
      1:100,000 Beatty, Saline Valley
Maptech CD-ROM: Kings Canyon/Death
      Valley; Las Vegas/Henderson/ Laughlin
Nevada Atlas & Gazatteer, p. 64
Southern & Central California Atlas &
      Gazetteer, pp. 29, 30
California Road & Recreation Atlas, p. 81
Trails Illustrated, Death Valley National
      Park (221)
Other: Free NPS Death Valley map

Route Directions

▼ 0.0   From Nevada 374, 6 miles southwest
        of Beatty, NV, zero trip meter and turn
        west on the graded dirt road, sign-
        posted to Titus Canyon.
        GPS: N36°51.56′ W116°50.70′

▼ 0.9   SO Track on left and track on right.
        GPS: N36°51.45′ W116°51.67′
▼ 1.8   SO Cattle guard and closure gate. Entering

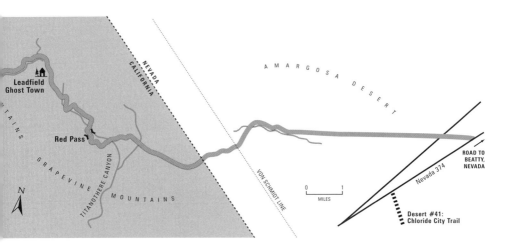

Death Valley National Park. Zero trip meter.

GPS: N36°51.31′ W116°52.68′

▼ 0.0   Continue to the southwest.

▼ 4.1   SO   Enter line of wash. Look back to see Bare Mountain.

▼ 5.3   SO   Exit line of the wash and cross the old Von Schmidt state line of 1873.

GPS: N36°50.20′ W116°57.58′

▼ 5.5   SO   Re-enter line of wash.

▼ 5.9   SO   Entering California—no sign.

GPS: N36°49.69′ W116°58.47′

▼ 7.2   SO   Exit line of wash.

▼ 7.3   SO   Saddle. Trail starts to descend.

▼ 8.4   SO   Cross through wash.

▼ 8.6   SO   Cross through wash.

▼ 8.8   SO   Cross through wash.

GPS: N36°49.68′ W117°01.27′

▼ 8.9   SO   Cross over wash.

GPS: N36°49.62′ W117°01.33′

▼ 10.1   SO   Red Pass. Trail now descends toward Titus Canyon. Zero trip meter in the cutting of the pass.

GPS: N36°49.72′ W117°01.89′

▼ 0.0   Continue to the west.

▼ 0.7   SO   Cross through wash.

▼ 1.2   SO   Cross through wash.

▼ 1.7   SO   Mine adit on far side of canyon.

GPS: N36°50.20′ W117°02.80′

▼ 2.2   SO   Pull-in on left and mine on left.

▼ 2.6   SO   Cross through wash.

▼ 2.7   SO   Cross through wash.

▼ 2.9   SO   Cross through wash.

▼ 3.0   SO   Ghost town of Leadfield. Zero trip meter at sign.

GPS: N36°50.90′ W117°03.50′

▼ 0.0   Continue to the northwest.

▼ 0.3   SO   Enter wash.

▼ 0.7   SO   Entering Titus Canyon.

GPS: N36°51.19′ W117°03.96′

▼ 2.4   SO   Klare Spring on right at palm trees. Petroglyphs are around the springs on the large gray boulder to the left of the sign. Zero trip meter at sign.

GPS: N36°50.47′ W117°05.38′

▼ 0.0   Continue to the southwest.

▼ 1.2   SO   Exit wash.

▼ 1.4   SO   Enter wash.

▼ 4.0   SO   Entering tight part of Titus Canyon.

▼ 5.6   SO   Exiting Titus Canyon into Death Valley. Closure gate and parking area. Trail is now suitable for two-way traffic. Zero trip meter. Fall Canyon Hiking Trail leaves on the north side of the parking lot.

GPS: N36°49.25′ W117°10.41′

▼ 0.0   Continue to the southwest.

▼ 2.5   Closure gate; then trail ends at T-intersection with North Highway. Turn right for Scotty's Castle; turn left for Stovepipe Wells.

GPS: N36º47.27' W117º11.44'

Chloride City Trail

STARTING POINT: Daylight Pass Road, 10 miles northeast of intersection with California 190

FINISHING POINT: Nevada 374 at the boundary of Death Valley National Park, 9.5 miles southwest of Beatty, NV

TOTAL MILEAGE: 15.4 miles, plus 2.4-mile spur to Chloride Cliff

UNPAVED MILEAGE: 15.4 miles, plus 2.4-mile spur

DRIVING TIME: 1.5 hours

ELEVATION RANGE: 3,300–5,200 feet

USUALLY OPEN: Year-round

BEST TIME TO TRAVEL: October to May

DIFFICULTY RATING: 3

SCENIC RATING: 10

REMOTENESS RATING: +1

Special Attractions

- Unparalleled view from Chloride Cliff overlooking Death Valley and the Amargosa and Panamint Ranges.
- Historic site of Chloride City.
- Quiet trail in Death Valley National Park and the Amargosa Desert.

History

While prospecting in the region in 1871, A. J. Franklin picked up a rock to kill a rattlesnake. He found silver ore beneath the rock and quickly established a mine at the site. However, by 1873 he had ceased operations, realizing that the cost of transporting ore from this remote location made the operation inefficient. There were no roads to the eastern section of Death Valley prior to the development of the Chloride Cliff Mine. A route was established from Barstow to the mine via Wingate Wash. This allowed Death Valley to be accessed from

the southwest for the first time. In time, the road was improved and used by borax mule trains.

In 1905, one year after Franklin's death and with the mine now owned by his son George, the success of the nearby Bullfrog strike spilled over to Chloride City. Water for the mines and its workers, a scarcity in these parts, was carted and later pumped from Keane Spring, just a few miles to the north in the Funeral Mountains.

Activity halted once again when the 1906 earthquake rattled San Francisco. Investors disappeared and life around Chloride City was quiet. The mines and cabins lay abandoned for the next few years. George sold the mine to a Pittsburgh syndicate. A resurgence in 1909 saw another wave of mining activity, which came and went, finally halting by 1940.

There are few structural remains in Chloride City today because most buildings were flimsy, temporary structures. A stamp mill and a half dozen wooden structures were built in the region; the rest of the miners were housed in tents.

Keane Wonder Mine, situated southwest of the spectacular Chloride Cliff, was an important mine in this region. Founded by an Irishman named Jack Keane and his partner Domingo Etcharren in 1904, the mine sold for more than $50,000, quite a sum of money at the time. It went on to produce almost $1 million. The new owners constructed a monumental 4,700-foot-long aerial tramway between the mine and mill.

Description

The undulating trail to Chloride City sees little vehicle traffic. Located on the eastern edge of Death Valley National Park, the well-formed trail travels between California and Nevada, passing through the northern end of the Funeral Mountains (part of the Amargosa Range).

The trail is rough in places, enough so that high-clearance 4WD is advised. There are few side trails, but one worthwhile spur travels a short distance down a narrow canyon to a deep pour-off in the wash. A hiking trail

The windy trail is rough in places

follows an old pack trail farther down the canyon. It heads past Monarch Spring on its way to Death Valley.

The ghost town of Chloride City and its associated mining area is a short distance from the main trail. The spur leads past the remains of the town and finishes on top of Chloride Cliff, arguably the best overlook in Death Valley. The final 0.1 miles of the spur is 4-rated. If you don't wish to tackle the final steep pinch, leave your vehicle at the bottom and hike the remaining distance. The view from the elevated point is stupendous. Death Valley and the Amargosa Range are spread out below you, and the Panamint Range borders the valley on the west side. This viewpoint alone makes this trail worthwhile.

There is a network of short trails to explore around Chloride City; many will take you past mines and old cabins.

Back on the main trail, the standard improves slightly, becoming smoother and easier going as it travels into Nevada. The trail comes to an end on Nevada 374 at the boundary of Death Valley National Park.

Current Road Information
Death Valley National Park
PO Box 579
Death Valley, CA 92328-0579
(760) 786-3200

Map References
BLM   Beatty
USGS 1:24,000   Daylight Pass, Chloride City, East of Chloride City, Gold Center
1:100,000 Beatty
Maptech CD-ROM: Kings Canyon/Death Valley
Nevada Atlas & Gazatteer, p. 64
Southern & Central California Atlas & Gazetteer, p. 30
California Road & Recreation Atlas, pp. 81, 88
Trails Illustrated, Death Valley National Park (221)
Other: Free NPS Death Valley map

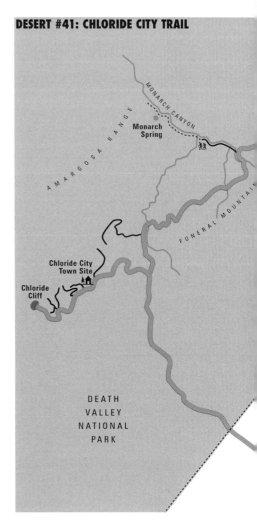

DESERT #41: CHLORIDE CITY TRAIL

Route Directions

▼ 0.0   From Daylight Pass Road in California, 10 miles northeast of intersection with California 190, zero trip meter and turn northeast on unmarked, formed dirt trail. There is no signpost at the intersection but the road is marked as recommended for high-clearance 4x4. Trail is traveling in the wash.

2.1 ▲   Trail ends on Daylight Pass Road in California, which becomes Nevada 374. Turn left for Stovepipe Wells; turn right for Beatty, NV.
   GPS: N36°45.03′ W116°56.15′

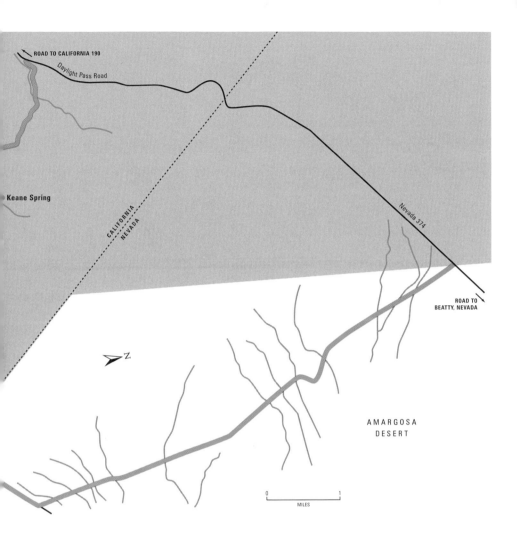

▼ 1.0　SO　Exit wash.
1.1 ▲　SO　Enter wash.
▼ 1.5　SO　Enter line of wash.
0.6 ▲　SO　Exit line of wash.
▼ 2.1　TL　Track on right travels 0.6 miles down a
　　　　　tight canyon to a large pour-off before
　　　　　turning into a hiking trail to Monarch
　　　　　Spring and Death Valley. Zero trip meter.
0.0 ▲　　　Continue to the north up wash.
　　　　GPS: N36º44.20′ W116º54.71′

▼ 0.0　　Continue to the east up wash.
2.9 ▲　TR　Track on left travels 0.6 miles down a
　　　　　tight canyon to a large pour-off before
　　　　　turning into a hiking trail to Monarch
　　　　　Spring and Death Valley. Zero trip meter.

▼ 0.3　SO　Tank on left. Exit line of wash.
2.6 ▲　SO　Enter line of wash. Tank on right.
　　　　GPS: N36º44.29′ W116º54.37′

▼ 1.0　SO　Cross through wash.
1.9 ▲　SO　Cross through wash.
▼ 1.3　SO　Cross through wash.
1.6 ▲　SO　Cross through wash.
▼ 1.6　SO　Cross through wash.
1.3 ▲　SO　Cross through wash.
▼ 2.2　BL　Bear left up wash.
0.7 ▲　BR　Bear right out of wash.
　　　　GPS: N36º43.08′ W116º53.74′

▼ 2.4　SO　Track on right.
0.5 ▲　SO　Track on left.

Climbing into the Grapevine Mountains

GPS: N36°43.04' W116°53.59'

▼ 2.8 SO Exit line of wash.
0.1 ▲ SO Enter line of wash.
▼ 2.9 BL Track on right at Mine Hazard sign is spur to Chloride City and Chloride Cliff. Zero trip meter.
0.0 ▲ Continue to the west.
GPS: N36°43.06' W116°53.06'

Spur to Chloride Cliff

▼ 0.0 Proceed southwest on formed trail at Mine Hazard sign.
▼ 1.0 TL T-intersection. Site of Chloride City. Zero trip meter.
GPS: N36°42.42' W116°53.07'

▼ 0.0 Continue to the east.
▼ 0.3 SO Track on right, track on left, and second track on right.

▼ 0.4 SO Track on right to cabin and mine.
▼ 0.5 SO Second entrance to cabin and mine on right.
▼ 0.8 TL Track ahead, two tracks on right, and track on left. Turn first left.
GPS: N36°41.97' W116°52.68'
▼ 1.1 SO Track on right.
▼ 1.2 SO Track straight ahead and track on left; then bear left at second track on left.
GPS: N36°41.82' W116°52.68'

▼ 1.3 SO Adit and tailings on right.
▼ 1.4 UT Spur ends at Chloride Cliff—unparalleled viewpoint over the Amargosa Range, Death Valley, and the Panamint Range.
GPS: N36°41.69' W116°52.75'

Continuation of Main Trail

▼ 0.0 Continue to the east.
3.9 ▲ BR Track on left at Mine Hazard sign is

View over Death Valley from Chloride Cliff

spur to Chloride City and Chloride Cliff.
Zero trip meter.
GPS: N36°43.06′ W116°53.06′

▼ 2.4　SO　Entering Nevada and leaving Death
Valley National Park (no signs).

1.5 ▲　SO　Entering California and Death Valley
National Park. Only sign is a "High
Clearance 4x4 Recommended" sign.
GPS: N36°43.82′ W116°50.94′

▼ 2.9　SO　Track on right.

1.0 ▲　SO　Track on left.

▼ 3.9　BL　Trail forks. Well-used track on right.
Zero trip meter.

0.0 ▲　　　Continue to the south.
GPS: N36°44.82′ W116°49.83′

▼ 0.0　　　Continue to the northwest. There are
many small wash crossings for the
next 6.5 miles.

6.5 ▲　BR　Well-used track on left. Zero trip meter.

▼ 1.1　SO　Cross through wash. Track on left up
wash.

5.4 ▲　SO　Cross through wash. Track on right up
wash.

▼ 1.5　SO　Faint track on left.

5.0 ▲　SO　Faint track on right.

▼ 6.5　　　Trail ends on Nevada 374 at the
boundary of Death Valley National Park
at the "Welcome to Nevada" sign. Trail
is unmarked. Turn right for Beatty, NV;
turn left for Death Valley.

0.0 ▲　　　Trail commences on Nevada 374, 9.5
miles southwest of Beatty, NV, on the
boundary of Death Valley National Park
at the "Welcome to Nevada" sign. Turn
is unmarked. Zero trip meter and turn
southeast on formed dirt trail across
the bajada. There are many small
wash crossings for the first 6.5 miles.
GPS: N36°49.94′ W116°52.76′

Cottonwood Canyon Trail

STARTING POINT: California 190 at Stovepipe Wells
FINISHING POINT: Wilderness boundary in Cottonwood Canyon
TOTAL MILEAGE: 17.4 miles (one-way)
UNPAVED MILEAGE: 16.6 miles
DRIVING TIME: 2 hours (one-way)
ELEVATION RANGE: 0–2,500 feet
USUALLY OPEN: Year-round
BEST TIME TO TRAVEL: October to May
DIFFICULTY RATING: 3
SCENIC RATING: 8
REMOTENESS RATING: +0

Special Attractions

■ Remote desert canyon within Death Valley National Park.
■ Petroglyphs in Marble Canyon.

History

Native American occupancy of Cottonwood Canyon is evidenced by the rock art inscribed at the lower entrance to this peaceful canyon. The upper canyon provided cool relief from the sweltering summer heat of the desert floor. The cottonwood trees that grow here, after which the canyon is named, are sometimes felled by flash flood waters.

The name at the starting point of this trail, Stovepipe Wells, comes from the original well that was located in the sand dune area of Death Valley. This water source was greatly valued by early inhabitants and travelers alike. Because shifting sands made finding the water difficult at times, a length of stovepipe was placed upright to mark the well. With time, the well became known as Sovepipe Well. As the nearby mining town of Skidoo developed in late 1906, the need for a stage line increased. Stovepipe Wells became a stage stop before the stagecoach tackled the long climb to Skidoo. A tent saloon, lodging house, and store all operated during this period.

In 1925, Herman Eichbaum and his wife realized that Death Valley might have a lot to offer as a backcountry vacation destination. They set about constructing a toll road from the base of Darwin Wash, across the wide depression of Panamint Valley, over Towne Pass in the Panamint Range, and down to the proposed location of their Death Valley resort. By 1926, they opened their resort, named Bungalow City, near Stovepipe Wells. Later the name Stovepipe Wells was transposed to their resort. Initially, it consisted of 20 tent platforms, a restaurant, tennis courts, and even a swimming pool. The first airstrip was built so visitors could reach the desert resort without enduring the long, rough roads into the region.

The Eichbaums soon found themselves competing with the revamped Furnace Creek Ranch. Both properties discovered their visitors were fascinated by the extremes of Death Valley. The Furnace Creek owners commissioned an access road to an excellent viewpoint. The outcome was Dantes View, set in the Black Mountains to the south of the Furnace Creek resort of the 1920s.

The Eichbaums counteracted in the winter of 1929 by constructing a road past Harrisburg to the crest of the Panamint Range, calling the spot Grand View. This viewpoint later became known as Aguereberry Point after a nearby prospector. Pierre "Pete" Aguereberry, from the Basque region, had been a shepherd until he was struck by gold fever at Rhyolite and Goldfield. From 1905 until his death in 1945, Pete and his friend Shorty Harris worked several claims in the surrounding region. At Aguereberry Point, visitors can see Mount Whitney to the west and Badwater to the east. Aguereberry Point, therefore, held a unique advantage for the Eichbaums. Their guests could see the highest and lowest points in the contiguous United States at the same time.

Description

Cottonwood Canyon is a picturesque canyon within Death Valley that has a vehicle route running along most of its length. The spur trail leaves Stovepipe Wells past the National

Park Service campground, taking the road toward the airstrip. At the airstrip, the paved road turns into a dirt trail and travels in a straight line toward the Cottonwood Mountains, part of the Panamint Range. The trail is sandy in places, rough and rocky in others

No camping is permitted for the first 8 miles of the trail. There is a good, although exposed, campsite at the mouth of the canyon. Within the canyon, options are limited.

Past the campsite, the trail drops into the loose and sandy wash of Cottonwood Canyon. There are some petroglyphs on the left-hand wall of the canyon near the entrance. However, the majority of rock art to be found along this trail is within Marble Canyon, an offshoot of the main trail.

Past an initial narrow section, the trail opens out to travel up the valley for a couple of miles before re-entering canyon narrows. A surprisingly large wind- and water-eroded cave is encountered on the eastern side of the canyon; camping is not advised in such a large wash setting. The trail finishes at the wilderness boundary where an indistinct hiking trail ultimately connects north to Marble Canyon, south to Lemoigne Canyon, and west to the old Goldbelt mining camp.

Current Road Information

Death Valley National Park
PO Box 579
Death Valley, CA 92328-0579
(760) 786-3200

Cottonwood Canyon opens out to this beautiful vista

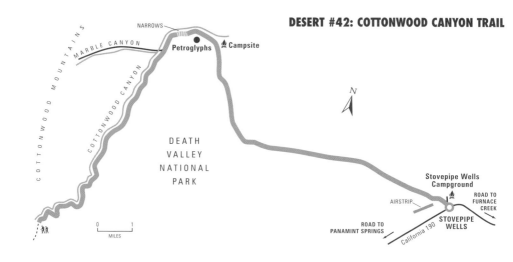

DESERT #42: COTTONWOOD CANYON TRAIL

Map References

BLM   Saline Valley
USGS   1:24,000   Stovepipe Wells, East of
       Sand Flat, Cottonwood Canyon
       1:100,000 Saline Valley
Maptech CD-ROM: Kings Canyon/Death
       Valley

Southern & Central California Atlas &
   Gazetteer, p. 29
California Road & Recreation Atlas, p. 88
Trails Illustrated, Death Valley National Park
   (221)
Other: Free NPS Death Valley map

Looking out from the natural cavern carved in the sediment of Cottonwood Canyon

Route Directions

▼ 0.0　At Stovepipe Wells on California 190, immediately west of the general store, zero trip meter and turn northwest into the entrance to the campground. Immediately bear left, leaving the campground on your right, and follow the paved road toward the airstrip.
GPS: N36°36.38′ W117°08.77′

▼ 0.8　BR　Bear right onto graded dirt trail. Airstrip is on the left. No vehicle entry into the airstrip.
GPS: N36°36.42′ W117°09.26′

▼ 8.4　BL　Campsite on right. Zero trip meter at sign.
GPS: N36°38.56′ W117°16.17′

▼ 0.0　Drop down and enter Cottonwood Canyon Wash, bearing northwest up wash.

▼ 0.4　SO　Petroglyphs on rock wall on left. Enter Cottonwood Canyon.
GPS: N36°38.68′ W117°16.63′

▼ 1.0　SO　Enter canyon narrows.

▼ 2.1　BL　Marble Canyon on right. Bear left at old signpost, remaining in Cottonwood Canyon, and zero trip meter.
GPS: N36°37.92′ W117°17.64′

▼ 0.0　Continue to the southwest.
t 6.9　Trail ends at wilderness boundary.
GPS: N36°33.40′ W117°20.10′

DESERT #43

Skidoo Road

STARTING POINT: Wildrose Road, 9 miles southeast of California 190
FINISHING POINT: Skidoo
TOTAL MILEAGE: 8.7 miles, plus 0.9-mile spur
UNPAVED MILEAGE: 8.7 miles, plus 0.9-mile spur
DRIVING TIME: 1 hour
ELEVATION RANGE: 4,900–5,900 feet

USUALLY OPEN: Year-round
BEST TIME TO TRAVEL: October to May
DIFFICULTY RATING: 2
SCENIC RATING: 9
REMOTENESS RATING: +0

Special Attractions
■ Historic site of Skidoo and Skidoo Mill.
■ Landscape and historic photography.

History

In 1905, prospectors Pete Aguereberry and Shorty Harris made a gold discovery at a location near Skidoo, which Shorty named Harrisburg. Very soon, other prospectors were drawn into the region. Two such hopefuls, John "One-eye" Thompson and John Ramsey, were prepared to join the strike at Harrisburg when they chanced upon some promising colored ledges to the north. The duo filed claims in 1906 that covered a broad region near their find, and they tried to keep things quiet. Word leaked out, though, and eventually reached the town of Rhyolite, Nevada.

Bob Montgomery recognized a potential winner and reportedly paid a total of $60,000 for what became known as Skidoo, which was a popular slang expression of the time meaning "skeedaddle." The mine faced the usual problem of a lack of water for milling purposes. Montgomery invested more than twice what he had paid for the claims to get water to the site. An 8-inch pipe was hauled in to draw water from Bird Spring, more than 20 miles away on Telescope Peak. This engineering feat was completed in 1907, and water from the spring powered the 15-stamp mill.

By this time, Skidoo had attracted more than 400 inhabitants. Several stores opened and restaurants, saloons, and associated businesses soon followed. Permanent commercial buildings were erected and a telephone line and stagecoach connected the new town to Rhyolite, the focal mining center of the region.

Skidoo was noted for, and often avoided because of, its peaceful nature. The town was considered to be boring. Interestingly enough,

Skidoo's old stamp mill sits at the head of a tight canyon

it was also the site of the only known hanging in the Death Valley region. In April 1908, a drunken Joe L. "Hootch" Simpson gunned down a local man named Jim Arnold. The townspeople wasted no time in retaliating, and Hootch Simpson was strung up on a telephone pole.

Skidoo endured highs and lows and remained active for more than 10 years. At its peak, almost 700 people lived here. But like all such mining towns, once the mine ceased operation the town's lifeline ended and the townsfolk moved away. Skidoo was just about the last real gold town in Death Valley. Many found it hard to just walk away from their town. Because it was too far to haul them away to erect elsewhere, many of the buildings remained. One prospector known as Old Tom Adams remained until 1922.

Skidoo was listed on the National Register of Historic Places in April 1974.

Description

Skidoo is a very popular site within Death Valley National Park. Photos of the historic mill, clinging precariously to the hillside above the valley, can be seen on many postcards. The entire length of road to the site is suitable for high-clearance 2WD vehicles. In addition, passenger vehicles can easily travel the graded dirt road as far as the Skidoo town site sign. Past here, the rough trail makes it risky for low-slung vehicles.

The road is heavily used, so it is often very washboardy. It winds around the southern side of Tucki Mountain, giving excellent views of Death Valley and the surrounding mountains.

The trail forks at the sign for Skidoo. The remains of the old Skidoo Mill are the most substantial in town. There are several vantage points from which to observe it. The left fork takes you past an old wooden hopper and several mine shafts to a point at the top of the mill. You will have to hike the last 600 feet. Note that the mill is unsafe, and it is highly dangerous to walk onto the structure. The right fork at the town site sign takes you around a small loop. From here you can gain excellent views of the mill from across the canyon, or you can hike to

the base of it. The loop continues around the hilltop, giving excellent views of the Panamint Range, before returning to its starting point. The loop is 2-rated in the direction mapped. If driven in reverse it is 3-rated and requires 4WD to ascend the hill.

The entire area is for day use only. Camping is prohibited, and trailers or vehicles longer than 25 feet are not permitted along the road. Skidoo Road is suitable for mountain bikes as well as vehicles.

Current Road Information

Death Valley National Park
PO Box 579
Death Valley, CA 92328-0579
(760) 786-3200

Map References

BLM   Darwin Hills
USGS 1:24,000   Emigrant Canyon,
        Tucki Wash
        1:100,000 Darwin Hills
Maptech CD-ROM: Kings Canyon/Death
        Valley
Southern & Central California Atlas & Gazetteer, p. 41
California Road & Recreation Atlas, p. 88
Trails Illustrated, Death Valley National
        Park (221)
Other: Free NPS Death Valley map

Route Directions

▼ 0.0   From Wildrose Road, 9 miles southeast of California 190, zero trip meter and turn east on graded dirt road at the sign for Skidoo. The trail initially crosses Harrisburg Flats.
             GPS: N36°23.15′ W117°09.00′

▼ 2.7   SO   Track on left passes mine shaft on its way to a cabin; then track on right to mine. Zero trip meter at track on right.
             GPS: N36°24.18′ W117°06.53′

▼ 0.0   Continue to the east.
▼ 0.2   SO   Track on right.
             GPS: N36°24.18′ W117°06.30′

The easygoing road passes around Tucki Mountain

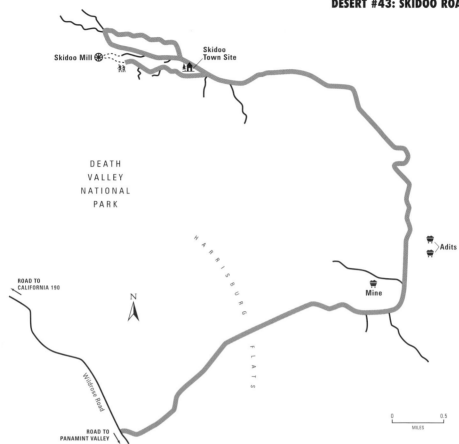

▼ 0.5   SO   Track on left to mines and old cabin.
       GPS: N36°24.39' W117°06.15'
▼ 0.9   SO   Timber-lined adits in hillside on left.
       GPS: N36°24.73' W117°06.11'

▼ 1.4   SO   Faint track on right.
▼ 1.9   SO   Pull-in on right for a view over Death
       Valley.
▼ 3.2   SO   Track on right.
▼ 3.7   SO   Two tracks on left.
▼ 3.8   SO   Track on left.
       GPS: N36°26.00' W117°07.97'

▼ 4.1   SO   Small track on left; then continue
       straight ahead on graded road. Graded
       road on left is spur to the top of Skidoo
       Mill. Zero trip meter.
       GPS: N36°26.07' W117°08.22'

Spur to the Top of Skidoo Mill

▼ 0.0   From the intersection of graded roads
       at the sign for Skidoo, zero trip meter
       and proceed west. This spur is suitable
       for high-clearance 2WD vehicles.
▼ 0.1   SO   Track on right.
▼ 0.4   SO   Track on left.
▼ 0.5   SO   Track on left.
▼ 0.7   BL   Track on left; then bear left past wood-
       en hopper. Track on right. There are
       other tracks on the left and right. Pass
       directly alongside the hopper.
       GPS: N36°26.13' W117°08.88'

▼ 0.9   UT   Spur ends at a locked gate. From here,
       it is a 600-foot hike to the mill.

Continuation of Main Trail

▼ 0.0   Continue to the northwest. Small track on right.

▼ 0.2   SO   Track on left.

▼ 0.3   SO   Track on left; then track on right is end of loop.
       GPS: N36°26.18′ W117°08.48′

▼ 0.5   BR   Track on left goes to a gate and a short hike to the base of the mill.
       GPS: N36°26.19′ W117°08.76′

▼ 0.7   SO   Cross through wash.

▼ 0.9   SO   Skidoo Mill is visible on the far side of the canyon. Track on left to viewpoint over the mill.
       GPS: N36°26.29′ W117°09.15′

▼ 1.0   TR   4-way intersection. Track on left goes 0.8 miles to more diggings. Turn right to continue around the loop.
       GPS: N36°26.39′ W117°09.25′

▼ 1.4   SO   Viewpoint.

▼ 1.9   End of loop. Turn left to exit the way you came.
       GPS: N36°26.18′ W117°08.48′

DESERT #44

Darwin Falls Trail

STARTING POINT: Main Street in Darwin

FINISHING POINT: California 190, 1 mile west of Panamint Springs

TOTAL MILEAGE: 12.1 miles, plus 1.2-mile spur to China Garden Spring

UNPAVED MILEAGE: 12 miles, plus 1.2-mile spur

DRIVING TIME: 1.5 hours

ELEVATION RANGE: 2,100–5,000 feet

USUALLY OPEN: Year-round

BEST TIME TO TRAVEL: October to June

DIFFICULTY RATING: 3

SCENIC RATING: 9

REMOTENESS RATING: +0

Special Attractions

- Pretty China Garden Spring.
- Hiking trail to Darwin Falls.
- Many old mining remains on Zinc Hill.
- Rugged Darwin Canyon.

History

One of the first white men through this region was Dr. Erasmus Darwin French, an early prospector who was hunting for the Lost Gunsight Mine with an Indian guide. French was unsuccessful in finding the mine. He had moved on by the time Darwin became a gold fever town in 1874.

The first recorded mine in the area was the Promontoria, which was established in 1874 by Rafael Cuervo. Other mines in the area quickly took off. Darwin became the main commercial center for the developing New Cosco Mining District.

By 1875 the town supported more than 70 businesses with 2 smelters, 20 mines, many wooden houses, and a population nearing 700. Just two years later, 3,000 people had taken up residency in the booming town. Darwin and nearby Lookout were two of the most productive desert mining locations of the 1870s. The Christmas Gift, the Defiance (which was named after legal wranglings over the ownership of the claims), and the Lucky Jim were some of the biggest producers. Like many western mining towns, saloon brawls and shootings were not uncommon in these early years.

The future looked good for Darwin until the nation's economic woes of the late 1870s and more impressive strikes at Bodie to the north were enough to spell the demise of Darwin. Labor forces were on the move to more promising claims and a devastating fire in 1879 destroyed much of the town's commercial center. As has always been the case for this persistent community, Darwin never actually became a ghost town. Mining activity continued at a low level and the saloon continued to operate.

Changing market needs brought a resurgence to Darwin around 1906, with copper now a valued mineral. Earlier tailings that contained copper-bearing ore were greatly

Goldfish in the clear waters of China Garden Spring

Old commercial building in Darwin

valued. By the late 1910s, silver was the sought-after commodity. The Darwin region was a notable producer, putting the town back on the map. In fact, most metallic minerals were being found in the region during the 1920s. Silver, lead, copper, gold, and tungsten were all in production. By the 1930s, more than $3 million worth of ore had been extracted from the region. Mining and milling activities continued in varying degrees until the 1950s. Though many mining structures have been torn down over the decades, several latter-day structures have survived. These remains provide a slight insight into a town driven mainly by mining prospectors.

Darwin Falls Trail follows a section of the old toll road, officially known as Eichbaum Toll Road, which was developed in 1925 by the Eichbaums as the first vehicle route into Panamint Valley and Death Valley from the west. The influx of visitors to their resort near Stovepipe Wells brought a lot of auto traffic through Darwin, which was developing quite a name for its fine Panamint Shoshone basketry.

In 1937, Darwin was bypassed by the construction of California 190 to the north. The passing tourist trade was gone. Darwin seemed like a dead end street to Death Valley visitors; it was no longer the Gateway to Death Valley. Advertisements put out by the Death Valley Hotel Company in 1938 renamed Lone Pine as the new "Gateway." Darwin was left off their mileage charts. These changes may have played a part in the economic demise of the town, yet they may also have been the town's savior. Darwin persists with its own ever-evolving character and characters.

Darwin Falls is fed by an underground spring that surfaces at the canyon floor. Over the centuries, the spring and the falls have been enjoyed by natives and travelers alike. During Darwin's early mining days in the 1870s, this spring was an asset to one settler who established vegetable gardens downstream from the falls. He had an excellent market for his produce with the booming population of nearby Darwin.

Description

The small town of Darwin still has a number of year-round residents, but it is a lot smaller now than it was at the height of its mining boom. As you enter the town from California 190, the old Ophir Mine and its extensive buildings are on the left, perched on the flank of Ophir Mountain. This mine is privately owned and posted, but a good view can be obtained from the main road. It has been renamed the Darwin Mine by the owners.

There are many old buildings in Darwin that are worth a look—the old dance hall, the post office, and many buildings constructed of corrugated iron, a common construction material in mining camps throughout the West.

The trail starts at the intersection in the center of Darwin and heads east toward the Darwin Hills. There are many tracks on the left and right, many of which lead to the remains of what were once active mines. The road is roughly graded as it snakes through the Darwin Hills to drop into the loose and gravelly Darwin Canyon Wash. Darwin Canyon is not deep, but its striated layers of rock and twisting path make it an interesting drive.

A worthwhile spur trail leads 1.2 miles to China Garden Spring. This little oasis is sheltered under large cottonwoods. The clear waters of the spring contain large numbers of introduced goldfish. The spring makes an excellent spot for a picnic. The remains of a mine and cabin are nearby. The spur trail

ends at the Darwin Falls Wilderness boundary. A 20-minute hike along the canyon floor takes you to Darwin Falls and a second lush spring. Darwin Falls is easiest approached from the northern end of the canyon, farther along the main trail.

The main trail leaves the canyon to wind around the western side of Zinc Hill where more mining remains dot the hillside. The trail around Zinc Hill is the roughest part, with some loose, rocky sections.

The main hiking access to Darwin Falls is passed at a small parking area. The 1-mile hike (each way) includes a year-round stream crossing and some rock scrambling. The small metal pipeline that you see coming out of the canyon at this point is the public water supply for the Panamint Springs Resort in Death Valley. Darwin Falls is a wetland habitat, and there are many birds, amphibians, reptiles, and mammals that use the springs for water. The 30-foot-high falls are fed by an underground spring, which bubbles to the surface through the volcanic rock of Darwin Canyon.

Past the hiking access, the trail is an easy-going graded road as it heads out to join California 190, 1 mile west of Panamint Springs.

Current Road Information

Death Valley National Park
PO Box 579
Death Valley, CA 92328-0579
(760) 786-3200

Bureau of Land Management
Bishop Field Office
351 Pacu Lane, Suite 100
Bishop, CA 93514
(760) 872-5000

Map References

BLM   Darwin Hills
USGS 1:24,000   Darwin, Panamint
            Springs
            1:100,000 Darwin Hills
Maptech CD-ROM: Kings Canyon/Death
            Valley
Southern & Central California Atlas &
            Gazetteer, p. 40

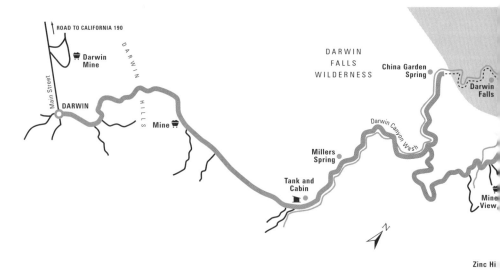

DESERT #44: DARWIN FALLS TRAIL

California Road & Recreation Atlas, p. 87
Trails Illustrated, Death Valley National
 Park (221)
Other: Free NPS Death Valley map; Tom
 Harrison Maps—Death Valley
 National Park Recreation map

Route Directions

▼ 0.0   At the 4-way intersection in the center
         of Darwin, zero trip meter and turn
         northeast on paved road. The Darwin
         Dance Hall, old Out Post store, and gas
         station are at the intersection. Pass
         many side streets on the way out of
         town.
6.1 ▲   Trail ends at Main Street intersection
         in Darwin. Turn right onto Main Street
         to exit to California 190.
         GPS: N36°16.10′ W117°35.47′

▼ 0.1   SO Road turns to graded dirt.
6.0 ▲   SO Road is now paved.
▼ 0.4   BL Track on right goes to mines. Remain
             on main dirt road.
5.7 ▲   SO Track on left goes to mines.
▼ 0.6   SO Track on right.
5.5 ▲   SO Track on left.
▼ 0.8   SO Track on right.
5.3 ▲   SO Track on left.

▼ 1.0   SO Track on left.
5.1 ▲   SO Track on right.
▼ 1.8   SO Track on left.
4.3 ▲   SO Track on right.
▼ 2.1   SO Mine on right.
4.0 ▲   SO Mine on left.
         GPS: N36°16.86′ W117°34.21′

▼ 2.2   SO Track on right.
3.9 ▲   SO Track on left.
▼ 2.3   SO Faint track on right.
3.8 ▲   SO Faint track on left.
▼ 2.7   SO Track on right.
3.4 ▲   SO Track on left.
▼ 3.3   SO Faint track on right.
2.8 ▲   SO Faint track on left.
▼ 3.6   SO Track on right to mine.
2.5 ▲   SO Track on left to mine.
         GPS: N36°16.82′ W117°32.50′

▼ 3.8   BL Enter wash down narrow Darwin
             Canyon. Vehicles travel up wash to the
             right.
2.3 ▲   BR Exit Darwin Canyon; then bear right
             and exit wash. Vehicles continue up
             wash.
         GPS: N36°16.88′ W117°32.31′

▼ 3.9   SO Tank and old cabin on left.
2.2 ▲   SO Tank and old cabin on right.

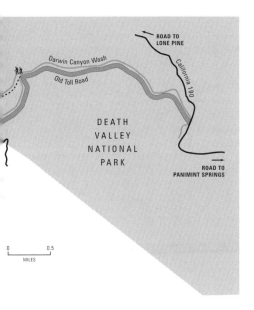

```
0        0.5
|_____|
   MILES
```

▼ 4.1 SO Two tracks on left to mine.
2.0 ▲ SO Two tracks on right to mine.
       GPS: N36°17.07′ W117°32.14′

▼ 4.6 SO Millers Spring on left.
1.5 ▲ SO Millers Spring on right.
       GPS: N36°17.54′ W117°32.17′

▼ 6.1 TR Well-used track on right leads out of
           Darwin Canyon Wash up a smaller
           side canyon. Turn right up this track
           and zero trip meter. Trail continuing
           down the wash is spur to China
           Garden Spring.
0.0 ▲   Continue to the southeast up the wash.
       GPS: N36°18.19′ W117°31.43′

Spur to China Garden Spring

▼ 0.0   Continue down wash to the northwest.
▼ 1.0 SO China Garden Spring on left under large
           cottonwoods. Stone and brick founda-
           tions of old pump house; then track on
           left to cabin and mine.
       GPS: N36°18.84′ W117°31.85′

▼ 1.2 UT Spur ends at boundary of the Darwin
           Falls Wilderness.
       GPS: N36°18.91′ W117°31.79′

Continuation of Main Trail

▼ 0.0   Continue to the east and climb out of
           Darwin Canyon.
2.1 ▲ TL T-intersection with wash in Darwin
           Canyon. Zero trip meter. Track down
           wash to the right is spur to China
           Garden Spring.
       GPS: N36°18.19′ W117°31.43′

▼ 0.9 SO Two tracks on right.
1.2 ▲ SO Two tracks on left.
▼ 1.9 SO Cross through wash.
0.2 ▲ SO Cross through wash.
▼ 2.1 SO Two tracks on right. Take first track on
           right to travel 0.3 miles to a mine on
           the hillside with an excellent view of
           the Darwin Hills. Zero trip meter.
0.0 ▲   Continue to the southwest.
       GPS: N36°18.48′ W117°30.66′

▼ 0.0   Continue to the north.
1.6 ▲ SO Two tracks on left. Take second track
           on left to travel 0.3 miles to a mine on
           the hillside with an excellent view of
           the Darwin Hills. Zero trip meter.
▼ 0.1 SO Track on right at loading hoppers and
           stone ruins on right.
1.5 ▲ SO Track on left at loading hoppers and
           stone ruins on left.
       GPS: N36°18.58′ W117°30.66′

▼ 0.8 SO Cross through wash. Track on right up
           wash. Trail now follows line of wash.
0.8 ▲ SO Exit wash. Track on left up wash.
       GPS: N36°19.02′ W117°30.57′

▼ 0.9 SO Track on left.
0.7 ▲ SO Track on right.
▼ 1.6 SO Parking area on left for hiking trail to
           Darwin Falls. Zero trip meter.
0.0 ▲   Continue to the southeast up line
           of wash.
       GPS: N36°19.68′ W117°30.81′

▼ 0.0   Continue to the north, re-entering
           Darwin Canyon and following line of
           wash.
2.3 ▲ BL Parking area on right for hiking trail
           to Darwin Falls. Zero trip meter.
▼ 2.3   Trail ends at T-intersection with

Mine on western face of Zinc Hill overlooks Darwin Canyon

	California 190. Turn right for Panamint Springs and Death Valley; turn left for Lone Pine.
0.0 ▲	Trail commences on California 190, 1 mile west of Panamint Springs. Zero trip meter and turn west on graded dirt road at sign for Darwin Falls.
	GPS: N36°20.40′ W117°28.76′

DESERT #45

Cactus Flat Road

STARTING POINT: US 395, 2 miles south of Olancha, opposite the Olancha Fire Station
FINISHING POINT: US 395, at Coso Junction
TOTAL MILEAGE: 23.5 miles
UNPAVED MILEAGE: 22.2 miles
DRIVING TIME: 2 hours
ELEVATION RANGE: 3,300–5,400 feet

USUALLY OPEN: Year-round
BEST TIME TO TRAVEL: Dry weather, fall to spring
DIFFICULTY RATING: 3
SCENIC RATING: 8
REMOTENESS RATING: +1

Special Attractions

- Joshua trees at the northern limit of their range.
- Many mining remains.
- Lightly traveled network of trails in the Inyo Mountains.

History

Haiwee Reservoir is named after the Panamint word for dove. Coso, a name that applies to both Coso Junction and the Coso Range, comes from the Panamint word for a burned region. The Coso Range contains a number of petroglyphs. Current land divisions place the range within the China Lake Naval Weapons Center.

The navy has used China Lake Naval Weapons Center since 1943 for the deployment, testing, and development of air to target missiles and weaponry. At approximately one million acres, China Lake is the largest region available to the navy for such activities.

The Coso Petroglyphs have been conserved by the navy, which allows controlled entry to the sites at certain times of the year. Details of entry and tours can be obtained from the interagency office in Lone Pine. The sites were listed on the National Register of Historic Places in 1964 as Little Petroglyphs Canyon.

Description

The trail travels through a band of BLM land in the Inyo Mountains. It is bounded on the east by the China Lake Naval Weapons Center, and on the west by US 395. The area contains many Joshua trees, the signature plant of the Mojave Desert. Although this area is the northernmost extremity of their distribution, Joshua trees grow in abundance on Cactus Flat and in other valleys throughout the region.

The trail leaves Olancha along a graded dirt road that drops in standard to become a well-used, formed trail after the entrance to a pumice mine. The trail becomes smaller and lesser used as it winds along Cactus Flat, offering wide ranging views of the Inyo Mountains.

A few mining remains can be seen along the trail. There is a small stone cabin tucked under a large granite overhang at the McCloud Mine, and a well-preserved wooden headframe near the Five Tunnels Mine. Both mines have tailings heaps, shafts, and adits.

From the McCloud Mine on, the trail earns its 3-rating for difficulty, becoming rougher and more eroded. Navigation also becomes more difficult, especially around the Five Tunnels Mine, where small tracks intersect frequently. The trail crosses a claypan, which quickly becomes impassable when wet. Please remain on the main trail through

Cactus Flat Road passes alongside Haiwee Reservoir

the claypan to avoid leaving scars of additional tire tracks.

The trail leaves McCloud Flat through a gap in the range, running close to the China Lake Naval Weapons Center. The area is fenced, and there is no public admittance to the center. Please be sure to remain on public land. The trail follows a good, graded dirt road before joining paved Gill Station Road to exit to Coso Junction.

Generally, animal life in the area is not readily apparent, although coyotes, jackrabbits, and a wide variety of reptiles live in the region. Raptors are occasionally seen circling overhead. Overall, the area is incredibly quiet and still, and it is a wonderful place for solitude and relaxation.

Current Road Information
Bureau of Land Management
Bishop Field Office
351 Pacu Lane, Suite 100
Bishop, CA 93514
(760) 872-5000

Map References
BLM   Darwin Hills
USGS 1:24,000   Vermilion Canyon, Haiwee
       Reservoirs, Upper Centennial Flat,
       Cactus Peak, Coso Junction
       1:100,000 Darwin Hills
Maptech CD-ROM: Kings Canyon/Death
       Valley
Southern & Central California Atlas & Gazetteer, pp. 39, 40
California Road & Recreation Atlas, p. 87
Other: Panamint Desert Access Guide

Route Directions

▼ 0.0   Trail begins on US 395 south of
           Olancha, opposite the fire station. Turn
           east along paved Cactus Flat Road and
           zero trip meter.
4.1 ▲   Trail ends on US 395. Turn right for
           Olancha; turn left for Ridgecrest.
           GPS: N36°15.31' W117°59.52'

▼ 0.4   SO Graded road on left into private property.
3.7 ▲   SO Graded road on right into private property.

▼ 1.3   SO Road turns to graded dirt.
2.8 ▲   SO Road is now paved.
▼ 1.6   SO Cattle guard.
2.5 ▲   SO Cattle guard.
▼ 2.1   SO Track on right.
2.0 ▲   SO Track on left.
▼ 2.4   SO Cross through wash. Track on left
           up wash.
1.7 ▲   SO Cross through wash. Track on right
           up wash.
▼ 2.5   SO Haiwee Reservoir on right.
1.6 ▲   SO Haiwee Reservoir on left.
▼ 2.6   SO Road is paved as it ascends the hill;
           then track on right.
1.5 ▲   SO Track on left; then road is paved as it
           descends the hill.
▼ 2.9   SO Track on right.
1.2 ▲   SO Track on left.
▼ 3.6   SO Two tracks on left.
0.5 ▲   SO Two tracks on right.
▼ 4.1   SO Graded road on left into pumice mine.
           Continue along smaller graded road
           and zero trip meter. Small track on
           right. Road is marked with BLM marker
           for 4WDs, ATVs, and motorbikes.
0.0 ▲   Continue to the northwest.
           GPS: N36°13.21' W117°56.07'

▼ 0.0   Continue to the southeast.
4.4 ▲   SO Graded road on right into pumice mine.
           Join larger, graded dirt road and zero
           trip meter. Small track on left.
▼ 0.2   SO Cross through wash.
4.2 ▲   SO Cross through wash.
▼ 0.7   SO Cross through wash.
3.7 ▲   SO Cross through wash.
▼ 1.0   BL Track on right down wash.
3.4 ▲   BR Track on left down wash.
           GPS: N36°12.54' W117°55.37'

▼ 1.5   SO Cross through wash.
2.9 ▲   SO Cross through wash.
▼ 2.1   SO Track on right.
2.3 ▲   SO Track on left.
▼ 2.3   SO Track on left.
2.1 ▲   SO Track on right.
▼ 2.4   SO Track on left. Trail is entering Cactus Flat.
2.0 ▲   SO Track on right. Trail is leaving Cactus Flat.
           GPS: N36°12.28' W117°53.88'

DESERT #45: CACTUS FLAT ROAD

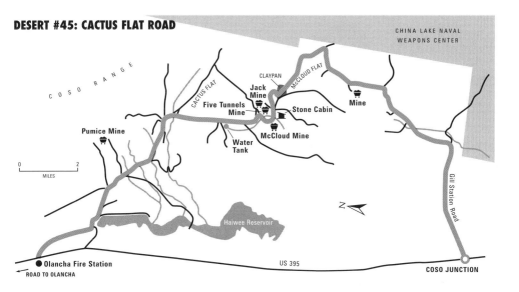

▼ 2.5　SO　Track on left.
1.9 ▲　SO　Track on right.
▼ 2.8　SO　Track on left; then cross through wash; then second track on left.
1.6 ▲　SO　Track on right; then cross through wash; then second track on right.
▼ 4.3　SO　Track on right.
0.1 ▲　SO　Track on left.
▼ 4.4　SO　Track on right at water tank. BLM trail marker at intersection. Road is marked for 4WDs, ATVs, and motorbikes. Zero trip meter.
0.0 ▲　　　Continue to the north.
　　　GPS: N36°10.60' W117°53.49'

▼ 0.0　　　Continue to the south.
1.3 ▲　SO　Track on left at water tank. BLM trail marker at intersection. Road is marked for 4WDs, ATVs, and motorbikes. Zero trip meter.
▼ 0.7　SO　Track on right.
0.6 ▲　SO　Track on left.
　　　GPS: N36°09.95' W117°53.40'

▼ 1.3　BR　Bear right onto smaller trail. Track ahead goes 0.1 miles to remains of the Jack Mine—a stone chimney and mine are visible farther up the hillside. Zero trip meter.
0.0 ▲　　　Continue to the west.

　　　GPS: N36°09.55' W117°53.08'

▼ 0.0　　　Continue to the southeast.
4.9 ▲　BL　Bear left onto larger formed trail. Track on right goes 0.1 miles to remains of the Jack Mine—a stone chimney and mine are visible on hillside to the right. Zero trip meter.
▼ 0.1　SO　Second entrance to Jack Mine on left.
4.8 ▲　SO　Track on right to Jack Mine, which is visible on hillside to the right.
▼ 0.2　SO　Cross through wash.
4.7 ▲　SO　Cross through wash.
▼ 0.6　SO　Cross through wash. Remains of the McCloud Mine on right. Small stone cabin on right.
4.3 ▲　SO　Remains of the McCloud Mine on the left. Small stone cabin on left. Cross through wash.
　　　GPS: N36°09.12' W117°53.07'

▼ 0.7　SO　Cross through wash; then track on right, which rejoins at top of rise.
4.2 ▲　SO　Track on left, which rejoins immediately; then cross through wash.
▼ 0.9　BL　Track on right and track straight on; bear left toward the headframe visible on hillside to the left.
4.0 ▲　SO　Two tracks on left.
　　　GPS: N36°09.07' W117°52.78'

Old stone cabin at the McCloud Mine built under a granite overhang

▼ 1.1 BR Track on left.
3.8 ▲ BL Track on right.
GPS: N36°09.15' W117°52.60'

▼ 1.2 BL Track on right.
3.7 ▲ SO Track on left.
GPS: N36°09.17' W117°52.48'

▼ 1.4 BL Bear left toward mine, tailings heaps, and wooden remains. Track on right.
3.5 ▲ SO Track on left.
GPS: N36°09.21' W117°52.31'

▼ 1.5 TR Mine on left. Turn right and then immediately left.
3.4 ▲ TL Turn right toward the mine and immediately left, just below the mine.
GPS: N36°09.22' W117°52.22'

▼ 1.6 SO Track on left; then bear right following around edge of claypan. Do not cut across the claypan.
3.3 ▲ BL Swing left away from the claypan toward the mine visible on the hill; then bear left, leaving a second track on right.

▼ 1.7 TL Rejoin track that bypassed the mine. Turn left (southeast), skirting edge of the claypan.
3.2 ▲ TR Turn right (northeast) around edge of claypan.
GPS: N36°09.08' W117°52.22'

▼ 1.8 BL Bear left and cross claypan. Trail you are heading for is visible on the far side. Track on right and track straight ahead.
3.1 ▲ BR Leave claypan and bear right alongside it. Track on left and track straight ahead.
GPS: N36°09.02' W117°52.17'

▼ 2.1 SO Exit claypan. Track on right and track on left.
2.8 ▲ SO Start to cross claypan. Track on right and track on left.
GPS: N36°08.90' W117°51.95'

▼ 3.0 SO Trail passes through gate.
1.9 ▲ SO Trail passes through gate.
GPS: N36°08.60' W117°51.07'

▼ 3.3 BR Bear right, remaining on most-used trail. Track on left goes to the boundary of the China Lake Naval Weapons Center.
1.6 ▲ BL Bear left, remaining on most-used trail. Track on right goes to the boundary of the China Lake Naval Weapons Center.
GPS: N36°08.55' W117°50.69'

▼ 4.1 TR Turn right onto well-used track that can be seen leading out of the valley. Track straight ahead leads to the boundary of the China Lake Naval Weapons Center.
0.8 ▲ TL T-intersection with well-used track. Track on right leads to the boundary of the China Lake Naval Weapons Center.
GPS: N36°07.90' W117°50.30'

▼ 4.9 TL Pass through wire fence line; then T-intersection. Turn left down valley. Zero trip meter.
0.0 ▲ Continue to the northeast.
GPS: N36°07.60' W117°51.04'

▼ 0.0 Continue to the south.
2.0 ▲ TR Turn right through wire fence line. Zero trip meter.
▼ 0.6 BL Small track on right goes to mine.
1.4 ▲ BR Small track on left goes to mine.
GPS: N36°07.10' W117°51.30'

▼ 2.0 TR T-intersection with main graded dirt road. Zero trip meter.
0.0 ▲ Continue to the northwest on small trail.
GPS: N36°05.95' W117°51.38'

▼ 0.0 Continue to the south on graded dirt road.
3.1 ▲ TL Turn left onto small well-used trail, marked by a BLM jeep trail marker with no number. Trail heads over the ridge. Zero trip meter.
▼ 0.9 SO Track on right.
2.2 ▲ SO Track on left.
▼ 1.4 SO Graded road on right.
1.7 ▲ SO Graded road on left.
GPS: N36°05.09' W117°52.39'

▼ 1.7	SO	Cross through wash.
1.4 ▲	SO	Cross through wash.
▼ 3.0	SO	Cross through wash.
0.1 ▲	SO	Cross through wash.
▼ 3.1	BR	T-intersection with paved road. Bear right, heading into the Owens Valley. Zero trip meter.
0.0 ▲		Continue to the northeast.

GPS: N36°03.68′ W117°52.98′

▼ 0.0		Continue to the west.
3.7 ▲	BL	Bear left onto large graded dirt road at unmarked intersection. Zero trip meter.
▼ 3.7		Trail ends at intersection with US 395 at Coso Junction.
0.0 ▲		Trail commences on US 395 at Coso Junction. Zero trip meter and turn east on paved road. There is a rest area at the intersection.

GPS: N36°02.76′ W117°56.76′

DESERT #46

Saline Valley Road

STARTING POINT: California 190, 9.5 miles east of the intersection with California 136.
FINISHING POINT: California 168, 2.5 miles east of Big Pine and the intersection with US 395
TOTAL MILEAGE: 91.4 miles
UNPAVED MILEAGE: 78.8 miles
DRIVING TIME: 5.5 hours
ELEVATION RANGE: 1,000–7,600 feet
USUALLY OPEN: Year-round, higher elevations may be closed during winter
BEST TIME TO TRAVEL: October to May, for the lower elevations
DIFFICULTY RATING: 2
SCENIC RATING: 10
REMOTENESS RATING: +2

Special Attractions

■ Old salt works and tramway.
■ Saline Valley Dunes.
■ Many old mining camps and remains in Saline Valley and Marble Canyon.
■ Remote desert experience.

History

Saline Valley, along with the Death Valley area in general, has a long history of mining activity. Saline Valley is best known for salt and borax mining operations. Borax was discovered in Saline Valley in 1874. The Conn and Trudo Borax Works operated in the valley from the late 1880s to the early 1900s. Saline Valley, along with Calico in San Bernardino County, was the principal producer of borax between 1888 and 1893. The valley's salt reserves were first worked around the same time, but they didn't become a large concern until 1903. The need to freight salt to the ferry and railroad on the western side of the Inyo Mountains for shipment across what was then Owens Lake led to the development of the salt tramway. The tramway, which was constructed between 1911 and 1913, runs from the floor of Saline Valley, up and over the Inyo Mountains, to Swansea in the Owens Valley. More about the tramway can be read in the history in Desert #48: Swansea–Cerro Gordo Road. The Saline Valley Salt Tram owners claim it to be "the most scenic, historic, best preserved, oldest, and largest of its kind remaining today." It is listed on the National Register of Historic Places.

Gold mining activity in Marble Canyon, to the north of Saline Valley, began as limited placer mining in 1882. Lack of transportation into the region meant that the canyon remained quiet until the 1930s, when there was a slight revival of gold mining. The gold in Marble Canyon is unusual in that large nuggets can be found on top of the bedrock beneath a deep gravel layer. The region was active until 1960, when it once again became quiet.

In October 1944, a B-24 bomber with a crew of seven was on a routine training mission when engine trouble developed. The plane crashed on the dry lake in Saline Valley. With their radios damaged in the crash, the crew, which had one man seriously injured, wrote the word "plasma" in 6-foot-high letters on the dry salt bed. A rescue team was dispatched to the site. After hours of arduous travel and numerous flat tires, the team reached the crash site. The injured man had a severed leg, and although the rescue

Salt-encrusted pilings at evaporation ponds at Salt Marsh

team tried their best, he died on the way to Big Pine.

Description

Saline Valley Road is a long, mainly dirt road that takes the traveler from California 190 to California 168, finishing near Big Pine. The historic road is suitable for high-clearance 2WDs in dry weather, but it is not a journey to be taken lightly by anyone. The dusty road can be extremely corrugated and there are no facilities or fuel anywhere along the way. In summer, temperatures reach extreme levels at the lower elevations, and in winter, there is often snow at the higher elevations that may require the use of chains in order to pass through safely.

The trail commences along the original Saline Valley Road, which is now less used than the new route that begins farther east on California 190. The old and new routes merge 8.3 miles from the start of the trail. The first part of the route travels through the Talc City Hills, close to the site of several old mines, before ending at the broad Santa Rosa Flat. The Santa Rosa Hills separate the flat from Lee Flat, a broad valley with abundant Joshua trees.

From the intersection with Desert #49: Hidden Valley Road, the trail winds down the twisting Grapevine Canyon. The trail crosses the creek several times. These crossings are likely to be dry in summer but may be icy in winter. The route spills out of Grapevine Canyon and heads down into the wide, sage-covered Saline Valley. A well-used track to the right is the rougher, more difficult Desert #50: Lippincott Mine Road, which connects with Desert #51: Racetrack Road. Saline Valley Road is well defined but dusty and washboardy, as it runs down the length of Saline Valley with the Nelson Range on the left. There are several small tracks that lead to the base of the range and the remains of various mining camps. One noteworthy feature is the remains of the old salt works at Salt Marsh. A spur leads a short distance to the edge of the marsh, where you can view the evaporation ponds and remains of the tramway.

The Saline Valley Dunes, a low range of sand dunes that are lightly vegetated with creosote bush, are a great place for photographs. No vehicles are allowed on the dunes, which are in a wilderness area. However, the road runs close enough that it is a very short, easy hike to the dunes.

The start of the more difficult Steels Pass Trail is the next major intersection. Travelers who do not wish to drive this route may still wish to detour for the first few miles of this trail to check out Palm Spring Hot Springs. Nudity is the norm at these popular springs, so if this offends you, you are better off staying on the main road.

The trail continues down the broad Saline Valley, passing side tracks that lead to old mining camps. The trail climbs out of the valley into the higher elevations up to 7,000 feet. There are several higher elevation campsites tucked into the pinyons and junipers. No campfires are allowed at any time of year within Death Valley National Park.

The trail joins paved Eureka Canyon Road and passes the northern end of Harkless Flat Trail and Papoose Flat Trail, before finishing at the intersection with California 168, a short distance east of Big Pine. The trail is normally open year-round, but some sections may be impassable at times. Even light rainfall can make the trails in this region impassable, and they may be temporarily closed by the National Park Service.

Current Road Information

Death Valley National Park
PO Box 579
Death Valley, CA 92328-0579
(760) 786-3200

Maps References

BLM   Saline Valley, Last Chance Range, Bishop, Darwin Hills
USFS Inyo National Forest
USGS 1:24,000 Talc City Hills, Santa Rosa Flat, Lee Wash, Jackass Canyon, Nelson Range, West of Ubehebe Peak, Craig Canyon, Lower Warm Springs, Pat Keyes

Canyon, Waucoba Canyon,
Waucoba Spring, Waucoba Mtn.,
Cowhorn Valley, Uhlmeyer Spring,
Big Pine
1:100,000 Saline Valley, Last Chance
Range, Bishop, Darwin Hills
*Southern & Central California Atlas &
Gazetteer,* pp. 40, 28, 27
Northern California Atlas & Gazetteer, p. 124
California Road & Recreation Atlas,
pp. 87, 80, 79
Trails Illustrated, Death Valley National
Park (221)
Other: Free NPS Death Valley map; Tom
Harrison Maps—Death Valley
National Park Recreation Map

Route Directions

▼ 0.0   Trail commences on California 190,
         9.5 miles east of the intersection with
         California 136. Zero trip meter and turn
         north on small paved road. Intersection
         is unmarked.
1.9 ▲   Small paved road on left is Talc City
         Road; then trail ends at intersection
         with California 190. Turn right for Lone
         Pine; turn left for Death Valley.
         GPS: N36°19.84′ W117°42.84′

▼ 0.1   SO Track on left.
1.8 ▲   SO Track on right.
▼ 0.7   SO Track on left joins S9.
1.2 ▲   SO Track on right joins S9.
▼ 1.2   SO Track on left and track on right; then
             second track on left to Viking and
             White Swan Mines; then second track
             on right.
0.7 ▲   SO Track on left; then track on right to
             Viking and White Swan Mines; then
             second track on left and second track
             on right.
         GPS: N36°20.65′ W117°42.22′

▼ 1.4   SO Cross through wash.
0.5 ▲   SO Cross through wash.
▼ 1.8   SO Track on right is S5, suitable for 4WDs,
             ATVs, and motorbikes, and goes
             toward the Sierra Mine.
0.1 ▲   SO Track on left is S5, suitable for 4WDs,

ATVs, and motorbikes, and goes
toward the Sierra Mine.
▼ 1.9   SO Track on left is S9, suitable for 4WDs,
             ATVs, and motorbikes, and goes to the
             Viking Mine, which is visible on the
             hillside to the left. Zero trip meter.
0.0 ▲   Continue to the south.
         GPS: N36°21.20′ W117°41.74′

▼ 0.0   Continue to the north.
4.6 ▲   SO Track on right is S9, suitable for 4WDs,
             ATVs, and motorbikes, and goes to the
             Viking Mine, which is visible on the
             hillside to the right. Zero trip meter.
▼ 0.5   SO Track on left to mine.
4.1 ▲   SO Track on right to mine.
         GPS: N36°21.56′ W117°41.50′

▼ 1.6   SO Track on left.
3.0 ▲   SO Track on right.
▼ 1.7   SO Cross through wash.
2.9 ▲   SO Cross through wash.
▼ 2.1   SO Track on right.
2.5 ▲   SO Track on left.
▼ 3.1   SO Many small wash crossings for the
             next 1.5 miles.
1.5 ▲   SO End of wash crossings.
▼ 3.7   BR Graded road on left is Santa Rosa Road.
0.9 ▲   SO Graded road on right is Santa Rosa Road.
         GPS: N36°23.95′ W117°40.25′

▼ 4.6   BR Track on left is S5 for 4WDs, ATVs,
             and motorbikes. Zero trip meter.
0.0 ▲   Continue to the south. Trail is leaving
         Santa Rosa Flat. Many small wash
         crossings for the next 1.5 miles.
         GPS: N36°24.72′ W117°39.91′

▼ 0.0   Continue to the northeast. End of wash
         crossings.
1.8 ▲   BL Track on right is S5 for 4WDs, ATVs,
             and motorbikes. Zero trip meter.
▼ 0.4   SO Cross through large wash.
1.4 ▲   SO Cross through large wash.
         GPS: N36°24.86′ W117°39.49′

▼ 1.1   SO Faint track on right.
0.7 ▲   SO Faint track on left.
▼ 1.5   SO Cross through two channels of Santa
             Rosa Wash.

0.3 ▲   SO Cross through two channels of Santa
             Rosa Wash.
▼ 1.8   SO Join larger road that was once paved
             and zero trip meter. Alternate Saline
             Valley Road on right returns to
             California 190 in 4.7 miles. Intersection
             is unmarked.
0.0 ▲   Continue to the southwest toward
             Santa Rosa Flat.
             GPS: N36°25.71' W117°38.39'

▼ 0.0   Continue to the northeast through the
             Santa Rosa Hills.
3.3 ▲   BR Bear right onto smaller graded road,
             which is the original Saline Valley
             Road. Larger road ahead that was
             once paved is Alternate Saline Valley
             Road, which joins California 190 in 4.7
             miles. Intersection is unmarked. Zero
             trip meter.
▼ 0.5   SO Track on left past cabin.
2.8 ▲   SO Track on right past cabin.
▼ 1.1   SO Track on right to Lee Mines.
2.2 ▲   SO Track on left to Lee Mines.
             GPS: N36°26.10' W117°37.33'

▼ 1.3   SO Track on left to mine.
2.0 ▲   SO Track on right to mine.
▼ 2.5   SO Entering Death Valley National Park
             at sign.
0.8 ▲   SO Leaving Death Valley National Park
             at sign.
             GPS: N36°27.20' W117°37.38'

▼ 3.3   BR Desert #47: Cerro Gordo Road on left.
             Intersection is large, but unmarked.
             Small track on right. Zero trip meter.
0.0 ▲   Continue to the southeast.
             GPS: N36°27.91' W117°37.55'

▼ 0.0   Continue to the north.
7.1 ▲   SO Desert #47: Cerro Gordo Road on
             right. Intersection is large, but
             unmarked. Small track on left. Zero
             trip meter.
▼ 1.5   SO Track on left. Track on right to site of
             Wilson Ranch.
5.6 ▲   SO Track on left to site of Wilson Ranch.
             Track on right.
             GPS: N36°29.13' W117°36.97'

Saline Valley Dunes

Large, jumbled boulders at the south end of Saline Valley

▼ 3.1 SO Cross through wash.
4.0 ▲ SO Cross through wash.
▼ 4.9 SO Diggings on left.
2.2 ▲ SO Diggings on right.
        GPS: N36°30.53' W117°34.44'

▼ 5.4 SO Track on left past corral.
1.7 ▲ SO Track on right past corral.
        GPS: N36°30.82' W117°34.04'

▼ 6.8 SO Turnout on right gives views of the Panamint Dunes.
0.3 ▲ SO Turnout on left gives views of the Panamint Dunes.
▼ 7.1 SO Well-used track on right is Desert #49: Hidden Valley Road. Zero trip meter. Intersection is unmarked.
0.0 ▲ Continue to the south.
        GPS: N36°31.62' W117°32.75'

▼ 0.0 Continue to the northwest.
10.0 ▲ SO Well-used track on left is Desert #49: Hidden Valley Road. Zero trip meter. Intersection is unmarked.

▼ 2.6 SO Cross through Grapevine Canyon Creek many times in the next 1.6 miles.
7.4 ▲ SO Final crossing of Grapevine Canyon Creek.
        GPS: N36°32.91' W117°34.37'

▼ 4.2 SO Final crossing of Grapevine Canyon Creek.
5.8 ▲ SO Cross through Grapevine Canyon Creek many times in the next 1.6 miles.
▼ 4.8 SO Track on right.
5.2 ▲ SO Track on left.
▼ 7.8 SO Cross through wash.
2.2 ▲ SO Cross through wash.
▼ 10.0 SO Graded track on right is Desert #50: Lippincott Mine Road. Intersection is unmarked apart from a large cairn. Zero trip meter.
0.0 ▲ Continue to the southeast.
        GPS: N36°37.20' W117°38.88'

▼ 0.0 Continue to the northwest.
10.6 ▲ SO Graded track on left is Desert #50: Lippincott Mine Road. Intersection is unmarked apart from a large cairn. Zero trip meter.

DESERT #46: SALINE VALLEY ROAD

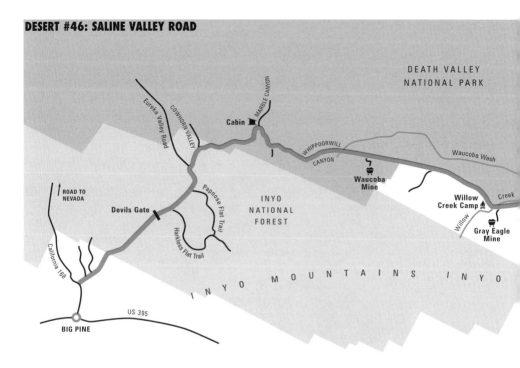

▼ 2.9   SO Track on right.
7.7 ▲   SO Track on left.
> **GPS: N36°39.38′ W117°40.58′**

▼ 10.3   SO Track on left.
0.3 ▲   SO Track on right.
▼ 10.6   SO Track on left follows route of abandoned aerial tramway and heads toward Big Silver Mine. Track on right goes to the edge of Salt Lake with its old salt evaporator and some remains of the salt tramway. Zero trip meter.
0.0 ▲   Continue to the east.
> **GPS: N36°41.07′ W117°48.90′**

▼ 0.0   Continue to the west.
8.1 ▲   SO Track on right follows the route of the abandoned aerial tramway and heads toward Big Silver Mine. Track on left goes to the edge of Salt Lake with its old salt evaporators and some remains of the salt tramway. Zero trip meter.
▼ 0.1   SO Track on left.
8.0 ▲   SO Track on right.
▼ 1.4   SO Track on right across cattle guard.
6.7 ▲   SO Track on left across cattle guard.

> **GPS: N36°41.91′ W117°49.86′**

▼ 1.8   SO Track on left toward Vega Mine and the start of the old steep pack route to Burgess Mine in the Inyo Mountains. Track on right.
6.3 ▲   SO Track on right toward Vega Mine and the start of the old steep pack route to Burgess Mine in the Inyo Mountains. Track on left.
> **GPS: N36°42.25′ W117°49.67′**

▼ 2.2   SO Track on right.
5.9 ▲   SO Track on left.
▼ 2.4   SO Track on left goes to old works area.
5.7 ▲   SO Track on right goes to old works area.
> **GPS: N36°42.74′ W117°49.90′**

▼ 2.5   SO Track on right.
5.6 ▲   SO Track on left.
▼ 4.2   SO Track on left to Snowflake Mine.
3.9 ▲   SO Track on right to Snowflake Mine.
> **GPS: N36°43.85′ W117°50.51′**

▼ 4.3   SO Track on left to Snowflake Mine and track on right.

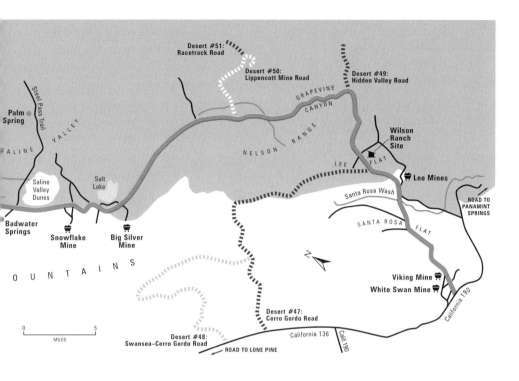

3.8 ▲ SO Track on right to Snowflake Mine and
            track on left.
        GPS: N36º43.89' W117º50.52'

▼ 4.7   SO Track on right.
3.4 ▲   SO Track on left.
▼ 4.9   SO Track on left to Snowflake Mine.
3.2 ▲   SO Track on right to Snowflake Mine.
        GPS: N36º44.37' W117º50.96'

▼ 5.0   SO Track on left and track on right.
3.1 ▲   SO Track on right and track on left.
▼ 5.6   BR Graded road on left.
2.5 ▲   SO Graded road on right rejoins.
        GPS: N36º44.81' W117º51.41'

▼ 6.3   SO Saline Valley Dunes are on the right.
1.8 ▲   SO Saline Valley Dunes are on the left.
▼ 6.6. SO Graded road on left rejoins.
1.5 ▲   BL Graded road on right.
▼ 7.1   SO Track on left.
1.0 ▲   SO Track on right.
▼ 8.1   SO Well-used track on right is Steel Pass
            Trail. Zero trip meter. Intersection is
            unmarked.
0.0 ▲   Continue to the southeast.

        GPS: N36º46.68' W117º52.74'

▼ 0.0   Continue to the northwest.
4.5 ▲   SO Well-used track on left is Steel Pass
            Trail. Zero trip meter. Intersection is
            unmarked.
▼ 0.4   SO Track on left to Badwater Springs.
4.1 ▲   SO Track on right to Badwater Springs.
▼ 0.8   SO Track on left.
3.7 ▲   SO Track on right.
▼ 1.7   SO Cross through wash.
2.8 ▲   SO Cross through wash.
▼ 3.3   SO Track on left.
1.2 ▲   SO Second entrance to track on right.
        GPS: N36º49.30' W117º54.35'

▼ 3.4   SO Second entrance to track on left.
1.1 ▲   SO Track on right.
▼ 4.1   SO Track on left to Gray Eagle Mine.
0.4 ▲   SO Second track on right to Gray Eagle Mine.
        GPS: N36º49.89' W117º54.79'

▼ 4.2   SO Second track on left to Gray Eagle Mine.
0.3 ▲   SO Track on right to Gray Eagle Mine.
▼ 4.4   SO Track on left; then cross through
            Willow Creek Wash.

0.1 ▲ SO Cross through Willow Creek wash; then track on right.

▼ 4.5 BR Graded road on left goes into Willow Creek Camp. Zero trip meter.

0.0 ▲ Continue to the southeast.
GPS: N36°50.16' W117°54.97'

▼ 0.0 Continue to the north, following sign for Big Pine, and cross through wash.

19.3 ▲ BL Cross through wash; then graded road on right goes into Willow Creek Camp. Zero trip meter.

▼ 0.1 SO Track on left.

19.2 ▲ SO Track on right.

▼ 0.6 SO Cross through many washes for the next 3.4 miles.

18.7 ▲ SO Cross through wash. End of wash crossings.

▼ 4.0 SO Cross through wash. End of wash crossings.

15.3 ▲ SO Cross through many washes for the next 3.4 miles.

▼ 5.4 SO Well-used track on left.

13.9 ▲ SO Well-used track on right.
GPS: N36°54.69' W117°54.50'

▼ 7.8 SO Cross through wash.

11.5 ▲ SO Cross through wash.

▼ 8.6 SO Track on left.

10.7 ▲ SO Track on right.

▼ 8.7 SO Cross through wash.

10.6 ▲ SO Cross through wash.

▼ 9.8 SO Track on left goes to Waucoba Mine.

9.5 ▲ SO Track on right goes to Waucoba Mine.
GPS: N36°58.54' W117°55.88'

▼ 10.7 SO Cross through wash.

8.6 ▲ SO Cross through wash.

▼ 11.5 SO Cross through Waucoba Wash.

7.8 ▲ SO Cross through Waucoba Wash.

▼ 12.0 SO Cross through wash.

7.3 ▲ SO Cross through wash.
GPS: N37°00.41' W117°56.54'

▼ 12.3 SO Cross through wash.

7.0 ▲ SO Cross through wash.

▼ 12.6 SO Enter line of wash. Trail follows in or alongside wash, crossing it often for the next 2 miles.

6.7 ▲ SO Exit line of wash.

▼ 14.6 SO Exit line of wash and Whippoorwill Canyon.

4.7 ▲ SO Enter line of wash and Whippoorwill Canyon. Trail follows in or alongside wash, crossing it often for the next 2 miles.

▼ 15.0 SO Track on left. Entering Whippoorwill Flat.

4.3 ▲ SO Track on right. Exiting Whippoorwill Flat.
GPS: N37°02.06' W117°58.41'

▼ 15.3 SO Track on left.

4.0 ▲ SO Track on right.

▼ 16.2 SO Track on left.

3.1 ▲ SO Track on right.
GPS: N37°03.06' W117°58.47'

▼ 17.3 SO Track on left.

2.0 ▲ SO Track on right.

▼ 17.6 SO Track on left.

1.7 ▲ SO Second entrance to track on right.
GPS: N37°04.27' W117°58.65'

▼ 17.8 SO Second entrance to track on left. Trail enters Opal Canyon.

1.5 ▲ SO Track on right. Trail enters Whippoorwill Flat.

▼ 18.0 SO Cross through wash.

1.3 ▲ SO Cross through wash.

▼ 19.3 BL Track on right goes down Marble Canyon to many mining remains. Bear left up Marble Canyon, remaining on main graded road, and zero trip meter. Marble Canyon intersects with Opal Canyon at this point.

0.0 ▲ Continue to the south.
GPS: N37°05.47' W117°57.82'

▼ 0.0 Continue to the west.

7.6 ▲ BR Track straight ahead continues down Marble Canyon. Bear right up Opal Canyon, remaining on main graded road, and zero trip meter. Marble Canyon intersects with Opal Canyon at this point.

▼ 0.1 SO Old miner's cabin on right. There are many mining remains scattered along the floor of Marble Canyon.

7.5 ▲ SO Old miner's cabin on left. There are many mining remains scattered along the floor of Marble Canyon.

▼ 0.7 SO Track on right to mine.

6.9 ▲ SO Track on left to mine.
        GPS: N37°05.35′ W117°58.53′

▼ 1.0 SO Entering Inyo National Forest.
6.6 ▲ SO Entering Death Valley National Park.
        GPS: N37°05.29′ W117°58.88′

▼ 1.2 SO Track on left.
6.4 ▲ SO Track on right.
▼ 1.3 SO Track on left; then cross through wash;
            then second track on left.
6.3 ▲ SO Track on right; then cross through
            wash; then second track on right.
▼ 1.5 SO Track on right.
6.1 ▲ SO Track on left.
▼ 4.4 SO Track on left to game tank.
3.2 ▲ SO Track on right to game tank.
▼ 4.5 SO Track on left.
3.1 ▲ SO Track on right.
▼ 4.8 SO Track on left.
2.8 ▲ SO Track on right.
▼ 4.9 SO Track on right.
2.7 ▲ SO Track on left.
▼ 5.9 SO Track on right enters Cowhorn Valley.
1.7 ▲ SO Track on left enters Cowhorn Valley.
        GPS: N37°08.15′ W118°01.52′

▼ 6.0 BR Trail forks. Take either trail.
1.6 ▲ SO Trail rejoins.
▼ 6.3 SO Trail rejoins.
1.3 ▲ SO Trail forks. Take either trail.
▼ 6.5 SO Old road cutting on left.
1.1 ▲ SO Old road rejoins.
▼ 6.6 SO Old road rejoins.
1.0 ▲ SO Old road cutting on right.
▼ 7.6 TL Track on left and track on right; then
            T-intersection with Eureka Valley Road
            (listed as Death Valley Road on some
            maps). Road on right is 9S18. Zero trip
            meter and turn left onto paved Eureka
            Valley Road.
0.0 ▲   Continue to the east. Track on left and
            track on right.
        GPS: N37°08.24′ W118°03.15′

▼ 0.0   Continue to the southwest.
1.8 ▲ TR Turn right onto graded dirt road, follow-
            ing the sign for Saline Valley Road, and
            zero trip meter. Paved road continues
            ahead and is marked 9S18.

▼ 1.2 SO Track on left.
0.6 ▲ SO Track on right.
▼ 1.8 SO Track on left is Papoose Flat Trail.
            Zero trip meter.
0.0 ▲   Continue to the northeast.
        GPS: N37°07.38′ W118°04.60′

▼ 0.0   Continue to the west.
2.0 ▲ SO Track on right is Papoose Flat Trail.
            Zero trip meter.
▼ 0.6 SO Track on right.
1.4 ▲ SO Track on left.
▼ 2.0 SO Track on left is Harkless Flat Trail
            (9S13). Zero trip meter.
0.0 ▲   Continue to the southeast.
        GPS: N37°08.04′ W118°06.64′

▼ 0.0   Continue to the northwest.
5.5 ▲ SO Track on right is Harkless Flat Trail
            (9S13). Zero trip meter.
▼ 0.2 SO Track on right.
5.3 ▲ SO Track on left.
▼ 1.1 SO Pass through Devils Gate; then cross
            through wash.
4.4 ▲ SO Cross through wash; then pass
            through Devils Gate.
        GPS: N37°08.66′ W118°07.47′

▼ 2.7 SO Track on left.
2.8 ▲ SO Track on right.
▼ 4.9 SO Track on left.
0.6 ▲ SO Track on right.
▼ 5.3 SO Track on right.
0.2 ▲ SO Track on left.
▼ 5.5 SO Exiting Inyo National Forest at sign.
            Zero trip meter.
0.0 ▲   Continue to the east.
        GPS: N37°10.20′ W118°11.81′

▼ 0.0   Continue to the west.
3.3 ▲ SO Entering Inyo National Forest at sign.
            Zero trip meter.
▼ 0.8 SO Cross through wash.
2.5 ▲ SO Cross through wash.
▼ 1.1 SO Track on right.
2.2 ▲ SO Track on left.
▼ 1.9 SO Track on right.
1.4 ▲ SO Track on left.
▼ 2.5 SO Track on right.
0.8 ▲ SO Track on left.

▼ 3.3 SO Trail ends at intersection with
California 168. Turn left for Big Pine;
turn right for Nevada.

0.0 ▲ Trail commences on California 168,
2.5 miles east of US 395 and Big Pine.
Zero trip meter and turn southeast on
paved Saline Valley Road. It is sign-
posted as Death Valley Road to
Scotty's Castle.

GPS: N37°11.10′ W118°15.13′

DESERT #47

Cerro Gordo Road

STARTING POINT: California 136 at Keeler, 12
miles east of Lone Pine
FINISHING POINT: Desert #46: Saline Valley
Road, 11.6 miles north of California
190
TOTAL MILEAGE: 23.7 miles
UNPAVED MILEAGE: 23.7 miles
DRIVING TIME: 2.5 hours
ELEVATION RANGE: 3,600–8,100 feet
USUALLY OPEN: Year-round (may be blocked
by snow in winter)
BEST TIME TO TRAVEL: Spring and fall
DIFFICULTY RATING: 2
SCENIC RATING: 9
REMOTENESS RATING: +1

Special Attractions

■ Lee Flat Joshua tree forest.
■ Cerro Gordo ghost town.
■ Alternate entry point to Desert #46:
Saline Valley Road and Death Valley
National Park.
■ Views of the Sierra Nevada, Saline Valley,
and Panamint Range.

History

Perched high in the Inyo Mountains, Cerro
Gordo (Spanish for "fat hill") was the greatest producer of silver and lead in California's
history. Rival cities competed to trade with
the mining district. Los Angeles won out
and Cerro Gordo became crucial in the development of the young city. Mexican

prospectors discovered the first silver deposits in 1865, but the area was largely ig-
nored until 1867 when Spanish-speaking
miners began bringing silver ore samples to
Virginia City, Nevada. Scores of fortune
seekers hurried to the region and the town
of Cerro Gordo soon sprang up to accommodate them.

The two biggest investors in Cerro Gordo were San Francisco mining engineer M.
W. Belshaw and his partner, storeowner Victor Beaudry. Belshaw constructed the Old
Yellow Grade Road, an expensive toll road
whose high rates helped bankrupt poor
miners. This enabled the investors to form a
monopoly on mining operations.

The ore was transported out of Cerro
Gordo using mule teams. After several years,
ferries began to carry silver over Owens Lake
(which was not yet dry). At its peak in the
mid-1870s, Cerro Gordo boasted a population of more than 2,000 and had many
stores. Soon, though, the silver and iron
mines played out, and the residents and
store owners moved to other locations. The
town reawakened several times, for zinc and
limestone mining, but in 1959 the remaining equipment was sold and Cerro Gordo
assumed its present, ghost town state. It is
now private property, and its current owner
rents out restored buildings to help fund
preservation of the site.

Description

Cerro Gordo Road follows close to the route
of the old toll road into Death Valley. It
travels up a steep canyon in the Inyo Mountains to Cerro Gordo ghost town and down
the east side to Desert #46: Saline Valley
Road in Lee Flat. The road leaves from Keeler, a small settlement on California 136.

The route is well graded, but surprisingly
steep as it travels into the Inyo Mountains.
Vehicles traveling the route in the reverse direction will need to watch their brakes.
There are some mining remains visible along
the length of the route. The upper sections
of the trail approaching Cerro Gordo travel a
narrow shelf road. The ghost town of Cerro
Gordo is privately owned. Please remain on

The Old Yellow Grade Road made its way up the best possible route through the canyon

the through-routes while on private property. Tours of the ghost town are offered; call ahead for details at (760) 876-5030.

Cerro Gordo sits on a saddle under the shadow of the hill from which it takes its name. From the saddle the road descends the east side of the range. The grade here is less steep than the west side, although the trail is slightly rougher. The vegetation is different on each side; the west has bare, sparsely vegetated hills scattered with a few Joshua trees, the east has pinyon and juniper at the higher elevations.

The trail comes to a T-intersection with the east-west running San Lucas Canyon. The trail is rougher and prone to washouts, but it is usually suitable for high-clearance vehicles. San Lucas Canyon spills out onto Lee Flat, where there are some of the densest stands of Joshua trees to be found in Death Valley. The trail then comes to an end at Desert #46: Saline Valley Road.

With care, passenger vehicles can access the trail as far as Cerro Gordo. High-clearance is required east of the town site.

Current Road Information

Death Valley National Park
PO Box 579
Death Valley, CA 92328-0579
(760) 786-3200

Map References

BLM   Saline Valley, Darwin Hills
USGS 1:24,000 Keeler, Cerro Gordo Peak,
         Nelson Range, Santa Rosa Flat
         1:100,000 Saline Valley, Darwin Hills
Maptech CD-ROM: Kings Canyon/Death
         Valley
*Southern & Central California Atlas &
         Gazetteer,* pp. 40, 28
California Road & Recreation Atlas, p. 87
Trails Illustrated, Death Valley National
         Park (221)
Other: Free NPS Death Valley map; Tom
         Harrison Maps—Death Valley
         National Park Recreation Map

Sierra Talc Company plant at Keeler

American Hotel in Cerro Gordo

Route Directions

▼ 0.0   From California 136 on the east side of Keeler, 12 miles east of Lone Pine, zero trip meter and turn northeast on graded dirt Cerro Gordo Road. There is a historical marker for Cerro Gordo at the intersection.

4.2 ▲   Trail ends on California 136. Turn left for Death Valley; turn right for Lone Pine. There is a historical marker for Cerro Gordo at the intersection.

       GPS: N36°29.19′ W117°51.94′

▼ 0.4   SO   Track on left along power lines.
3.8 ▲   SO   Track on right along power lines.
▼ 0.6   SO   Track on right to stone ruins.
3.6 ▲   SO   Track on left to stone ruins.

       GPS: N36°29.60′ W117°51.87′

▼ 3.4   SO   Track on right.
0.8 ▲   SO   Track on left.

       GPS: N36°30.97′ W117°49.76′

▼ 4.2   BL   Two tracks on right—first passes salt tramway tower. Zero trip meter.
0.0 ▲   Continue to the south, remaining on main graded road.

       GPS: N36°31.11′ W117°49.04′

▼ 0.0   Continue to the northwest, remaining on main graded road. Cross through wash.
3.4 ▲   BR   Cross through wash; then two tracks on left—second passes salt tramway tower. Zero trip meter.
▼ 0.3   SO   Track on right.
3.1 ▲   SO   Track on left.
▼ 1.5   SO   Track on left.
1.9 ▲   SO   Track on right.
▼ 1.7   SO   Track on left.
1.7 ▲   SO   Track on right.

       GPS: N36°32.09′ W117°48.85′

▼ 2.0   SO   Loading hopper on left.
1.4 ▲   SO   Loading hopper on right.
▼ 3.1   SO   Cross through wash.
0.3 ▲   SO   Cross through wash.

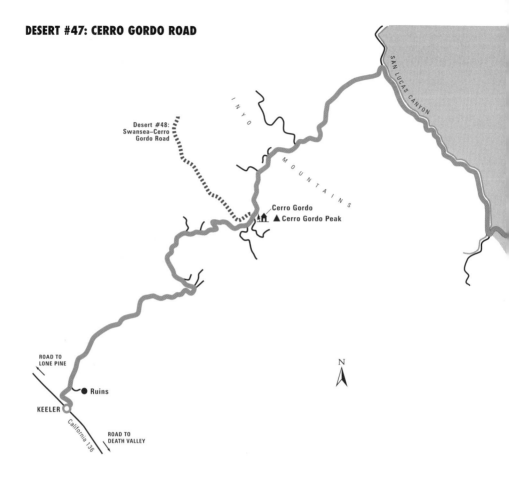

▼ 3.2   SO   Track on right on edge of Cerro Gordo.

0.2 ▲   SO   Track on left on edge of Cerro Gordo.

▼ 3.3   SO   Track on right is entrance to Cerro Gordo.

0.1 ▲   SO   Track on left is entrance to Cerro Gordo.

           GPS: N36°32.27' W117°47.64'

▼ 3.4   SO   Track on left is Desert #48: Swansea–Cerro Gordo Road. Track on right is private road into Cerro Gordo. Zero trip meter. Cerro Gordo Peak is on the right.

0.0 ▲   Continue to the south.

           GPS: N36°32.36' W117°47.62'

▼ 0.0   Continue to the north over the saddle and drop toward Saline Valley.

4.9 ▲   SO   Track on right is Desert #48: Swansea–Cerro Gordo Road. Track on left is private road into Cerro Gordo. Zero trip meter. Cerro Gordo Peak is on the left.

▼ 0.6   SO   Track enters line of wash.

4.3 ▲   SO   Track exits line of wash.

▼ 1.0   SO   Track on right is private.

3.9 ▲   SO   Track on left is private.

▼ 1.2   SO   Leaving private property of Cerro Gordo Mining District at sign.

3.7 ▲   SO   Entering private property of Cerro Gordo Mining District at sign.

           GPS: N36°33.08' W117°47.49'

▼ 1.3   SO   Track on left.

3.6 ▲   SO   Track on right.

▼ 1.6   SO   Two tracks on left.

3.3 ▲   SO   Two tracks on right.

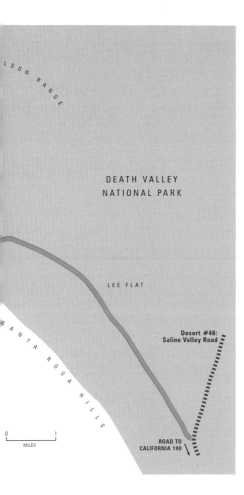

 L S O N R A N G E

DEATH VALLEY
NATIONAL PARK

LEE FLAT

S A N T A   R O S A   H I L L S

Desert #46:
Saline Valley Road

0   1
MILES

ROAD TO
CALIFORNIA 190

▼ 2.2   SO   Track on left.
2.7 ▲   SO   Track on right.
        GPS: N36°33.52' W117°46.66'

▼ 2.3   SO   Track on right.
2.6 ▲   SO   Track on left.
▼ 4.9   TR   T-intersection with bottom of San
             Lucas Canyon. Turn right and continue
             up wash in San Lucas Canyon. Zero
             trip meter.
0.0 ▲   Continue to the southwest.
        GPS: N36°34.85' W117°44.67'

▼ 0.0   Continue to the southeast.
4.4 ▲   TL   Turn left into line of wash, following
             BLM road marker for Cerro Gordo.
             Road continues ahead in San Lucas
             Canyon. Zero trip meter.

▼ 4.1   SO   Trail exits line of the wash.
0.3 ▲   SO   Trail enters line of the wash.
        GPS: N36°32.06' W117°42.55'

▼ 4.4   TL   T-intersection. Track on right is S5 for
             4WDs, ATVs, and motorbikes. Remain
             on main graded road. Zero trip meter.
             Trail is now entering Death Valley
             National Park (no sign).
0.0 ▲   Continue to the northwest.
        GPS: N36°31.85' W117°42.55'

▼ 0.0   Continue to the northeast.
6.8 ▲   TR   Track straight ahead is S5 for 4WDs,
             ATVs, and motorbikes. Turn right,
             remaining on graded road. Zero trip
             meter. Trail leaves Death Valley
             National Park (no sign).
▼ 2.2   SO   Cross through wash.
4.6 ▲   SO   Cross through wash.
▼ 2.3   SO   Cross through wash.
4.5 ▲   SO   Cross through wash.
▼ 2.4   SO   Cross through wash.
4.4 ▲   SO   Cross through wash.
▼ 3.0   SO   Well-used track on left.
3.8 ▲   SO   Well-used track on right.
        GPS: N36°30.78' W117°39.62'

▼ 3.1   SO   Track on left.
3.7 ▲   SO   Track on right.
▼ 5.1   SO   Track on left.
1.7 ▲   SO   Track on right.
        GPS: N36°29.23' W117°38.48'

▼ 6.6   SO   Track on left.
0.2 ▲   SO   Track on right.
▼ 6.8   Trail ends at intersection with Desert
             #46: Saline Valley Road on Lee Flat.
             Turn right for California 136; turn left
             to travel Saline Valley Road.
0.0 ▲   Trail commences on Desert #46:
             Saline Valley Road, 11.6 miles north
             of California 190 on Lee Flat. Zero trip
             meter at unmarked, well-used intersec-
             tion with graded dirt road and proceed
             northwest at the Y-intersection. Saline
             Valley Road continues to the north at
             this point.
        GPS: N36°27.91' W117°37.55'

Swansea–Cerro Gordo Road

STARTING POINT: California 136 at the site of Swansea, 9.1 miles east of Lone Pine

FINISHING POINT: Desert #47: Cerro Gordo Road at Cerro Gordo

TOTAL MILEAGE: 23 miles, plus 1.5-mile spur to Burgess Mine

UNPAVED MILEAGE: 23 miles, plus 1.5-mile spur

DRIVING TIME: 4.5 hours

ELEVATION RANGE: 3,700–9,500 feet

USUALLY OPEN: Year-round

BEST TIME TO TRAVEL: October to May

DIFFICULTY RATING: 5

SCENIC RATING: 10

REMOTENESS RATING: +1

Special Attractions

■ Remote, rugged trail that follows a corridor through the Inyo Mountains Wilderness.

■ Excellent example of an aerial tramway.

■ The privately owned ghost town of Cerro Gordo.

History

The Owens Lake Silver and Lead Company constructed a smelter at Swansea in 1869 to process ores from the many mining claims around Cerro Gordo. A section of the furnace is all that remains today. This was one of three smelters handling ores from the booming mining district. By the late 1860s, Mortimer Belshaw of San Francisco had gained control of a high percentage of the claims, and he was making every effort to develop full control. Victor Beaudry, a merchant from Lone Pine, moved in and set up a store. Beaudry also had a smelter in operation on the mountain. Belshaw and Beaudry joined forces and attempted to squeeze out the smelter operation at Swansea. They constructed a toll road that they called the Yellow Grade Road down from the mountain and charged enormous fees to the miners who used it.

James Brady, who ran the smelter at Swansea, was eager to cut ore transportation costs. He realized it would be faster and cheaper to ferry the enormous number of ingots across Owens Lake rather than hauling them around the lake through soft sand. He constructed a wharf at Swansea and acquired a steamboat, named *Bessie Brady* by his young daughter.

In 1872, a violent earthquake killed 27 people in Lone Pine and altered the bed of Owens Lake. The lake moved to the west, thereby necessitating a 150-foot extension to the planned wharf. The first voyage across the lake to a landing at Cartago was made in May 1872. The trip shaved two to three days off the traditional freight time. Belshaw and Beaudry built their own wharf at Keeler, where the Yellow Grade Road exited the Inyo Mountains, and bought the *Bessie Brady* as part of their expanding Cerro Gordo Freighting Company.

The aerial tramway encountered along this trail was part of the ambitious salt works located at Saline Lake. The salt was reportedly so pure that it was sold at market in an unrefined state. Like all other mining activities in Death Valley, freighting costs and the time involved were prohibitive. In order to cut several days off the transportation route, construction of the monumental aerial tramway was started in 1911, with the first shipment made in 1913. The tramway was almost 14 miles long, making it one of the longest in the world at the time. It traversed extremely rugged terrain. Twenty tons of salt an hour were hauled up nearly 7,000 feet to then drop down more than 5,000 feet to Swansea on the edge of Owens Lake for shipment to market. Three hundred buckets were constantly on the go.

The family who lived and maintained the tower at the top of the crest had a lonely existence. They greeted any visitors who came their way. The family could only occupy the cabin during the summer; winters were much too harsh.

Mining operations lasted into the early 1930s, when salt supplies were depleted. Investors moved on and the salt works closed down. A restoration program, coordinated by the Bishop office of the Bureau of Land Management, is attempting to save the remainder of the controller's cabin and the aerial tramway tower.

Description

The dramatic road that runs over the ridge tops of the Inyo Mountains is one of the most beautiful in the region. The trail also passes the well-preserved remains of the salt tramway.

The trail leaves Swansea, beside the tumbledown stone building that was once a stagecoach stop, and follows a single-lane, stony formed trail toward the Inyo Mountains. The trail is easy to follow for the most part; it is well used with few turns. It climbs up the alluvial fan to enter a canyon. As it climbs, there are good views back over Owens Lake to the Sierra Nevada.

The trail within the wash is lumpy, loose, and gravelly as it climbs gradually to enter a vehicle corridor through the Inyo Mountains Wilderness. As you climb into the mountains, the salt tramway becomes visible. Look for it standing out starkly on the crests of the hills. The wooden tramway towers are well preserved in this dry climate.

The trail undulates steeply as it enters the range, at times with grades up to 25 degrees. At some spots, it is difficult to get traction on the shale surface. The views improve as you climb, with the Sierra Nevada coming fully into view. Driver will want to keep their eyes on the road, particularly around some of the narrow and rough sections of shelf road. The shelf road is narrow, with very limited passing places at times.

A spur leads 1.5 miles to the site of the Burgess Mine, where there is an excellent view over Saline Valley and the Nelson and Panamint Ranges. There is a small cabin left at the mine, plus tailings heaps, diggings, and some stone foundations.

High above Saline Valley, aerial tramway timbers are preserved by the dry climate

Overlooking Owens Valley and the Sierra Nevada

The main trail now runs around the head of Craig Canyon, with a dizzying, sheer drop-off into the canyon, and down toward Saline Valley. It passes under a section of the salt tramway, which sits next to the control station tender's cabin. The cabin and tramway are listed on the National Register of Historic Places. This is one of the most accessible points along the trail to reach the tramway, where it plunges down off the range, heading north toward Saline Valley.

The trail finishes by wrapping down off the range to join Desert #47: Cerro Gordo Road at the ghost town of Cerro Gordo. The town site is privately owned, but tours can be arranged by calling ahead at (760) 876-5030.

The final section of the trail crosses private property around Cerro Gordo. Please remain on the main trail.

Current Road Information

Death Valley National Park
PO Box 579
Death Valley, CA 92328-0579
(760) 786-3200

Bureau of Land Management
Bishop Field Office
351 Pacu Lane, Suite 100
Bishop, CA 93514
(760) 872-5000

Map References

BLM   Saline Valley
USGS 1:24,000 Dolomite, New York
       Butte, Cerro Gordo Peak
       1:100,000 Saline Valley
Maptech CD-ROM: Kings Canyon/Death
       Valley
Southern & Central California Atlas &
       Gazetteer, pp. 27, 28
California Road & Recreation Atlas, p. 87
Trails Illustrated, Death Valley National
       Park (221)
Other: Free NPS Death Valley map; Tom
       Harrison Maps—Death Valley
       National Park Recreation Map

Route Directions

▼ 0.0   From California 136 at the site of
            Swansea, 9.1 miles east of US 395 and
            Lone Pine, zero trip meter and turn east
            on formed dirt trail. The turn is not well
            marked. It leaves immediately north of
            a private house and there is a small
            wooden "Welcome to Swansea" sign
            at the turn. The historical marker is
            opposite, set back from the road. There
            is a sign once you are on the road for
            the Swansea–Cerro Gordo Road.
12.3 ▲   Trail ends on California 136 at the site
            of Swansea. Turn right for US 395 and
            Lone Pine; turn left for Death Valley.
            GPS: N36°31.46′ W117°54.26′

▼ 0.3 SO Track on left.
12.0 ▲ SO Track on right.
▼ 1.2 SO Cross through wash.
11.1 ▲ SO Cross through wash.
         GPS: N36°32.43′ W117°53.97′

▼ 1.4 SO Cross through wash. Trail follows
            along line of wash.
10.9 ▲ SO Cross through wash. Trail leaves line
            of wash.
▼ 1.6 SO Track on left.
10.7 ▲ SO Track on right.
▼ 2.0 SO Remains of salt tramway on left and
            right on hill.
10.3 ▲ SO Remains of salt tramway on right and
            left on hill.

GPS: N36°33.04′ W117°54.04′

▼ 2.7 SO Enter wash in tight canyon.
9.6 ▲ SO Exit wash.
▼ 3.1 SO Exit wash up steep pinch; then cross
            through wash.
9.2 ▲ SO Cross through wash; then descend
            steep pinch to enter wash.
         GPS: N36°33.72′ W117°54.03′

▼ 3.2 SO Hiking trail on saddle on right goes
            to tramway support.
9.1 ▲ SO Hiking trail on saddle on left goes
            to tramway support.
▼ 3.5 SO Cross through wash and start to climb.
8.8 ▲ SO End of descent. Cross through wash.
▼ 4.2 SO End of climb.
8.1 ▲ SO Start to descend.
▼ 4.6 SO Enter wash.
7.7 ▲ SO Exit wash.
▼ 4.9 SO Exit wash.
7.4 ▲ SO Enter wash.
▼ 5.4 SO Enter wash.
6.9 ▲ SO Exit wash.
         GPS: N36°33.68′ W117°52.66′

▼ 7.9 SO Salt tramway remains up hillside on
            right and fallen remains on left.
4.4 ▲ SO Salt tramway remains up hillside on
            left and fallen remains on right.
         GPS: N36°35.31′ W117°52.04′

▼ 8.9 BL Exit wash.
3.4 ▲ BR Enter wash.
         GPS: N36°35.46′ W117°53.22′

▼ 9.0 SO Cross through wash. Enter line of
            wash, crossing it often.
3.3 ▲ SO Cross through wash. Exit line of
            wash.
▼ 10.0 SO Exit line of wash.
2.3 ▲ SO Enter line of wash, crossing it often.
         GPS: N36°36.21′ W117°53.68′

▼ 10.1 SO Campsite and viewpoint on left.
2.2 ▲ SO Campsite and viewpoint on right.
▼ 10.8 SO Track on left.
1.5 ▲ SO Track on right.
         GPS: N36°36.63′ W117°53.82′

DESERT #48: SWANSEA-CERRO GORDO ROAD

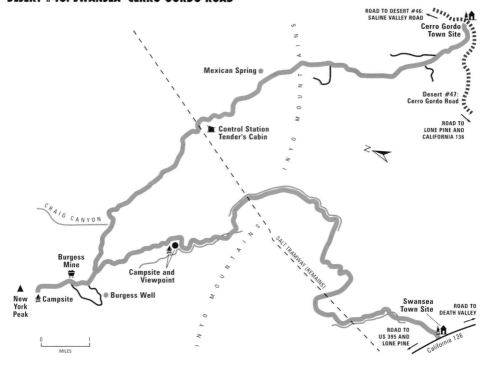

▼ 12.3 TR Well-used track on left in open flat area is spur to Burgess Mine. Zero trip meter. Intersection is unmarked.

0.0 ▲ Continue to the southeast.

GPS: N36°37.53' W117°54.69'

Spur to the Burgess Mine

▼ 0.0 Zero trip meter and proceed west on formed trail.

▼ 0.2 BR Track on left is a 1.3-mile loop past Burgess Well.

GPS: N36°37.62' W117°54.92'

▼ 0.7 BL Burgess Mine on right—many tailings heaps, old miner's cabin, and stone foundations remain. There is an exceptional view from this point east over Saline Valley and the Nelson and Panamint Ranges.

GPS: N36°37.96' W117°54.98'

▼ 1.4 SO Track on left.

▼ 1.5 Spur ends at turning circle and camp-

site at the base of New York Peak.

GPS: N36°38.49' W117°55.34'

Continuation of Main Trail

▼ 0.0 Continue to the east.

4.0 ▲ TL Well-used track straight ahead in open flat area is spur to Burgess Mine. Zero trip meter. Intersection is unmarked.

GPS: N36°37.53' W117°54.69

▼ 0.8 SO Sheer drop-off on left into Craig Canyon and down to Saline Valley.

3.2 ▲ SO Sheer drop-off on right into Craig Canyon and down to Saline Valley.

▼ 3.8 SO Salt tramway remains on left, immediately on the hill and farther down.

0.2 ▲ SO Salt tramway remains on right, immediately on the hill and farther down.

GPS: N36°36.54' W117°51.30'

▼ 4.0 SO Pass under aerial tramway. Zero trip meter.

0.0 ▲ Continue to the northwest.

▼ 0.0   Continue to the southeast. Control station tender's cabin on right.

6.7 ▲   SO   Control station tender's cabin on left; then pass under aerial tramway. Zero trip meter.

▼ 1.9   BR   Two tracks on left lead into wilderness and are closed to vehicles.

4.8 ▲   BL   Two tracks on right lead into wilderness and are closed to vehicles.
              GPS: N36°35.43′ W117°49.76′

▼ 2.5   SO   Mine below trail on left.

4.2 ▲   SO   Mine below trail on right.
              GPS: N36°34.98′ W117°49.36′

▼ 3.1   SO   Track on right. Start of steep, loose descent.

3.6 ▲   SO   Track on left. End of climb.
              GPS: N36°34.54′ W117°49.21′

▼ 4.2   SO   Enter wash.

2.5 ▲   SO   Exit wash.
              GPS: N36°33.69′ W117°49.19′

▼ 4.6   SO   End of descent. Trail starts to climb again.

2.1 ▲   SO   End of descent. Trail starts to climb again.

▼ 5.6   SO   End of climb. Well-used track on right; then track on left. Start of shelf road.

1.1 ▲   SO   End of shelf road. Track on right; then well-used track on left. Trail starts to descend.
              GPS: N36°32.73′ W117°48.48′

▼ 6.6   SO   Gate. Entering private property of Cerro Gordo.

0.1 ▲   SO   Gate. Leaving private property.

▼ 6.7   Join larger graded road and bear right, leaving both graded roads on left. Trail finishes on Desert #47: Cerro Gordo Road, immediately north of Cerro Gordo ghost town. Turn left to exit to Desert #46: Saline Valley Road; turn right to exit back to California 136 and Lone Pine.

0.0 ▲   Trail starts 0.1 miles north of Cerro Gordo ghost town on Desert #47: Cerro Gordo Road. Zero trip meter and proceed northwest on graded road and

immediately swing left onto unmarked, formed trail that wraps around the hill, leaving two graded roads on the right. You know you are on the correct trail when you pass the Swansea–Cerro Gordo Road warning sign, 0.1 miles from the start of the formed trail.
              GPS: N36°32.36′ W117°47.62′

DESERT #49

Hidden Valley Road

STARTING POINT: Desert #51: Racetrack Road, 21.3 miles from intersection with Big Pine Road

FINISHING POINT: Desert #46: Saline Valley Road, 15.5 miles north of California 190

TOTAL MILEAGE: 28.5 miles, including both spurs

UNPAVED MILEAGE: 28.5 miles

DRIVING TIME: 3 hours

ELEVATION RANGE: 4,100–7,300 feet

USUALLY OPEN: Year-round

BEST TIME TO TRAVEL: October to April

DIFFICULTY RATING: 2

SCENIC RATING: 9

REMOTENESS RATING: +1

Special Attractions

- Extensive remains of the Lost Burro Mine.
- The Ubehebe Talc Mine and other mining camps.
- Hiking access into Death Valley Wilderness.
- Can be combined with Desert #51: Racetrack Road and Desert #46: Saline Valley Road to form a loop trail from Scotty's Castle or Panamint Springs.

History

The site of what became the Lost Burro Mine was discovered in 1907 by Bert Shively. The prospector was chasing his straying burro when he picked up a rock that contained gold. There was a water-powered 5-

stamp mill at the site, running on water piped in from Burro Spring, 8 miles away. The mine had many different owners; its most profitable years were between 1912 and 1917.

Description

Hidden Valley Road leaves Desert #51: Racetrack Road at Teakettle Junction. The name of the intersection has resulted in a number of teakettles being hung from the signpost, many of them inscribed with the thoughts of passing travelers. The National Park Service removes some of them periodically, but they are typically replaced as quickly as they are removed. This unique piece of folk art makes the start of Hidden Valley Road difficult to miss.

A short distance from the start, the trail enters Lost Burro Gap, a narrow canyon of tilted, striated rock. The trail follows a gravelly wash through this short but picturesque gap.

A very worthwhile detour from the main trail is the short side trail to Lost Burro Mine. The site includes extensive mining remains set in a tight, small canyon. A miner's cabin, outhouse, and various wooden structures remain. Opposite the turn to Lost Burro Mine, a second trail leads to White Top Mountain.

Continuing along Hidden Valley Road, the trail dips down to enter the long, wide Hidden Valley. A saddle divides the valley from Ulida Flat. Several spur trails on both sides lead to the remains of old mining camps on the flat. One worthwhile trail is the spur to Ubehebe Talc Mine, where various remains can still be seen and photographed.

Past the flats and mining areas, the road climbs above 7,000 feet. The wide shelf road is easygoing as it twists through pinyons and junipers to wind along the top of Hunter Mountain. In winter, this section can be icy and may be blocked by snow. Chains should be carried in winter months.

The trail finishes by descending from Hunter Mountain to join Desert #46: Saline Valley Road at South Pass. The Panamint Dunes and Panamint Dry Lake can be seen

DESERT #49: HIDDEN VALLEY ROAD

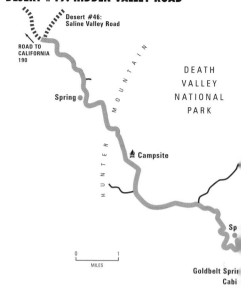

to the south from this intersection.

Current Road Information

Death Valley National Park
PO Box 579
Death Valley, CA 92328-0579
(760) 786-3200

Map References

BLM   Saline Valley
USGS   1:24,000   Teakettle Junction,
       Ubehebe Peak, Sand Flat, Harris
       Hill, Jackass Canyon
       1:100,000 Saline Valley
Maptech CD-ROM: Kings Canyon/Death
       Valley
Southern & Central California Atlas &
       Gazetteer, p. 28
California Road & Recreation Atlas, p. 87
Trails Illustrated, Death Valley National
       Park (221)
Other: Free NPS Death Valley map

Route Directions

▼ 0.0   From Desert #51: Racetrack Road at
         Teakettle Junction, 21.3 miles south of
         the intersection with Big Pine Road
         near Grapevine, zero trip meter and

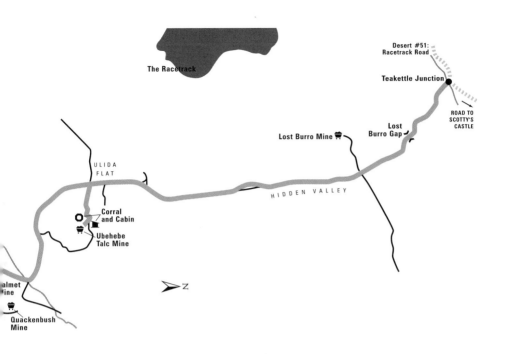

turn southeast on graded dirt trail,
following sign to Hunter Mountain.

3.1 ▲   Trail ends at Teakettle Junction on
Desert #51: Racetrack Road. Turn left
to visit The Racetrack; turn right to exit
via Racetrack Road to Scotty's Castle.
GPS: N36°45.61' W117°32.48'

▼ 0.1 SO Cross through wash.

3.0 ▲ SO Cross through wash.

▼ 1.2 SO Entering Lost Burro Gap. Trail is traveling in wash.

1.9 ▲ SO Exiting Lost Burro Gap and wash.
GPS: N36°44.91' W117°31.49'

▼ 1.8 SO Exiting Lost Burro Gap.

1.3 ▲ SO Entering Lost Burro Gap.

▼ 2.4 SO Exit line of wash.

0.7 ▲ SO Enter line of wash.

▼ 3.1 SO 4-way intersection. Track on right goes
1.2 miles to Lost Burro Mine. Track on
left travels toward White Top
Mountain. Zero trip meter.

0.0 ▲   Continue to the northwest, exiting
Hidden Valley.
GPS: N36°43.78' W117°30.26'

▼ 0.0   Continue to the southeast, entering
Hidden Valley.

6.4 ▲ SO 4-way intersection. Track on left goes
1.2 miles to Lost Burro Mine. Track on
right travels toward White Top
Mountain. Zero trip meter.

▼ 1.4 SO Track on left.

5.0 ▲ SO Track on right.

▼ 2.3 BR Track on left is old road (not used).
Deep, fine dirt traps for next 0.7 miles.

4.1 ▲ SO Track on right is old road rejoining.

▼ 3.0 SO Track on left is old road rejoining.

3.4 ▲ BL Track on right is old road (not used).
Deep, fine dirt traps for next 0.7 miles.

▼ 5.0 SO Track on right is a short dead end.

1.4 ▲ SO Second entrance to track on left.
GPS: N36°39.38' W117°29.95'

▼ 5.2 SO Second entrance to track on right.

1.2 ▲ SO Track on left is a short dead end.

▼ 5.3 SO Saddle. Leaving Hidden Valley and
entering Ulida Flat.

1.1 ▲ SO Saddle. Leaving Ulida Flat and entering
Hidden Valley.
GPS: N36°39.21' W117°30.08'

▼ 6.1 SO Track on left.

0.3 ▲ SO Track on right.

▼ 6.4 SO Well-used track on left is spur to

Lost Burro Mine cabin remains intact. High winds can be one of the most destructive forces in this region

Ubehebe Talc Mine. Also track on right. Zero trip meter.

0.0 ▲ Continue to the north.

GPS: N36°38.20' W117°30.07'

Spur to Ubehebe Talc Mine

▼ 0.0   Proceed east on well-used, unmarked trail.

▼ 0.1   SO   Track on right returns to main trail. Sign for Ubehebe Talc Mine.

▼ 0.4   SO   Enter line of wash.

▼ 0.6   SO   Exit line of wash and climb up side of hill.

GPS: N36°38.15' W117°29.41'

▼ 0.9   SO   Saddle. Remains of mine are visible ahead and on the right.

GPS: N36°38.21' W117°29.21'

▼ 1.0   BR   Cabin on left and old corral on right; then track on left down line of wash.

▼ 1.2   UT   Trail ends at Ubehebe Talc Mine.

GPS: N36°38.04' W117°29.08'

Continuation of Main Trail

▼ 0.0   Continue to the south.

3.1 ▲   SO   Well-used track on right is spur to Ubehebe Talc Mine. Also track on left. Zero trip meter.

GPS: N36°38.20' W117°30.07'

▼ 0.2   SO   Track on left is second entrance to Ubehebe Talc Mine spur.

2.9 ▲   SO   Track on right is alternate entrance to Ubehebe Talc Mine spur.

▼ 1.6   SO   Saddle. Exiting Ulida Flat.

1.5 ▲   SO   Saddle. Entering Ulida Flat.

GPS: N36°37.10' W117°29.24'

▼ 1.9   SO   Small track on left goes to mining camp.

1.2 ▲   SO   Small track on right goes to mining camp.

GPS: N36°37.15' W117°28.85'

▼ 2.3   SO   Cross through wash.

0.8 ▲   SO   Cross through wash.

▼ 2.6   SO   Enter line of wash.

0.5 ▲   SO   Exit line of wash.

▼ 2.8   SO   Exit line of wash.

0.3 ▲   SO   Enter line of wash.

▼ 3.1   BR   Trail forks. Track on left goes to mine.

		Bear right and zero trip meter.
0.0 ▲		Continue to the north.

GPS: N36°36.97′ W117°27.73′

▼ 0.0		Continue to the south and cross through wash.
0.9 ▲	SO	Cross through wash. Track on right goes to mine. Zero trip meter.
▼ 0.9	BR	Trail forks. Intersection is unmarked. Track on left is spur to Calmet and Quackenbush Mines. Zero trip meter.
0.0 ▲		Continue to the west.

GPS: N36°36.20′ W117°27.84′

Calmet and Quackenbush Mine Spur

▼ 0.0		Proceed east.
▼ 0.3	SO	Track on right rejoins main trail. Calmet Mine on left.

GPS: N36°36.11′ W117°27.57′

▼ 0.5	SO	Enter line of wash.
▼ 0.8	SO	Exit line of wash; then track on left to Quackenbush Mine.

GPS: N36°36.04′ W117°26.99′

▼ 1.0	BR	Track on left to old cabin.
▼ 1.1	UT	Spur ends at old mining remains near Goldbelt Spring, once the locality of Goldbelt mining camp.

GPS: N36°35.89′ W117°26.83′

Continuation of Main Trail

▼ 0.0		Continue to the south. Trail starts to climb.
3.6 ▲	BL	End of descent. Trail forks. Intersection is unmarked. Track on right is spur to Calmet and Quackenbush Mines. Zero trip meter.

GPS: N36°36.20′ W117°27.84′

▼ 0.4	SO	Track on left is second entrance to Calmet and Quackenbush Mine spur.
3.2 ▲	BL	Track on right is alternate entrance to Calmet and Quackenbush Mine spur.
▼ 1.2	SO	Spring on right.
2.4 ▲	SO	Spring on left.

Striated rock within Lost Burro Gap

Lost Burro Mine is well preserved in the dry atmosphere of the Panamint Range

GPS: N36°35.55' W117°27.82'

▼ 3.1   SO   End of climb. Trail is now running over
             Hunter Mountain.
0.5 ▲   SO   Start of descent off Hunter Mountain.
▼ 3.5   SO   Cattle guard.
0.1 ▲   SO   Cattle guard.
             GPS: N36°34.78' W117°28.65'

▼ 3.6   SO   Well-used track on right. Zero trip meter.
0.0 ▲   Continue to the north.
             GPS: N36°34.72' W117°28.70'

▼ 0.0   Continue to the south.
6.8 ▲   SO   Well-used track on left. Zero trip meter.
▼ 1.6   SO   Track on left over cattle guard.
5.2 ▲   SO   Track on right over cattle guard.
             GPS: N36°33.45' W117°29.02'

▼ 2.6   SO   Track on right and campsite on right.
4.2 ▲   SO   Track on left and campsite on left.
▼ 4.0   SO   Trail starts to descend toward Mill Canyon.
2.8 ▲   SO   End of climb. Trail is now running over
             Hunter Mountain.
▼ 4.9   SO   Spring on left.
1.9 ▲   SO   Spring on right.
             GPS: N36°32.44' W117°31.40'

▼ 5.2   SO   Track on right.
1.6 ▲   SO   Track on left.
             GPS: N36°32.39' W117°31.75'

▼ 5.7   SO   Track on right.
1.1 ▲   SO   Track on left.
▼ 6.8   Trail ends at intersection with Desert
             #46: Saline Valley Road on South
             Pass, 15.5 miles north of California
             190. Turn left for California 190; turn
             right to travel along Saline Valley Road.
0.0 ▲   Trail commences on Desert #46:
             Saline Valley Road on South Pass, 15.5
             miles north of California 190. Zero trip
             meter and turn north on unmarked,
             well-used graded dirt road that starts
             to climb Hunter Mountain. There are
             views south of Panamint Dry Lake and
             the Panamint Dunes.
             GPS: N36°31.62' W117°32.75'

Lippincott Mine Road

STARTING POINT: Desert #46: Saline Valley
Road, 10 miles north of intersection
with Desert #49: Hidden Valley Road
FINISHING POINT: Lippincott Mine
TOTAL MILEAGE: 8 miles
UNPAVED MILEAGE: 8 miles
DRIVING TIME: 1.5 hours
ELEVATION RANGE: 2,000–3,900 feet
USUALLY OPEN: Year-round
BEST TIME TO TRAVEL: October to May
DIFFICULTY RATING: 4
SCENIC RATING: 9
REMOTENESS RATING: +1

Special Attractions
■ Rugged, moderately challenging 4WD
  trail within Death Valley National Park.
■ Remains of the Lippincott Mine.
■ Trail provides a link between Desert #51:
  Racetrack Road and Desert #46: Saline
  Valley Road for high-clearance 4WD
  vehicles.

Description
Lippincott Mine Road is not signposted at either end, and it does not appear on the free
map handed out by the rangers when you enter the park. However, the road does exist and
it is well traveled by those in the know. The
trail connects dusty Desert #46: Saline Valley
Road with Desert #51: Racetrack Road, both
roughly graded dirt roads suitable for high-
clearance vehicles. Lippincott Mine Road,
however, requires a 4WD vehicle because of
the loose and lumpy nature of the trail and
the narrowness of the shelf road. In addition,
the trail receives little maintenance and is
quite eroded. Even a scant inch of rain can
cause the loose trail to wash out to the point
of impassability.
   The intersection at the start of the trail is
marked by a cairn and a sign warning about
the rough road ahead. The trail begins by
heading east from Saline Valley Road and
gradually climbing the bajada to the canyon.

Old mining equipment at the upper level of the Lippincott Mine overlooking The Racetrack

DESERT #50: LIPPINCOTT MINE ROAD

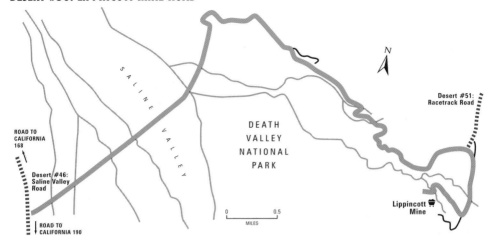

It winds into an unnamed, tight canyon and starts to climb, gaining nearly 2,000 feet in the next 5 miles.

The trail within the canyon is slow going. Large embedded boulders require careful wheel placement and some washouts reduce the trail to a single vehicle width. However, with a careful driver, the trail is traversable by most high-clearance 4WDs. Drivers should be aware that conditions can be worse than those described here because the trail receives little maintenance.

The trail snakes its way up, giving excellent views back toward the Saline Valley and the mountains beyond. From the top of the trail, the Lippincott Mine is visible on the far side of the canyon. The trail briefly joins the final graded section of road off of Desert #51: Racetrack Road, passing the end of this trail before dropping in standard again to a rough, loose 4WD trail. Two separate spurs lead to different parts of the Lippincott Mine; both have various remains.

The trail is usually open all year, though it may be closed after heavy rain. It is uncomfortably hot for both you and your vehicle in summer and it may be icy in winter.

Current Road Information
Death Valley National Park
PO Box 579
Death Valley, CA 92328-0579
(760) 786-3200

Map References
BLM   Saline Valley
USGS 1:24,000   Nelson Range, West of Ubehebe Peak, Ubehebe Peak
1:100,000 Saline Valley
Maptech CD-ROM: Kings Canyon/Death Valley
Southern & Central California Atlas & Gazetteer, p. 28
California Road & Recreation Atlas, p. 87
Trails Illustrated, Death Valley National Park (221)

Route Directions

▼ 0.0   Trail commences on Desert #46: Saline Valley Road, 10 miles north of the end of Desert #49: Hidden Valley Road. Zero trip meter and turn northeast on graded dirt track. Intersection is unmarked apart from a large cairn.

6.7 ▲   Trail ends on Desert #46: Saline Valley Road. Turn left to exit to California 190 and Lone Pine; turn right to exit to California 168 and the Owens Valley.
GPS: N36°37.20′ W117°38.88′

▼ 0.1   SO Warning sign for Lippincott Road.
6.6 ▲   SO Warning sign for Lippincott Road.
▼ 0.3   SO Cross through wash.
6.4 ▲   SO Cross through wash.
▼ 0.7   SO Cross through wash.

Lippincott Mine Road descends to Saline Valley

6.0 ▲   SO Cross through wash.
▼ 0.8   SO Cross through wash.
5.9 ▲   SO Cross through wash.
▼ 1.0   SO Cross through wide wash.
5.7 ▲   SO Cross through wide wash.
▼ 1.2   SO Cross through wash.
5.5 ▲   SO Cross through wash.
▼ 1.3   SO Cross through wash.
5.4 ▲   SO Cross through wash.
▼ 1.4   SO Cross through wash.
5.3 ▲   SO Cross through wash.
▼ 1.9   SO Cross through wide wash.
4.8 ▲   SO Cross through wide wash.
▼ 2.1   SO Cross through wide wash.
4.6 ▲   SO Cross through wide wash.
▼ 2.3   SO Cross through wide wash. Leave baja-

da and start to climb away from Saline
Valley.
4.4 ▲   SO End of descent. Start to cross bajada.
        Cross through wide wash.
        GPS: N36°38.81′ W117°37.41′

▼ 2.5   SO Start of shelf road.
4.2 ▲   SO End of shelf road.
▼ 3.7   SO Faint track on left.
3.0 ▲   SO Faint track on right.
▼ 3.9   SO Track on left to mine.
2.8 ▲   SO Track on right to mine.
        GPS: N36°38.89′ W117°36.34′

▼ 4.1   SO Adit on left.
2.6 ▲   SO Adit on right.

▼ 4.2	SO	Old Death Valley National Park boundary at metal sign.
2.5 ▲	SO	Old Death Valley National Park boundary at metal sign.

GPS: N36°38.82′ W117°36.13′

▼ 4.4	SO	Cross through wash.
2.3 ▲	SO	Cross through wash.
▼ 4.6	SO	Cross through wash.
2.1 ▲	SO	Cross through wash.
▼ 4.8	SO	Cross through wash.
1.9 ▲	SO	Cross through wash.
▼ 5.2	SO	Cross through wash.
1.5 ▲	SO	Cross through wash.
▼ 5.9	SO	End of climb from Saline Valley. The Lippincott Mine is visible on the south side of the canyon wall.
0.8 ▲	SO	Start of descent to Saline Valley.
▼ 6.5	SO	Road standard improves to graded dirt at a small turning circle.
0.2 ▲	SO	Warning sign for Lippincott Road. Road standard is now a rough, formed trail that starts to descend toward Saline Valley.

GPS: N36°38.44′ W117°34.70′

▼ 6.7	BR	Trail forks. Graded road on left is Desert #51: Racetrack Road. Zero trip meter. Intersection is unsigned.
0.0 ▲		Continue to the south.

GPS: N36°38.47′ W117°34.51′

▼ 0.0		Continue to the east. Trail is now a spur.
▼ 0.1	SO	Second entrance to Desert #51: Racetrack Road.
▼ 0.2	SO	Start of Lippincott Mine Area. Camping permitted for next 0.2 miles.

GPS: N36°38.36′ W117°34.43′

▼ 0.3	BR	Track on left. There are a few exposed campsites in this area.
▼ 0.4	SO	Track on right joins. Trail drops to cross through wash.
▼ 0.5	SO	Cross through wide wash.
▼ 0.7	BR	Old yellow water tank on left; then track on left goes 0.5 miles to an upper level of the Lippincott Mine.

GPS: N36°37.93′ W117°34.43′

▼ 1.2	SO	Cross through wash.

▼ 1.3		Trail ends at the Lippincott Mine. Adit and various remains, including the loading hopper and part of the old tramway, are scattered around.

GPS: N36°38.08′ W117°34.84′

Racetrack Road

STARTING POINT: Big Pine Road, 2.7 miles west of Grapevine on North Highway

FINISHING POINT: Desert #50: Lippincott Mine Road, 1.3 miles west of Lippincott Mine

TOTAL MILEAGE: 30.5 miles

UNPAVED MILEAGE: 27.8 miles

DRIVING TIME: 2.25 hours

ELEVATION RANGE: 2,000–5,000

USUALLY OPEN: Year-round

BEST TIME TO TRAVEL: October to May

DIFFICULTY RATING: 2

SCENIC RATING: 9

REMOTENESS RATING: +1

Special Attractions
■ Ubehebe Crater.
■ Racetrack Playa and the mysterious moving rocks.

History
Ubehebe Crater was formed several thousand years ago by a volcanic eruption. Magma rose to the surface, contacting groundwater. The build-up of steam pressure caused an explosion of such force that it created the crater you see today. The crater is 500 feet deep and half a mile wide. Rock debris from the explosion covers an area of several square miles. Several smaller craters, formed at a later time, can be found to the south of the main crater. *Ubehebe* (pronounced "yew-beh-HEE-bee") is an Indian word meaning "big basket in the rock."

South of the crater, the Ubehebe Mine was first established in 1875, but was not developed until 1906. The mine produced copper, lead, and zinc. However, its remote location meant that it would not be profitable until the value of copper increased.

The huge pit of Ubehebe Crater was formed several thousand years ago by a volcanic eruption

This finally happened when copper wiring became essential for domestic electricity.

In 1906, Jack Salsberry purchased the mine. A tent city known as Salina City sprang up to service the mine. Situated in Racetrack Valley, Salina City had two saloons, a store, and a stage station. However it did not have a post office. Most of the workers lived in tents on the valley floor.

Jack Salsberry also surveyed a railroad grade that would connect the Ubehebe Mine to the Las Vegas & Tonopah Railroad tracks at Bonnie Claire, Nevada. The grade was supposed to run up Grapevine Canyon. Although construction of the line was started, the mine did not warrant the outlay and the railroad was abandoned. Racetrack Road follows the surveyed grade from Ubehebe Crater to the mine. The mine was last worked in 1951.

The famous moving rocks at The Racetrack are not the only example of this phenomenon to be found near Death Valley, but they are the best known. Other playas in the area also show evidence of the mysterious movement. The real reason the rocks move is unknown. It was originally thought that magnetic forces somehow caused the rocks to move. The current theory is that a combination of rain or ice on the playa makes its surface slick enough that the rocks are moved by gusts of high wind. Although it is a little hard to believe—some of the rocks weigh up to 500 pounds and the force needed to move them under any conditions would be considerable—nobody has come up with a more plausible explanation.

Description

Racetrack Road is a long, graded dirt road that runs from Ubehebe Crater down a long valley to The Racetrack—a dry lakebed, famous for its legendary moving rocks.

Initially, the road follows a small, one-way loop past the large deep pit of Ubehebe Crater. The graded dirt road starts here and heads south, down the long valley between the Panamint Range to the east and the Last Chance Range to the west. The valley is carpeted with sagebrush and creosote bush, interspersed with clumps of cotton-top cactus growing on the alluvial fan. The road can be very washboardy depending on how recently it was graded. But apart from the bumpy ride, it is an easy drive for high-clearance 2WD vehicles; on occasion passenger vehicles can make the trip.

The intersection with Desert #49: Hidden Valley Road comes at Teakettle Junction. The signpost is always adorned with a number of teakettles, some brand new, some old and battered. The kettles are hung in disarray on the signpost and passing travelers often leave their names and thoughts inscribed on them. When there are too many, park rangers remove some of the kettles, but they always leave a good selection.

The Racetrack playa comes into view 5.6 miles after Teakettle Junction. The smooth surface of the dry lake is broken by The Grandstand, an outcropping of rock that protrudes through the lakebed. The moving rocks can be found at the southern end of the playa. It is approximately a half-mile walk over the flat surface to reach the rocks. You can see rocks that have traveled (often a great distance) across the bed. The imprint of their tracks can clearly be seen. Why the rocks move is a mystery but it is these moving rocks that give The Racetrack its name.

Racetrack Road ends a couple of miles farther, at the intersection with Desert #50: Lippincott Mine Road. This rough trail is a shorter exit to Desert #46: Saline Valley Road, but it is suitable for high-clearance 4WD vehicles only.

Current Road Information

Death Valley National Park
PO Box 579
Death Valley, CA 92328-0579
(760) 786-3200

Map References

BLM   Last Chance Range, Saline Valley
USGS 1:24,000   Ubehebe Crater, Tin
        Mtn., Dry Mtn., White Top Mtn.,
        Teakettle Junction, Ubehebe Peak
        1:100,000 Last Chance Range,
        Saline Valley
Maptech CD-ROM: Kings Canyon/Death
        Valley
Southern & Central California Atlas &

DESERT #51: RACETRACK ROAD

Gazetteer, p. 28
California Road & Recreation Atlas,
     pp. 80, 87
Trails Illustrated, Death Valley National
     Park (221)
Other: Free NPS Death Valley map

The Grandstand on the Racetrack playa

Route Directions

▼ 0.0   From Big Pine Road, 2.7 miles west of
          Grapevine on North Highway, zero trip
          meter and proceed northwest on
          paved road following the sign to
          Ubehebe Crater. Big Pine Road contin-
          ues as a graded dirt road to the north.
2.4 ▲   Trail ends on Big Pine Road. Continue
          to the east on Big Pine Road to exit to
          Grapevine and Scotty's Castle.
          GPS: N37°01.07′ W117°24.63′

▼ 0.3 SO Cross through Death Valley Wash.
2.1 ▲ SO Cross through Death Valley Wash.
▼ 2.4 BR Road on left is exit from Ubehebe
          Crater. Start of one-way road section.
          Zero trip meter and continue reading
          Forward Directions
0.0 ▲ SO Road on left is entry to Ubehebe
          Crater. End of one-way road.
          GPS: N37°00.86′ W117°27.18′

Forward Directions

▼ 0.0   Continue to the northwest.
▼ 0.3 TR Turn right onto graded dirt Racetrack
          Road at sign. Zero trip meter. Ubehebe
          Crater is straight ahead. To visit the
          crater, follow around the loop and
          return to this point.
          GPS: N37°00.78′ W117°27.41′

Reverse Directions

0.0 ▲   Continue to the southeast.
0.3 ▲ SO Ubehebe Crater on right.
          GPS: N37°00.67′ W117°27.24′

0.6 ▲   End of one-way section. Zero trip
          meter. Turn left to continue along
          Racetrack Road; turn right to continue
          the trail in the reverse direction to Big
          Pine Road.
          GPS: N37°00.86′ W117°27.18′

DEATH VALLEY

Located on the northern edge of the great Mojave Desert, Death Valley is characterized by one of the harshest climates in the world. It was a thoroughfare for some early travelers into California, but one that they may have preferred to avoid. Water is scarce, and the few oases are widely spaced. The region receives less than 2 inches of rain per year, and daytime summer temperatures regularly exceed 120 degrees Fahrenheit. Truly the area has earned its name; more than 500 people have perished in the heat. Local place names express the forbidding nature of the land: Hells Gate, Coffin Peak, Funeral Peak, Badwater Basin, and Dantes View. Local Indian tribes called the area To-me-sha, which means "ground on fire."

Situated between the Amargosa Range and Black Mountains to the east and the Panamint Range to the west, Death Valley is a youngster in geological terms. Like the coastal ranges and the Sierra Nevada, it was created by a complex series of tectonic movements. It sits on the continental North American plate and has faults that occur as the plate stretches and moves. The result is what geologists call a pull-apart basin. The bordering mountains rise as the valley sinks or subsides.

Volcanic activity is frequently associated with such tectonic movements, and there are numerous lava flows and craters throughout the region. The Ubehebe Crater, along Desert #51: Racetrack Road in the north-central part of the park, is just one example.

Death Valley

Also found along that trail are Death Valley's famous moving rocks (pictured above). Within the park, Telescope Peak (11,049 feet) is not far from Badwater Basin (-282 feet), the lowest point in the Western Hemisphere. Mount Whitney, the highest point in the coterminus United States, is fewer than 100 miles away. These extremes typify the astounding difference in relief and the wide variety of landforms within the park. From Zabriskie Point, you can see badlands, evidence of volcanic activity, salt flats, and alluvial fans.

Continuation of Main Trail

▼ 0.0   Continue to the west on graded dirt road. End of one-way road. No camping allowed for next 2 miles.

18.6 ▲   Turn right onto paved road into Ubehebe Crater. No entry to road on left, part of the one-way system around the crater. Zero trip meter and continue reading Reverse Directions.
         GPS: N37°00.78' W117°27.41'

▼ 2.9   SO Track on left.
15.7 ▲   SO Track on right.
         GPS: N36°58.40' W117°28.16'

▼ 3.2   SO Cross through wash.
15.4 ▲   SO Cross through wash.
▼ 12.8   SO Largest peak on left is Tin Mountain.
5.8 ▲   SO Largest peak on right is Tin Mountain.
         GPS: N36°50.27' W117°30.15'

▼ 16.4   SO Cross through wash.
2.2 ▲   SO Cross through wash.
▼ 18.5   SO Cross through wash.
0.1 ▲   SO Cross through wash.
▼ 18.6   SO Teakettle Junction. Zero trip meter and continue on Racetrack Road, following

Teakettle Junction

sign to The Racetrack. Track on left is Desert #49: Hidden Valley Road.

0.0 ▲   Continue to the northeast.
         GPS: N36°45.61' W117°32.48'

▼ 0.0   Continue to the southwest.
2.2 ▲   SO Teakettle Junction. Zero trip meter and continue on Racetrack Road. Track on right is Desert #49: Hidden Valley Road.
▼ 0.3   SO Cross through wash.
1.9 ▲   SO Cross through wash.
▼ 2.1   BL Track on right joins Ubehebe Mine track. Second track on right.
0.1 ▲   SO Track on left and second entrance to Ubehebe Mine on left.
▼ 2.2   SO Graded road on right goes 0.7 miles into the Ubehebe Mine. Zero trip meter.
0.0 ▲   Continue to the north.
         GPS: N36°44.66' W117°34.45'

▼ 0.0   Continue to the southeast.
5.3 ▲   BR Graded road on left goes 0.7 miles into the Ubehebe Mine. Zero trip meter.
▼ 3.4   SO Pull-in for The Grandstand on left.
1.9 ▲   SO Pull-in for The Grandstand on right.
         GPS: N36°41.66' W117°34.24'

▼ 5.3   SO Turnout on left is viewing point for the moving rocks. Zero trip meter.
0.0 ▲   Continue to the north.
         GPS: N36°39.95' W117°34.04'

▼ 0.0   Continue to the south.
1.7 ▲   SO Turnout on right is viewing point for the moving rocks. Zero trip meter.
▼ 1.7   Trail ends at T-intersection with Desert #50: Lippincott Mine Road. Turn left to visit the Lippincott Mine; turn right to exit to Desert #46: Saline Valley Road. NOTE that Lippincott Mine Road is 4-rated and suitable for high-clearance 4WD vehicles only.
0.0 ▲   Trail commences along Desert #50: Lippincott Mine Road, 1.3 miles west of the Lippincott Mine. Zero trip meter and turn north on graded dirt road. Intersection is unmarked.
         GPS: N36°38.47' W117°34.51'

Selected Further Reading

Beck, Warren A., and Ynez D. Haase. *Historical Atlas of California*. Norman, Okla.: University of Oklahoma Press, 1974.

Belden, L. Burr, and Mary DeDecker. *Death Valley to Yosemite: Frontier Mining Camps and Ghost Towns*. Bishop, Calif.: Spotted Dog Press, Inc., 1998.

Boessenecker, John. *Gold Dust and Gunsmoke*. New York: John Wiley & Sons, Inc., 1999.

Bright, William. *1500 California Place Names*. Berkeley and Los Angeles: University of California Press, 1998.

Broman, Mickey, and Russ Leadabrand. *California Ghost Town Trails*. Baldwin Park, Calif.: Gem Guides Book Co., 1985.

Casebier, Dennis G. *Mojave Road Guide*. Essex, Calif.: Tales of the Mojave Road Publishing Company, 1999.

Clarke, Herbert. *An Introduction To Southern California Birds*. Missoula, Mont.: Mountain Press Publishing Company, 1997.

Dunn, Jerry Camarillo, Jr. *National Geographic's Driving Guides to America: California and Nevada and Hawaii*. Washington, D.C.: The Book Division National Geographic Society, 1996.

Durham, David L. *Durham's Place-Names of California's Eastern Sierra*. Clovis, Calif.: Word Dancer Press, 2001.

———. *Durham's Place-Names of California's Desert Counties*. Clovis, Calif.: Word Dancer Press, 2001.

Florin, Lambert. *Ghost Towns of The West*. New York: Promontory Press, 1993.

Gersch-Young, Marjorie. *Hot Springs and Hot Pools of the Southwest*. Santa Cruz, Calif.: Aqua Thermal Access, 2001.

Gudde, Erwin G. *1000 California Place Names*. Berkeley and Los Angeles: University of California Press, 1959.

———. *California Place Names*. Berkeley and Los Angeles: University of California Press, 1998.

Hart, James D. *A Companion to California*. New York: Oxford University Press, 1978.

Heizer, Robert F. *The Destruction of California Indians*. Lincoln, Nebr.: University of Nebraska Press, 1993.

The Historical Guide to North American Railroads. Waukesha, Wisc.: Kalmbach Publishing, 2000.

Hirschfelder, Arlene. *Native Americans*. New York: Dorling Kindersley Publishing, Inc., 2000.

Holmes, Robert. *California's Best-Loved Driving Tours*. New York: Macmillan Travel, 1999.

Hoxie, Frederick E., ed. *Encyclopedia of North American Indians*. Boston: Houghton Mifflin Company, 1996.

Huegel, Tony. *California Desert Byways*. Idaho Falls, Idaho: The Post Company, 1995.

The Indians of California. Alexandria, Va.: Time-Life Books, 1994.

Keyworth, C. L. *California Indians*. New York: Checkmark Books, 1991.

Kirk, Ruth. *Exploring Death Valley*. Stanford, Calif.: Stanford University Press, 1981.

Kroeber, A. L. *Handbook of the Indians of California*. New York: Dover Publications, Inc., 1976.

Kyle, Douglas E. *Historic Spots in California*. Stanford, Calif.: Stanford University Press, 1990.

Lamar, Howard R., ed. *The New Encyclopedia of the American West*. New Haven, Conn.: Yale University Press, 1998.

Lawlor, Florine. *Mohave Desert OHV Trails*. Glendale, Calif.: La Siesta Press, 1989.

Lewellyn, Harry. *Backroad Trips and Tips*.

Costa Mesa, Calif.: Glovebox Publications, 1993.

Lewis, Donovan. *Pioneers of California*. San Francisco: Scottwall Associates, 1993.

Lindsay, Lowell, and Diana Lindsay. *The Anza-Borrego Desert Region*. Berkeley: Wilderness Press, 1998.

Martin, Don W., and Betty Woo Martin. *California-Nevada Roads Less Traveled*. Henderson, Nev.: Pine Cone Press, Inc., 1999.

Milner, Clyde A., II, Carol A. O'Conner, and Martha A. Sandweiss, eds. *The Oxford History of the American West*. Oxford: Oxford University Press, 1996.

Mitchell, James R. *Gem Trails of Southern California*. Baldwin Park, Calif.: Gem Guides Book Co., 1998.

Mitchell, Roger. *Death Valley Jeep Trails*. Glendale, Calif.: La Siesta Press, 1969.

Nadeau, Remi. *Ghost Towns and Mining Camps of California*. Santa Barbara, Calif.: Crest Publishing, 1999.

National Audubon Society Field Guide to North American Birds: Western Region. New York: Alfred A. Knopf, Inc., 1998.

National Audubon Society Field Guide to North American Trees: Western Region. New York: Alfred A. Knopf, Inc., 1996.

Pepper, Choral. *Desert Lore of Southern California*. San Diego: Sunbelt Publications, 1999.

Poshek, Lucy, and Roger Naylor, comps. *California Trivia*. Nashville, Tenn.: Rutledge Hill Press, 1998.

Powers, Stephen. *Tribes of California*. Berkeley and Los Angeles: University of California Press, 1976.

Rae, Cheri, and John Mckinney. *Mojave National Preserve: A Visitor's Guide*. Santa Barbara, Calif.: Olympus Press, 1999.

Rolle, Andrew. *California: A History*. Wheeling, Ill.: Harlan Davidson, Inc., 1998.

Sagstetter, Beth, and Bill Sagstetter. *The Mining Camps Speak*. Denver: Benchmark Publishing, 1998.

Schuler, Stanley, ed. *Cacti and Succulents*. New York: Simon and Schuster, Inc., 1985.

Secrest, William B. *California Desperadoes*. Clovis, Calif.: Word Dancer Press, 2000.

Sharp, Robert P., and Allen F. Glazner. *Geology Underfoot in Southern California*. Missoula, Mont.: Mountain Press Publishing Company, 1993.

Starry, Roberta Martin, and Suzanne Knudson. *Exploring the Ghost Town Desert: A Guide to the Rand Mining Area*. Woodland Hills, Calif.: Engler Publishing, 2000.

Sullivan, Noelle. *It Happened in Southern California*. Helena, Mont.: Falcon Publishing, Inc., 1996.

Taylor, Colin F. *The Native Americans: The Indigenous People of North America*. London: Salamander Books Ltd., 2000.

Thrap, Dan L. *Encyclopedia of Frontier Biography*. 3 vols. Lincoln, Nebr.: University of Nebraska Press, 1988.

Varney, Philip. *Southern California's Best Ghost Towns*. Norman, Okla.: University of Oklahoma Press, 1990.

Waldman, Carl. *Encyclopedia of Native American Tribes*. New York: Facts on File, 1988.

Selected Web sources

California Historical Society, http://californiahistoricalsociety.org

California Missions, http://www.californiamissions.com

Death Valley National Park, http://nps.gov/deva/

Desert USA, http://desertusa.com/

Ghost Town Explorers, http://www.gjpsttpwmexplorers.org/

GORP.com, http://gorp.away.com

Joshua Tree National Park, Joshua.tree.national-park.com

Mojave National Preserve,
http://www.nps.gov/moja

National Center for Disease Control:
Hantavirus Pulmonary Syndrome,
http://www.cdc.gov/ncidad/diseases/hanta/hps/

National Historic Route 66 Federation,
http://national66.org

National Park Service, http://nps.gov/

Pacific Southwest Railway Museum,
http://www.sdrm.org

San Bernardino County, California,
http://www.usgennet.org/usa/ca/county/
sanbernardino/

Twenty Mule Team Museum, Boron,
California,
http://www.20muleteammuseum.org

U.S. Bureau of Land Management,
California, http://www.blm.gov/ca

Photo Credits

Unless otherwise indicated in the following list of acknowledgments (which is organized by page number), all photographs were taken by Bushducks—Maggie Pinder and Donald McGann.

38 San Diego Museum of Man; **39** (upper right and bottom left) San Diego Museum of Man; **94** California Historical Society, San Francisco; **116** Huntington Library; **171** (right and left) Corel.

Cover photography: Bushducks—Maggie Pinder and Donald McGann

About the Authors

Peter Massey grew up in the outback of Australia, where he acquired a life long love of the backcountry. After retiring from a career in investment banking in 1986 at the age of thirty-five, he served as a director for a number of companies in the United States, the United Kingdom, and Australia. He moved to Colorado in 1993.

Jeanne Wilson was born and grew up in Maryland. After moving to New York City in 1980, she worked in advertising and public relations before moving to Colorado in 1993.

After traveling extensively in Australia, Europe, Asia, and Africa, the authors covered more than 80,000 miles touring the United States and the Australian outback between 1993 and 1997. This experience became the basis for creating the Backcountry Adventures and Trails guidebook series.

As the research team grew, a newcomer became a dedicated member of the Swagman team.

Angela Titus was born in Missouri and grew up in Virginia, where she attended the University of Virginia. She moved to Alabama and worked for *Southern Living Magazine* traveling, photographing, and writing about the southeastern U.S. She moved to Colorado in 2002.

Since research for the Backcountry Adventures and Trails guidebooks began, Peter, Jeanne, and Angela have traveled more than 75,000 miles throughout the western states.

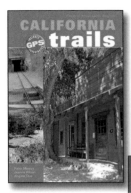

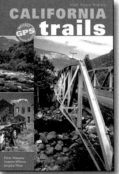

more california trails
backroad guides

California Trails—Central Mountains
This guide is comprised of painstaking detail and descriptions for 52 trails located near the towns of Big Sur, Fresno, San Luis Obispo, Santa Barbara, Bakersfield, Mojave, and Maricopa. **ISBN-10, 1-930193-19-X; ISBN-13, 978-1-930193-19-2; Price $19.95**

California Trails—High Sierra
This guidebook navigates and describes 50 trails located near the towns of Fresno (north), Oakhurst, Lone Pine, Bishop, Bridgeport, Coulterville, Mariposa, and Mammoth Lakes. **ISBN-10, 1-930193-21-1; ISBN-13, 978-1-930193-21-5; Price $19.95**

California Trails—North Coast
This guide meticulously describes and rates 47 off-road routes located near the towns of Sacramento, Redding (west), Red Bluff, Clear Lake, McCloud, Mount Shasta, Yreka, Crescent City, and Fort Bidwell. **ISBN-10, 1-930193-22-X; ISBN-13, 978-1-930193-22-2; Price $19.95**

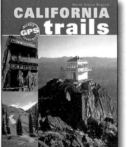

California Trails—Northern Sierra
This book outlines detailed trail information for 55 off-road routes located near the towns of Sacramento (east), Red Bluff (east), Truckee, South Lake Tahoe, Sonora, Susanville, Chico, Oroville, Yuba City, Placerville, Stockton (east), Jackson, and Sonora. **ISBN-10, 1-930193-23-8; ISBN-13, 978-1-930193-23-9; Price $19.95**

California Trails—South Coast
This field guide includes meticulous trail details for 50 trails located near the towns of Los Angeles, San Bernardino, San Diego, Salton Sea, Indio, Borrego Springs, Ocotillo and Palo Verde. **ISBN-10, 1-930193-24-6; ISBN-13, 978-1-930193-24-6; Price $19.95**

to order
call 800-660-5107 or
visit 4WDbooks.com

arizona trails
backroad guides

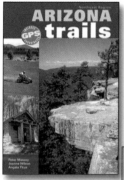

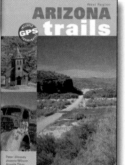

Arizona Trails–Northeast

This guidebook consists of meticulous details and directions for 47 trails located near the towns of Flagstaff, Williams, Prescott (northeast), Winslow, Fort Defiance and Window Rock. **ISBN-10, 1-930193-02-5; ISBN-13, 978-1-930193-02-4; Price $19.95**

Arizona Trails–West

This volume consists of comprehensive statistics and descriptions for 33 trails located near the towns of Bullhead City, Lake Havasu City, Parker, Kingman, Prescott (west), and Quartzsite (north). **ISBN-10, 1-930193-00-9; ISBN-13, 978-1-930193-00-0; Price $19.95**

Arizona Trails–Central

This field guide includes meticulous trail details for 44 off-road routes located near the towns of Phoenix, Wickenburg, Quartzsite (south), Payson, Superior, Globe and Yuma (north). **ISBN-10, 1-930193-01-7; ISBN-13, 978-1-930193-01-7; Price $19.95**

Arizona Trails–South

This handbook is composed of comprehensive statistics and descriptions for 33 trails located near the towns of Tucson, Douglas, Mammoth, Reddington, Stafford, Yuma (southeast), Ajo and Nogales. **ISBN-10, 1-930193-03-3; ISBN-13, 978-1-930193-03-1; Price $19.95**

to order
call 800-660-5107 or
visit 4WDbooks.com

4WDBOOKS.COM

utah trails
backroad guides

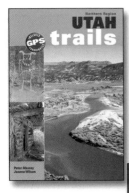

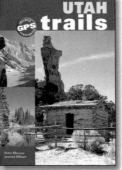

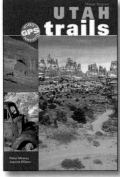

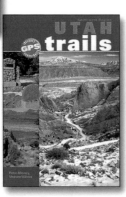

Utah Trails—Northern
This field guide includes meticulous trail details for 35 off-road routes near the towns of Vernal, Logan, Salt Lake City, Price, Wendover, Beaver, and Milford. **ISBN-10, 1-930139-30-0; ISBN-13, 978-1-930193-30-7; Price $16.95**

Utah Trails—Central
This volume is composed of comprehensive trail statistics for 34 trails near the towns of Green River, Richfield, Hanksville, Crescent Junction, and Castle Dale. **ISBN-10, 1-930193-31-9; ISBN-13, 978-1-930193-31-4; Price $16.95**

Utah Trails—Moab
This guidebook contains detailed trail information for 57 trails in and around Moab, Monticello, Canyonlands National Park, Arches National Park, Green River, Mexican Hat, Bluff, and Blanding. **ISBN-10, 1-930193-09-2; ISBN-13, 978-1-930193-09-3; Price $19.95**

Utah Trails—Southwest
This travel guide outlines detailed trail information for 49 off-road routes in the Four Corners region and around the towns of Escalante, St. George, Kanab, Boulder, Bryce Canyon, Hurricane, and Ticaboo. **ISBN-10, 1-930193-10-6; ISBN-13, 978-1-930193-10-9; Price $19.95**

to order
call 800-660-5107 or
visit 4WDbooks.com

4WDBOOKS.COM

colorado trails
backroad guides

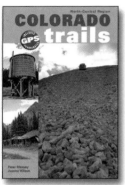

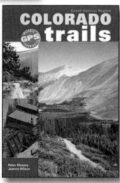

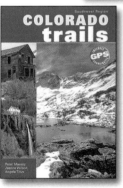

Colorado Trails–North-Central

This guidebook is composed of comprehensive statistics and descriptions of 28 trails, including 8 trails additional to those profiled in the Adventures Colorado book, around Breckenridge, Central City, Fraser, Dillon, Vail, Leadville, Georgetown, and Aspen. **ISBN-10, 1-930193-11-4; ISBN-13, 978-1-930193-11-6; Price $16.95**

Colorado Trails–South-Central

This edition of our Trails series includes meticulous trail details for 30 off-road routes located near the towns of Gunnison, Salida, Crested Butte, Buena Vista, Aspen, and the Sand Dunes National Monument. **ISBN-10, 1-930193-29-7; ISBN-13, 978-1-930193-29-1; Price $16.95**

Colorado Trails–Southwest

This field guide is comprised of painstaking details and descriptions for 31 trails, including 15 trails additional to those described in the Adventures Colorado book. Routes are located around Silverton, Ouray, Telluride, Durango, Lake City, and Montrose. **ISBN-10, 1-930193-32-7; ISBN-13, 978-1-930193-32-1; Price $16.95**

to order

call 800-660-5107 or
visit 4WDbooks.com

backcountry adventures
guides

Each book in the award-winning *Adventures* series listed below is a beautifully crafted, high-quality, sewn, 4-color guidebook. In addition to meticulously detailed backcountry trail directions and maps of every trail and region, extensive information on the history of towns, ghost towns, and regional history is included. The guides provide wildlife information and photographs to help readers identify the great variety of native birds, plants, and animals they are likely to see. This series appeals to everyone who enjoys the backcountry: campers, anglers, four-wheelers, hikers, mountain bikers, snowmobilers, amateur prospectors, sightseers, and more...

Backcountry Adventures Northern California

Backcountry Adventures Northern California takes readers along 2,653 miles of back roads from the rugged peaks of the Sierra Nevada, through volcanic regions of the Modoc Plateau, to majestic coastal redwood forests. Trail history comes to life through accounts of outlaws like Black Bart; explorers like Ewing Young and James Beckwourth; and the biggest mass migration in America's history—the Gold Rush. Contains 152 trails, 640 pages, and 679 photos.
ISBN-10, 1-930193-25-4; ISBN-13, 978-1-930193-25-3
Price, $39.95.

Backcountry Adventures Southern California

Backcountry Adventures Southern California provides 2,970 miles of routes that travel through the beautiful mountain regions of Big Sur, across the arid Mojave Desert, and straight into the heart of the aptly named Death Valley. Trail history comes alive through the accounts of Spanish missionaries; eager prospectors looking to cash in during California's gold rush; and legends of lost mines. Contains 153 trails, 640 pages, and 645 photos.
ISBN-10, 1-930193-26-2; ISBN-13, 978-1-930193-26-0
Price, $39.95.

to order
call 800-660-5107 or
visit 4WDbooks.com

backcountry adventures
guides

Backcountry Adventures Utah

Backcountry Adventures Utah navigates 3,721 miles through the spectacular Canyonlands region, to the top of the Uinta Range, across vast salt flats, and along trails unchanged since the riders of the Pony Express sped from station to station and daring young outlaws wreaked havoc on newly established stage lines, railroads, and frontier towns. Trail history comes to life through the accounts of outlaws like Butch Cassidy; explorers and mountain men; and early Mormon settlers. Contains 175 trails, 544 pages, and 532 photos.
ISBN-10, 1-930193-27-0; ISBN-13, 978-1-930193-27-7
Price, $39.95.

Backcountry Adventures Arizona

Backcountry Adventures Arizona guides readers along 2,671 miles of the state's most remote and scenic back roads, from the lowlands of the Yuma Desert to the high plains of the Kaibab Plateau. Trail history is colorized through the accounts of Indian warriors like Cochise and Geronimo; trailblazers; and the famous lawman Wyatt Earp. Contains 157 trails, 576 pages, and 524 photos.
ISBN-10, 1-930193-28-9; ISBN-13, 978-1-930193-28-4
Price, $39.95.

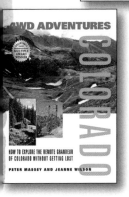

4WD Adventures Colorado

4WD Adventures Colorado takes readers to the Crystal River or over America's highest pass road, Mosquito Pass. This book identifies numerous lost ghost towns that speckle Colorado's mountains. Trail history is brought to life through the accounts of sheriffs and gunslingers like Bat Masterson and Doc Holliday; millionaires like Horace Tabor; and American Indian warriors like Chief Ouray. ains 71 trails, 232 pages, and 209 photos.
ISBN 0-9665675-5-2.
Price, $29.95.

to order
call 800-660-5107 or
visit 4WDbooks.com

4WD BOOKS.COM